Design and Covid-19

Illustrations

Figures

1.1	NHS Covid-19 mobile application	14
1.2	Wingcopter drone used in Scotland during the pandemic	15
1.3	New Zealand government Covid-19 poster	19
1.4	Data visualization showing rise and fall of Covid-19 infections (2020)	20
1.5	Data visualization showing how contagious Covid-19 was in 2020	21
1.6	Home-made mask (left) and fashion mask produced by British designer (right)	22
2.1	Design intervention data collection example	38
2.2	An example page from our book highlighting one of the 500+ design interventions we have assembled as part of this ongoing work. The 500+ design interventions were collected over a period of 152 days	39
2.3	Design intervention data highlights	39
2.4	Design interventions framework	41
2.5	Design interventions development (actions) – citizens and government	42
2.6	Design interventions development (masks)	44
2.7	Dilemmas and paradoxes	45
2.8	Design interventions graphics (posters) from educational to political	46
2.9	Design interventions – face shields simplification	47
4.1	Impact of social distancing metric on room capacity of 100 m^2	67
4.2	Examples of different brand images by UK Government and Designer Bespoke	68
4.3	Codification of signage influenced by UK Traffic signs	70
4.4	Workflow for social distance optimization using Grasshopper	72
4.5	Voronoi median line diagram (left) and analysis of surface clash detection	73
4.6	Visibility graph analysis indicating fixed view projected onto surfaces	73
4.7	Installation of the signage in the Storey Building, Lancaster, UK. Installation took 18 h and twenty-four local businesses visited the space	74
4.8	Comparison of (a) human-designed plan and (b) automated Grasshopper definition	75
4.9	Grasshopper definition applied to the Lancaster Health Innovation Campus	76
4.10	Open Source Social Distance Signage Pack	76
5.1	Countries analyzed at the first research stage	85

5.2	Analysis of language and message framing by country	87
5.3	Analysis of visual design by country	88
5.4	Italian Ministry of Health leaflets on handwashing	89
5.5	Communication material on social distancing by the Yukon regional government in Canada	90
5.6	Draft recommendations	93
6.1	Daily data of cases confirmed, active and recovered – Covid-19 Chile	102
6.2	Evolution of cases confirmed by region – 100,000 habitants – Covid-19 Chile	102
6.3	Total number of cases confirmed by gender and group of age – Covid-19 Chile	103
6.4	Territorial viewfinder – Covid-19 Chile	103
6.5	Options of visualization territorial viewfinder – Covid-19 Chile	103
6.6	Fake news in Columbia – Covid-19 visualization. Project COLEV	104
6.7	Facial shield made at the Pontificia Universidad Católica de Chile, Chile	106
6.8	Ventilator PersoCO – Universidad de los Andes, Colombia	107
6.9	SOFA – Project Facial Cushion for Covid-19 Patients – Chile	108
6.10	SOFA – Project Facial Cushion for Covid-19 Patients – Chile	109
6.11	SOFA – Project Facial Cushion for Covid-19 Patients – Chile	109
7.1	Advertisement on the New Zealand campaign-style based on a haiku by Meria Marom 'We isolate now / So when we gather again / No one is missing'	115
7.2	The graph shows the Covid-19 Alert System Timeline from 21 March 2020 to 2 December 2021. It is based on graphs done by Vinay Ranchhod and published by RNZ in March 2021, one year into the pandemic (Strongman et al., 2021)	117
7.3	*Unite against COVID-19*. Licensed by CC BY-NC 4.0	119
7.4	Images from the campaign	120
7.5	Users download and actively use the app, creating a digital diary of visited places by scanning the official QR codes or manually entering location data	125
7.6	A sample of the visual language applied in different media for diverse purposes since first created in 2020 to January 2021	127
8.1	(a) 'Map UI information design application in the reaction stage: (A-1) "Coronavirus Infectious Disease-19" Homepage Screen in 2020'. (b) Map UI information design application in the reaction stage: (A-2) Goodoc mask scanner app*. (*This is a healthcare super app providing users with various functions in line with the pandemic, including a corona mask scanner, a cost comparison service for Covid-19 testing and non-face-to-face treatment.) (c) Map UI information design application in the reaction stage: (A-2) 'NAVER app place service indicating mask holding status'. (d) Map UI information design application in the reaction stage: (A-3) Corona 100m Alert App*. (*This is a self-developed app created	

	by Tina3D for the purpose of visualizing information about coronavirus in 3D and providing a notification service to prevent the spread of corona. Its main function is to induce a detour by sending a notification when a confirmed person approaches within 100 m of the current location.)	145
8.2	(a) Cases of action induction using PR campaign and character design in the adaptation stage: (B-3) Citizen participatory advertisement as part of the 'Mask is the answer!' campaign. (b) Cases of action induction using PR campaign and character design in the adaptation stage: (B-5) '30 Second Song Soap' promotion using the Baby Shark character	147
8.3	Cases of the healthcare environment and user experience design in the adaptation stage: (B-1) (a) Untact screening clinic in Seocho-gu; (b) it's moving line plan*. (*The entire process, from epidemiological investigations to specimens, is a non-contact walk-through with patients, allowing medical staff to work in a safe and pleasant environment without protective clothing.). Cases of the healthcare environment and user experience design in the adaptation stage: (B-2) (c) Mobile Clinic Module (MCM)* developed by the Korea Aid for Respiratory Epidemic initiative at KAIST; (d) contactless meal delivery to patients; (e) negative pressure ward UI for patients. (*MCM wins Best of the Best at 2021 Red Dot Design Award, simultaneously in the Product Design and Brand & Communication Design categories. Related information will be continuously updated on mcm.kaist.ac.kr.)	148
8.4	A case of online-based exhibition design in the adaptation stage: (B-8) Busan Biennale 2020 Online Exhibition* 3D viewing room. (*Biennale in the era of non-face-to-face aims to maximize the three-dimensional effect and synesthetic experience the audience feels when meeting on-site work by utilizing the latest IT technologies, such as 3D stereoscopic images and virtual reality (VR).)	149
8.5	(a) Cases of design for social communication using Metaverse in the recovery and resilience stage: a. (C-1) Soonchunhyang University entrance ceremony based on Metaverse platform*. (*Students created their own avatars and participated in the campus playground of a three-dimensional virtual world where the boundary between reality and virtuality disappeared.). (b) Cases of design for social communication using Metaverse in the recovery and resilience stage: b. (C-6) Metaverse community platform 'ZEPETO' with its unique avatar worldview	151
8.6	(a) Cases of design of user interaction with robots and IoT devices in the recovery and resilience stage: a. (C-4) Food-delivery app Baemin's serving robot 'Dilly plate'. (b) Cases of design of user interaction with robots and IoT devices in the recovery and resilience stage: b. (C-9) Non-face-to-face care service robot, 'Kimi' that combines the roles of a guidance robot	

	and a quarantine robot. (c) Cases of design of user interaction with robots and IoT devices in the recovery and resilience stage: c. (C-7) Smart medicine refrigerator temperature management system UI by VITCON. (d) Cases of design of user interaction with robots and IoT devices in the recovery and resilience stage: d. (C-8) Smart IoT air shower installed at a day care centre in Gyeyang-gu, Incheon	153
8.7	Analysis of problem-solving methods and strategic goals for Covid-19 response stage	157
8.8	Comprehensive analysis of design and technology use according to strategic purposes	158
9.1	Prototype of the 'Askin Napkin' activity during family meals	169
9.2	Storyboard for the 'Askin Napkin' activity during family meals	170
9.3	Proposal for a vacant lot on East 163rd Street recreates the classic New York City stoop as hub to engage neighbours with play and programming and invites the community to shape the long-term vision of the space	174
9.4	April 2021 clean-up day led by Banana Kelly community organizers to prepare a recently acquired vacant lot as a participatory stage for temporary design interventions and neighbourhood programming	175
9.5	Vibrant mural designs bring colour to the College Avenue Garden and a visual identity that unites all Banana Kelly's community gardens, activating existing wall and ground planes while featuring designated space for youth to leave their mark	176
10.1	Most stores put burglary warnings at the windows when they have to shut	192
10.2	Prototype designs extending the core Orbit concept to communicate richer information	197
10.3	A set of icons for legible AI is being tested in a co-creation workshop	197
11.1	As well as highlighting the design process, Design Council's framework for innovation also includes the key principles and design methods that designers and non-designers need to take, and the ideal working culture needed, to achieve significant and long-lasting positive change. We see orchestration as the activity that keeps all of these elements flowing together	203
11.2	Timeline of about four months, describing the five main stages in light blue, and all activities in dark blue. Results are outlined in the white boxes below and the red squiggly line suggests the process is not as linear and boxed-in as it may seem	206
11.3	Example of a gathering on a virtual whiteboard (we used Miro) during one of the online workshops where we worked around five virtual tables in Zoom and Miro at the same time, with five participants, a facilitator and two observers at each table	207
11.4	One of the activities we designed focused on the hopes (esperanzas) and fears (miedos) of the twenty-five participants	

	for the future of the cultural sector in Jalisco. This required them to look ahead and create 'dots on the horizon' that the policy recommendations we wanted to develop jointly would have to respond to	209
11.5	The diversity of unique perspectives that the participants brought to the *Innovation for Culture* programme was crucial to its success. We needed to communicate the extent of this diversity to the participants, who largely did not know each other yet. We achieved this by inviting everyone to introduce themselves in a virtual museum (on a virtual whiteboard) where we created an empty frame for each participant to fill with images and a caption that represented what culture in Jalisco looks like and feels like to them	212
11.6	To put EDI at the core of *Innovation for Culture*, we had to improvise and improve. This ranged from 'translating' visual, virtual whiteboards into word docs that screen readers can work with, to sign language interpreters on Zoom calls who later were	213
11.7	A more intimate space for conversation, in a Zoom breakout room and around a table on the Miro board, with the participants visible around the table as well as on the Zoom tiles	214
11.8	Interactive timeline of cultural policy in Jalisco, Mexico for the past hundred years, with detailed stories about each element of the timeline that pop up when the item is clicked. When building common ground, it is important to know the ground that you are standing on, with all its sensibilities as well as possibilities. Maps of the past like these offer a shared reference (even if it is contested) for discussions about possible policy futures	216
11.9	Hopes and Fears of twenty-five participants and their peers on the virtual whiteboard, an exercise that developed over the course of several weeks in between two workshop sessions	217
11.10	Dot Voting on the headlines of the future speculative magazine from 2024, which contained articles created from analysis of the Hopes and Fears exercise the participants did in an earlier workshop and fieldwork with their peers. Here, participants are adding post it notes with their names to articles they strongly support	219
11.11	The magazine from the future with votes from participants to prioritize certain future situations and ambitions was consequently used to steer conversations in three groups, at three virtual round tables	219
11.12	Discussing an early version of the policy recommendations with the participants in a Zoom breakout room, using screen share and the chat channel. External experts were involved in the discussions to offer suggestions on, for instance, the feasibility of policy directions that the participants desired	220
12.1	Basic requirements to improve general levels of health and well-being in cities	231

14.1	Digital resources produced for the (a) designing research ecosystems at DRS and (b) festival of social sciences workshops	255
14.2	Example physical card sets from left to right, Visitor Box, Mixed Reality Game Cards and Moral-IT cards	257
14.3	Gather Town: Four instances of experimental spaces. Top to bottom: Imagination Exhibition Space, *The Egg, Ways of Seeing*, the Lancaster Design Studio	262

Tables

4.1	Result of Plan Comparisons and Survey of Designers	75
5.1	Framework Guidelines Employed for Data Analysis	83
8.1	Stages of Pandemic Progression	132
8.2	Roles of Social Problem-Solving Design	133
8.3	Promotion of Social Innovation Design (Manzini, 2014)	133
8.4	Covid-19-Related Technology Keywords	135
8.5	List of Selected Cases	137
8.6	Example of a Case Study Framework	143
8.7	Synthetic Analysis of Reaction Stage Cases	146
8.8	Synthetic Analysis of Cases in the Adaptation Stage	152
8.9	Synthetic Analysis of Cases in the Recovery and Resilience Stage	154
9.1	Family Pockets by Sour	168
9.2	South Bronx Community Gardens Activation	171
9.3	Design Agency and the Design for Social Innovation Lens	177
9.4	Impact of Covid-19 on Design Research and Co-design Processes	181

Contributor Biographies

Editors:

Louise Mullagh is Senior Researcher (Design for Policy) in ImaginationLancaster. Her cross-disciplinary design research explores design and its roles in the development and implementation of policy at global, national and regional levels. Her previous research explored the role of design in sustainability, and her dissertation explored how design principles can be deployed to bring about balance between data-driven and situated understandings of place. She is interested in developing collaborations both within academia and beyond to explore the implications of design within the creation of policies in a range of areas, including emerging technologies, urban environments and other complex issues.

Rachel Cooper, OBE, is Distinguished Professor of Design Management and Policy at Lancaster University. She is a director of ImaginationLancaster and also chair of Lancaster Institute for the Contemporary Arts. Professor Cooper's research interests cover design thinking, design management and design policy; across all sectors of industry, Cooper has a specific interest in design for well-being and socially responsible design. She has published extensively on these topics, including books *Designing Sustainable Cities* and *The Handbook of Wellbeing and the Environment*. She was founding editor of *The Design Journal* and also founding president of the European Academy of Design.

Contributing Authors:

Mariana Amatullo's scholarship bridges the design and management fields with publications that examine the cognitive capacity of design to advance innovation in organizations and environments of social complexity. Her latest publication (co-editor) is *Design for Social Innovation: Case Studies from around the World* (2021). Dr Amatullo serves on the Board of Aalto University; she is Honorary President of the Cumulus Association, a Salzburg Global Fellow and a Fellow with the Royal Society of the Arts. Dr Amatullo holds a PhD in Management from Case Western Reserve University; an MA in Art History and Museum Studies from the University of Southern California and a Licence en Lettres Degree from the Sorbonne University, Paris, where she also studied Art History at L'Ecole du Louvre

Megan Anderson is a design researcher based in London. She worked at STBY at the time of co-writing the chapter for this book, where she worked with a range of public and private sector clients from across the globe. Her graduate research at Leiden University focused on collaboration and innovation in the public safety sector. She is currently working at D-Ford.

Steve Benford is the Dunford Professor of Computer Science at the University of Nottingham where he founded the Mixed Reality laboratory in 2000. He has directed the Horizon Centre for Doctoral Training since 2009 and leads the University's Smart Products research beacon. His research explores artistic and creative applications of mixed reality technologies and he has employed ideation cards in teaching this for many years. He previously held an EPSRC Dream Fellowship, was elected to the CHI Academy and was awarded the Prix Arts Electronica Golden Nica for Interactive Art. He is a keen amateur musician.

Christopher Boyko is a senior lecturer in urban design at Lancaster University. He explores critical connections between urban design and behaviour, informing both design practice and policy. He has undertaken research on the relationship between well-being, sharing and the design of neighbourhoods for the *Liveable Cities* project; urban density and decision-making processes on *Urban Futures*; and the sustainable urban design decision-making process for *VivaCity2020*. His most recent project, *Remembering Resistance*, focused on the relationship between women's activism and public space.

Craig Bremner is an adjunct professor of design at Charles Sturt University (CSU), Australia. Before moving to France to start a design consultancy he was Professor of Design at the University of Southern Denmark. Prior to these positions, he was Professor in Design Pedagogy at Northumbria University UK, and before that Professor of Design at the University of Canberra, where he was also dean of the Faculty of Design & Architecture. He is a signatory to the *Lancaster Care Charter* and his most recent books are *A Design History of the COVID-19 Virus* and *118 Theories of Design[ing]*.

Camilla Buchanan is a researcher, policy maker and strategic designer working to introduce design to new environments. She currently co-leads the Policy Lab, a design team set up to help UK Government departments to use design in policymaking. Before joining government, Camilla was part of the UK Design Council's policy team, where she first started teaching design to policymakers. Camilla has been a visiting scholar at Parsons' School of Design and a Fellow of The Public Policy Lab since 2015 – the first public sector design non-profit in the United States, and holds a PhD in Strategic Design from Lancaster University.

Elisavet Christou is a transdisciplinary researcher and educator in Digital Arts, Internet studies, Design and Evaluation research. She has worked extensively in the creative industries sector as communications, marketing and advertising strategist and manager. She is currently a post-doctoral research associate at the ImaginationLancaster design-led research group and an associate lecturer in Arts Management at Lancaster University. In her current role, she researches creative evaluation methodologies, tools and methods for transdisciplinary research and practice.

Ana Rute Costa is an architect and an educational researcher with expertise in Learning and Teaching spaces. Her research and professional practice focus on analysing the impact of the built environment on teaching and learning using ethnography and visual research techniques. She is currently developing a research project about the spaces and tools for learning, and she is interested in the policies and practices that affect the design of spaces and tools/products that enable learning to take place.

Peter J. Craigon is a research fellow at Horizon Digital Economy, previously a research fellow in ethics legislation and engagement at the Future Food Beacon, both at the University of Nottingham. He has a multidisciplinary background including History, Animal Behaviour, Science and Technology Studies, Responsible Innovation and Ethics. These interests come together and underpin his current work on Responsible Innovation where he seeks to engage researchers and technology developers with responsibility concerning their work. To this end, he has developed approaches and tools, particularly card-based tools including sets on technology ethics, ethics of research and Equality Diversity and Inclusion, for example.

Dimitrios Darzentas is an interdisciplinary lecturer in the School of Computing, Engineering, and the Built Environment at Edinburgh Napier University, and formerly a research fellow in the Mixed Reality Lab of the University of Nottingham. His work is situated at an intersection between Human-Computer Interaction and Design with a broad scope including Mixed Reality Technologies, Experience Design, MXR Storytelling and Cultural Heritage, Physical/Digital Service Design, Playful Interactions, Wellbeing, Sustainability and Political Engagement, among others. His current research interests include Creative Technology, Hybrid Physical/Digital Experiences and Data-Supported Creativity.

Des Fagan is the Head of Architecture at Lancaster and Chair of the National RIBA Practice and Policy Committee. Des's field of research interest is in optimization and Deep Learning (AI) for Decision Support Systems in AEC. He is particularly interested in the impact that Machine Learning will have on design processes and the regulatory and policy implications for the RIBA and ARB. Prior to working in academia, he worked on several international award-winning projects as project architect for the London Olympic Village for GHA and Glasgow Transport Museum for Zaha Hadid Architects, winner of European Museum of the Year.

Mariana Fonseca-Braga is interested in design capability building for tackling global challenges (Sustainable Development Goals [SDGs]), such as Water, Sanitation and Hygiene (WASH), antimicrobial resistance (AMR) and other community resilience challenges. She looks into how design capabilities can effectively contribute to a shared, equitable, fair and plural future, feeding policy planning and implementation. She enjoys (co-)crafting better futures, and helping non-expert (non-designer) teams apply human-centred, participatory and other design approaches (strategic design, product-service systems, design-driven innovation) to their businesses, organizations and communities.

Isabella Gady is Chief Experience and Peoples Officer at Wonderwerk, a strategic design studio based in Vienna. She has worked locally, nationally and internationally as design researcher, strategist and executive coach co-creating organizational change and leadership programmes. Fuelled by the desire to imagine the Future of Work, she fuses elements from many disciplines with design – drawing from anthropology, the behavioural sciences and psychology. Isabella has worked with organizations including the United Nations, UN Women, the City of New York, ideo.org, 3x3 Design, Snowcone and Haystack and Spark Microgrant. She co-founded the New York Digital Diplomacy Chapter and served as spokeswoman and special advisor for International Development at the Austrian Federal Ministry for Europe, Integration and Foreign Affairs.

Rosendy Galabo is a post-doctoral research associate for the Beyond Imagination project at Lancaster University. He has an interdisciplinary expertise in Human-Computer Interaction, Creative Engagement and Co-design. His research focuses on how technologies can enable and support communities and public sector professionals to co-design new sustainable ways of living and working together. His current research interest focuses on developing new distributed co-design approaches, sustainable practices and creative interactions.

Fernando Galdon is a lecturer on the double masters Innovation Design Engineering at the Royal College of Art and Imperial College. His research focuses on design theory, trust, sustainability and applied ethics. His research has been published and presented internationally at conferences at MIT, the University of Cambridge, the University of Manchester, the RCA, the University of Côte d'Azur, UNISINOS Brazil, CHUV Lausanne, The European Academy of Design and the Design Museum in London.

Tomás Garcia Ferrari is a senior lecturer at the Department of Design, University of Waikato in New Zealand. Previously, he held academic positions at the University of Otago (New Zealand), the Burg-Giebichenstein School of Art and Design (Germany) and the University of Buenos Aires (Argentina). He formerly worked as a design consultant for companies and institutions in Latin America, Europe and Oceania.

Tomás has a postgraduate specialization in Communication Design Theory and a Graphic Design degree from the University of Buenos Aires (UBA), Argentina.

David Green is a senior researcher at Lancaster University, with interdisciplinary expertise in Human-Computer Interaction, Documentary Studies and Design. With a background in participatory filmmaking, his work responds to the social impacts of technology through design and collaborative, cross-disciplinary research. His previous affiliations include MIT Open Documentary Lab, Department of Film & Journalism at UWE Bristol, and Open Lab, Newcastle University.

David Hands is a design researcher who explores the emerging role design can play towards building resilience in an era of uncertainty. David has also written and published extensively on design management and design as a strategic resource for both profit and non-profit organizations alike.

Ricardo J. Hernandez is an adjunct assistant professor of engineering design at the Pontificia Universidad Católica de Chile. He is also the director of sustainability at New Future Consulting. Previously, Ricardo was an assistant professor of design and innovation at ImaginationLancaster, a design lab part of Lancaster University in the UK. Ricardo holds a PhD in Sustainable Product Service Systems Design from Loughborough University in the UK, a Master Research in Industrial Engineering from the Institute National Polytechnic of Grenoble in France and a Master of Science in Industrial Engineering from the Universidad de Los Andes in Colombia.

Naomi Jacobs is lecturer in Design Policy and Futures Thinking at Lancaster University, researching technology and society, and the nature of digital public spaces. Naomi's work focuses primarily on interaction; between individuals, communities, disciplines or sectors, and between people and technology and the media they consume. Much of her current research relates to how design research can be used in policymaking, particularly in the context of ensuring new technologies and digital platforms and services are ethical, transparent, trustworthy and respect privacy. This work often uses speculative methods such as design fiction to think about what possible futures might look like.

Yoori Koo is an associate professor of Service Design at the Graduate School of Industrial Arts, Hongik University in Seoul, Korea. She completed her PhD in Design at Lancaster University, UK. Her research interest covers co-creative, empathic research and the design of product-service systems focused on the well-being of people. She is currently engaged with developing future vision scenarios for the Disabled and the Elderly at the Ministry of Health and Welfare. She is a committee member of the International Association of Societies of Design Research and won the Best Paper Award from the Korean Society of Design Science in 2016.

Boyeun Lee is a qualitative researcher focusing on design and innovation strategy surrounding data and data systems. She has worked as a service design researcher for several years in South Korea, through which she gained a wide range of public and commercial experience across sectors and projects, such as service design policy, design audits for NGOs and design research for EV users. She is currently a post-doctoral research fellow for The DigitLab Project at the University of Exeter Business School. Her research focuses on data-driven design, design with AI and design intervention in the value creation of emerging technologies.

Joseph Lindley is a senior research fellow and leads Design Research Works, a project dedicated to progressing and promoting Design Research as a key means for addressing emerging socio-technological challenges. He is an alumnus of the PETRAS Centre for Excellence for IoT Cybersecurity and the ACM Future of Computing Academy, held the AHRC's Challenges of the Future Fellowship in AI & Data, and has published widely on the Adoption and Acceptability of emerging technologies.

Zach Mason is a PhD researcher at Lancaster University exploring the perception and accessibility of virtual spaces. Through Co-Design and Design Research, he works with charities and private sector organizations aiming to improve people's lives through better accessibility for blind and visually impaired people. Recently, his research has explored the design of non-visual games, using sound as primary feedback. This research stemmed from a dissatisfaction with the design of emerging virtual web conferencing systems because of their failure to account for users who may need accessibility features.

Alejandro Moreno Rangel is lecturer in Building Performance Evaluation and Net Zero Design. Alejandro's main research interests are sustainable architecture and the indoor environment, indoor air quality (IAQ) and thermal comfort, particularly Passivhaus buildings. Ultimately, the connections between sustainable architecture to health and human behaviours to create healthy homes can be achieve through the use of design research methods. Recently, Alejandro has developed an interest in using low-cost sensors as research tools and their effect on residential behaviour, design and human health & well-being. Alejandro is also a certified Passivhaus Designer.

David Perez is a lecturer in Radical Co-Design at Lancaster University. His research focuses on the emergence and adoption of new creative and collaborative practices from collaborative design projects. He works with public and third sector organizations and with local communities in projects aiming to improve people's lives. He has worked with a wide range of partners including social entrepreneurs, national and local museums, people with lived experience of food poverty, food delivery workers, and local and national authorities. His research utilizes a variety of methods and theories such as design-led research approaches, co-design, participatory design and practice theories.

Bas Raijmakers is a design researcher based in London and Amsterdam. He co-founded his design research studio STBY in 2003 in London and Amsterdam. He worked for a long list of clients in the public, private and non-profit sectors. Bas holds a PhD in design interactions from the Royal College of Art, which introduces documentary film approaches and techniques in design research.

Paul A. Rodgers is professor of design at the University of Strathclyde, Department of Design, Manufacturing and Engineering Management (DMEM). He has over twenty-five years of experience in product design research and has led research projects for UK Research and Innovation (UKRI), the Arts and Humanities Research Council (AHRC), and design projects funded by the Scottish government and The Lighthouse (Scotland's National Centre for Architecture, Design and the City). He is the author of more than 170 papers and 14 books. His books have been translated into several languages including Spanish, Italian, Chinese and Taiwanese.

Justin Sacks conducts research on commons-making through #commonize studio, a design studio that supports partners to make commons through studio experimentation. He is a member of the International Association for the Study of the Commons and Community Economies Research Network. He holds degrees in architecture from Yale University and economic history from the London School of Economics. Justin is completing his PhD in design at Lancaster University and is a visiting scholar at the Ostrom Workshop at Indiana University.

Carolina Short is a design lecturer at the University of Waikato, New Zealand. Previously, she held academic positions at the University of Otago (New Zealand), the Burg-Giebichenstein School of Art and Design (Germany) and the University of Buenos Aires (Argentina). She founded (bi)gital» in 1996 and, since then, has worked for companies and institutions in Latin America, Europe and New Zealand as a designer and consultant. Carolina has a master's in Communication Design Theory and a Graphic Design degree from the University of Buenos Aires (UBA), Argentina.

Lisa Thomas is a lecturer in design whose research explores how design can contribute to developing more sustainable ways of living. Lisa is particularly interested in how design education engages with sustainability and has developed methods and tools for supporting design students to challenge dominant, potentially unsustainable eco-modern values.

Emmanuel Tsekleves leads Design for Global Health at ImaginationLancaster, Lancaster University. Driven by the UN's Sustainable Development Goals, his research focuses on tackling community health challenges across the world. He is currently working on understanding cleaning practices and driving infections from homes in Ghana, developing health care policies for senior citizens in Malaysia and promoting seafood across Europe through novel packaging design

Hanne G. Wagner is a lecturer in applied informatics at Edinburgh Napier University, previously working as a research fellow with the Mixed Reality Lab and the Horizon Digital Economy Research Institute at the University of Nottingham. With a multidisciplinary background in computing, psychology, law and politics, she is interested in a vast area of topics in the area of Human-Computer Interaction. Hanne's current main research interests are in the fields of policy, public engagement and eGovernment as well as digital health, mental health and well-being. Other areas she has worked on as part of her research include Trust in Autonomous Systems, Responsible Research and Innovation (RRI), Robot-Human-Interaction and card-based design tools.

Acknowledgements

We would like to thank Jane Quin for her dedication, persistence and support in helping us bring this book together; our task would have been much more difficult without her support. We would also like to thank all the contributors, who responded rapidly to our invitation to write a chapter, during challenging times both professionally and personally. Finally, we would like to acknowledge the support of Research England who funded our Beyond Imagination project and the appointment of Louise Mullagh.

Introduction

LOUISE MULLAGH AND RACHEL COOPER

The 2018 Global Risk Report (WEF 2018) reported that the likelihood of the spread of an infectious disease was below average and above average for impact. We have certainly seen how impactful Covid-19 has been. This pandemic has dramatically changed our lives, in ways we could not have predicted three years ago. As we write this introduction, in 2022, the pandemic has still not disappeared and case numbers are still high. We are facing the need to learn to live with the virus as it mutates, adapting to new ways of living and working amidst the need to stay safe and healthy. Our experience should help us to live with future infectious diseases as this is now sixth in the WEF (2022) lists of risks for 2022.

Indeed outbreaks of viruses and disease have shaped our world throughout history (Honigsbaum, 2020). However, the Covid-19 pandemic has spread more quickly around the globe than previous viruses due to our increased mobility (Hâncean et al., 2020). This is also the first pandemic which has been tracked almost in real time, using the vast amount of data that have been gathered globally. Unlike pandemics throughout history, those fortunate enough to do so have been able to communicate with the outside world, while being isolated at home. As a result of the virus, we have seen huge disparities arise around the world. Access to basic healthcare, green spaces and healthy housing have become priorities during the pandemic. Many of these issues existed prior to Covid-19, but have been exacerbated by the unique challenges the pandemic has posed.

As with major world events in the past, Covid-19 has demanded myriad applications of design to shape not only the physical products required for tackling the pandemic, but also in the rethinking and re-formation of services, complex systems and governance. We have seen much of the world, where resources are available and able, go online. Education, healthcare and social lives were moved onto digital platforms while huge swathes of the population complied with shelter-in-place orders. The disproportionate effect of the need to live our lives distanced from one another upon those able to do so, and those who have been forced to remain in work and unable to benefit from state-provided healthcare and financial support, has been highlighted around the world. Governments had to simultaneously cope with rising infection and death rates, while trying to balance already precarious economies (Sridhar, 2022), while those without adequate resources were left scrabbling for equipment and vaccines. We saw communities drawn together to offer support to frontline workers and those who were isolated, while fractures along the lines of differing opinions as to the best way of tackling the pandemic appeared across societies. The pandemic highlighted the state of global health, of which Sridhar (2022, p. 11) states we saw 'the massive progress in rich countries over the last century in reducing child mortality, increasing life expectancy and eliminating infectious diseases . . . set against that of poorer countries, where we still see the rampant spread of preventable diseases'. At a smaller scale, families and communities were split as to whether they should follow rules or guidelines implemented by governments, in addition to decisions around getting vaccinated. The criminalization of behaviour such as holding social gatherings and legal requirements to self-isolate caused further societal discord, even at the level of governments (Cabinet Office, 2022).

As design researchers and practitioners, we have been embedded within this rapidly changing environment, living through our own experiences both professionally and personally. For many of us, this period has meant changing the focus of our research and adjusting to new ways of working that are located both in the digital and physical world. For example, those of us who engage in design and research 'with' people have had to change our practices and develop new ways of distributed working online (Davis et al., 2021). We have seen design deployed at varying degrees of success around the world at differing scales, from the graphic design of government public health campaigns and data visualization, down to collective community action of mask design that resulted from a lack of PPE in the early stages of 2020. Large-scale design, such as the design of cities and the need for adequate green space provision and healthy homes and workplaces, has also been foregrounded over the last two years. The need for design to be used in the creation of policies and strategies has also been highlighted, as we have seen governments create and implement policies in rapid response, using prototyping as they went.

The pandemic has also brought into focus the need for design research to engage meaningfully not only with the impact of Covid-19, but also the coexisting global challenges such as climate change and the vast inequalities in health and social care. These changes have had profound impacts on the way we undertake design research now, the fields we engage with now and in the future, highlighting the need for designers and researchers around the world to unite and share our learnings.

Around the world we saw drastically different reactions from governments, with some moving immediately to track and trace systems that prevented lockdowns during the first wave, while others being slow to react, meaning full lockdowns were implemented. The rapid development of vaccines around the world meant those countries who could afford to vaccinate much of their population were able to reopen and begin to recover, while those who were further down the queue were left with vulnerable populations, many of whom were already struggling with vast health and economic inequalities prior to the outbreak of Covid-19 (Sridhar, 2022).

Certain governments around the world failed to learn lessons from previous pandemics (Science Committee, 2021), while others, predominantly in Asia, illustrate the value of learning lessons from severe acute respiratory syndrome and Middle East respiratory syndrome. We witnessed complacency across rich countries, including the UK, United States and around Europe, linked to the fact that these countries had not seen the destructive effect of infectious diseases in the recent past. However, in places such as West Africa, governments deployed their post-Ebola structures towards Covid-19 because they knew that an infectious disease can run through society, shut down schools and hospitals, stop vaccination campaigns and paralyse society. They were the ones who reacted much faster, but of course with far fewer resources. In these situations, we saw that when a community sets out to design the process it can be used anywhere. While the COVID-19 pandemic is still not over at the time of writing this book, in 2022, reflections and learning about this latest virus are beginning to emerge. We are now urged to 'learn to live with' the virus, as controls have been lifted and responsibilities for preventative actions have shifted from governments to the individual.

The pandemic has made it ever more apparent that design needs to be involved in creating new modes of existence that not only ensures a more sustainable future, but one that is also more equitable. As Fry and Nocek (2020, p. 6) state 'Design can't limit itself to changing the patterns of human consumption, to altering its supply chains, or to sourcing biodegradable materials. It must envision the possibility of designing *new conditions for being human*.' Within the context of interconnected and related crises such as climate change, unequal access to basic health care and future pandemics, it is also vital that we begin to understand how we might design for a complex world (Escobar, 2018, p. 49). Design is seen as having the potential to create possible futures and to explore the developing emergencies we face around the world (Rawsthorne and Antonelli, 2022). During the last two years much has been made about the need to redesign many aspects of societies, where the glaring disparities in access to safe work, health care and education have appeared. While design offers opportunities to tackle these issues and there is a great deal of optimism (Rawsthorne and Antonelli, 2022), it is not a panacea.

The brief for this edited volume was to capture a wide range of global design interventions deployed during the pandemic, both successful and unsuccessful. The examples gathered from colleagues around the world and presented here offer rich insights across geographies and contexts, as well as from a range of design disciplines. We present a wide range of ways in which design has been deployed, from the design of new products, to complex systems and the rapid deployment of new technologies and policies around the world. We have structured the book into three parts – *Reaction*, *International Reaction and Adaptation*, and *Recovery and Resilience: Building for the Future* – to encompass different scales and contexts that reflect the key stages of the pandemic.

Part I: *Reaction* charts the early stages on the pandemic through the lens of global design interventions, looking at attempts to utilize strategic design and the emergence of design for social distancing during this period. Chapters 1 and 2 chart the emergence of design interventions at different scales, exploring the maturity of both professional and informal design. Chapter 1, *Design Reactions* through understanding the pandemic using a four-stage framework, surveys interventions across design disciplines to understand where we might draw insights and principles for the future in tackling the vastly complex challenges we face. The notion of 'care' in design is explored in Chapter 2, *The Usefulness of Imperfect Design.* The authors survey a wide range of design interventions around the world and challenge us to consider the benefits of design that is 'imperfect', rather than as a finished product, as we have traditionally understood and practised design. These opening chapters highlight the necessity of design as prototyping and the importance of considering less-than-perfect design products and artefacts that have been produced by non-designers or communities. Chapter 3 offers insights into the operation of the UK Government's Policy Lab throughout the pandemic, exploring how strategic design was employed and what lessons can be extracted for the future. That chapter reflects both upon the practice of policy making and the practice of using design within policy making during an immensely challenging period.

Part II: *International Reaction and Adaptation* offers a global perspective on design from the initial stages of reaction and adaptation. Chapter 4 presents a case study of design for social distancing developed and deployed during the early stages of the pandemic. The chapter highlights the ways in which our use of buildings changed rapidly during the early stages of the pandemic and offers insights into how a unique methodology might be deployed rapidly in future to enable buildings to generate bespoke graphics and social distancing layouts.

Examples are presented through the lens of public health communication design around the world in Chapter 5, for instance the authors offer principles for effective public health messaging for future crises. Chapter 6 shines the spotlight on South America, taking examples of design from Chile and Colombia. The chapter explores the need for multidisciplinary approaches that are located within complex systems in order to tackle future challenges, highlighting the value of design across a range of examples from this period. New Zealand's response is presented in Chapter 7, in which the authors highlight the effective use of strategies that sought to bring the country together through design. The responses from New Zealand were effective in both uniting the country and ensuring lower cases than elsewhere around the world. Chapter 8 explores the response of South Korea's government, which was seen by many to be one of the more effective strategies. The chapter highlights the convergence of ICT design in the country and offers suggestions for designers for future challenges.

Part III: *Recovery and Resilience: Building for the Future* offers possibilities for design across a range of areas that might help us both recover and build stronger resilience for future crises. The first chapter in this part comes from New York. The authors present two case studies that foreground the need to work across disciplines, adopt systemic approaches and reflect on the agency of designers in challenging times.

Chapter 10 reflects on the impacts of businesses during the pandemic, offering insights from a range of case studies that explore the move towards digital retail around the world. A musical approach to exploring cultural policy post-Covid-19 is presented in Chapter 11, offering a creative approach to ways we can design our futures. The impact of past public health crises and the need to design resilient cities are explored in Chapter 12. The authors present work that highlights the need to consider density in urban places in order to ensure they are healthy and resilient in future. Principles for designing healthy and resilient cities are offered, along with the call for designers to be trained more effectively in the design of future cities. Chapter 13 presents new ideas for the design of education spaces post-Covid-19. The rapid re-imagining of education provision during the pandemic highlighted not only the inequity inherent within the move to online learning, but also the need for more engaging, flexible and healthy learning environments in the future. Chapter 14 presents a range of case studies exploring the rapid move to the digital during the pandemic. The authors highlight a range of different design responses that have been both successful and unsuccessful and collectively offer a range of insights and recommendations for the use of digital technologies in the future.

The chapters included here offer a diverse array of design responses from across a range of disciplines, exploring tangible, physical artefacts and places, as well as less tangible policies and strategies. While the authors all present heterogeneous approaches for design, they all share a hopefulness that by working as a community we might take the lessons learned and build them in to our shared visions of the future. The contributions in this book offer us the opportunity to collectively reflect upon the experiences of the last two years and to explore what learning can be embedded as we move beyond the recovery phase and into resilience. It is vital that we pay attention to the broad range of issues presented here and to maintain the momentum that has built across the design community during this period of great uncertainty. By reflecting upon the myriad of ways in which design has been used around the world since 2020, we hope that this book will provide learning from a range of practitioners. While we have still not emerged fully from the pandemic at the time of writing this introduction, we feel it is now time to reflect upon what has happened and to explore how these lessons might be embedded into our design research and practice in the future.

This book begins the journey of reflection on where design has been implemented successfully and where it has been less successful in a range of disciplines and across disciplinary practice. Writing a book about a pandemic with authors based in different locations around the world while experiencing one has been a challenge, as literature and design examples emerged at different rates. The emergence of literature and design examples during the period in which the authors were writing the chapters in this volume means some literature published during the last two years may not be included. Our final chapter draws together the opportunities and challenges for design research and practice not just for addressing future pandemics but also the very complex challenges that face us in relation to climate change, political disharmony, an ageing population and the social and environment dimensions related to these. This book offers a snapshot, a period in time when we all had to adapt to new ways of living and working, and which will have profound impacts on our lives in the future, and which will of course change designers and design research and practice.

References

Cabinet Office (2022). *Findings of Second Permanent Secretary's Investigation into Alleged Gatherings on Government Premises During Covid Restrictions*. London: HM Government. https://assets.publishing.service.gov.uk/government/uploads/system/uploads/attachment_data/file/1078404/2022-05-25_FINAL_FINDINGS_OF_SECOND_PERMANENT_SECRETARY_INTO_ALLEGED_GATHERINGS.pdf.

Davis, A., Niki, W., Langley, J., & Ian, G. (2021). Low-contact co-design: Considering more flexible spatiotemporal models for the co-design workshop. *Strategic Design Research Journal*, 14(1), 124–37.

Escobar, A. (2018). *Designs for the Pluriverse: Radical Interdependence, Autonomy, and the Making of Worlds*. Durham: Duke University Press.

Fry, T., & Nocek, A. (2020). Editor's introduction: "Design in crisis, introducing a problematic". In Tony Fry and Adam Nocek (Eds.), *Design in Crisis: New Worlds, Philosophies and Practices*. London: Routledge, 17–25.

Hâncean, M.G., Slavinec, M., & Perc, M. (2020). The impact of human mobility networks on the global spread of COVID-19. *Journal of Complex Networks*. https://doi.org/10.1093/comnet/cnaa041.

Honigsbaum, M. (2020). *The Pandemic Century: A History of Global Contagion from Spanish Flu to Covid-19*. London: Penguin.

Rawsthorne, A., & Antonelli, P. (2022). *Design Emergency: Building a Better Future*. London: Phaidon.

Sridhar, D. (2022). *Preventable: How a Pandemic Changed the World & How to Stop the Next One*. London: Penguin Random House.

UK Parliament Science Committee (2021). Science and Technology Committee: Oral Evidence Report: The role of technology, research and innovation in the COVID-19 recovery, HC 95. https://committees.parliament.uk/event/14114/formal-meeting-oral-evidence-session/.

World Economic Forum (2018). *The Global Risks Report*. Geneva: WEF, ISBN: 978-1-944835-15-6.

PART I   Reaction

This section illustrates the immediate reaction to the pandemic from a design perspective at both a practical and a strategic level, in response to societies, communities and government needs, addressing products, places and policies.

1 Design reactions

LOUISE MULLAGH, RACHEL COOPER, LISA THOMAS AND JUSTIN SACKS

Covid-19 has been described as a 'transboundary crisis' (Bryce et al., 2020), which has presented unprecedented pressures upon organizational, personal and community resilience. It has highlighted the nature of complexity and interconnectedness, while simultaneously bringing to the fore social, economic and structural inequalities. Since the beginning of the pandemic, we have seen that the use of design has gone beyond the production of products and services, to think about how we might design or redesign societies, governance and complex systems, such as healthcare, welfare and education. The pandemic has also, as Cohen and Cromwell (2021) state, 'significantly expanded the scope of possible problems to solve while also constraining the resources available to develop solutions to those problems'.

As we write this chapter we are still in a pandemic and even though some aspects of our lives have returned to normal, largely as a result of vaccination, we still live under the threat of rising cases over winter and new virus variants (Callaway, 2021; Chen et al., 2021). It is inevitable that there will be more pandemics in the future, and possibly sooner than later (Mackenzie, 2020, pp. 47–8), therefore it is essential that lessons are learned quickly and embedded in policy and societies for the future. The threats of future pandemics arise from the increasingly crowded cities and global mobility (Mackenzie, 2020), global health inequalities and the entanglements between humans and wildlife. Changing environments and the encroachment of humans into more habitats, resulting in the reduction of biodiversity (Akomolafe, 2020) and the movement of many animal populations (Fry & Nocek, 2020), mean we are more susceptible than ever in catching zoonotic diseases (Matthews, 2020).

This chapter explores the following research question:

What role can design play in the recovery from Covid-19 and in building resilience for future pandemics and global emergencies?

The chapter presents an overview of a range of design interventions that were created or implemented throughout the Covid-19 pandemic in order to draw out insights and develop principles for the future. We begin by presenting our methodology and research questions, followed by the presentation of the key themes identified through developing the database (Stage 1: Reaction; Stage 2: Adaptation) and a discussion in relation to the research question in order to understand how design has been deployed during this period. As the database is a work in progress, and we have not yet reached stages 3 (Recovery) and 4 (Resilience), we explore how design can contribute here through the development of principles for recovery and resilience. The chapter concludes with reflections upon how we move forward as designers and researchers, and how we might set an agenda for recovery and resilience, post-Covid-19.

Methodology

Our methodology was shaped by undertaking the task during lockdown in the UK. Our key aim was to build a database to capture a wide range of design interventions specifically targeted at the Covid-19 pandemic around the world, to understand where and how design was being used now and what this might mean for the future.

An online search using the terms 'design and pandemics', 'design and Covid-19', 'design and coronavirus' was undertaken. The main criteria were that the design intervention or proposal was related specifically to Covid-19. The success or roll-out of the design was not important, so examples included speculative designs, designs that were rolled out and were both successful and unsuccessful. A database was created using Excel, capturing key information about each example and the entries were categorized according to the following design disciplines:

1. Technology design and use (e.g. contact tracing mobile applications)
2. PPE equipment production (e.g. masks)
3. Graphic design and communication
4. Data visualization
5. Healthcare/medical equipment design and production
6. Cities/public space/architecture
7. Creative responses (e.g. design provocation)
8. Service design
9. Design methods

Examples were collated and assigned to four key stages of the pandemic that were identified through reviewing literature that was emerging throughout the early stages of the pandemic (the stages are defined in the following section):

1. Reaction
2. Adaptation
3. Recovery
4. Resilience

Although our experiences as researchers are rooted within the UK, the examples were chosen globally, in order to develop a rich picture of how design is being deployed around the world and in different circumstances. This enables comparison both geographically and temporally to understand the type of design interventions being developed and how they are compared. From this we were able to understand the differing approaches, their impact and potential for contributing to recovery, stability and resilience.

Undertaking this research during a period of rapid and profound change has been challenging, with a substantial body of literature, much of which was not peer reviewed appearing daily. Examples of design interventions have also been numerous, and as such, this research does not seek to offer an exhaustive account of examples, but instead offers a range of examples from a moment in time, as we collectively lived through the early stages of the pandemic. The research is ongoing and we are continuing to build the database, with a plan to make it available online to enable others to contribute.

Reaction, adaptation, recovery and resilience: Four stages of a pandemic

There have been pandemics throughout history, which have reshaped our social and physical environments (Budds, 2020), having profound effects upon urban design and infrastructure to create healthier towns and cities. This pandemic is no different in that respect, as we need to tackle issues such as high-density cities, unequitable access to technologies that we have become so reliant upon during the pandemic and ways in which we can remain connected socially and work from a distance if, or when, we experience future pandemics.

As we write this chapter we do not appear to have entered the recovery phase, s we face a winter with emerging variants and uncertainty as to how vaccinations will protect against them. However, we do appear to be moving forward as vaccinations and boosters are rolled out globally, but some countries around the world are still lagging with vaccinations due to lack of availability and cost implications (Sing et al., 2021).

Development of the framework: Enables design to be seen against the four key stages, to place examples against this backdrop, and to analyse and draw insights as to how design has been used this far, and how it might develop in the latter stages (recovery and resilience).

The four-stage framework is based on examples we found when creating the database and on literature relating to a range of emergency situations and recovery from them. The four stages encompass different scales, from the personal and domestic, to organizations, and to governments, both locally, nationally and global organizations. The stages are not exclusive and do not all occur individually from each other. For example, during the reaction phase, huge adaptations in myriad areas of life occurred, from our own domestic activities through to governments. This adaptation continued throughout the pandemic, as we continued to adapt our behaviours and at the wider scale, with organizations changing the ways in which they work, and governments adapting policies and legal frameworks.

Reaction: The initial stage of the pandemic varied around the world, with some countries quicker to impose lockdowns than others, with some relying upon track and trace systems in place of large-scale lockdowns. To restrict the spread of the virus new laws and policies are rapidly designed and implemented. Those countries who could afford to provide financial support for businesses and individuals to protect economies during the worst of the crisis. Many countries imposed lockdowns or strict track and trace systems due to rising cases. New laws and policies were rapidly designed and implemented, and the economy might be shut down, with only essential businesses allowed to open. Some governments implemented systems without enforcing them, where citizens voluntarily implement social distancing or other measures, whereas other countries (including China) imposed strict 'zero tolerance' policies. Communities came together and we saw the emergence of mutual aid groups that filled gaps between provision of care and services from governments around the world.

Adaptation: After the initial shock and rapid changes to lives in March, systems began to adapt and gradually society became used to a 'new normal'. Citizens adapted to new measures of social distancing and became accustomed to often severe measures, including leaving home to exercise or for essential activities. Around the world people found ways of connecting online, for social, work and educational purposes. However, this situation highlighted a digital divide, where those unable to access lives online were excluded. During this period governments rapidly developed vaccines, which were seen as fundamental to entering the recovery phase. Rhetoric from governments and NGOs highlighted the need for societies to be redesigned post-Covid-19, to 'build back better' and to tackle challenging and interconnected challenges, including climate change, societal unrest and health inequalities.

Recovery: This stage is only possible once large swathes of populations are vaccinated and levels of the virus decrease. During the summer and autumn of 2021, we saw slow recovery in economies, with industries including retail, hospitality and travel beginning to reopen fully. However, the recovery seems to have been short lived as Covid-19 variants emerge. Life feels uncanny, almost back to 'normal', but with underlying and profound changes, coupled with economic challenges.

Resilience: Post-pandemic, all lockdown measures and social distancing relaxed. The term 'resilience' has been used frequently throughout the pandemic, both in terms of examining how resilient societies were prior to the outbreak, and how it might be built as we emerge out of the other side. Resilience is a term that has multiple definitions, many of which refer to the return to an original state after going through stress or challenge, or 'bouncing back'. In relation to Covid-19, resilience has been embedded in political rhetoric, calling for societies to 'build back better'. To build resilience, it is vital that lessons are learned through reflection, in order to bring about lasting and meaningful change that will enable governments and communities around the world to cope with future crises.

Designing for and in pandemics: A database

This section presents key findings from each of the design phases. We have encountered the *reaction* and *adaptation* phases of the pandemic, and we are now beginning to tentatively enter the *recovery* phase. At the time of writing, it feels as though we are not at the *resilience* phase and we have certainly not emerged from the pandemic. Therefore, we offer speculations, or principles, as to how design can encourage and be embedded within resilience as we move forward, rather than offering examples of designs that have been created or deployed.

1. Technology design and use

Stage 1: Reaction: The rush to design and implement technologies in the tracking of the virus in order to limit its spread was seen worldwide (Ada Lovelace Institute, 2020). However, many of the designs for mobile applications and wearables to track citizens or the use of AI and IoT did not take fully into account issues such as privacy, data protection or ethics by design, an area that has received significant attention in various areas of design research in recent years (Lindley et al., 2018; Veale et al., 2018).

Contact tracing mobile applications: The use of mobile applications to trace contacts and alert those who might be at risk of contracting the virus has been seen as a key tool in the fight against the pandemic and a key enabler to governments in reopening their economies (Ada Lovelace Institute, 2020). We tracked a range of applications from the initial reaction stage, through to the adaptation stage in order to understand how governments and private developers were designing and implementing them, and at the time of writing, more than thirty public and private systems were being developed or in use around the world (GDPR Hub, 2020) (Figure 1.1).

We found significant variation in the speed at which they were designed and deployed and the ensuing issues, for example. The earliest countries to be exposed to the virus implemented a range of solutions, from private and government apps in South Korea, the use of QR codes to enable access to citizens China, TraceTogether in Singapore (TraceTo) and the StayHomeSafe app in Hong Kong. However, the use of mobile applications to combat the spread of a virus such as Covid-19 relies upon a high percentage of the population downloading the app, which proved to be an issue in Singapore, where only 12 per cent of the population had downloaded it by mid-April. The key to combatting the virus in the early stages was the design of comprehensive track and trace systems, which deployed both analogue and digital methods rather than relying solely upon apps. This approach was utilized by South Korea, one of the only countries to avoid significant lockdowns, but this was due to a national network of contact tracers who interviewed infected people and traced those who had been in contact with them. Phone alerts were used, but not through the kind of mobile application being developed in other countries (Nature, 2020). The UK announced early in the pandemic that NHSx, the digital transformation arm

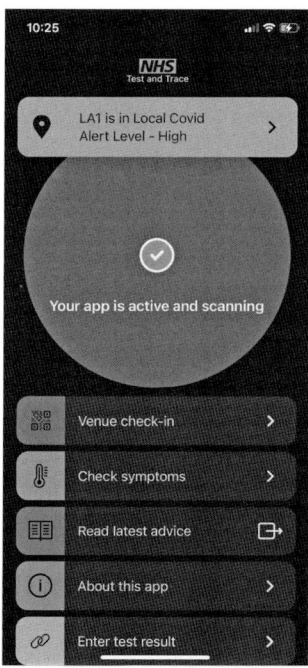

Figure 1.1 NHS Covid-19 mobile application. Image courtesy of UK Government (Open Government Licence v. 3.0).

of the NHS, was developing their own mobile app but this was delayed and then abandoned in favour of using the Google and Apple framework. By July, the UK had not deployed the application and it has been reported that when released it will include wider functionality and features such as a map warning people about areas with many infections, a countdown timer that helps people track the duration of a period of self-isolation and barcodes for buildings that would enable offices and restaurants to know if someone infected with the virus had visited (Skippervold and Wheller, 2020).

In recent years, issues relating to data security and privacy by design have been explored in areas of design research (Lindley, Coulton and Cooper, 2018), and through following literature relating to these apps, we have found the reliance upon their implementation alone, without also designing in robust and often analogue contact tracing, was widely challenged in the early stages of the pandemic (Ada Lovelace Institute, 2020; Morley et al., 2020; Stokel-Walker, 2020). At this early stage we see the lack of consideration of not only usability and access to mobile technologies, but the lack of designing ethics and privacy into the applications (Ada Lovelace Institute, 2020; Morley et al., 2020).

Drones: The use of drones during the pandemic has largely been focused on delivery of supplies to those self-isolating and to hospitals, and as a mode of surveillance to ensure social distancing and isolation measures are adhered to. Existing drones have been repurposed with new software and have been subject

Figure 1.2 Wingcopter drone used in Scotland during the pandemic. Akash 1997, CC BY-SA 4.0.

to revised airspace regulations (in the USA) to enable operators to carry out their new roles. In our database we found that very few examples exist in the UK and that USA and China have been the key sites of drone use during the pandemic. It is not necessarily the design of the drone itself we ought to consider in light of their use during epidemics, but the infrastructure and practices they are embedded within and the impact upon the populations for which they are operating, particularly where concerned with surveillance and privacy (Figure 1.2).

In China, the Shenzhen Smart Drone UAV has been deployed to aid in disease detection and crowd management, using thermal sensors, high-definition zoom lenses, loudspeakers and chemical spray jets to disinfect large areas (Liu, 2020). Through redesigning the application of the drones, it is hoped that less human contact will be had and the virus would not spread as quickly. However, this raises issues around privacy and the use of drones in surveillance. Similar drones were banned in France as they were deemed to constitute 'a serious and manifestly unlawful infringement of privacy rights' (Fouquet and Sebag, 2020). In USA, drones have been deployed to deliver groceries for those who are self-isolating, with Google's parent company Alphabet Inc. deploying their machines which can make deliveries without having contact with customers (Block, 2020). Medical supplies and Covid-19 test samples have also been carried to medical facilities in USA, where the FDA have relaxed rules to enable drones to operate in their airspace during the pandemic. Zipline drones have collaborated with a health network in North Carolina to deliver medical supplies using contactless on-demand delivery of PPE and medical supplies using drones that can fly at speeds of up to 80 miles per hour and at a range of over 100 miles (Wong, 2020). They faced issues in urban areas due to regulations around air restrictions, but policies were redesigned quickly to enable them to access airspace.

While drones present opportunities for non-contact delivery, surveillance and large-scale disinfecting, it is important to remember that they often operate in environments that have not been designed for them. Furthermore, 'the technology has arrived before society is ready. It is quite Utopian in a sense but we need to figure out how we actually use it and for whose benefit' (Cureton, 2020). In the UK, where policy is currently being designed to control the illegal use of drones and encourage those uses which have wider benefits, such as in emergencies (UK Parliament, 2020), drones have not been widely used during the current pandemic. They were trialled in delivering medical equipment in the Isle of Wight (Southampton, 2020) and in Scotland to deliver PPE to the remote Island of Mull (BBC, 2020), but were not used as extensively as in China and the United States. If drones are to become more commonplace, as predicted, it is not only privacy and consideration for the public who move around in the space below their flight paths that need to be designed into their operating systems, but also the design of the built environment will need to be reconsidered. Longer term use will require adaptations such as landing pads, solar photovoltaic panels for energy efficiency, charging points for delivery drones and landscaping to mitigate noise emissions (Cureton, 2020).

Robots: During the pandemic, robots have been deployed in settings such as hospitals and public parks with all the examples included in the database being repurposed for carrying out new tasks, as this enabled rapid deployment and ease of use by their operators. As with the issues we identified (above) with contact tracing apps and drone use, the deployment of robots also needs careful consideration and ethics carefully designed into their use.

In Singapore and China, dog robots produced by Boston Dynamics which feature cameras and speakers, enabling operators to view the park and communicate with visitors, were deployed to ensure social distancing was adhered to in parks (Neira, 2020). In hospitals, robots have been deployed to ensure cleaning could be carried out without the need for people, which enabled the disinfection of patient rooms and operating theatres (Ackerman, 2020). We also found examples of robots being used to provide contact-free support in a variety of healthcare roles, from carrying out basic monitoring and testing in hospitals, to providing remote care for vulnerable patients or those diagnosed with the virus (Spears, 2020).

Robots have been used in healthcare settings prior to the pandemic, but this period has demonstrated their value in protecting healthcare workers and limiting their contact with infected patients. 'Tommy' the robot nurse was used in Italy to monitor patients who were not in a critical state in order to free up doctors. The child-sized machine with large blinking eyes had a microphone to communicate, as well as a tablet and the ability to measure blood pressure and oxygen saturation (Romero, 2020). However, issues remain around the need to provide face-to-face care for vulnerable patients, which should be considered as part of a human-centred approach for the holistic implementation of technologies within healthcare settings both during and after the current crisis ends. When robots are deployed in public places, issues arise regarding the potential to cause fear and confusion, particularly during times of crisis when being outside might be traumatic for some. Deploying the dog robots might have been a rapid option, but they are not the friendliest looking machines and have the potential to cause fear. The physical design of machines that might be deployed in the future should be considered in order to reassure citizens, rather than causing fear.

Stage 2: Adaptation: As we moved into the adaptation phase, the use of mobile tracing apps, drones and robots continued. The mobile tracing apps developed around the world as the virus spread at different speeds and governments attempted to understand the challenges of designing and implementing complex systems. The use of wearable devices, in particular fitness trackers in the form of bracelets and watches, began to develop as governments and private developers started to explore their potential in tracking the health of citizens (Venkataramakrishnan, 2020).

We found examples using existing technologies, such as Fitbit and the Apple watch, as an early warning system to monitor signs such as heartbeat before the symptoms occur. This might enable the monitoring of symptoms ahead of second wave outbreaks around the world, as a high proportion of those infected remain asymptomatic (Giles and Brown, 2020). South Korea utilized the 'Safe Korea' bracelet to enforce quarantine rules after people were caught leaving the house without their smartphones to avoid detection (BBC, 2020b). Hong Kong also deployed electronic bands to inform police if those in quarantine left their homes and India manufactured thousands of temperature and location monitoring bands for those in quarantine. Liechtenstein was the first European country to introduce biometric monitoring using bracelets to implement a real-time tracking system (Privacy International, 2020) and was followed by Belgium where bands are used for social distancing and vibrate if they come within 3 metres of another band (BBC, 2020b) and Bulgaria where the Comarch Life Wristbands developed in Poland were introduced (Comarch, 2020). Oura's smart rings have also been the subject of rapid studies to explore their efficacy of symptom prediction through using AI to analyse user data. The platform monitors the human operating systems as wearers log symptoms into an app and the ring tracks physiological data like body temperature, heart rate and sleep patterns.

While wearable devices offer a passive experience and can be produced relatively inexpensively (such as South Korea and Belgium's examples), they once again pose potential issues of data creep, where more data than originally intended can be collected and their use can be enforced post-pandemic (Privacy International, 2020). Designing such systems to be used during and beyond the pandemic once again, as with the tracking apps, robots and drones, requires not only high standards of user interfaces and person-centred design, but ethics and privacy should be at the forefront. As we move onto the third and fourth stages of recovery and resilience, the designers of these technologies, while under pressure from governments during the initial stages, should ensure that the lessons learned from the current crises are reflected upon and folded into future uses for similar purposes.

2. Graphic design and communication

Stage 1: Reaction: Clear communication has been vital during all stages of the pandemic thus far, but particularly so in the early stages as governments rushed to roll-out social distancing guidance and the processes entailed in track and trace systems.

Government communications: As none of us had lived through a pandemic before Covid-19, the new situation had the potential to cause widespread panic or misunderstanding of the rules which would have a direct impact on the spread of the virus. During times of stress and anxiety, clear communication has been vital and governments have had to design and deliver information and messages accurately with as little room for interpretation as possible. . . . 'Design has a key role to play in distilling this information' (Dixon, quoted in Wong 2020b). The information communicated by governments evolved rapidly and was disseminated through multiple online and analogue channels. Clear and simple typography, colour and images were key in delivering unambiguous messages, as was demonstrated by the New Zealand government in their 'Unite against COVID-19' campaign (New Zealand Government, 2020). Bold colours, predominantly yellow and black, were used alongside simple images and text to communicate messages in a straightforward, unambiguous manner. In the UK, the government was criticized for a lack of coherence in their messaging and imagery, demonstrating how designing campaigns rapidly and under pressure can directly impact the public's perception and understanding of key communications (Moore, 2020).

The use of 'Stay home, protect the NHS, save lives' in the first stage follows the rule of three often adopted in campaigns, which was used in addition to 'Catch it, bin it, kill it' on public health posters and films. The 'Stay home . . .' image was coloured red with chevrons to denote the severity of the situation (Ivey-Williams et al., 2020) and communicate clearly what was expected of the public. During the easing of the lockdown in May, the messaging changed to 'Stay alert, protect the NHS, save lives', and the red changed to green, which was criticized for being less clear, in particular it was often unclear what was meant by 'stay alert' and indicated that rules were being relaxed due to the association of green with 'go'.

Public health: In April, the World Health Organisation (WHO) launched a competition – 'Global Call out to Creatives' (WHO, 2020). The aim was to translate public health messages such as the importance of hand washing, sneezing and coughing into tissues and physical distancing into clear messages using creative design. The submissions were all made available on the WHO platform to be used in any kind of campaign and designers consented to the open use of their work on submission. This is an example of how design can be harnessed to communicate across cultures and the keenness of designers to become involved in global campaigns.

Global branding: Global brands including Volkswagen, McDonald's and Audi all released Covid-19-related campaigns in around April to show solidarity and encourage social distancing (image); however, these received negative attention as

Figure 1.3 New Zealand government Covid-19 poster. Covid19.govt.nz Images. Owned by The Crown. Licensed by CC BY-NC 4.0.

they were seen to be marketing gimmicks by large organizations who were able to support workers in tangible ways to help tackle the spread of the virus (Figure 1.3).

Stage 2: Adaptation: Design has continued to play a vital role in communicating messages at all levels, from the hyper-local to the global, with creativity proving a salve in such turbulent times. Images of rainbows in support of the NHS on windows have been seen in the UK, created by school children to professional artists and designers. One key image that has been consistent throughout the pandemic is that of the virus itself. The image has become widely used and shared globally, after its release by the Centers for Disease Control and Prevention (CDC) in USA. It was felt the virus should be given an identity in order to be able to communicate the risk and make something that seemed so abstract into a tangible entity. Designers wanted to create 'a realistic virus that people can envision when walking into public places or coming into close contact with strangers. . . . Something that says the virus is real and needs to be taken seriously' (CDC, 2020). This image has been adapted countless times during the pandemic and is now recognized as shorthand for Covid-19, the embodiment of a virulent and unbelievably disruptive virus that has now become tangible.

3. Data visualization

Stage 1: Reaction and Stage 2: Adaptation: Throughout the pandemic, line graphs, bar charts and choropleth maps have become a vital method of communication by governments and the media around the world (Kennedy, 2020) to visualize the spread of the disease and death rates. The images have remained at a similar level of design maturity throughout the pandemic, but the data they are based on have changed rapidly, meaning they can become out of date very quickly. An early example of informative and interesting visualization came from New Zealand and demonstrated how the virus could spread depending upon people's interactions with others.

While charts, graphs and infographics have become essential in providing vital information, there are issues relating to literacy, of being able to understand visualizations, the bias that resides in the choices of data made and the accuracy of data (Kennedy, 2020). Visualizations can be beautiful, as we see in the Information is Beautiful dashboard, but there is a risk of form outweighing function, with the elegance of the designs giving legitimacy to the data and its interpretation. In the UK, the government gave daily briefings which centred around graphs, including the globally synonymous 'curve' diagram that demonstrated daily infection rates (UK Government, 2020) (Figure 1.4).

The Information is Beautiful website, created by the author of the book with the same title (McCandless), has become widely seen as a benchmark in creating aestheticized data visualization. The site hosts a wide range of Covid-19-related infographics and visualizations that are interactive and present a variety of data from around the world. Perhaps the most trusted source of data and visualizations during the pandemic has been the Johns Hopkins data repository (Johns Hopkins, 2020). As experts in global public health and infectious diseases, they have been a source of data and information that is widely trusted, so the visualizations we see are led by

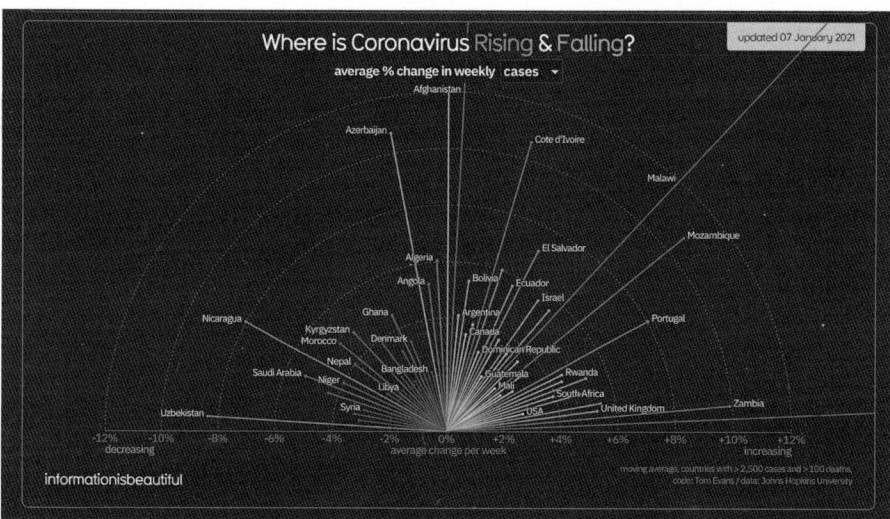

Figure 1.4 Data visualization showing rise and fall of Covid-19 infections (2020). 'Where is coronavirus rising and falling' graphic from Information is Beautiful website (Information is Beautiful, 2020).

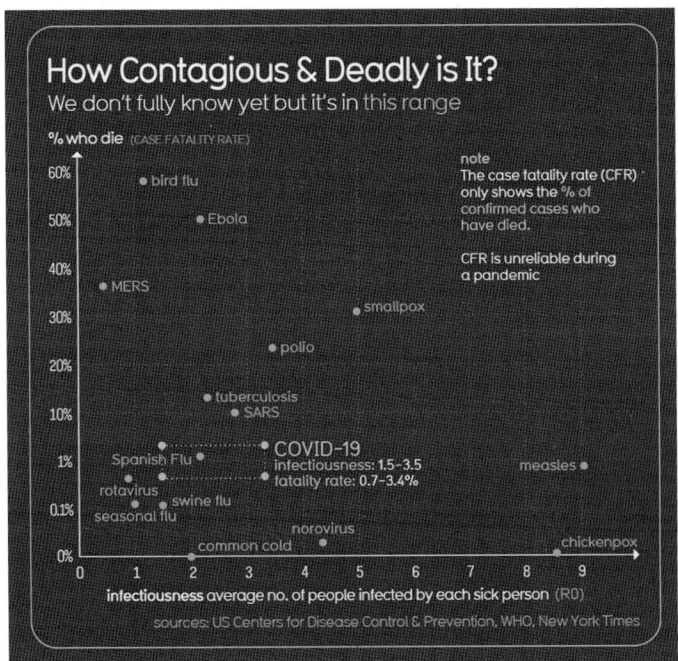

Figure 1.5 Data visualization showing how contagious Covid-19 was in 2020. Information is Beautiful, 2020.

a deep understanding of the data and the science behind it, with text to accompany the visualizations that provide context. The danger in presenting highly aestheticized visualizations of such complex data, as we see on many web-based platforms, is that 'visualizations can do ideological work, privileging certain views of the world and hiding others, or perpetuating existing power relations' (Kennedy, 2020). The data presented are not neutral and the ways in which they are presented rely on the values and choice of the designer (Figure 1.5).

4. Personal protective equipment and medical equipment

From the very beginning of the pandemic, governments around the world struggled to cope with demand for PPE equipment (masks, aprons, gloves, face shields) for frontline healthcare workers. China made half the world's masks before Covid-19 emerged there and it expanded production; however, due to the scale of the outbreak in the country much of the stock remained there. In the very early stages of the pandemic, innovation flourished in homes and factories, as people rushed to help in the production of masks, scrubs and ventilators. Issues with ventilators also became apparent very quickly as many patients infected with the virus required ventilation in intensive care units, placing huge pressure on supplies of the machines.

Huge demand placed on health services, particularly with the NHS and the need for ventilators. Government put out competition call for companies to provide ventilators and for the usual bureaucracy in this area to be temporarily reduced. Healthcare professionals have called for greater input from designers in both the design of medical equipment and the physical environments that have been placed under immense strain during the pandemic. We found many examples of design innovation, both in the design and production of PPE equipment such as masks and medical equipment, in particular ventilators.

Stage 1: Reaction:

Personal protective equipment: Shortages of PPE equipment such as face masks and shields, scrubs and aprons meant many organizations such as Burberry and Barbour switched production from their normal products to making masks and non-surgical gowns (Burberry, 2020; Barbour, 2020). In the UK, the wearing of masks by the public has only been made legal while travelling on public transport and there has not been widespread use. This is mostly down to differing advice as to whether or not wearing masks in public helps to prevent the spread of the virus (Rawlinson, 2020) and suggestions that not wearing them should be treated as socially unacceptable as drink-driving (Rawlinson, 2020). Furthermore, in the UK, mask wearing as of late April was around 25 per cent, despite the WHO and CDC in the United States issuing guidance suggesting that people should wear masks in public places where there is greater transmission of the virus (WHO, 2020; CDC, 2020). When PPE was made available it was mostly disposable, which has already been shown to affect the environment adversely. All single use PPE in the NHS is discarded after one use and the waste labelled as either 'infectious', 'offensive' or 'municipal' and is either disposed of through burning in incinerators or sent to landfill, or in rarer exceptions, recycled (Temple, 2020) (Figure 1.6).

During March and April, we found many examples of masks being made at home by individuals (Freesewing, 2020) or by professionals with making skills who were furloughed, such as television costumiers (BBC, 2020; Yale University, 2020). This highlighted that during the early stages of the pandemic where people were socially and physically isolated, there was a desire to be involved in making

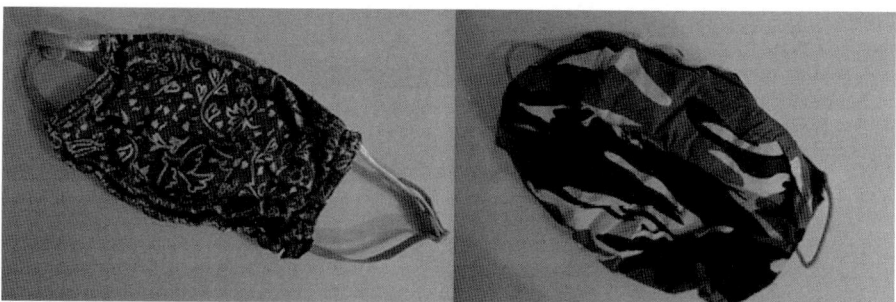

Figure 1.6 Home-made mask (left) and fashion mask produced by British designer (right). Copyright (both images) Louise Mullagh. Mask (on left) designed by Rixo.

things, with the materiality and processes that are positive for mental health. The use of platforms such as Facebook also enabled makers, both amateur and professionals, to join together from a distance to help counter the issues with the lack of PPE equipment (Murray, 2020), with many designs shared online, mirroring a 'commoning' approach where private organizations and individuals made their products available. However, due to strict guidelines relating to the production of medical equipment, it is not clear as to how many of the amateur ventilators or parts were utilized in hospitals. Exhaustive testing is also required, which has been very difficult to carry out under such demanding timescales. A huge amount of demand was also placed on materials required to produce ventilators, which would be wasted by those products that did not make it into hospitals but were produced by well-meaning volunteers.

Stage 2: Adaptation:

Personal protective equipment: As we moved into the later stages, masks were produced using high-quality fabrics from fashion designers, for example the British Fashion Council's 'Great British Designer Face Coverings' (British Fashion Council, 2020). We also found that factories which usually produce fashion garments, including Burberry and Barbour, redesigned their production lines to produce masks and scrubs for frontline staff (Burberry, 2020).

We also found issues relating to accessibility as we moved from the reaction to the adaptation stage. In particular, the issues of masks being problematic for people with hearing issues, who rely on seeing mouths to lip read, began to emerge during this stage. A student developed a mask that is partially see-through, with a transparent mouth area, but this isn't a fully resolved design due to the need to see not only the mouth but the full chin area (Azzarello, 2020). A more developed and mature design that tackles the issue with viewing the mouth is the 'HelloMask' (Houser, 2020) – a product created by scientists who experienced the 2015 Ebola outbreak in Africa that has been in development prior to the pandemic but will not be ready for full production until 2021.

During the adaptation stage, we see provocations such as Ai Weiwei's mask series that comment on various aspects of the pandemic globally (Myers, 2020), home-grown generative masks that could be grown from microbial cellulose, meaning masks could be made by individuals from materials that are effective and compostable, and masks that can be made from any see-through material and clipped onto a plastic frame. As we move out of the adaptation stage, it is clear that masks will be required in the future and that the approach taken during the Covid-19 pandemic will not be adequate.

Ventilators: Covid-19 lifted the mechanical ventilator from obscurity to a piece of equipment that was vital in treating millions of people around the world. In our database we came across a wide range of machines that were designed and produced by individuals using their own 3D printers at home (BBC, 2020b), girls in Afghanistan making ventilators from car parts (Haidare, 2020), the repurposing of diving snorkels into low-cost machines, to large global companies such as Dyson (2020) and the Formula One motor racing team (Mercedes Petronas, 2020).

The UK Government launched their Ventilator Challenge in March 2020 and spent £454 million to incentivize private companies to innovate design and escalate production of ventilators (Kinder et al., 2020) before cancelling all design innovations in June 2020 (Tovey and Roberts, 2020). Dyson spent £21 million rapidly developing, prototyping and producing their machine in thirty days, only for the machines to not be required in the UK (Dyson, 2020). The Penlon's Prima ES02 was a simplification of Penlon's proprietary ES02 ventilator (Penlon, 2020) and was created in response to the government's call. The proprietary design lies in opposition to the open designs we gathered for the database, in particular those such as the OVSI ventilator system, a product of the Open Ventilator System Initiative (OVSI). This machine is a generative concept design, signalled by OVSI's commitment to the Open Covid-19 Pledge (OVSI, n.d.) and the CERN Open Hardware License. The decentralized, open approach represented by OVSI aims to create 'inclusive innovation ecosystems . . . to enable local manufacturing and maintenance of the OVSI ventilator systems' (OVSI, n.d.).

5. Cities and public space

During the pandemic the places we inhabit have been largely empty while lockdowns have been enforced. For those buildings and spaces still open to the public, they have been adorned by rainbows of tape to direct where we can and can't go and to denote social distancing enforcement. The urban environment has long been shaped by crises, with buildings, infrastructure and green spaces all being affected historically (Budds, 2020) and as we emerge from the current pandemic they will be shaped once again.

Stage 1: Reaction: The immediate reaction in public places and essential businesses who were allowed to remain open (in the UK) was to deploy *ad hoc* markings on floors in order to change behaviour and enforce social distancing. This was seen around the world and was documented on social media, with accounts such as @Tape_measure on Instagram capturing thousands of examples. During the reaction stage, speed was of the essence, and as we have not lived through a pandemic before, there have been no prior precedents in terms of the most effective way of designing and implementing such measures. Supermarkets quickly designed and installed vinyl floor markings (Image) to visualize the required distances and to guide shoppers through one-way systems. They also quickly released visual campaigns in stores and on television explaining their operating methods and to reassure shoppers. The issues faced during this time were that wayfinding measures were often hastily designed and were often ignored where they were ineffective.

Stage 2: Adaptation: As we moved deeper into the pandemic, we found more refined designs being created to enforce social distancing measures. In the near future, as people return to public spaces, it is vital that the *ad hoc* taping we saw during Stage 1 is replaced with more refined and elegant designs in order to reassure people as they move around towns and cities, but that are also adaptable enough to be changed as social distancing measures change (e.g. in the UK the distance was reduced from 2 metres to 1 metre in June). An innovative project created by ImaginationLancaster at Lancaster University and in partnership with Lancaster City Council explores generative social distancing that offers businesses in the city attractive and effective wayfinding graphics and social distancing measures. Using Grasshopper and Rhino computer software a risk analysis of existing floor plans is generated to identify areas of social distance non-compliance. Using generative design methods, the work will automate and implement optimized wayfaring designs to ameliorate the risk of areas identified as non-compliant (Fagan, 2020). A live test case has been developed at a council building in the city centre that houses an information centre, café, performance spaces and a hub for small businesses. Floor markings and clear wayfinding graphics are generated for local businesses according to their individual floor plans and are printed by the design agency who has been working in partnership with ImaginationLancaster. Heat mapping tracking and a user survey will provide qualitative data on experience and operational success.

We have also found more refined and elegant social distancing markers in public spaces, such as the wave themed street signage in Paris (Norman, 2020) and white squares made from removable paint located in an Italian Plaza (Hitti, 2020), both demonstrate the efficacy of considered designs as we move deeper into the pandemic. Public spaces are also being reconsidered in the light of social distancing requirements, such as the design for a socially distanced park (Neira, 2020b) that takes the shape of a fingerprint.

Principles for designing towards recovery and resilience

Through understanding and learning from how design has contributed to the first two stages of the pandemic, we have developed principles to consider for the future stages of recovery and resilience. There has been a rapid refining of design interventions that become more elegant and considered as we move from the reaction and adaptation stages towards recovery and resilience. As countries reopen and embark upon a new way of operating, with localized outbreaks still occurring, vigilance is still fundamental. Designers and design researchers must carefully consider how we design for the latter two stages, recovery and resilience. From the findings presented above, we have identified key themes across all disciplines to consider how we might move forward into the recovery and resilience stages.

Effective, clear and consistent communication

Throughout the pandemic we have seen different responses from governments and public health organizations in communicating new laws, health messages and visualizations of the impact of the virus. Some of the campaigns have been more successful than others (Kennedy, 2020; Moore, 2020) and demonstrate the importance of having a clearly defined strategy for graphic communication and data visualization. Designers are uniquely placed to work across disciplines in governments, healthcare and NGOs to develop clear communication strategies and data visualization due to their ability to absorb and disseminate complex data and information.

- Governments and organizations should prioritize design in communicating their messages.
- Designers, governments and NGOs should engage more with what the data means, how we make sense of it and how this is balanced with the aesthetic elements of visualizing complex, global epidemiological data.

Design of, with and for community

The global and collective experiences of the pandemic have highlighted various versions of 'being in it together', from governments and organizations, or through the grassroots community mutual aid groups that have emerged. People wanted to make things and have a physical connection with material and objects: everyone can be a designer, whether through the production of face masks or 3D printed products at home. This democratization, or opening up of design, demonstrates the importance of the making process and its potential for supporting positive mental health through unprecedented and stressful periods.

- Designers have a role in developing digital and analogue products and services to support individuals and communities to build resilience (economic, health, and social) into their lives.

Equitable access to and ethical design of technologies

While the pandemic has seen a huge rise in the use of digital technologies, it has also highlighted issues of digital divide and inequitable access to internet and equipment such as smartphones and laptops (Berners-Lee, 2020). Also, the speed at which new technologies have been designed and deployed has led to complex issues relating to security, privacy and equitable access and potential to undermine public trust.

- It is vital that both analogue and digital systems are designed for those without digital access (Ada Lovelace Institute, 2020).
- It is vital that privacy and ethical principles are embedded by design from the outset (Morley et al., 2020).

Designing collaboratively

The sharing of designs for ventilators, associated spare parts and face shields has demonstrated an economic imaginary that can be termed commonism. In short, commonism is a mode of production in which open generative systems create common products (also called commons) for decentralized peer governance (Dyer-Witheford, 2007). While we saw individuals sharing designs online, we also saw different examples of operation that included large organizations sharing their proprietary operations.

- Mobilization of design and implementation through commons will be important in ensuring resilience.

Design agility and speed

Throughout the pandemic we have seen design and implementation of products and services occur at high speed. Layers of bureaucracy have been removed, as seen with the CDC in USA, who relaxed strict testing protocols to get medical equipment into hospitals, or rapid passing of policy to enable the closure of large swathes of the economy, or writing social distancing regulations into law, 'speed is, of course, of the essence – but so is due diligence and due process' (Nature, 2020).

- Utilizing well tested design methods such as rapid prototyping or design sprints will enable multidisciplinary teams to come together and work through complex issues.

Designing sustainably

The heavy use of disposable PPE in medical, social and domestic settings is unsustainable due to its negative environmental impacts (Ip et al., 2020). New forms of PPE must improve human well-being while not diminishing planetary well-being. Disposable PPE equipment, particularly masks used in public settings, are increasingly being discarded after use, rather than being disposed of adequately. While home-made masks are often reused and have greater potential to encourage sustainable behaviours, it is important for governments to begin to publicize the need for greater care in disposing of masks and for more sustainable alternatives to be developed, in line with the move towards circular economies.

- Designers can contribute to the development of sustainable PPE in two main ways: through the design of PPE that demonstrates adequate environmental sustainability through the design and disposal processes of equipment (particularly to members of the public) and through the design of persuasive and informative communications about PPE and the need for reusable equipment made from sustainable materials with robust disposal methods.

Conclusions and future work

As a reactive piece of research, this chapter explores a range of design interventions and propositions during the early stages of the pandemic. The authors continue to gather examples of design as the pandemic progresses and develop more nuanced and in-depth analysis to understand the potential strengths, issues and impacts of the interventions and propositions. We have demonstrated that during the pandemic a light has been shone upon many inequalities across societies and demonstrated the need to redesign at different scales, from the hyper-local to the societal level. There have been repeated calls to design a better society as a whole and we are mindful that design is only part of a solution in a crisis. Much of the work to enable recovery and build resilience is the responsibility of national governments and their collaboration with key agencies around the world. However, as demonstrated in this initial stage of this research, designers are able to connect across a wide range of disciplines and organizations to enable innovative and creative solutions.

Covid-19 has highlighted the need to rethink the nature of the complex and interrelated problems we face, as well as the ways in which design can be positioned to explore possible solutions (Fry and Nocek, 2020). The pandemic has shone a light upon myriad inequalities around the world, including access to basic healthcare and vaccines, safe working conditions and economic support (Singh et al., 2020). This situation also presents opportunities to rethink and redesign societies from the ground up. There have been calls for this to be the time we collectively reconsider many aspects of our lives and rebuild in ways that are socially equitable and more sustainable. This approach is echoed by the UN secretary general who said

> We are in an unprecedented situation and the normal rules no longer apply. We cannot resort to the usual tools in such unusual times. The creativity of the response must match the unique nature of the crisis – and the magnitude of the response must match its scale.
>
> (Guterres, 2020)

While we can present potential future scenarios for design, we are still experiencing profound uncertainty about the ways in which we emerge from the pandemic. What is evident, however, is a need for innovative, collaborative and cross-disciplinary approaches, which will result in future resilience. The notion of design and its role in creating a more resilient future is also being questioned. As Fry and Nocek (2020, p. 6) suggest, 'Design can't limit itself to changing the patterns of human consumption, to altering its supply chains, or to sourcing biodegradable materials. It must envision the possibility of design *new conditions for being human*.'

This places design in a strong position to be able to contribute to the ways in which we collectively move forward and build resilience at all scales of society. There is also a recognition globally that new ways of thinking at all scales, from the hyper-local to the global, are required and this situation also presents opportunities to rethink and redesign societies from the ground up. This unique period in time offers an opportunity to collectively reconsider many aspects of our lives and to rebuild in ways that are socially equitable, ethically responsible and more sustainable.

References

Ada Lovelace Institute (2020). *Confidence in a Crisis: Building Trust in a Contact Tracing App*. https://www.adalovelaceinstitute.org/wp-content/uploads/2020/08/Ada-Lovelace-Institute_COVID-19_Contact_Tracing_Confidence-in-a-crisis-report-3.pdf.

Ackerman, E. (2020). Autonomous Robots are Helping Kill Coronavirus in Hospitals, *IEEE Spectrum*.https://spectrum.ieee.org/automaton/robotics/medical-robots/autonomous-robots-are-helping-kill-coronavirus-in-hospitals (Retrieved 10 June, 2020).

Akomolafe, B. (2020). *Mushroom Newsletter*. The Emergence Network. www.emergence-network.org.

Azzarello, N. (2020). Student creates transparent masks for the deaf and hard of hearing community. *Designboom*. https://www.designboom.com/design/student-creates-transparent-masks-deaf-hard-of-hearing-04-08-2020/ (Retrieved April 9, 2020).

Barbour (2020). *Barbour Service Update*. https://uk.burberry.com/burberry-supports-the-fight-against-covid-19/ (Retrieved June 10, 2020).

BBC (2020b). Coronavirus: TV costume makers create scrubs for NHS Staff. *BBC Website*. https://www.bbc.co.uk/news/av/uk-wales-52273528/coronavirus-tv-costume-makers-create-scrubs-for-nhs-staff (accessed 15 April 2020).

Berners-Lee (2020), COVID-19 makes it clearer than ever: access to the internet should be a universal right. *The Guardian*. https://www.theguardian.com/commentisfree/2020/jun/04/covid-19-internet-universal-right-lockdown-online (Retrieved June 5, 2020).

Block, I. (2020). *Google's Wing Drones Deliver Essentials during Coronavirus Pandemic*. https://www.dezeen.com/2020/04/15/google-wing-drone-delivery-coronavirus-virginia/.

British Fashion Council (2020). *Great British Designer Face Coverings*. https://www.britishfashioncouncil.co.uk/About/Great-British-Designer-Face-Coverings (Retrieved June 10, 2020).

Bryce, C., Ring, P., Ashby, S., & Wardman, J. K. (2020). Resilience in the face of uncertainty: Early lessons from the COVID-19 pandemic. *Journal of Risk Research*, 23(7–8), 880–7. doi:10.1080/13669877.2020.1756379.

Budds, D. (2020). *Design in the Age of Pandemics*. https://www.curbed.com/2020/3/17/21178962/design-pandemics-coronavirus-quarantine.

Burberry (2020). *Burberry supports the fight against COVID-19*. https://uk.burberry.com/burberry-supports-the-fight-against-covid-19/ (Retrieved 20 June 2020).

Calder-Gerver G., Mazeri S., Haynes S., Simonet C., Woolhouse M., & Brown H. (2021). Real-Time Monitoring of Covid-19 in Scotland. *Journal of the Royal College of Physicians of Edinburgh*, 51(1_suppl), 20–25. doi:10.4997/jrcpe.2021.237.

Callaway, E. (2021). *Heavily Mutated Omicron Variant Puts Scientists on Alert, Nature*. https://www.nature.com/articles/d41586-021-03552-w.

Centres for Disease Control and Prevention (CDC) (2020). *Use of Cloth Face Coverings to Help Slow the Spread of COVID-19*. https://www.cdc.gov/coronavirus/2019-ncov/prevent-getting-sick/diy-cloth-face-coverings.html (accessed 7 July 2020).

Chen, J., Gao, K., Wang, R., & Wei, G. (2021). Preparation and mitigation of mutation threats to COVID-19 vaccines and antibody therapies. *Royal Society of Chemistry*, 12, 6929–48. https://pubs.rsc.org/en/content/articlehtml/2021/sc/d1sc01203g.

Christakis, N. A. (2020). *Apollo's Arrow: The Profound and Enduring Impact of Coronavirus on the Way We Live*. New York: Little, Brown Spark.

Cohen, A. K., & Cromwell, J. R. (2021). How to respond to the COVID-19 pandemic with more creativity and innovation. *Population Health Management*, 24(2), 153–5. doi:10.1089/pop.2020.0119.

COMARCH, (2020). *Quarantined Sofia residents to receive Comarch LifeWristbands*. https://www.comarch.com/press-center/news/corporate/quarantined-sofia-residents-to-receive-comarch-lifewristbands/ (Retrieved 30 April, 2020).

Cureton, P. (2020). *How Drones and Aerial Vehicles Could Change Cities*. https://theconversation.com/how-drones-and-aerial-vehicles-could-change-cities-140907.

Dyer-Witheford, N. (2007). Commonism. *Turbulence*, 1(1). http://www.turbulence.org.uk/turbulence-1/commonism/index.html (Retrieved June 8, 2020).

Dyson (2020). *Ventilator Update*. https://www.dyson.co.uk/newsroom/overview/update/ventilator-update.html (Retrieved 20 June 2020).

Escobar, A. (2018). *Designs for the Pluriverse: Radical Interdependence, Autonomy, and the Making of Worlds*. Durham, NC: Duke University Press.

Fouquet, H., & Sebag, G. (2020). French covid-19 drones grounded after privacy complaint. *Bloomberg*, 18 May. https://www.bloomberg.com/news/articles/2020-05-18/paris-police-drones-banned-from-spying-on-virus-violators (accessed 20 June 2020).

Freesewing (2020). *Calling All Makers: Here's a 1-page PDF Facemask Pattern; Now Go Make Some and Help Beat This Thing*. https://freesewing.org/blog/facemask-frenzy (Retrieved 6 June 2020).

Fry, T., & Nocek, A. (2020). Editor's introduction: 'Design in crisis, introducing a problematic'. In Tony Fry and Adam Nocek (Eds.), *Design in Crisis: New Worlds, Philosophies and Practices*. London: Routledge, 1–17.

GDPR Hub (2020). *Projects Using Personal Data to Combat SARS-CoV-2*. https://gdprhub.eu/index.php?title=Projects_using_personal_data_to_combat_SARS-CoV-2 (accessed 6 June 2020).

Guterres, A. (2020). *United Nations Secretary General's Open Remarks at Virtual Press Conference on COVID-19*. https://www.un.org/sg/en/content/sg/speeches/2020-03-19/remarks-virtual-press-encounter-covid-19-crisis.

Haidare, S. (2020). Coronavirus: Afghan girls make ventilators out of car parts, *BBC*. https://www.bbc.co.uk/news/world-asia-52738668 (Retrieved July 1, 2020).

Hitti, N. (2020). *Caret Studio installs gridded social-distancing system inside Italian piazza*. https://www.dezeen.com/2020/05/12/caret-studio-social-distancing-stodistante-installation-vicchio/.

Honigsbaum, M. (2020). *The Pandemic Century: A History of Global Contagion from the Spanish Flu to Covid-19*. London: WH Allen.

Houser, K (2020). *Fully see-through face mask ready for mass production*. https://www.freethink.com/articles/see-through-face-mask (Retrieved June 11, 2020).

Ip, V., Özelsel, T., Sondekoppam, R., Tsui, B. (2012). *COVID-19 Pandemic: Is Sustainability the Answer to Personal Protective Equipment (PPE) Shortages?*. https://www.asra.com/page/2934/covid-19-pandemic-is-sustainability-the-answer-to-personal-protective-equipment?_zs=OS9cX&_zl=AT162 (Retrieved June 10, 2020).

Ivey-Williams, K., Allers, M., Dub, S. (2020). *Designing the GOV.UK coronavirus page*. https://designnotes.blog.gov.uk/2020/06/08/designing-the-gov-uk-coronavirus-page (Retrieved June 7, 2020).

Jessop, Z. M., Dobbs, T. D., Ali, S. R., Combellak, E., Clancy, R., Ibrahim, N., Jovic, T. H., Kaur, A. J., Nijran, A., O'Neilll, T. B., & Whitaker, I. S. (2020). Personal protective equipment for surgeons during COVID-19 pandemic: Systematic review of availability, usage and rationing. *British Journal of Surgery*, 7(10), 1262–80. https://doi-org.ezproxy.lancs.ac.uk/10.1002/bjs.11750.

Johns Hopkins University (2020). *Global COVID-19 Data and Visualizations*. https://coronavirus.jhu.edu (Retrieved July 1, 2020).

Kennedy, H. (2020). Simple data visualisations have become key to communicating about the COVID-19 pandemic, but we know little about their impact. *LSE Blog*. https://blogs.lse.ac.uk/impactofsocialsciences/2020/05/04/simple-data-visualisations-have-become-key-to-communicating-about-the-covid-19-pandemic-but-we-know-little-about-their-impact/.

Kinder, T., Foster, P., & Pooler, M. (2020). *Ventilator challenge to cost government £450m despite cancellations*. https://www.ft.com/content/8df85bb4-4e2e-41f3-bb51-c7d046d23455 (Retrieved May 20, 2020).

Lindley, J., Coulton, P., & Cooper, R. (2018). Informed by design. In *Living in the Internet of Things: Cybersecurity of the IoT – 2018*. London, 1–12. doi:10.1049/cp.2018.0022.

Liu, Y. (2020). China adapts surveying, mapping, delivery drones to enforce world's biggest quarantine and contain coronavirus outbreak. *South China Morning Post*, 5 March. https://www.scmp.com/business/china-business/article/3064986/china-adapts-surveying-mapping-delivery-drones-task (accessed 3 June 2020).

Mackenzie, D. (2020). *COVID-19: The Pandemic that Never Should Have Happened, and How to Stop the Next One*. London: The Bridge Street Press.

Martindale, A., Armstead, C., & Mckinney, E. (2021). 'I'm not a doctor, but I can sew a mask': The face mask home sewing movement as a means of control during the COVID-19 pandemic of 2020. *Craft Research*, 12(2), 205–23, doi:10.1386/crre_00050_1.

Matthews, A. (2020). *Review of Mark Honigsbaum (2020). The Pandemic Century—A History of Global Contagion from the Spanish Flu to Covid-19*. Cambridge, MA: Penguin. 321p. ISBN 9780753558287 [published online ahead of print, 2020 July 20]. *Postdigital Science and Education*. 2020;1–9. doi:10.1007/s42438-020-00170-z.

Mercedes Petronas (2020). *Designs for Life-saving Breathing aid to be Made Freely Available*. https://www.mercedesamgf1.com/en/news/2020/04/ucl-uclh-f1-project-pitlane-start-delivery-breathing-aids-nhs-hospitals/ (Retrieved April 30, 2020).

Meyer, A. (1982). Adapting to environmental jolt. *Administrative Science Quarterly*, 27(4), 515–37.

Moore, R. (2020). The UK Government Coronavirus Strategy: Shoddy by design? *The Guardian*. https://www.theguardian.com/artanddesign/2020/jun/14/the-uks-government-coronavirus-strategy-shoddy-by-design (Retrieved June 14, 2020).

Morley, J. C., Taddeo, M., & Floridi, L. (2020). Ethical guidelines for covid-19 tracing apps: Protect privacy, equality and fairness in digital contact tracing with these key questions. *Nature Online*. https://www.nature.com/articles/d41586-020-01578-0 (accessed 6 June 2020).

Murray, J. (2020). Volunteers stitch together to make scrubs for the NHS, *The Guardian*. https://www.theguardian.com/world/2020/apr/13/volunteers-stitch-together-make-scrubs-for-nhs (Retrieved April 14, 2020).

Myers, L. (2020). *Ai Weiwei Designs Face Masks for Charity*. https://www.designboom.com/art/ai-weiwei-designs-coronavirus-masks-for-charity-middle-finger-05-28-2020 (Retrieved 20 May 2020).

Nature (2020). Covid-19 digital apps need due diligence. *The International Journal of Science Nature*, 580, 30 April. https://media.nature.com/original/magazine-assets/d41586-020-01264-1/d41586-020-01264-1.pdf (Retrieved 15 June 2020).

Neira, J. (2020a) *Singapore deploys dog robots to remind people of safe distancing measures*. https://www.designboom.com/technology/singapore-deploys-dog-robots-safe-distancing-measures-05-08-2020/ (Retrieved June 15, 2020).

Neira, J. (2020b). *Parc de la Distance, Design Boom*. https://www.designboom.com/design/wave-themed-street-signage-system-by-studio-5•5-encourages-parisians-social-distance-05-26-2020/.

Norman, L. (2020). *Wave Distinction Line for Paris against Covid-19, Design Boom*. https://www.designboom.com/design/wave-themed-street-signage-system-by-studio-5•5-encourages-parisians-social-distance-05-26-2020/.

Olatunbosun-Alakija, A. (2021). Unless we address the inequity in global health, then the world will not be prepared for the next pandemic. *BMJ*, 375, n2848. https://www.bmj.com/content/375/bmj.n2848.

OVSI. (n.d.). *Mission – Open Ventilator System Initiative. OVSI – Open Ventilator System Initiative*. https://ovsi.org/mission (Retrieved June 29, 2020)

Penlon (2020). *COVID-19 Simple Alternative Ventilator Solution from Penlon*. https://www.penlon.com/Blog/March-2020/Simple-Alternative-Ventilator-Solution-from-Penlon.

Privacy International (2020a). *Tracking the Global Response to COVID-19*. https://privacyinternational.org/examples/tracking-global-response-covid-19 (Retrieved July 1, 2020).

Rawlinson, K. (2020). Refusal to wear mask should be as taboo as drink-driving, says Royal Society Chief. *The Guardian*. https://www.theguardian.com/world/2020/jul/07/refusal-to-wear-mask-should-be-as-taboo-as-drink-driving-says-royal-society-chief?utm_source=Nature+Briefing&utm_campaign=13e014bf84-briefing-dy-20200707&utm_medium=email&utm_term=0_c9dfd39373-13e014bf84-45504658 (accessed 7 July 2020).

Rittel, H. W. J., & Webber, M. M. (1973). Dilemmas in a general theory of planning. *Policy Sciences*, 4(2), 155–69. doi:10.1007/bf01405730.

Romero, M. L; Martirosyan, L. (2020) *Tommy the robot nurse helps Italian doctors care for COVID-19 patients*. https://theworld.org/stories/2020-04-08/tommy-robot-nurse-helps-italian-doctors-care-covid-19-patients.

Singh, S., Bartos, M., Abdalla, S., Legido-Quigly, H., Nordström, A., Johnson Sirleaf, E., & Clark, H. (2021). Resetting international systems for pandemic preparedness and response. *The BMJ*, 375, e067518.

Skippervold and Wheller (2020). *COVID-19 and the Internet of Things Briefing*. PETRAS IOT. https://petras-iot.org/update/covid-19-the-internet-of-things-and-cybersecurity/.

Spears, T. (2020). *Boston Dynamics spot robot dog helps doctors treat COVID-19 patients*. https://www.designboom.com/technology/boston-dynamics-spot-robot-dog-doctors-covid-19-04-24-2020/ (Retrieved June 15, 2020)

Stokel-Walker, C. (2020). Smartphone contact-tracing technology has played a role in easing lockdown in china, and other countries are following suit. But are contact-tracing apps all they're cracked up to be? *BBC Future*. https://www.bbc.com/future/article/20200415-covid-19-could-bluetooth-contact-tracing-end-lockdown-early (accessed 6 June 2020).

Tonkinwise, C. (2020). Sacrifices that do not work in a crisis. In T. Fry & A. Nocek (Eds.), *Design in Crisis: New Worlds, Philosophies and Practices*. London: Routledge, 43–56.

Tonkinwise, C. (2021) Sacrifices that do not work in a crisis. In T. Fry & A. Nocek (Eds.), *Design in Crisis: New Worlds, Philosophies and Practices*. Abingdon, Oxon: Routledge, 43–56.

Tovey, A., & Roberts, L. (2020, June 10). All new ventilator models abandoned by ministers. *The Telegraph*. https://www.telegraph.co.uk/business/2020/06/10/new-ventilator-models-abandoned-ministers/ (Retrieved June 27, 2020)

TraceTogther (2020) *Singapore's Track and Trace mobile application*. https://www.tracetogether.gov.sg (Retrieved June 1, 2020).

UK Parliament (2020). *Misuse of Civilian Drones*. Postnote number 610, January. https://www.google.com/url?sa=t&rct=j&q=&esrc=s&source=web&cd=&ved=2ahUKEwj5kpflmLvqAhVEQEEAHUQVDKQQFjAEegQIBBAB&url=http%3A%2F%2Fresearchbriefings.files.parliament.uk%2Fdocuments%2FPOST-PN-0610%2FPOST-PN-0610.pdf&usg=AOvVaw0CX_PK4uGHJ_UE92HTvFbL.

Veale, M., Binns, R., & Ausloos, J. (2018). When data protection by design and data subject rights clash. *International Data Privacy Law*, 8(2), 105–23. doi:10.1093/idpl/ipy002.

Venkataramakrishnan, S. (2020). *Researchers turn to wearable tech in race to track COVID-19, Financial Times*. https://www.ft.com/content/f13106bd-dc49-455e-ad9c-5aec256f9aa8 (Retrieved June 11, 2020).

Wong, H. (2020). *"Government needs to make people care": designers on coronavirus communications*. https://www.designweek.co.uk/issues/23-29-march-2020/coronavirus-communications-government/ (Retrieved April 10, 2020).

World Health Organisation (WHO) (2020). *Shortage of Personal Protective Equipment Endangering Health Workers Worldwide*. https://www.who.int/news/item/03-03-2020-shortage-of-personal-protective-equipment-endangering-health-workers-worldwide.

2 The usefulness of imperfect design

PAUL A. RODGERS, CRAIG BREMNER AND
FERNANDO GALDON

Introduction

We, the authors, have been probing the state of the gesture of care for nearly a decade, and we staged our first international symposium to begin a process of reformulating the conceptual basis of care from the point of view of design in Copenhagen in 2015. A few years and events later the first 'Does Design Care . . .?' workshop at ImaginationLancaster in 2017 asked participants to respond to what we had identified as ten problems with care including – What might a theory of care look and feel like? How can care be made more explicit? How do we get to better care and what will it be like? Is inconsistent, unpredictable and ever-changing care desirable? How do we create attractive personalized and customized care? Since then, the concept of 'care' has become very popular with a booming literature very little of which sees any problems associated with care other than the need for more of it.

In addition to the ten problems with care we started with, the first 'Does Design Care . . .?' workshop produced some problems with the problems. We wondered whether it was worth asking how much care, in particular health and social care, is just opportunistic. It is not enough for me to care – the other must need care. So, people appearing to need care are perfect, soft targets for something that we design and call care, that is, something easily imitating care. We also wonder what is the attraction for design to want to get into bed with health and social care when the invisible gesture of care is so complex – care is always care of the other, care for the other, care to be cared for by the other, care for what the other cares for.

And when an emerging platform we could call design and care comes into existence why do all the anecdotes paraded as design solutions appear to validate the design actions, especially when anecdotes never have currency in the disciplines? We could see why it was attractive to equate care with historic misconceptions of utopia because mixing design with care reprises the unfictionable ideals of design. But why does design need the increasingly popular 'fictions' to approach care? Does that make care a fiction? The trickiest issue for us was the carefully circumvented question of how design can avoid getting entangled in care's transactional platform? Was care simply another opportunity for design in its pact with capital? With the maturing of the service economy eventually people just wanted to be served, so with the rapid rise and maturing of the caring economy is it likely that people will just want to be cared for? If so, this is perfect for the business of care but what about the design of care? Keep in mind that service design is largely just transactional affairs sold under the guise of friendship (Rodgers and Bremner, 2018). Also, can design distinguish between interactional care and transactional care? The former is a basic gesture most of us engage in instinctively while the latter is an uncharitable trick of the capital project.

Initially, it appears that all of the design proceedings pushing the issue of care are confronting basic questions such as what do we mean when we speak of care and what do we mean when we think care? But it is now appearing to be easier for conferences and authors to sidestep these basic questions and leap straight to the managerial 'case-study' model. We were still interested in where we locate care (as gesture) or where we locate the idea of care (as value)? Does care initiate a process of production (e.g. via gestures)? Or do our habitual actions produce care (i.e. is care an end product or by-product)? Perhaps the most troubling question for design is whether design is attempting to give care agency or turn care into an agent, and as such, the relational design/product/service par excellence?

What made us even more suspicious was design's sudden predilection to chronicle its actions – its case studies and anecdotes – as acts of empathy, which prompted us to ask – what was design doing before it discovered empathy? But is design aware that empathy makes designers imagine they are people they are not (Solnit, 2015) and that 'empathy is, in a word, selfish . . . is biased . . . is short sighted' (Serpell, 2019).

Almost all of the above questions were answered in a matter of months – specifically the months from 1 January to 31 May 2020 – the period during which we collected design responses in the form of products, systems, graphics, shelters, networks and direct action to the Covid-19 pandemic. As the projects rapidly accumulated from all corners of the globe, we analysed and assembled them into a book that we published soon after (Rodgers et al., 2020). This chapter tells the story of this work and the resulting book – *A Design History of the Covid-19 Virus*.

We documented hundreds of projects many of which might have saved lives. All were produced as quickly as possible with designed outcomes getting more and more rudimentary – imperfection was irrelevant. Use was king. Lifesaving designs, absolutely essential and useful but all imperfect. Perfection would have been deathly! But long before we witnessed this absolute utility of imperfection in hundreds of design responses to the Covid-19 pandemic, Andrea Branzi wrote in his *Introduction to Italian Design* (2008) that imperfection had already superseded perfection as the archetype of design:

> The activity of innovation, which today design is called to respond to, follows strategies completely different from those past, committed to realising definitive products, that is industrial archetypes destined for large numbers to mass markets, and exemplified by great elegance by our masters. It is the opposite

today. . . . One must point to individualised models 'reversible, provisional, perfectible' that leave large margins for future action, market adjustment, but also the advent of new market spaces. One isn't dealing only with updating product aesthetics, but to individualise dynamic devices that will never reach a definitive equilibrium. Paradoxically, perfection creates rigidity, fragility and the risk of precocious aging of the brand.

(Branzi, 2008, p. 190)

Similarly, David Pye, the well-known architect, industrial designer and wood craftsman who also worked on the theory of design and workmanship, spoke widely on imperfection in design, stating:

Nothing we design or make ever really works. Never do we achieve a satisfactory performance. Things simply are not 'fit for their purpose'. Everything we design and make is an improvisation, a lash-up, something inept and provisional

(Pye, 1978, pp. 13–14).

In addition, in 'Towards Relational Design' (2008), Andrew Blauvelt proposed that we are moving towards a type of design that is relationally based and contextually specific. In his account, he structures the evolution of design into three main epochs: modern design, post-modern design and relational design. Modern design ranges from 1900 to 1950 and focused on *forms*, which were disseminated rationally and potentially universally. Post-modern design ranged from 1960 to 2000 and focused on design's *meaning-making* potential, symbolic value, semantic dimension and narrative potential. Finally, relational design ranges from 2000 to the present and focuses on effects on users, pragmatic and programmatic constraints, rhetorical impact and the ability to facilitate social interactions. He presents IDEO and Anthony Dunne and Fiona Raby as primary practitioners in this new evolution. In his account, he describes relational design as including performative, pragmatic, programmatic, process-oriented, open-ended, experiential and participatory elements, moving away from designing discrete objects 'to the creation of systems and more open-ended frameworks for engagement: designs for making designs' (Blauvelt, 2008). With the Covid-19 crisis we might argue for a fourth wave of design based on events.

The first wave of design offered us a multiplicity of forms, the second a multiplicity of meanings and interpretations and the third wave presented a multiplicity of contingent, boundaried or conditional solutions: open-ended rather than closed systems; real-world constraints and contexts over idealized utopias; relational connections instead of reflexive imbrication; 'the end of discrete objects, hermetic meanings, and the beginning of connected ecologies' (Blauvelt, 2008, p. 6). The fourth wave seems to present trust as a fundamental element to design: unsupervised versus supervised systems; unintended consequences versus control; readiness versus perfection, care versus profit; resilience versus comfort; not fully knowing versus fully knowing; reparation and accountability versus empathy and the ubiquity of fluid cyber-blended and hyper-connected interdependent ecologies.

The relationship between the imperfect and trust is being played out in the development of the vaccines. Every vaccine was developed in the 'just-in-time' method with each in varying degrees imperfect but imperfect just enough to be able to be customized to combat the coming virus variations. However, it appears that this same useful (by design) imperfection is making it difficult to convince everyone to put their trust in a vaccine's efficacy.

What we did

In our book – *A Design History of the Covid-19 Virus* – we documented the Covid-19 crisis as it evolved every day from 1 January 2020 to 31 May 2020. This temporal span encompassed the outbreak, the first lockdown and reopening. We looked at all of this care and caring from the point of view of design and, by the sheer volume of design interventions we have documented, illustrate that design really does care.

What the Covid-19 pandemic has illustrated is that for the first time in modern history capital was totally irrelevant. Money could not save your life. Only design could. Rapidly designed masks, shelters, hospitals, instructional posters, infographics, dashboards, respirators, sanitizers, virtual and local communities emerged to save us. From 1 January 2020, design became king. The Covid-19 global pandemic presented an ontological reality; design is more than margins or profit. In fact, design became extremely valuable when it stopped concentrating on those things and started to care about peoples' lives. This brief episode in history is repositioning the status of design and reconfiguring its signifier from consumption to care.

Given the very peculiar Covid-19 circumstances, to assemble our book – *A Design History of the Covid-19 Virus* – we simply collected everything as a type of diary entry form of data collection. We saw it as the best possible method to gather the collected experience of the material culture, body of experience, skill and understanding embodied in the arts of planning, inventing, making and doing related to the event. Also, the infinite array of digital tools enabled us to collect the interventions from our desks. In this context, photos, videos and text were collected using a variety of online apps and tools that allowed us to collect the design interventions dealing with an unexpected event. Here we are not investigating how people changed over time, but how practice, in this case design, adapted through time and circumstances to address readiness, appropriateness and preparedness.

In the development of our book, we adopted what could be objectively characterized as an elicitation perspective. This consisted of capturing media as soon as the phenomenon occurs to record examples of pandemic design as soon as they were found in the digital landscape. By assembling the cases in chronological order, the book functions as a history of the Covid-19 pandemic design interventions. It is a 'research-in-the-moment project' where we illustrated our thoughts and insights in

Title	COVID-19 Coronavirus Map: Global Outbreak Dashboard
Author	The New York Times
Published	2020-01-28T22:57:20.000Z
URL	https://www.nytmes.com/interactve/2020/world/coronavirus-maps.html
Keywords	days, reported, outbreak, rate, global, countries, average, coronavirus, map, deaths, cases, tracking
Description	The virus has infected more than 2,843,000 people in at least 177 countries.
Country	USA

Figure 2.1 Design intervention data collection example. © Paul A. Rodgers, Craig Bremner and Fernando Galdon.

tables, charts and diagrams. We accepted all design interventions as valid and gave them the same role and status by presenting each on a single page. No curation. No selection. No position. Figure 2.1 shows an example of the information we collected in each design intervention case.

In order to frame the intended outcome, a progressive and systematic integrative review was conducted. We decided to use this approach to insert flexibility into the cataloguing of the event. The search criteria were articulated based on their relevance to the subject. Design blogs and specialist websites were searched daily. These online sources articulated the views of relevant and amateur practitioners. We also included reports from news platforms to complement and expand data collection to insert a broader and more inclusive and representative perspective. The criterion for inclusion was the relevance to the practice of design.

The selection was conditioned by our searches; therefore, it was somewhat arbitrary. The design cases collected in our book represent a sample of data of the event. The date represented in the cases is an estimation. Online tools such as scraping data tools were used to determine the date of publication. However, as the tool in itself claims, it is just an estimation. In cases where we could not determine the date, we used the day it was encountered. We were not interested in documenting what happened with exactitude – this job belongs to sociologists and anthropologists. Rather, we were interested in documenting a sample of data to extract high patterns of knowledge to build 'knowledge for future actions' (Glanville, 2005).

In this process, as Figure 2.2 illustrates, sixty-three different types of design intervention were collected from fifty-four countries. There are six main *categories* of design intervention (Figure 2.2 top left) – Actions, Graphics, Networks, Products, Shelters and Systems; twenty-four *subcategories*, and eight *enablers* (i.e. who has supported the creation of the intervention – Independent, Private, Government, University, Citizens, Consortium, NGO, Professional Association). The example also shows further information – *country of origin*, *type of intervention* (e.g. mask, robot, mechanism, wearable, shield, test), *author*, *definition*, *source of information*, the *main image* and the *intervention title* at the bottom of the figure.

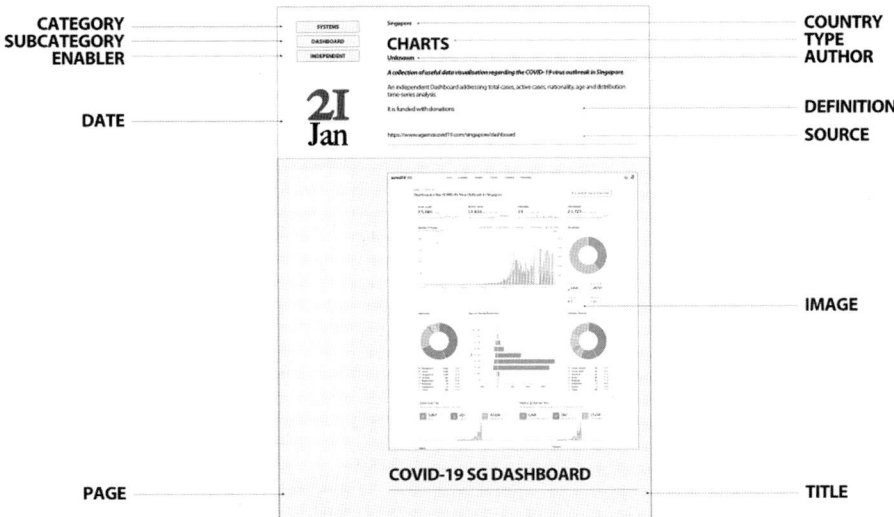

Figure 2.2 An example page from our book highlighting one of the 500+ design interventions we have assembled as part of this ongoing work. The 500+ design interventions were collected over a period of 152 days. © Paul A. Rodgers, Craig Bremner and Fernando Galdon.

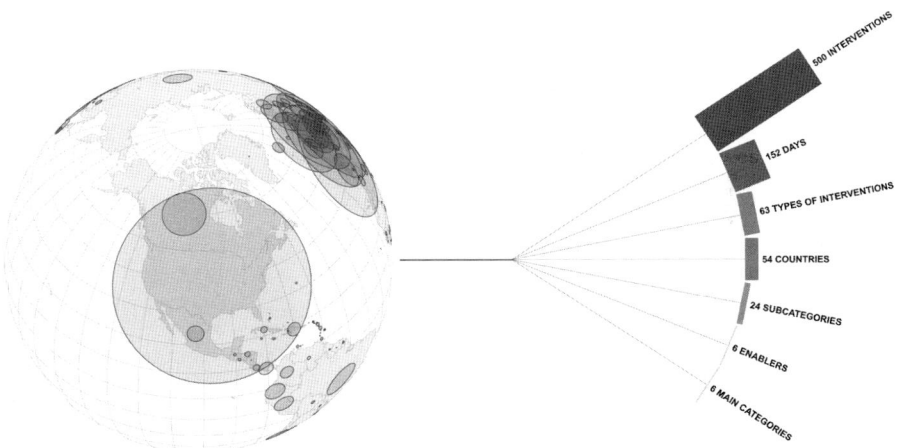

Figure 2.3 Design intervention data highlights. © Paul A. Rodgers, Craig Bremner and Fernando Galdon.

In total, we collected five hundred cases, during 152 days. As we assembled the cases, we identified six main categories, twenty-four subcategories, sixty-three types of embodiments and six types of enablers, which we illustrate in Figure 2.3.

The five hundred cases operated as a sizable sample of data from which to extract patterns of activity. The classification of the interventions into categories emerged in the process of collecting. There was no preliminary hypothesis as nobody was expecting this event to happen. Furthermore, there was no reference in the field of design research in how to conduct or catalogue pandemic design. The classification of cases into categories and subcategories presented challenges. What is the ontological nature of a mobile test unit? Is it a product, a service, a tester, a system, a shelter or an action? This kind of complexity led to a dynamic classification and categorization process that was executed 'in the moment' influenced by contextual elements and personal interpretations, knowledge, experiences and judgements. This aspect may result in variability in the assessment. However, as stated earlier, we were not so much concerned with exactitude, but recollection to underpin emerging patterns for future actions.

Review of early insights – one year on

The main design interventions framework, which includes six main design categories – Actions, Graphics, Networks, Products, Shelters and Systems, presented in our book (Figure 2.4) is potentially transferable to other pandemic events. This aspect is very relevant since the rate at which novel viruses are emerging means other pandemics and emergency events will occur. It is clear public administrations across the world will need to take seriously the need for preparedness for such circumstances.

We see the main categories as universally transferable to other types of pandemics and we see the subcategories as operational contextually. Some of the subcategories, for example dashboards, may be transferable to any pandemic event but others, like respirators, may not. With the exception of the introduction of vaccines, the first categorization we implemented still remains valid. So far, we have not been able to find other categories.

In terms of actions, the early citizen-driven portals and platforms gave way to government regulations in the form of specifications on behaviour. This aspect was also illustrated in our research (Figure 2.5).

Another early stage insight was related to the irrelevance of digital technologies to deal with this event. Governments, contrary to the preliminary insight we produced, keep pumping millions into their development but none of the variations of tracing has worked effectively. Even the main initiative developed by Google didn't work. A UK Government Public Accounts Committee (PAC) report earlier this year said test and trace (T&T) had 'minimal impact on transmission despite receiving £37billion of funding'. The Commons PAC said in March 2021 there was no evidence the tracing scheme had made a dent in Covid-19 transmission, despite its 'unimaginable' budget. In 2020, the UK Prime Minister's office spent £22billion on T&T and the UK chancellor promised to throw another £15billion at it in 2021, bringing the total cost to £37 billion. The PAC report said the UK Government was treating British taxpayers 'like an ATM machine' (PAC, 2021).

Despite the failure of digital solutions, the processes we traced enabled us to infer preliminary knowledge by implementing evolutionary traces. For instance, we observed that masks were first instantiated by citizens for free, but as manufacturing shifted its production masks became an object of profit and this tendency of

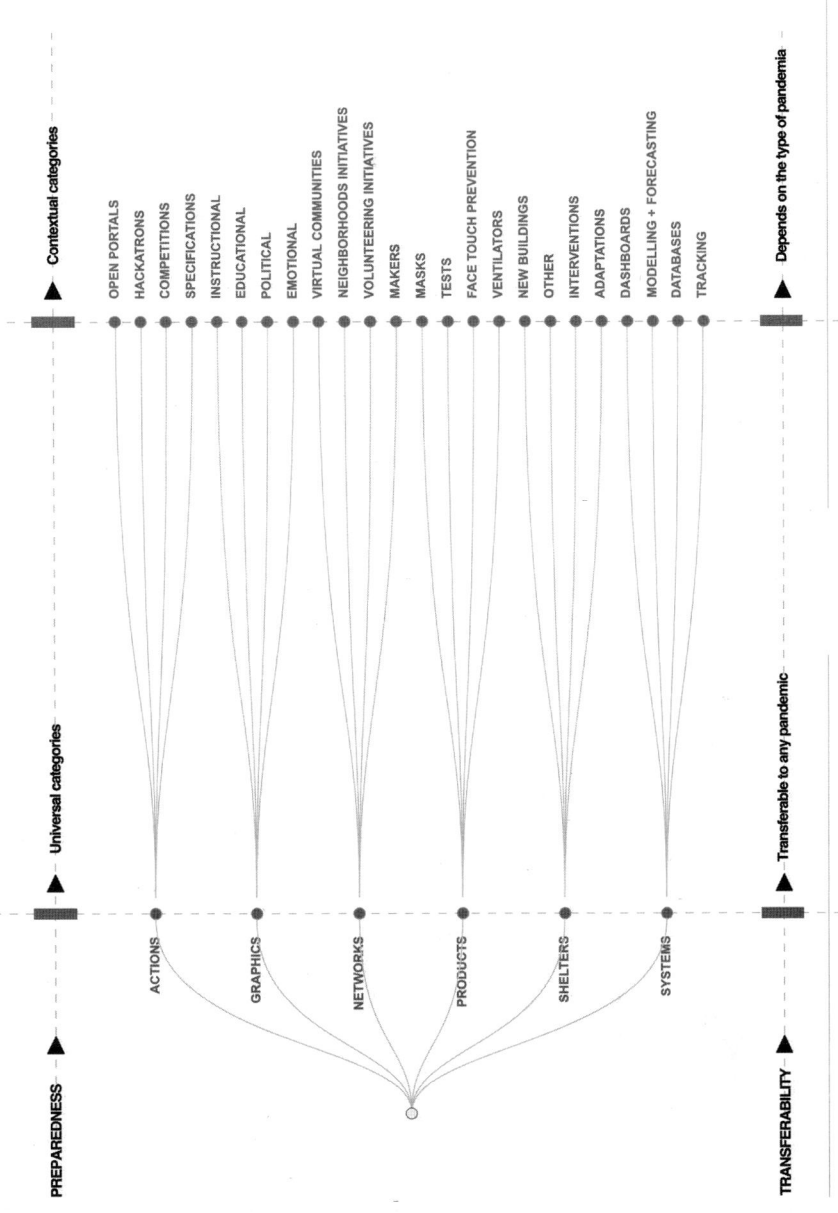

Figure 2.4 Design interventions framework. © Paul A. Rodgers, Craig Bremner and Fernando Galdon.

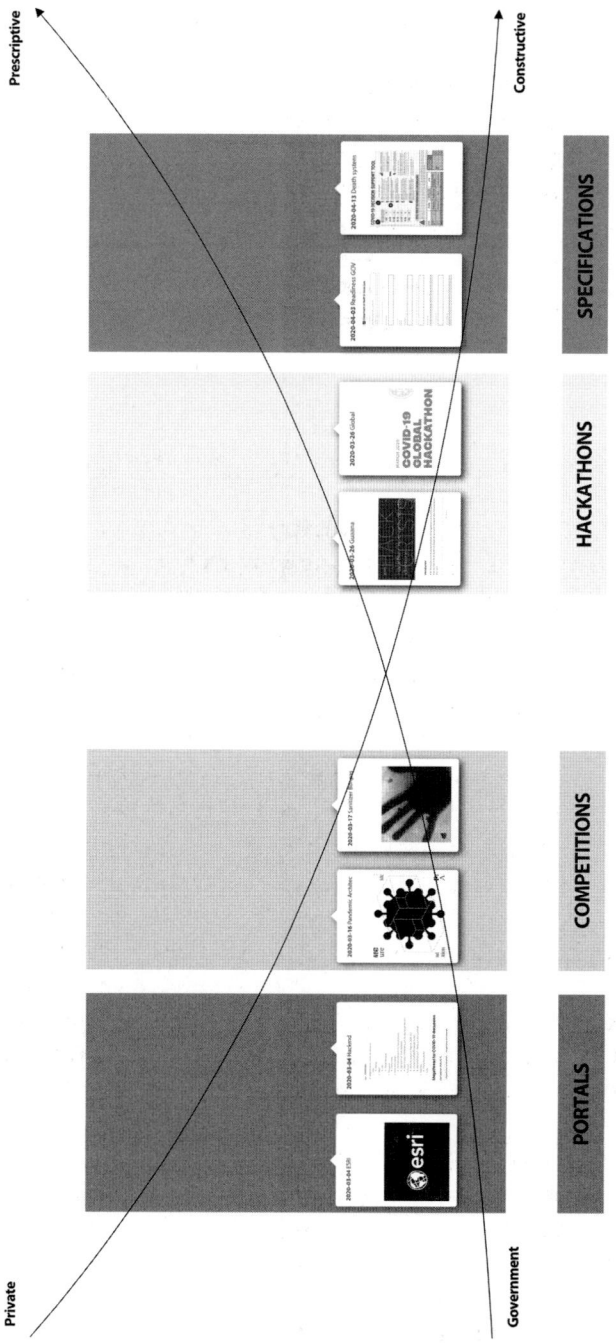

Figure 2.5 Design interventions development (actions) – citizens and government. © Paul A. Rodgers, Craig Bremner and Fernando Galdon.

liberal capital has been repeated. For instance, with vaccines, in the early stages, promises were made about distributing them at cost price – promises never fulfilled by the manufacturers even though millions of taxpayers' money were invested in their development.

Together with masks (Figure 2.6), dashboards became the main design intervention. One year later, they still remain as the main embodiment to convey information.

In our book, we illustrated how the ingenuity, practicality and willingness of designers also generated a range of dilemmas and paradoxes to consider. Our analysis has identified a number of key categories and needs, but also a range of worries, concerns and challenges to be addressed in the future by design and public policy (Figure 2.7). These dilemmas and paradoxes include maintaining privacy while tracking people, ensuring quality control measures while encouraging DIY and home manufacturing interventions, and encouraging originality versus derivative design.

Why everything was useful

In our approach to writing a design history of the Covid-19 pandemic we decided at the outset that everything we would collect would be useful. Because every design was aimed to help fill the vacuum of administrations that had planned for pandemics but were unprepared for the event it would have been ruthless and inappropriate to imagine selecting 'good' designs or classifying one design better or more worthy than the next one.

So, in our work we are comfortable with stating that every design project we found was as useful as the next one. In the midst of the quarantine in Italy, Franco 'Bifo' Berardi wrote: 'Use value, long expelled from the field of the economics, is back, and the useful is now king' (Berardi, 2020). The 500+ design projects here add up to a history of the Covid-19 crisis and we expect much of what is illustrated will disappear – so more than likely, as a document, the book will be extremely useful for a long time to come.

In compiling all of these cases, we accepted all design interventions as valid and gave them the same role and status by presenting each of them on a single page. No curation. No selection. No hierarchy. No status. No position. As the Covid-19 pandemic continues to roll on, wave after wave, the tasks of critical analysis and debate are still to follow – perhaps by us, perhaps by other authors in this book, but certainly by others. At this stage of the Covid-19 pandemic, where the book functions as an integral project of response/protest, any attempt to designate, distinguish or select projects will promote a notion of a 'good design' and by default demote the rest. This is a typical approach applied by the museum sector concerned with the classification of types.

Already some of the projects collected here are finding their way into the time capsules of museums via projects like Pandemic Objects at the V&A, London. In contrast to these archival practices, the rapid spread of the Covid-19 pandemic around the globe mirrors the fluid global information flows.

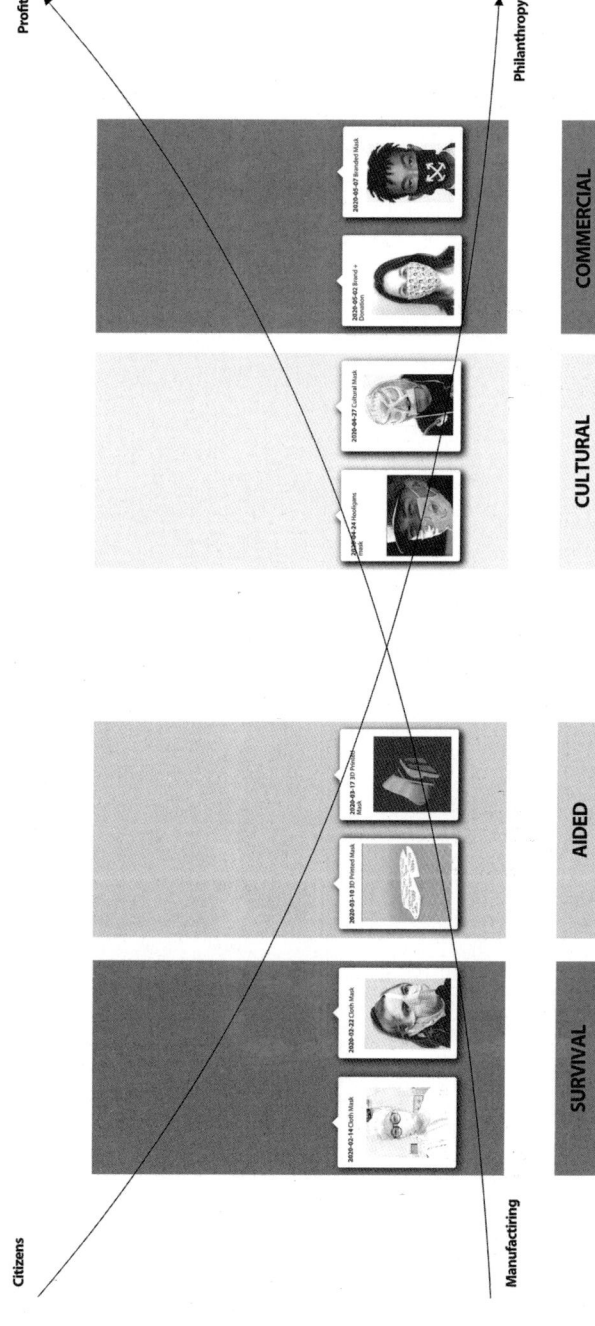

Figure 2.6 Design interventions development (masks). © Paul A. Rodgers, Craig Bremner and Fernando Galdon.

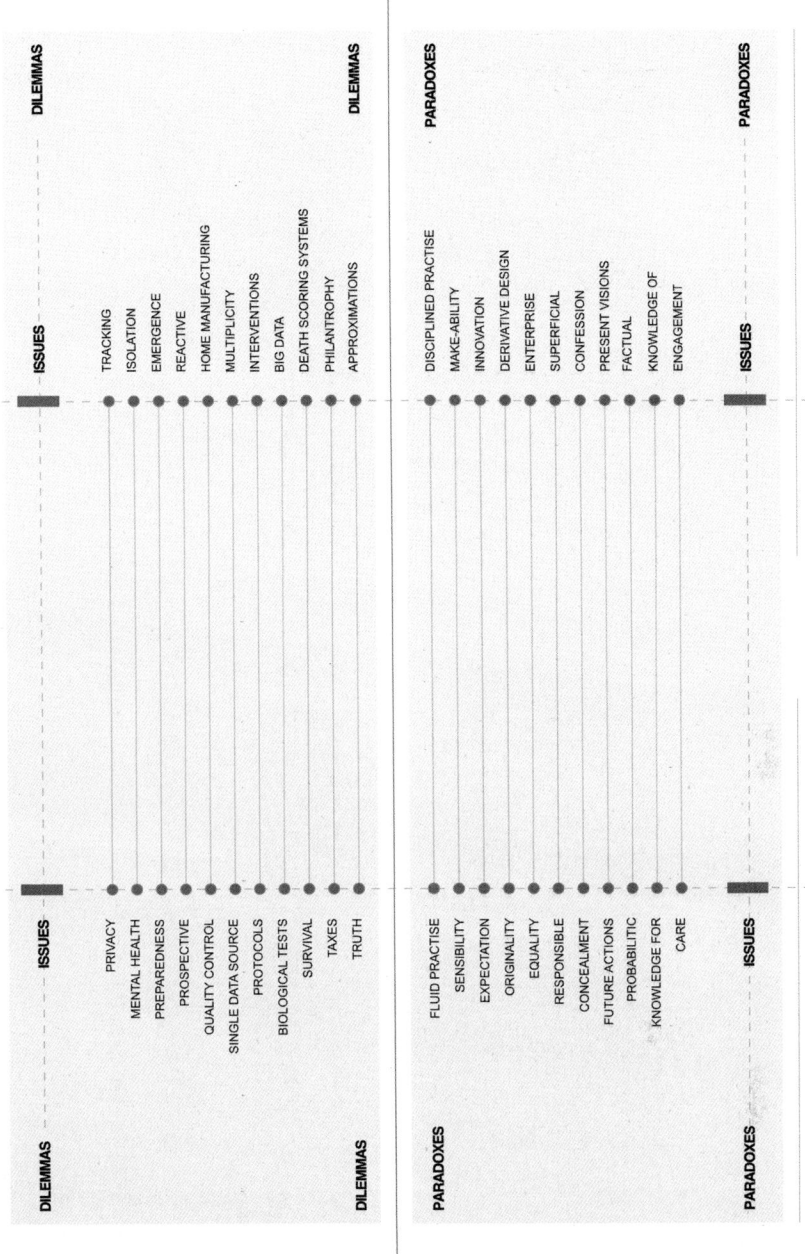

Figure 2.7 Dilemmas and paradoxes. © Paul A. Rodgers, Craig Bremner and Fernando Galdon.

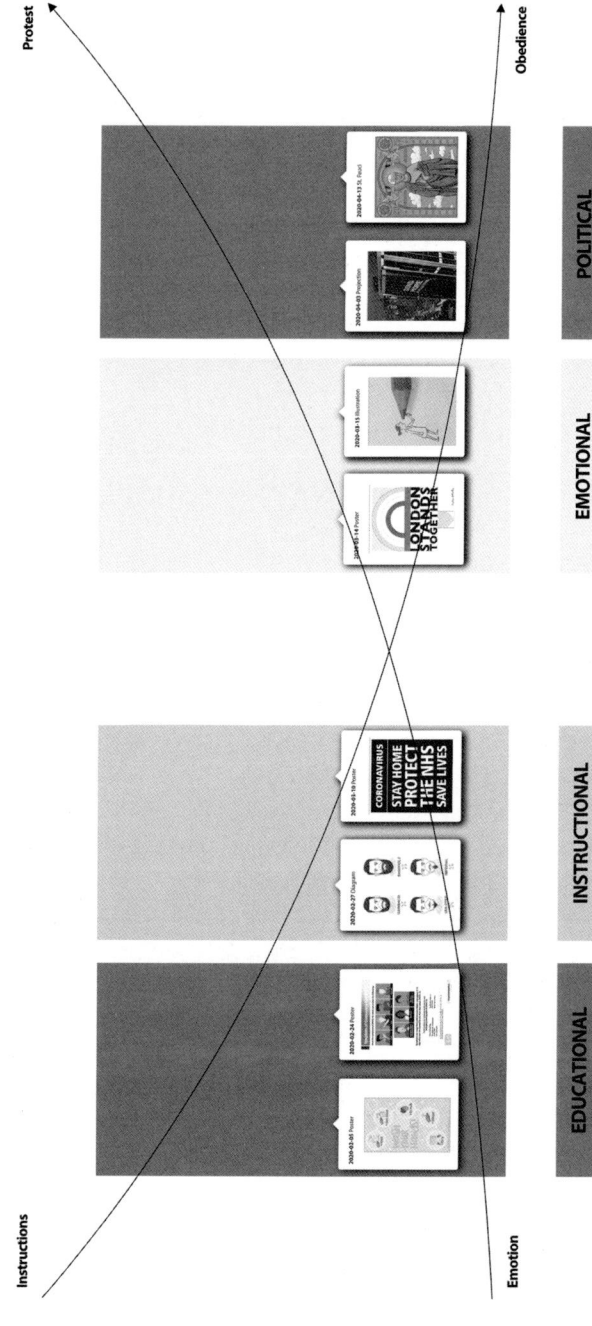

Figure 2.8 Design interventions graphics (posters) from educational to political. © Paul A. Rodgers, Craig Bremner and Fernando Galdon.

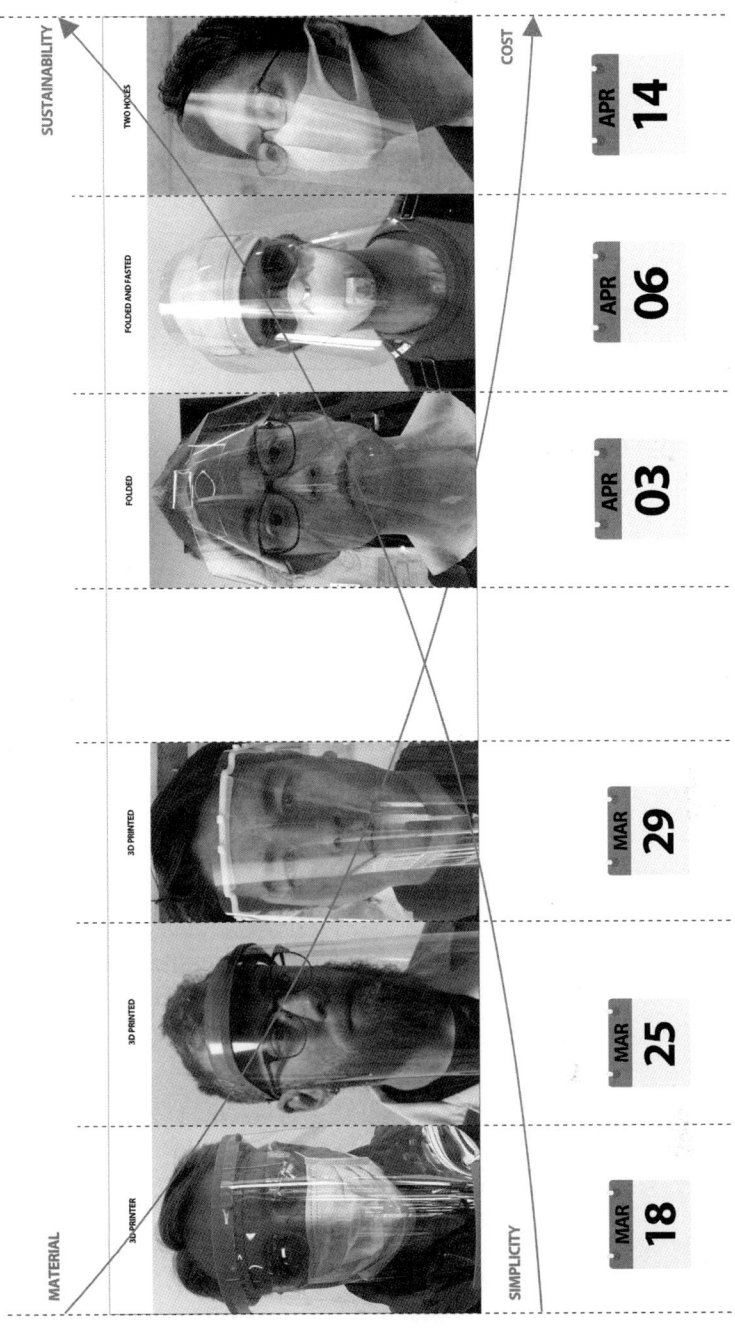

Figure 2.9 Design interventions – face shields simplification. © Paul A. Rodgers, Craig Bremner and Fernando Galdon.

The usefulness of imperfect design

As stated, the chronological structure of our book operates as a type of index system that we operationalized by articulating several graphic organizational frameworks enabling projects to be cross-referenced. From this point we were able to organize graphic material progressively to further analyse its evolution. By using chronology to frame the assembly of the book we uncovered evolutive traces; for instance, graphics and posters are first instructional, then emotional and then they became political (Figure 2.8).

In terms of personal protective equipment, we observed transparent face shields becoming simplified over time. The first models were complex and 3D printed. The final models were a sheet of plastic with two holes and a band, thereby removing the need for 3D printers. They were not perfect but their rudimentary fabrication enhanced production and sustainability in the process (Figure 2.9).

Furthermore, we discovered how at the beginning of the Covid-19 pandemic crisis, due to a shortage of products, it was a combination of professionals, individuals, groups and communities that stepped forward to fill the gaps left by aberrant public policy, government planning and preparedness. We witnessed that once the systems of production adapted and started to produce/import those goods, the civil production of initiatives/goods decreased in cycles in different countries. The process we adopted for our initial analysis illustrates a design-led alternative to pure statistical and mathematical models.

In this chapter, we have told the story of what we did during the first wave of the Covid-19 pandemic – we collected every design intervention we could – and we did this because we predicted that potentially everything would be useful. And having done this, our book illustrates the usefulness of imperfect design. As 'products' became more imperfect, simpler, rudimentary and targeted to vital demand, the more it became clear that design cares and really cares. And we did this because we, the authors, have a history of caring about design.

In a 2017 exhibition and catalogue entitled 'Nobody's Perfect' by Gaetano Pesce – the well-known Italian architect and designer of the twentieth century likened imperfect design to 'our bodies, all different and all, in a way, disabled'.

Grammatically, the imperfect (from the Latin *imperfectus*) is a verb tense that refers to a progressive or continuous action unfinished at the time of expression and something immature. The equivalent Ancient Greek term was *paratatikós* meaning prolonged. The Covid-19 virus is now a pandemic prolonged by variants, all immature and disabling to varying degrees. What is evident from the collection of design interventions in our book – *A Design History of the Covid-19 Virus* – is that imperfection can be a lifesaving 'accident' and this points to the thought that perhaps it is time for design to give up on designing as it is currently enacted (and taught) and rather acknowledge that an imperfect design will always be a work in progress and as such wholly useful.

References

Berardi, F.B. (2020). Beyond the breakdown: Three meditations on a possible aftermath. *e_flux Conversations*, 1 March. https://conversations.e-flux.com/t/beyond-the-breakdown-three-meditations-on-a-possible-aftermath-by-franco-bifo-berardi/9727.

Blauvelt, A. (2008). Towards relational design. *Design Observer*, 11 March. https://designobserver.com/feature/towards-relational-design/7557.

Branzi, A. (2008). *Introduzione al Design Italiano: Una Modernità Incompleta*. Milano: Baldini Castoldi Dalai Editore. (Translation by authors).

Glanville, R. (2005). Design propositions. In M. Belderbos & J. Verbeke (Eds.), *The Unthinkable Doctorate*. Brussels: Sint Lucas, 115–29.

Pesce, G. (2017). *Réinventer Le Monde Sensible*. Buchet-Chastel: Entre Tiens, Paris.

Imparfait: Nobody's Perfect (exhibition and sales) at Merci (shop) Paris (2017). https://www.elladoran.co.uk/blogs/news/imparfait-imperfect-merci-store.

Pye, D. (1978). *The Nature & Aesthetics of Design*. Bethel, CT: Cambium Press.

Rodgers, P.A., & Bremner, C. (2018). The design of nothing: A working philosophy. In P. Vermaas & S. Vial (Eds.), *Advancements in the Philosophy of Design*. Berlin: Springer Press, 549–64.

Rodgers, P.A., Galdon, F., & Bremner, C. (2020). *A Design History of the COVID-19 Virus*. Lancaster: Lancaster University.

Serpell, N.L. (2019). The banality of empathy. *The New York Review of Books*, 22 March.

Solnit, R. (2015). Men explain Lolita to me. *Literary Hub*, 17 December. http://lithub.com/men-explain-lolita-to-me/.

UK Government Public Accounts Committee (PAC) (2021). *Covid-19: Test, Track and Trace (Part 1)*. https://publications.parliament.uk/pa/cm5801/cmselect/cmpubacc/932/93202.htm.

3 Strategic design in a pandemic
CAMILLA BUCHANAN

Introduction

Design has been long associated with problem solving. However, more recently the places where designers and design are appearing, and the types of problems being addressed, have expanded enormously. New contexts for design include government agencies, healthcare systems, business and organizational strategies and complex systems that encompass several different fields (Banerjee, 2014; Irwin, 2015; Lurås, 2016). In the past two decades the public sector and other organizations or networks delivering social systems and services – including foundations and charities – have been places of huge growth for design (Bason, 2010; Mulgan, 2014; Prendiville and Sangiorgi, 2017). Latterly design has also percolated into the worlds of policy making and strategy development where, although it is now more present, it is arguably underdeveloped in theory and practice (Clarke and Craft, 2019).

This chapter looks at how design is being used in more strategic and systemic contexts with reference to recent work during the Covid-19 pandemic. It sets out a broad definition of 'strategic design' and refers to applied work. First, some context is provided. Second, key ideas about design and its link to strategic situations from the literature are outlined. Third, a definition of strategic design is given. Finally, a practical context where design has been used during the Covid-19 crisis is described, using examples from work in the Policy Lab.

A note on context

At the start of the Covid-19 pandemic, in early 2020, I was completing my doctoral research in 'strategic design' having worked in design and policy making for the best part of a decade. To get the work done I had been writing in relative solitude and I experienced disjuncture between the technical, cerebral new discipline I was researching and the immediacy and chaos of certain mega events. I had also noticed unease among the fifteen expert design practitioners and commissioners from around the world, who had contributed their insights as part of the project, about the ability of design to deliver on its early promise in the public and civic sectors (Buchanan, 2020).

Some people I interviewed expressed impatience for the field as a whole to be more ambitious and strategic. There was an uncomfortable sense that in the face of very real pressures design activity is still immature. Although these leading practitioners were sometimes uncertain about whether current practice is equal to the challenges presented by new environments, they also expressed ambition and sensitivity about the potential of design. Overall it was framed both as an alternative way of working in difficult situations and an approach that is yet to build sufficient capacity to demonstrate its value. For example, one designer I spoke to commented:

> We are doing things we haven't done before, these need a very different leadership model and I don't see that space in the public sector and, in fact now that we are increasingly facing austerity and populist pressure for different kind of reform, that space is vanishing. My overarching fear is that we are running out of time. The space around institutions is vanishing, we don't have the design capacity to do it. We haven't shown enough evidence.
>
> (p. 221)

At the end of the PhD thesis I had to reflect on whether 'strategic design' – which I had spent the best part of five years defining – was too lofty and theoretical to meet the immediate demands of sudden crises or if it was a viable alternative, concluding:

> there is a danger that strategic design remains a technocratic, abstract practice, this would be a wasted opportunity for an emerging field with deep roots in material and participatory ways of working. To fulfil its potential and promise, the practitioners of strategic design will have to learn how to make their work more accessible to non-designers, mobilise quickly and take active steps to consolidate the field as a valid response to these increasingly frequent global disruptions.
>
> (p. 256)

This approach to the research was prior to the pandemic when people were lucky to live in relative stability, including most policymakers, even with the worsening backdrop of social and environmental chaos the eye of the storm had usually seemed far away. That changed with Covid-19, when most people were required to engineer some form of adaptation in their own lives, at least in the UK. This is not to say the pandemic was not many things to different people; it intensified systemic and personal fragilities and made new opportunities, at least for some – indicated for example by the ballooning private testing industry. The crisis has also been complicated for public institutions where, in many instances rightly, their values and structure have been questioned deeply.

In the context of such upheaval design is a drop in the ocean, but it is at least one field where a growing number of people are considering the possibilities of responding to complex needs and crises in different ways. This chapter highlights one such set of adaptations and situations – work at the Policy Lab where I am joint head.

Theories of design and strategic challenges

A considerable portion of recent literature discusses changes within design methods and the expanding contexts for design activity.

The strategic potential of design

Different labels and frameworks are associated with new strategic or systemic forms of design. In his concept of 'fourth-order' design, Buchanan (2019) argues that 'this new practice of design engages some of the most complex and difficult creative work that designers have been called on to address' (p. 11). Buchanan's theoretical assessments of design, dating back to the early 1990s, established the potential for design activity to shape complex systems well before the current surge in practice, and more recently he argues that 'interior design, from its beginning, has been a fourth-order design practice', design activity focused on the creation of systems and environments (2019, p. 11). This implies that while the theory has long identified the strategic potential of design activity, this recognition is still relatively new in applied contexts. Building on Buchanan's concept of 'fourth order design', Banerjee (2014) puts forward the idea of the 'design of large-scale transformations', where he argues that a new class of 'super-wicked problems' distinct for their scale and complexity now require designers to take a broad systems view and to facilitate collaboration between disciplines; he describes this practice as 'fifth-order design' (p. 74).

Other theorists underline the cross-disciplinary nature of emerging design activity. Hunt (2012) uses the concept of 'transdisciplinary design' as a response to the increasing complexity of today's problems, observing that, 'transdisciplinary design situates its practices within new kinds of contexts – public health, government services, humanitarian relief, public education, infrastructure – and generates outcomes that might range from protocols, platforms, services and systems to those whose forms we cannot even predict' (p. 8). Hunt (2012) emphasizes the multidisciplinary and participatory aspects of this new design activity. Peruccio (2017) also underlines the integration with other disciplines, arguing in a historical account of systemic design that the 'task of the contemporary designer is to confront and find innovative solutions for humankind, and this is achieved by opening the doors to dialogue with other disciplines with the aim of enhancing communities and territories' (pp. 71–2).

Irwin (2015) emphasizes the environmental sustainability principle at the core of some contemporary design activity, and her theory of 'transition design' is of a transdisciplinary and collaborative practice that takes a systemic view to complex, global challenges such as 'climate change' and 'income inequality' (p. 229). She argues that transition design is 'based on longer-term visioning and recognition of the need for solutions rooted in new, more sustainable socioeconomic and political paradigms' (p. 230). Manzini (2016) highlights the fledgling and distributed status of new design activity and describes the change in current design practice in his theory of 'emerging design', a new 'problem-based, solution-oriented design' that is not yet mainstream but 'more or less consciously' appearing in different design theories and areas of work (p. 52).

Some theorists argue that developments in where design is now being used are a direct response to the increasing complexity. Banerjee (2014) describes a new class of 'super-wicked' problems that are 'simultaneously massive, integrated, pressing and highly complex'. Such problems entail the redesign of whole ecosystems and require designers to integrate their work with other disciplines (p. 71). Similarly, Irwin (2015) argues that major societal shifts have resulted in complex challenges and that 'fundamental change at every level of our society, and new approaches to problem solving are needed to address twenty-first-century wicked problems' (p. 229). In a recent study Lurås (2016) argues that to function effectively the products of design need to sit within systems, which entail the specific design at hand, the system that design seeks to influence and the wider system in which this is situated, for example an organizational context, 'There are no strict boundaries among the systems; they are intertwined and form a system in themselves' (p. 35).

Design in strategic contexts in the public and civic sectors

The public and civic sectors are major new contexts for design activity, and in the past 5–10 years design has been increasingly used in strategic areas such as the design of policy, governance and legislation (Bason, 2014; Kimbell and Bailey, 2017; Junginger, 2013; Clarke & Craft, 2019). The new interest in policy and strategy design is sometimes framed as an extension of service design. Prendiville and Sangiorgi (2017) observe that service design has expanded to more systemic issues, 'as part of the service design sphere, the hidden organisational systems and process behind the interface with users' (p. 3). While exposure to service design is likely to have been a catalyst for explorations of more strategic activity in large bureaucracies and systems, strategic and service design have different focuses.

Junginger (2013) offers a helpful definition of policy as 'a guideline or framework that delineates the kinds of services and products, the relationships and the manner of the interactions that are possible, encouraged or discouraged within and by a particular human system' (p. 5). Bailey (2017) further clarifies the distinction between policy making and policy delivery, arguing that 'Policymaking is a discrete (although somewhat ill-defined) activity in government, concerned with strategy and direction-setting. Distinct from the delivery of public services, which are one way of enacting a policy intention (as are laws, regulations, "nudges", incentives, etc.), it's as "upstream" as you can get in government decision-making without intervening directly in politics' (p. 43). Overall, design is impacting both strategic intent and policy implementation or the activities through which intent is accomplished, such as services, regulation and funding – the former 'policy/strategy intent' is a newer area for design.

However, there is a gap in the literature regarding the plural way in which social and policy challenges are met – by entities outside and inside of government institutions – and the wider ecosystem of 'civic sector' actors using design, in organizations such as foundations and charities, has received far less attention. Although some theorists and practitioners describe the growth of more strategic design activity in broad terms, Boyer et al. (2011), writing about the Helsinki Design Lab, observed that a growing community of designers were tackling large-scale 'social and public policy challenges' (p. 15), suggesting they were imagining wider potential than policy making. There are also concerns around design and policy or strategy work, where designers can consciously or unconsciously reinforce power structures and make decisions with the potential to impact thousands of lives (Buchanan et al., 2017). The field as a whole is largely silent on ethical guidance and the power dynamics that designers stepping into these new roles may enable and need to navigate.

Although the strategic potential of design is well established in the literature, its practical use in policy and other strategic contexts is more recent and less studied, particularly in the civic sectors. Despite various labels associated with new forms of design activity, there is commonality, for example in its multidisciplinarity and focus on systemic activities. There are also gaps relating to the ethical dimensions of design activity at the strategic level and scrutiny of its potential as well as its limitations. Furthermore, the literature is yet to catch up with the encompassing crisis of Covid-19 and the ways in which design has been used.

What is strategic design?

In light of some of these gaps and observations made in practice, I wanted to be more precise about where design was appearing in the public and civic sectors and how it could be framed through doctoral research. This research offered insights into the attributes of 'strategic design' and a simple definition. It argued that in applied situations, practical design work is catching up with the strategic potential which has been long recognized in academic theory, and that strategic design is emerging as a new design sub-discipline. The research used survey work, interviews and a case study, as well as practice-led insights, and the idea of 'strategic design' it developed is outlined below (Buchanan, 2020).

Overall, this research found that 'strategic design' has developed beyond work by isolated individuals or organizations in the public and civic sectors to become a distinct – albeit nascent – design sub-discipline. It demonstrated that design is being used in high-profile contexts across a wide range of sectors: the participants in the research were from design consultancies, government organizations, foundations, non-profit organizations, large charities and universities, in multiple different countries around the world. Many common experiences using design were found in these diverse situations, and the research expanded concepts of strategic design activity by making the case that a complex and diffuse ecosystem of organizations are using design activity to meet strategic objectives relating to social challenges, both within and beyond government policy making (p. 229).

Defining strategic design

Strategic contexts were defined as 'situations where a policy goal or another form of strategic intent is framed and articulated, resulting in concrete actions such as the development of new services, systems or regulations' (p. 246). The research argued that design is now influencing the development and articulation of strategic intent and the subsequent activities that this sets in place, in a wide range of settings (e.g. government policy making, large charities, foundations). It found that in strategic contexts design activity is being used to understand *strategic challenges, articulate a strategic goal and to develop practical responses to address that goal* (Buchanan, 2020).

An explanation of the attributes of strategic design and a definition were also created through this doctoral research, and its key features can be explained in the following statements:

- Strategic design is a broad and practical approach to *problem framing* and *problem solving*, which is increasingly underpinned by common methodologies and approaches, and where the imagination and creativity of individual designers play a crucial role.
- Strategic design is a fundamentally *material practice*. Its outputs are diverse, including tangible artefacts as well as new meanings and relationships. Making is used variously through the design process to: create new knowledge, 'making to learn'; develop practical design outputs, 'making to build'; and in 'making to speculate' about the future.
- Strategic design is *human centred and participatory*. Understanding human needs is a common entry point for strategic design activity, although in strategic contexts designers are also making decisions about and the role of the designer is increasingly to engender the participation of diverse groups.

From these features a description of strategic design was developed, and it was defined as 'a creative problem-framing and problem-solving activity which relies on material and participatory ways of working and is actively focused on understanding, articulating and responding to strategic challenges' (p. 253).

With this definition in mind, it is important to distinguish between the strategic aspects of all design activity and design work which is focused explicitly on strategic situations. Even in tangible design contexts such as product development, the system – or 'ecology' as Krippendorff (1995) would argue – in which a design artefact is situated becomes a consideration for design. However, while strategic considerations are generally a feature of design activity, 'strategic design' is a new and distinct sub-discipline that focuses on responses to strategic challenges, such as the creation of new policies or strategies to meet a variety of social needs. Here, the task of the designer is to define both a subject matter for design and its boundaries as well as the medium through which to create a design output, that is graphic or service (p. 246).

The research found that strategic design has many strengths. It offers pragmatic ways of working that provide the mindset and methods to cope with complex problems and focus on people's needs. It can also be used to establish new participatory and creative cultures in entrenched bureaucracies. It offers unifying potential for different groups and barriers of access can be reduced by design artefacts which are often easier to engage with than conventional institutional communications. Design is also highly versatile, and the 'making to learn' which takes place during the design process means that this activity can be applied to an incredible breadth of circumstances.

However, my research also argued that the field is facing a number of challenges. It is limited by the lack of clear terminology and approaches to evidencing impact. There are also structural challenges relating to factors such as training and recruitment. Perhaps most significantly, the ethical stance and values promoted through design activity in strategic contexts have not been adequately expressed or interrogated. For example, the research highlighted potentially far-reaching impacts of strategic design and that its presence in overtly power-laden or political environments raises questions about the diversity of its practitioners, including their class, ethnicity, sexuality and geography, as well as gender. Debates about representation are not well advanced in this area of design; they must be developed given its new strategic situations.

The term 'strategic design' is not new. It was used by a number of participants in the research itself – although they often struggled to explain it and no common definition was given – as well as notably by the Helsinki Design Lab, among others, to describe their work in the early to mid-2000s (Boyer et.al., 2011, 2013; Hill, 2012). However, this new design activity has grown considerably in the past 5–10 years, and in the public and civic sectors design activity is now being used more frequently to understand strategic challenges, articulate a strategic goal and to develop practical responses to address that goal – this includes new work which has taken place during the Covid-19 pandemic.

How has design been used in the pandemic?

Finally, this chapter looks at an applied design context in relation to Covid-19, with examples of recent experience from the Policy Lab where I work. There are two aspects to this: specific examples of design work related to issues arising from or exacerbated by the Covid-19 pandemic and the adaptations required to undertake design work itself.

Policy Lab was established in 2014 as a multidisciplinary team which has grown to around twenty people working across the UK Government – bringing skills such as ethnography, systems thinking, art, futures and design to policy making. The team aims to apply these varied skills to policy challenges, and we try to make it a place of inspiration and creativity for colleagues and our commissioners across government. The lab operates on a cost recovery basis, meaning it is funded entirely by commissions from government departments as well as local government and, on occasion, outside organizations. To date, Policy Lab has worked on around 130 projects – many of which are relatively large scale. Throughout the pandemic the lab used its methodologies to consider how different groups, such as people shielding, disabled people and those from a range of different ethnic backgrounds, have been affected variously by Covid-19 and the associated lockdowns.

Experiences of life with a disability during the Covid-19 pandemic: For example, during the first summer of Covid-19, Policy Lab partnered with the UK Government's Disability Unit[1] to gather insights about the lives of adults living with disabilities. Policy Lab and the Disability Unit had already worked together in 2019 to understand the daily experiences of twelve adults living with disabilities. This first project had a broad span and used a range of methods, including in-depth interviews, ethnographically led film work, journey mapping and diary writing. It created a picture of first-hand, daily experiences of life in the UK with a disability.

Policy Lab and the Disability Unit, returned to many of the same participants to understand what had changed for them as a result of Covid-19, using insights from the first project as a baseline. The second research project took place over six weeks between July and September 2020. During this time, further knowledge about disabled people's daily experiences was developed, focusing on impacts associated with Covid-19. Research comprised longer interviews, weekly tasks and check-ins conducted over WhatsApp as well as a final speculative design exercise to develop imagined futures with the participants, which were expressed in illustrated sketches.

The themes uncovered are, in part, a set of polarities around feelings such as 'dependence/independence', 'intimacy/functionality' and 'safety/risk'. The research also resulted in granular and practical knowledge about aspects of everyday life, including feelings of increased vulnerability when receiving social care or healthcare and uncertainty around the changing Covid-19 rules. There were occasional moments of positivity, and some participants even sought ways to enhance their independent living during the lockdowns (Cabinet Office, Disability Unit, 2021). More broadly the project developed near real-time insights of how the pandemic was being experienced at the granular, human, level. It foregrounded the personal situations of a group of individuals at a time when at least some of the existing data about how people live had been quickly invalidated by the disruptions associated with Covid-19. Insights were also used to understand the experiences behind data, and quotes from the research were used by the Office for National Statistics to illustrate their statistical data releases about lives of disabled people during this time (Office for National Statistics, 2020).

Aspects of this project tally with the definition of strategic design given above – as a creative problem-framing approach that relies on material and participatory ways of working. The Policy Lab – with its combination of design and research skills – was commissioned to understand changed realities resulting from Covid-19 for adults living with a disability. Although the work was largely remote, the material aspects of design were still in place – represented by video clips, audio recordings, photographs and sketches. The project was also commissioned intentionally to understand human needs and experience. Furthermore, it illustrates a policy team's desire to inform policy intent using design methodologies; the Disability Unit's stated aim for the work was to 'identify problems that could be resolved through policy change' (Cabinet Office, Disability Unit, 2021).

However, there is an important difference – while strategic design was used to inform policy intent, in this case it has not yet been part of policy implementation. This may indicate several things: as design becomes more strategic, parts of the design process are being valued more than others (e.g. problem framing); it is challenging for design teams to be involved in both 'policy intent' and 'policy implementation' because of the distinctions often made between these sets of processes in government; or more simply, not enough time has passed to determine how design will be used in policy implementation in this case. Overall, the attention of designers and commissioners needs to be astutely focused where this work can have the biggest impact.

There is no inherent problem with design work targeted at problem framing alone. In some cases better framing or understanding may be all that is needed, and upstream (strategic) changes can have huge impacts. Part of the power of design activity in policy making is that it brings downstream considerations to strategic contexts, illustrated by the desire from the Disability Unit to use design to understand granular individual experiences. This kind of work can make the factors that influence strategic decisions far more human and tangible. However, given the fundamentally material and pragmatic qualities of design, opportunities may be missed where it is used solely as a research tool and particular effort needs to be put into the hard work of 'problem solving' as well as 'problem framing'. Practitioners and commissioners need to ensure they are bold in using design to both 'learn' and 'do', so that the places where it is used are a matter of careful choice rather than a lack of access or significant capability in the field.

Broader adaptations

Finally, during this period there are many ways in which the Policy Lab team have had to adapt, this of course includes the personal changes that team members were required to make as a result of Covid-19.

Shifts include a move in the lab's ethnographic and social research to participant-led approaches. In several projects during the Covid-19 pandemic, individuals have collected their own data, either independently or with the support of our researchers, through artefacts such as film clips, digital photographs and collages. While participant-led work has always been a facet of Policy Lab's work, the circumstances of Covid-19 have amplified our use of these methods significantly. This has meant we can now work with people further afield and do research over time more easily, which is not to say that we will replace in-person work all together but that we have better developed some of our alternative methods.

We have also had to make changes to the 'materiality' of our practice, which had always been an important way of establishing the presence of a new culture as well as a means to enable participation – for example, through shared engagement with different objects – from simple cards and maps to speculative flags and system diagrams. While the emphasis on materiality was not lost during the Covid-19 pandemic, our work necessarily shifted to being more digital. Aspects of inclusivity are significantly increased by this shift, but there is also a loss for those who are not digitally able with the change to online living. For example, digital work emphasizes the visual and oral, but lacks some of the haptic and interpersonal aspects of physical design research. This has created a dualism in how we are able to work. Some of our engagement work is now more easy to undertake but in other instances we are having to, rightly, go slower and engage people offline in their own terms. Overall as practitioners we should be advocating for the widest possible entry points to participate in design activity.

Conclusion

The countless near universal adaptations required on a daily basis in the lives of millions of people are the real story of the Covid-19 pandemic, where the demands on individuals, even where they have been mundane, are staggering. This is painfully evident in the published findings of the work by Policy Lab and the Disability Unit discussed in this chapter. Probably, the bulk of the design work that has taken place during this time is at the level of the 'everyday' where, as Manzini argues, widespread disruptions now mean that 'more subjects must learn to design their own lives' (2016, p. 31) – the period of Covid-19 has surely been a wholesale example of the kind of lay design Manzini describes. However, inevitably, there have also been more coordinated and professional design responses.

This chapter has defined strategic design and discussed how it was used in the context of the UK Government, identifying it as an approach to develop new understandings of major problems, to foreground the micro experiences of individuals and as a way of working that is inclusive and clear through its materiality. It has also argued that strategic design has been used to inform 'policy intent'. Overall the chapter argues that designers and commissioners need to be persistent and aware in order to make use of the full spectrum of possibilities offered by strategic design. This includes defining both strategic intent and implementation.

Note

1. Disability Unit: see https://www.gov.uk/government/organisations/disability-unit

References

Bailey, J. (2017). Elements of novelty: Designer as policymaker. In S. Barbero (Eds.), *Systemic Design Method Guide for Policymaking. A Circular Europe on the Way*. [report]. Italy: Retrace Interreg Europe. https://www.interregeurope.eu/retrace/news/news-article/1772/retrace-method-guide-forpolicymaking/ (accessed April 2020).

Banerjee, B. (2014). Innovating large scale transformations. In C. Bason (Eds.), *Design for Policy*. Dorset: Gower, 71–87.

Bason, C. (2010). *Leading Public Sector Innovation: Co-Creating for a Better Society*. Bristol: Policy Press.

Bason, C. (ed.). (2014). *Design for Policy*. Dorset: Gower.

Boyer, B., Cook, J.W., & Steinberg, M. (2011). *In Studio: Recipes for Systemic Change*. [e-book]. Helsinki: Sitra. http://helsinkidesignlab.org/instudio/ (accessed December 2021).

Boyer, B., Cook, J.W., & Steinberg, M. (2013). *Legible Practices*. [e-book]. Helsinki: Sitra. http://www.helsinkidesignlab.org/legiblepractises/ (accessed December 2021).

Buchanan, C. (2020). What is strategic design: An examination of design in the public and civic sectors. [PhD text]. (accessed December 2021).

Buchanan, C., Junginger, S., & Terry, N. (2017). Service design in policymaking. In D. Sangiorgi & A. Prendiville (Eds.), *Designing for Service*. Fakenham: Bloomsbury, 183–98.

Buchanan, R. (2019). Surroundings and environments in fourth order design. *Design Issues*, 35(1), 4–22.

Cabinet Office, Disability Unit (2021). *Exploring the Everyday Lives of Disabled People*. [Online report]. https://www.gov.uk/government/publications/exploring-the-everyday-lives-of-disabled-people (accessed December 2021).

Clarke, A., & Craft, J. (2019). The twin faces of public sector design. *Governance*, 32(1), 5–21.

Hill, D. (2012). *Dark Matter and Trojan Horses: A Strategic Design Vocabulary*. Moscow, Russia: Strelka Press.

Hunt, J. (2012). Letter from the editor. *The Journal of Design Strategies: Transdisciplinary Design*, 5(1), 5–10.

Irwin, T. (2015). Transition design: A proposal for a new area of design practice, study, and research. *Design and Culture*, 7(2), 229–46.

Junginger, S. (2013). Design and innovation in the public sector: Matters of design in policy-making and policy implementation. In *Proceedings from the 10th European Academy of Design Conference, 'Crafting the Future'*, April. Gothenburg: European Academy of Design.

Kimbell, L., & Bailey, J. (2017). Prototyping and the new spirit of policy-making. *CoDesign*, 13(3), 214–26.

Krippendorff, K. (1995). On the essential contexts of artefacts or on the proposition that 'Design Is Making Sense (of Things)'. In R. Buchanan & V. Margolin, (Eds.), *The Idea of Design*. Cambridge, MA: MIT Press, 156–87.

Lurås, S. (2016). Systems intertwined: A systemic view on the design situation. *Design Issues*, 32(3), 30–41.

Manzini, E. (2016). Design culture and dialogic design. *Design Issues*, 32(1), 52–9.

Mulgan, G. (2014). Design in public and social innovation: What works and what could work better. [pdf] *Nesta*. media.nesta.org.uk/documents/design_in_public_and_social_innovation.pdf (accessed December 2021).

Office for National Statistics (2020). *Coronavirus and the Social Impacts on Disabled People in Great Britain: July 2020*. [article]. https://www.ons.gov.uk/peoplepopulationandcommunity/healthandsocialcare/disability/articles/coronavirusandthesocialimpactsondisabledpeopleingreatbritain/july2020 (accessed December 2021).

Peruccio, P.P. (2017). Systemic design: A historical perspective. In S. Barbero (Eds.), *Systemic Design Method Guide for Policymaking. A Circular Europe on the Way*. https://www.interregeurope.eu/retrace/news/news-article/1772/retrace-method-guide-for-policymaking/ (accessed August 2019).

Prendiville, A., Sangiorgi, S., & Rickets, A. (2014). *Mapping and Developing Service Design Research in the UK*. https://www.researchgate.net/publication/263255940_SERVICE_DESIGN_RESEARCH_UK_NETWORK_Mapping_and_developing_Service_Design_Research_in_the_UK (accessed December 2020).

Sangiorgi, D., & Prendiville, A. (Eds.). (2017). *Designing for Service*. Fakenham: Bloomsbury.

PART II International Reaction and Adaptation

This section provides some insights into how design was used in reacting and adapting to the local challenges across the world. It illustrates the instrumental value of design as an important tool in enabling society to react and adapt to contemporary challenges.

4 Designing for social distancing
DES FAGAN

Covid-19 has had an unprecedented impact on the way we design, operate, use and experience buildings. One consequence of this is likely to be an enduring medium- and long-term change to the arrangement of building layouts. In order to study the impact of distancing on spatial planning early on in the pandemic, our project the *Social Distance Lab* used computing software (Rhino3D and Grasshopper) to provide a unique methodology to redesign any interior layout with compliant social distancing at optimal user capacity. The method was tested in a 'live lab' at the Storey Building in Lancaster during the first UK lockdown in June 2020. We developed a unique automated methodology for building operators to redesign their layouts to instantly comply with social distancing. The objective was to reduce timescales for reopening and adaptation in the event of revised government advice, local lockdown or further variant outbreaks; benefitting building user health through verification of distances, while improving the efficiency of building operation through the optimization of capacity.

Scientific and contextual background

The science to support the efficacy of social distancing originated as early as the nineteenth century, with a series of experiments conducted by Flugge (1899), demonstrating that people located within 1–2 metres of the infected are more susceptible to contamination through aerosol and droplet inhalation. The 1–2 metre rule is based on a long-standing framework of classifying respiratory droplets into two sizes – large and small – with the size of a droplet determining how far it will travel from the infected person (Jones et al., 2020). Large droplets fall through the air more quickly than they evaporate and typically land within a 1–2 metre range, framing the parameters of social distance.

Initial governmental advice across the globe did, however, highlight differing scientific approaches to this metric of social distance: the UK and Canada, for example, initially advocated for a distance of 2 metres; the United States advised 1.8 metres; South Korea, 1.4 metres; and China, France and Hong Kong, just 1 metre. Hasan et al. (2021) describe how differing cultural and economic value systems may have led to the incongruence. Notwithstanding this range of values, countries across the world began to implement some form of social distance restrictions with hastily passed laws. On 4 July 2020, the UK Government signalled the reopening of buildings post-lockdown, guided by a series of documents; most notably 'Keeping workers and customers safe during COVID-19 in restaurants, pubs, bars and takeaway services' (Department for Business, Energy & Industrial Strategy, 2020) which required all business owners to protect the health and safety of their workers and customers through a series of layout and operational changes, including:

> Reconfiguring indoor and outdoor seating and tables to maintain social distancing guidelines (2m, or 1m with risk mitigation where 2m is not viable, is acceptable) between customers of different households or support bubbles. For example, increasing the distance between tables.

The government placed no legal responsibility for social distance compliance on the user of the building being occupied; rather, penalty for infringement was placed on business owners through a breach of the health and safety law. Thus began the disparate and urgent response from UK business owners to comply with revised laws by redesigning and reconfiguring their layouts for reopening.

Limitations on building capacity

With this exercise came the rapid realization that social distancing would have a profoundly negative impact on profitability and, in some cases, economic viability. The benefit of mid- to long-term economic recovery through social distancing measures would need to be weighed against the severe impact of short-term restrictions, and the sectors most affected by social distancing were labour intensive, including restaurants, hotels and bars, as a direct result of reduced building capacity. Many bars and restaurants delayed reopening altogether, citing that social distance restrictions applied to their existing floor layouts would be prohibitive. Accommodation and food services sectors in the UK furloughed three times the proportion of their workforce (27 per cent) compared with 8 per cent across all sectors during the pandemic (HM Government, 2021). The problem is outlined in Figure 4.1 which describes the space planning impact of both '1m+' (with risk mitigation) and 2-metre spacing for a 'typical' restaurant with social distance measures implemented.

The figure demonstrates (A) full capacity, (B) '1m+' social distancing as 60 per cent of full capacity and (C) 2-metre social distancing at 40 per cent of full capacity. The design exercise is a gross oversimplification by not integrating circulation routes, one-way systems, means of ordering or social 'bubbles', but serves as a useful comparator. The 1m+ (with risk mitigation) rule delivered much improved outcomes for capacity compared with the 2-metre distance, primarily as a consequence of the 'standard' 1-metre depths of tables which would exclude any other seated

Figure 4.1 Impact of social distancing metric on room capacity of 100 m². © Des Fagan.

person. The '1m+' rule came with an additional requirement for risk mitigation, which comprised of 'providing clear guidance on social distancing and hygiene to people on arrival, for example, signage, visual aids' (Department for Business, Energy & Industrial Strategy, 2020). The provision of plastic screening also constituted a potential 'mitigating factor' by virtue of blocking aerosol and droplet spread, as indicated in Figure 4.1B.

Social distance: Research questions

The timescale for implementation of building changes from the publishing of this new guidance on 23 June 2020 to the reopening on 4 July 2020 was just eleven days. Thus began the largest exercise in rapid public building layout redesign and signage design the UK has ever seen. At the University of Lancaster, we were approached by stakeholder groups, including the local county Covid-19 response team the *Lancashire Resilience Forum*, to explore the application of our experience and expertise in the optimization of spatial planning and wayfinding. Three key research questions were framed in the course of these discussions, focusing predominantly on wayfinding in space:

- *How does signage branding affect people's response to social distancing?*
- *How does signage design affect people's response to social distance measures?*
- *Can social distancing guidance be automated using optimization software?*

To evaluate these research questions, Lancaster City Council (LCC) became our client for a pilot project to test a 'live' site, automating the design of the interior layout and wayfinding signage of the ground floor of a public building complex they owned: the Storey Building in Lancaster City centre. The *Social Distancing Lab* was to be opened to key stakeholders prior to 4 July reopening, providing opportunity for local business owners to explore a building altered to comply with social distance restrictions, with the dual purpose of collecting evaluation data from users active in the space.

Question 1: How does signage branding affect people's response to social distancing?

In order to understand the best approach to social distance signage, we created five distinct signage branding approaches that we asked the public to respond to. The images were created as collages and respondents were asked by questionnaire what they thought the most effective branding approach was for social distance signage (Figure 4.2).

The most effective signage type was 'Designer Bespoke' signage, at 72 per cent total effectiveness compared with the other branding approaches: Universal/Emergency Signage (63 per cent), UK Government Signage (60 per cent), City Council Signage (65 per cent), Store Specific Signage (51 per cent) and Designer Bespoke Signage (72 per cent). Qualitative feedback from research participants suggested that *Universal* signage appeared too 'off-brand' and risked being ignored, *Government* branding within private stores was too 'harsh' and authoritarian in a place for customers, *City Council* branding appeared out of place in a private store and *Store* branding did not stand out sufficiently well from the context of its background. The most effective signage at 72 per cent effective was *Designer Bespoke*. Respondents thought that the new pandemic deserved a new approach to signage – one that didn't need to respond to existing brands or styles – this was a new problem, which required a new solution.

Figure 4.2 Examples of different brand images by UK Government and Designer Bespoke. © Des Fagan.

Question 2: How does signage design affect people's response to social distance measures?

As building users indicated a preference for a new, bespoke social distance signage, we began to design a new comprehensive social distance signage pack with designers Wash Studio based in Preston. In order to contextualize our approach to the type of signage, we compiled initial research into UK legislation governing the design of emergency spatial planning and signage. The Health and Safety (Safety Signs and Signals) Regulations (HM Government, 2020) require employers in the UK to provide specific safety signs whenever there is a risk that has not been avoided or controlled by other means. However, as neither the classification nor the messaging of the specific signs included in the Regulations (*Prohibition, Warning, Mandatory and Emergency*) was appropriate to the complex wayfinding guidance in the new context of the pandemic, we discounted this limited library of signs.

Expanding on the historical use of emergency signage, we identified a series of studies that described the rapid comprehension of instruction through bespoke signs for people in a dynamic and unfamiliar context. We thought these particularly relevant in informing our research questions, as building users would encounter an entirely new context of instructions for wayfinding during the pandemic. Tang et al. (2009) conducted a wayfinding study involving emergency signs with three scenarios. The study found that the absence of signs resulted in significantly slower escape times (123.8 seconds) than either old signs (75.6 seconds) or new signs (84.8 seconds). The study verifies that signage does help wayfinding tasks and that shape and form truly matter.

Due to the prevalence of flooding in Malaysia, research on the implementation of a national flooding signage system by Vikneswaran et al. (2018) found that the majority of respondents strongly agreed that signage with symbols improved the clarity of their route to safety in the event of a flood. A study on the design of tsunami warning signage in Japan and Thailand by Ongkrutraksa (2015) highlighted the importance of shape and colour in the interpretation of warning signs, reaching a similar conclusion to Blees and Mak (2012), who found that comprehension of signage between the Dutch and Chinese was highly dependent on cultural interpretation. Although historical knowledge informed understanding, they concluded that given clarity of text, message and consistency, users from different backgrounds were able to appropriately comprehend and interpret signage. Ng and Chan (2007) performed a quantitative analysis to find out whether 'universal' design features of Chinese traffic signs influenced comprehension of these signs by Hong Kong Chinese participants. These features, formulated by McDougall et al. (1999), included familiarity and physical resemblance.

What became clear from these studies is that familiarity with previous signage had a significant influence on comprehension. As such, we looked carefully at the context of UK signage, particularly that of UK road traffic signs; perhaps the most prevalent type of signage in the UK, accessible to a diverse demographic of ages and

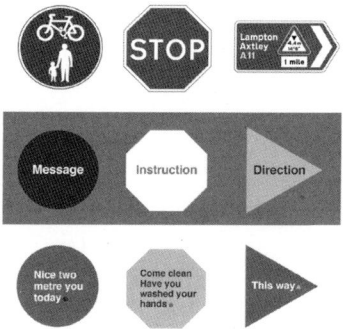

Figure 4.3 Codification of signage influenced by UK Traffic signs. © Des Fagan.

backgrounds. Generally, for UK traffic signs, circular signs are used to give orders, triangular signs are used to warn and directional signs are in the shape of an arrow. The hexagonal sign is reserved for just one sign: STOP, highlighting importance (Department for Transport, 2021). Colours are used to signify context, with red reserved for warnings, blue signs for motorways and brown for tourist destinations. Using this semantic structure, we developed our own new signage system for social distancing, building on familiarity of UK road signage, with circular signs representing 'message', hexagonal 'instruction' and arrow signs as 'directional' to align with existing meanings (Figure 4.3).

In relation to colour, the existing colour codification of UK traffic signals and use of primary colours; blue, green and red, offered insufficient variation and tone for a legally non-enforceable set of guidance. Given that the 'enforcer' of social distance is the building operator, not the police, businesses would need to make their users feel welcomed as customers, but at the same time, ensure they comply with social distancing through signage. As such, we felt that primary colour use, more traditionally seen in road traffic instruction and emergency signage, did not suit this 'new' role.

Silic and Silic (2016) found that colour enhances the effectiveness of a warning message and highlights the importance of critical messages. The use of non-primary colours in emergency signage is less well studied, but the study of colour emotion and its impact on products and branding is. Elliot and Maier (2014) found that colour meanings and colour effects are context specific. Baxter et al. (2018) found that while a generic colour may be intrinsically associated with a particular personality trait (e.g. purple is exhilarating), a distinctive colour is effective for creating a stronger brand identity (Simonson and Schmitt, 1997) and aids the portrayal of specific brand associations.

As such, the design team decided to trial a distinct colour palette to evoke feelings of well-being and positivity, with 'warm' hues of blue, green and yellow. The tone of voice would be friendly and reassuring, cognisant of the hybrid role of these signs as representing both the welcoming host *and* the enforcer. Signage would be created in a simple Sans Serif typeface, providing clarity and ease of comprehension. Eventually, an Open Source Social Distance Signage Pack (Fagan, 2020) would be authored as part of the research, providing fully customizable signs to complement the variable optimized outcomes of the research. This comprised sixty-five unique signs with 1,040 possible directional iterations available for public download.

Question 3: Can social distancing guidance be automated using optimization software?

Building on the concurrent design of social distance signage, we tested the automation of social distance layouts through the application of parametric software. This comprised of an automated and instant design rearrangement exercise, using software, to provide a layout complaint with social distance guidance. Our approach was to build a multi-criteria optimization definition using parametric software Grasshopper (e.g. Saremi et al., 2017) to generate a redesigned floor layout and signage positions with minimal human design input. This would generate an idealized location of tables, chairs, signs and user routes for an existing building layout made to comply with social distancing of any metric, with optimized capacity.

A review of existing research on layout optimization revealed that no existing study provided practical development, testing and evaluation of optimized floor layout design in relation to social distancing – an expected consequence of the short time since the start of the pandemic. Of the papers that explored spatial layouts in the context of Covid-19, most referred to speculative or theoretical guidance as opposed to means-tested outcomes: Fischetti et al. (2020) considered a mathematics-based approach to social distancing, exploring the effect of aerosol spread on spatial layouts. Banon and Banon (2020) investigated shape grammar optimization by mathematical formula. Yet no existing research at the time evaluated the complexity of practical application considering new signage typologies, real-world influences including multiple paths, wayfinding and unpredictable user behaviour.

Of the significant research completed on multi-criteria optimization of design for spatial layout studies pre-pandemic, Guo and Li (2017) explored a multi-agent evolutionary optimization process to define office and housing layouts. The introduction of pedestrian flow for multi-objective optimization presented by Huang et al. (2018) provides insight into the potential of agent-based modelling on wayfinding cognition. More recent research by Dubey et al. (2021) proposed a new system for the automated positioning of signage based on a multi-criteria optimization approach, referencing theories of Space Syntax and behavioural and cognitive science. Yet, as a consequence of the rapid onset of the pandemic, none had investigated automated optimization of layouts in the setting of social distancing restrictions. Given this knowledge gap, the work proposed a new methodology to bridge between theory and practical evaluation of layout optimization and signage in the new context of the pandemic.

To generate the redesigned and optimized building layout incorporating: (a) user routes; (b) user destinations (e.g. seating/toilets) and (c) signage locations, a simplified AutoCAD 2D building plan of the building was used as input. The workflow method is summarized in Figure 4.4.

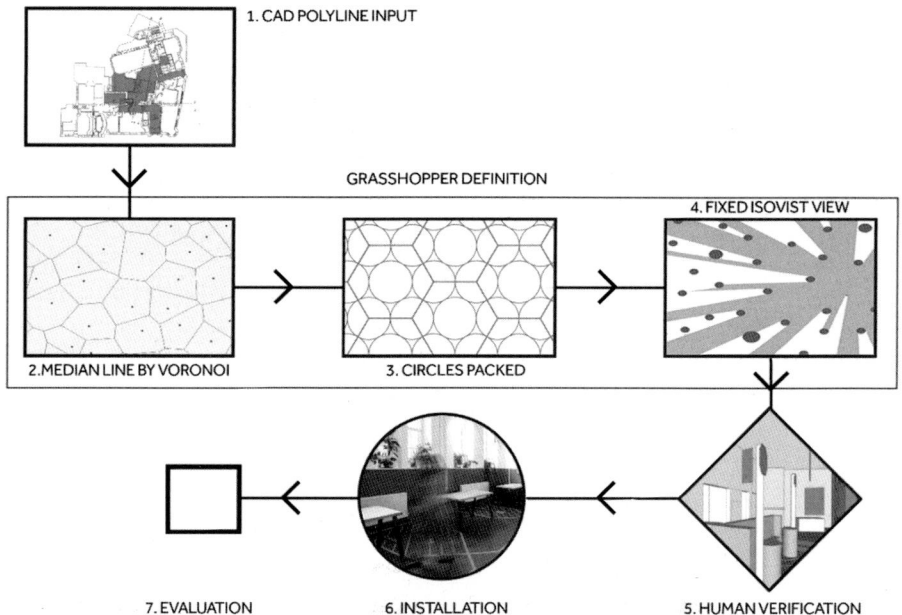

Figure 4.4 Workflow for social distance optimization using Grasshopper. © Des Fagan.

A Voronoi offset was applied to the AutoCAD building plan in a Grasshopper definition, providing a median line which was then simplified to establish a user route centred between adjacent fixed structures. An exclusion zone representing the social distance offset on either side of the median line was tracked onto plans, and areas highlighted at risk of non-compliance were identified using attractor points checking collision on an analysis surface. This provided an early visual risk analysis through colour codification of existing non-compliant spaces and routes (Figure 4.5). All routes needed to be bidirectional to avoid the scenario of users having to exit the building to return to a place of origin. As the width of circulation was insufficient to provide space for passing along the length of the median line, the method proposed the establishment of crossing regions that provide a place to give way to others on the same route. Crossing regions occurred at points of route intersection with three or more interconnected paths; a waiting spot was defined automatically adjacent to each crossing region.

As the Storey Building contained a cafeteria, it was important to establish a method for the optimization of seating locations for eating and drinking. The seating region was defined by subtracting the offset median line from the building outline. To provide optimal seating capacity within this region, circles offset from a point were packed using the Grasshopper Kangaroo Pack function (Piker, 2013) to fit wholly within the region. Using the Wallacei plugin, fitness functions of capacity and useable area were tested using the NSGA-II algorithm. The analysis tools contained within Wallacei, including the Parallel Coordinate Plot, were used to identify preferred outputs on the basis of the fitness functions (e.g. Petrov and Walker, 2018). Using the

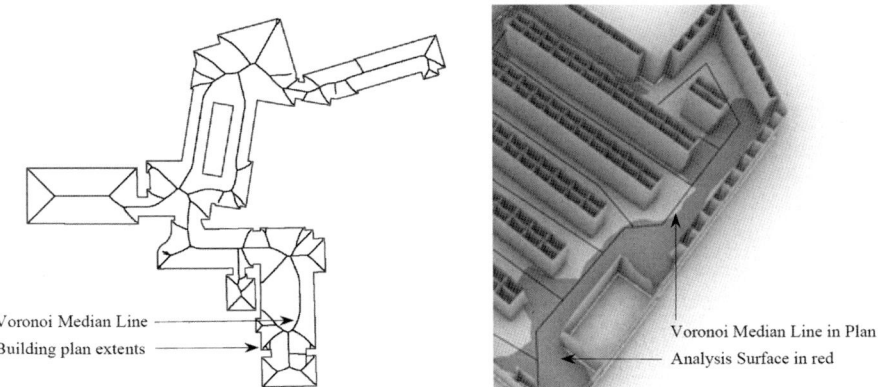

Figure 4.5 Voronoi median line diagram (left) and analysis of surface clash detection. © Des Fagan.

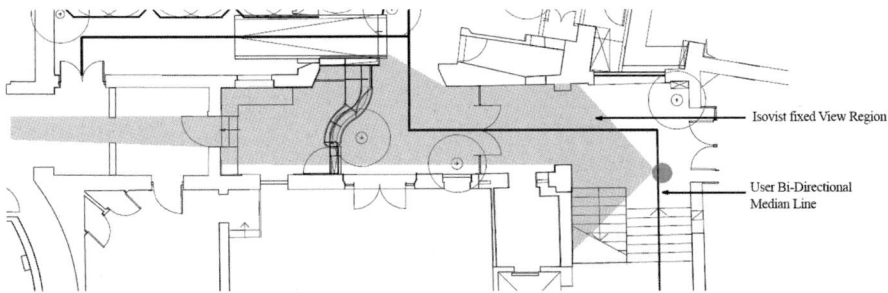

Figure 4.6 Visibility graph analysis indicating fixed view projected onto surfaces. © Des Fagan.

Decoding Spaces 2D Isovist definition, a visibility graph analysis was generated to indicate the relative visibility of walled surfaces using a restricted field of view isovist in the direction of the path of movement (Figure 4.6). This subsequently influenced the physical location of wayfinding signage.

Directed by the output of the Grasshopper definition and the associated visibility graph, the design team verified signage design and location with clients' LCC to establish final plans for fabrication and installation. Variable inputs were retained as customizable sliders, to allow for responsive alteration in the event of changing social distance legislation.

The Social Distance Lab: Installation, testing and results

The time for installation, from signage printing to layout rearrangement, took approximately 18 hours. The floor signage was installed using vinyl material, with wall signs mounted on foamboard and adhered to wall positions guided by the Grasshopper definition (Figure 4.7). Once fully installed, local businesses were then invited to provide feedback on the effectiveness of the signage by questionnaire and

Figure 4.7 Installation of the signage in the Storey Building, Lancaster, UK. Installation took 18 h and twenty-four local businesses visited the space. © Des Fagan.

interview. Key stakeholder evaluation by invited businesses showed that 92 per cent (22/24) of visitors to the Social Distance Lab thought the social distance measures installed were effective, and 92 per cent (22/24) thought they were visually clear. Comments in response to how distancing measures may have been improved include: 'it's a bit busy in places, I can see some getting quite confused' but most responses were positive: 'great presentation and space that gives us lots of examples'; 'The layout is attractive, it works in the background.'

In order to quantify the differences between human-designed and automated layouts, five designers were asked to draw a plan with identical parameters of input prior to viewing the automated outcome (Figure 4.8). The human-designed plans included, on average, thirty-two seated locations compared with forty in the automated layouts, a 25 per cent increase in total capacity. The percentage of useable space, defined as the seating region, is improved by 12 per cent in the automated layout. On verifying accuracy, the human-designed plans included three locations that infringe upon the 2-metre social distance.

The designers completed a questionnaire after installation of the optimized layout and signage, with results indicating the process was effective, accurate and that it facilitated design thinking (Table 4.1).

Future work

This research has provided a methodology that successfully automates social distancing guidance using optimization software in the context of the case study

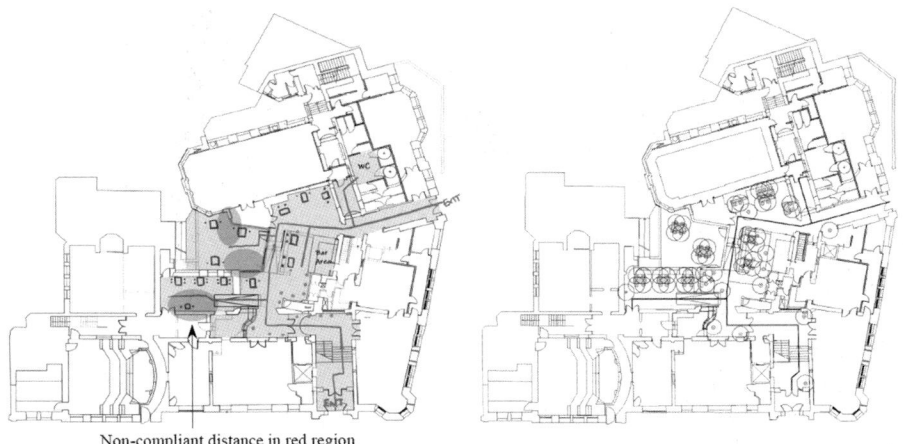

Non-compliant distance in red region

Figure 4.8 Comparison of (a) human-designed plan and (b) automated Grasshopper definition. © Des Fagan.

Table 4.1 Result of Plan Comparisons and Survey of Designers

	Human Designed	Generative Designed	Diff
Useable net seating (m^2)	210	224	14
Length of path (m)	52	48	−4
Number of seats	32	40	8
Instances of sub 2-m compliance	3	0	−3

building. The results confirm that the method generates automated socially complaint plan designs, providing improved outcomes of capacity and accuracy compared with human-designed layout. Subsequent user evaluation in the live lab proves the method presents visually clear and effective signage and social distancing measures. As the definition retains variable inputs, crucially social distance, the layout may be redesigned instantly to comply with any value of distance, providing an agile and responsive means to comply with changing social distance advice, and an essential resource to support reopening and resilience against future viral variants.

The method is not yet a fully automated process that can provide the content, direction, text and positioning of wall signage to complement floor signage locations. The current model requires final human verification of content, direction and positioning of this signage. Further work may therefore build upon the research of Dubey et al. (2020) to propose auto positioning and auto content to reduce person-hours and thus streamline the process.

Other work will explore the application of the method to other building case studies, evaluating a variety of space uses including hospitals, schools, care homes and offices to verify and refine the approach. This work is currently underway in part: with the method

Figure 4.9 Grasshopper definition applied to the Lancaster Health Innovation Campus. © Des Fagan.

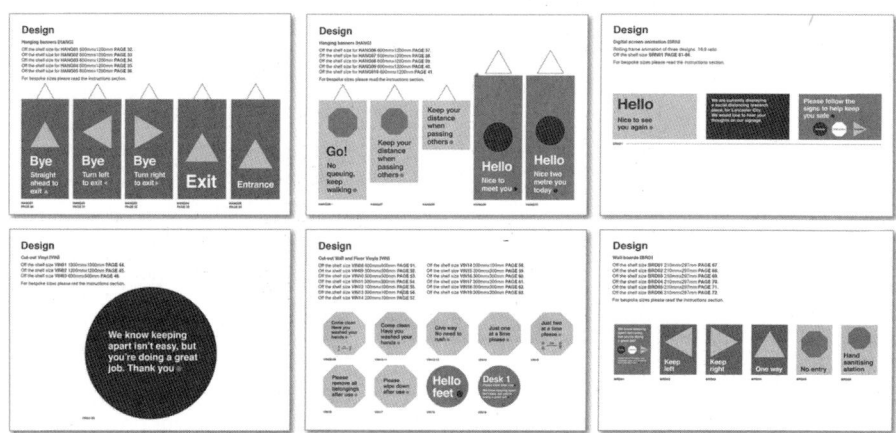

Figure 4.10 Open Source Social Distance Signage Pack. © Des Fagan.

being tested, refined and applied to layouts on the diverse Estate of the University of Lancaster Campus (Figure 4.9) to test the methodology in a different context.

Finally, we continue to track the downloads and global destinations of the Open Source Social Distance Signage Pack (Figure 4.10) which to date has been downloaded 158 times and applied in sixteen unique locations, which will provide useful data and insight into the variability of customization for wayfinding signage and its further application to diverse use cases.

References

Bañón, L., & Bañón, C. (2020). Improving room carrying capacity within built environments in the context of COVID-19. *Symmetry*, 12(10), 1–13. https://doi.org/10.3390/sym12101683.

Baxter, S.M., Ilicic, J., & Kulczynski, A. (2018). Roses are red, violets are blue, sophisticated brands have a Tiffany Hue: The effect of iconic brand color priming on brand personality judgments. *Journal of Brand Management*, 25(4), 384–94. https://doi.org/10.1057/s41262-017-0086-9.

Blees, G.J., & Mak, W.M. (2012). Comprehension of disaster pictorials across cultures. *Journal of Multilingual and Multicultural Development*, 33(7), 699–716. https://doi.org/10.1080/01434632.2012.715798.

Department for Business, Energy & Industrial Strategy, HM Government (2020). *Keeping Workers and Customers Safe during COVID-19 in Restaurants, Bars and Takeaway Services*. https://assets.publishing.service.gov.uk/media/5eb96e8e86650c278b077616/working-safely-during-covid-19-restaurants-pubs-takeaway-services-091120.pdf.

Department for Transport (2021). *Traffic Signage Manual*. https://www.gov.uk/government/publications/traffic-signs-manual.

Dubey, R.K., Khoo, W.P., Morad, M.G., Hölscher, C., & Kapadia, M. (2020). Autosign: A multi-criteria optimization approach to computer aided design of signage layouts in complex buildings. *Computers and Graphics (Pergamon)*, 88, 13–23. https://doi.org/10.1016/j.cag.2020.02.007.

Dubey, R.K., Thrash, T., Kapadia, M., Hoelscher, C., & Schinazi, V.R. (2021). Information theoretic model to simulate agent-signage interaction for wayfinding. *Cognitive Computation*, 13(1), 189–206. https://doi.org/10.1007/s12559-019-09689-1.

Elliot, A.J., & Maier, M.A. (2014). Color psychology: Effects of perceiving color on psychological functioning in humans. *Annual Review of Psychology*, 65, 95–120. https://doi.org/10.1146/annurev-psych-010213-115035.

Fagan, D. (Artist). (2020). Signage Pack – Social Distancing Signage for Retail, Commercial and Service Application: Open Source. Design.

Fischetti, M., Ab, V., Fischetti, M., & Stoustrup, J. (2020). Mathematical optimization for social distancing. 1, 1–20. https://doi.org/10.13140/RG.2.2.35799.91049.

Flugge C. (1899). Die Verbreitung der Phthise durch staubformiges Sputum und durch beim Husten verspritzte Tropfchen. *Z Hyg InfektKr*, 30, 107.

Guo, Z., & Li, B. (2017). Evolutionary approach for spatial architecture layout design enhanced by an agent-based topology finding system. *Frontiers of Architectural Research*, 6(1), 53–62. https://doi.org/10.1016/j.foar.2016.11.003.

Hasan, S.S., Kow, C.S., & Zaidi, S.T.R. (2021). Social distancing and the use of PPE by community pharmacy personnel: Does evidence support these measures? *Research in Social and Administrative Pharmacy*, 17(2), 456–9. https://doi.org/10.1016/j.sapharm.2020.04.033.

HM Government (2020). Keeping workers and customers safe during COVID-19 in restaurants, pubs, bars and takeaway services. November, 1–51. https://assets.publishing.service.gov.uk/media/5eb96e8e86650c278b077616/working-safely-during-covid-19-restaurants-pubs-takeaway-services-091120.pdf.

HM Government (2021). Social distancing review: Report, July, 967. https://doi.org/10.1007/978-3-319-95714-2_300243.

Huang, H., Lin, N.C., Barrett, L., Springer, D., Wang, H.C., Pomplun, M., & Yu, L.F. (2018). Automatic optimization of wayfinding design. *IEEE Transactions on Visualization and Computer Graphics*, 24(9), 2516–30. https://doi.org/10.1109/TVCG.2017.2761820.

Jones, N.R., Qureshi, Z.U., Temple, R.J., Larwood, J.P.J., Greenhalgh, T., & Bourouiba, L. (2020). Two metres or one: What is the evidence for physical distancing in covid-19? *BMJ (Clinical Research Ed.)*, 370, m3223. https://doi.org/10.1136/bmj.m3223.

McDougall, S. J. P., Curry, M. B., & de Bruijn, O. (1999). Measuring symbol and icon characteristics: Norms for concreteness, complexity, meaningfulness, familiarity, and semantic distance for 239 symbols. *Behavior Research Methods, Instruments & Computers*, 31(3), 487–519. https://doi.org/10.3758/BF03200730.

Ng, A.W.Y., & Chan, A.H.S. (2007). The guessability of traffic signs: Effects of prospective-user factors and sign design features. *Accident Analysis and Prevention*, 39(6), 1245–57. https://doi.org/10.1016/j.aap.2007.03.018.

Ongkrutraksa, W. (2015). International natural disaster communications: An exploratory study of signage for tsunami, earth quake and flood in Japan and Thailand. *Journalism and Media*, 283(8), 7–19.

Petrov, M., Walker, J., Optimization, A.D., Space, D., Optimization, M., & Algorithms, G. (2018). Optioneering methods for optimization. *Methods of Exploring Primary and Secondary Performance Criteria in Urban*, 1, 29–36.

Piker, D. (2013). Kangaroo: Form finding with computational physics. *Architectural Design*, 83(2), 136–7. https://doi.org/10.1002/ad.1569.

Saremi, S., Mirjalili, S., & Lewis, A. (2017). Grasshopper optimisation algorithm: Theory and application. *Advances in Engineering Software*, 105, 30–47. https://doi.org/10.1016/j.advengsoft.2017.01.004.

Silic, M., & Silic, D. (2016). The effects of colour on users' compliance with warning banner messages across cultures. https://www.alexandria.unisg.ch/248784/1/ECIS 2802.pdf.

Simonson, A., & Schmitt, B. H. (1997). *Marketing Aesthetics: The Strategic Management of Branding, Identity and Image* (1st American Edition). Simon & Schuster. ISBN: 9780684826554.

Tang, C. H., Wu, W.T., & Lin, C.Y. (2009). Using virtual reality to determine how emergency signs facilitate way-finding. *Applied Ergonomics*, 40(4), 722–30, ISSN 0003-6870, https://doi.org/10.1016/j.apergo.2008.06.009.

Vikneswaran, M., Raffiee, R., Yusof, M., Yahya, M., Subramaniam, S., Loong, W., Othman, M., & Galerial, J. (2018). Implementation of safety signage to ease transportation system in disaster prone area. *AIP Conference Proceedings*, 2 February 1930(1), 020060. https://doi.org/10.1063/1.5022954.

5 International public health communication design

EMMANUEL TSEKLEVES, MARIANA FONSECA-BRAGA AND ALEJANDRO MORENO RANGEL

Introduction

The coronavirus 2019 (Covid-19) pandemic has ushered a new era of increased conspiracy theories, fake news and misinformation about the aetiology, outcomes, prevention and cure of the virus (Tasnim et al., 2020; Van Bavel et al., 2020). This has overloaded and overburdened the public, in their effort to distinguish scientific evidence and facts from less reliable sources of information, often leading to counterproductive practices that increase the spread of the virus.

In addition to this, governmental agencies rely too on public affairs messaging to address public health crisis (Barbour et al., 2016). In this unprecedented situation, governments across the globe and policymakers have been looking at each other for solutions, inspiration, trialled policies and interventions they can implement by their own national and regional authorities. Despite this, there has been no universal effort at establishing international cooperation and knowledge exchange to cope with this challenge of Covid-19 public health information communication.

In response to that, the Design Research Society Special Interest Group on Global Health has developed an open access repository containing crowdsourced information on Covid-19 public health messages and information set by official national and international bodies (DRS SIG, 2021). The aim has been twofold. First, to develop an official repository of data on public messages and information on Covid-19 that researchers, public health authorities and policymakers can access. Second, to conduct a multinational, visual and language communication analysis of the Covid-19 public health messages included in it, in order to develop relevant communication recommendations. It is the latter that is outlined in this chapter.

Background and related work

The infodemic challenge of Covid-19

'Infodemic' refers to an exponential increase in the volume of information associated with a global issue such as an epidemic (WHO, 2020). As Covid-19 has been a relatively unknown virus, in terms of the impact on humans, we are witnessing a rapid rate of new scientific information being published (Eysenbach, 2020).

Since the Ebola outbreak in West Africa, in 2014–16, the health sector has learned that trust in health authorities, community engagement and accurate information can go a long way to help the public comply with public health measures (Gilmore et al., 2020). The need for official messaging during the Covid-19 pandemic is arguably far greater than in more commonly encountered hazard settings, and the demands on communicators to inform and motivate are higher (Sutton et al., 2020).

Governments and international health bodies are engaging the scientific community for evidence-based recommendations on how to minimize harms and better manage the pandemic (Sutton et al., 2020). The widespread misinformation related to the diagnosis and prevention of Covid-19 has confused both the general population and policymakers who are regularly issuing new and revised guidelines for disease prevention and treatments (Tasnim et al., 2020). The main challenge here is not just the sheer volume of information, but critically its translation and communication into actionable recommendations that are contextually, socially and culturally relevant for different audiences across different parts of the world, especially among countries with low income, low life expectancy and less education (Savoia et al., 2013; Gagliardone, 2016; Brisset-Foucault, 2016).

The Covid-19 pandemic has resulted in an enhanced requirement for communication with the public on an ongoing basis, not only to pass on warnings and alerts, but also to inform, educate and continuously motivate individuals in their roles as *de facto* responders in the ongoing disaster (Sutton et al., 2020). There is a need for more targeted public health information within communities and for partnerships between public health authorities and trusted organizations that are integral to these communities (Van Bavel et al., 2020; Srinivasan and Lopes, 2020).

Lessons from past epidemics/pandemics

As demonstrated by recent public health crises, such as the global Ebola outbreak, it is clear that threats to public health do not respect national boundaries (Barbour et al., 2016).

Communication of timely risk information is absolutely vital for behavioural change to protect public health and safety. However, prior work on messaging in response to emerging health threats such as Zika and Ebola has shown that effective messaging strategies can depend upon details of the threat itself (Sutton et al., 2020).

Analysis of previous outbreaks, such as Ebola and the Zika virus, shows that effective communication about the outbreak to the public and how to prevent its transmission take time and offer lessons for the current Covid-19 pandemic public health communication messaging (WHO, 2015; WHO, 2016). Covid-19 presents a challenging context for communication about prevention, containment and treatment as well. Rather than a single, one-time big event, we have seen that Covid-19 presents as a rising tide or prolonged risk incident with several waves of occurrence.

Public health officials and scholars agree that cultural values and traditions significantly influence responses to pandemic (Vaughan and Tinker, 2009; Lin et al., 2014). As in the cases of responses to influenza, Covid-19 risk information is influenced by existing psychological, social, cultural, health and socio-economic factors, which greatly affect how individuals interpret health risk communications, as well as their willingness and ability to act in a timely manner. Lessons learned from historical and recent public health crises suggest that inappropriate communications and insufficient planning can greatly compromise risk reduction (Maunder, 2004; Vanderford et al., 2007; Vaughan and Tinker, 2009).

Research methodology and data analysis

The methodology was developed around the following research question: How might communication design analysis of official Covid-19 public health material help develop recommendations that are contextually, socially and culturally relevant for public audiences across different parts of the world?

The study included two parts. The first part of this study comprised documentary research of crowdsourced information on Covid-19 public health messages and information, set by official national and international bodies, such as government, ministries and international health organizations. This has led to an open repository, which included data from forty-six countries from across five continents at the time of writing, of which data from thirty-one countries were analysed and presented in this chapter. These were collected between April and November 2020.

The second part included the information design analysis through language and message framing, as well as visual design framework. The analysis of the language and message framing was done through fifteen points divided into five themes: culture, language, social, structure and inclusivity. While the visual design framework analysed another fifteen aspects divided into four themes: impact, structure, colour and inclusivity.

A selection of key guidance documents about public health communication design were collected and reviewed (the *WHO Strategic Communications Framework for Effective Communications* (WHO, 2017); the Johns Hopkins Bloomberg School of Public Health, *A Field Guide to Designing a Health Communication Strategy* (O'Sullivan et al., 2003) and the US Centers for Medicare & Medicaid Services, The toolkit for making written material clear and effective (McGee, 2010)) in the development of the language and message framing and visual analysis framework the team used to analyse the public health Covid-19 communication documents.

The process followed the thematic analysis methodology by Braun and Clarke (2006). Once the team was familiarized with the documents, we began the code generation. This was done by looking at each document guideline and coding data by writing notes through the use of notes within the electronic version of the document. After the data coding and collation, we started to look for overarching themes based on the initial research questions. This process produced a number of guidelines, which were reviewed among the team and then consolidated and updated to provide the framework guidelines presented in Table 5.1. Although we recognize that designers employ picture, symbols, typography, colour patterns in an integrative manner to compose the final visual product, it was necessary for the purposes of our investigation to deconstruct the different visual elements to explore them both individually and as a whole message too.

Data analysis was carried out in two stages. The first stage was an analysis of the documents to evaluate the guidelines set above and how they were implemented. The data analysis included samples from each country that included a combination of text-based only (i.e. website information on Covid-19, FAQs, prevention instructions/ guidelines); visual and text (i.e. websites, posters on handwashing, mask wearing, prevention, self-isolating, etc.). Only documents targeting the general public were examined, as those aimed at expert and professional groups (such as healthcare professionals) were out of the scope of the study.

The data analysis is composed of language and message framing (Akl et al., 2011) and visual analysis (Welhausen, 2015) following the guidelines set in our message framing and visual analysis framework. To analyse the documents, a pool of eight researchers who have differing sociocultural backgrounds and understood the first language of the document being analysed. From this pool two researchers scored independently (scale 1–5) the documents sampled from a country and added notes. These were reviewed by a third researcher who scored them also in cases where there was a large score discrepancy (more than two points).

The second stage comprised of a more in-depth content analysis of the subsample of the documents that were explored in stage one. This focused on further analysing good and bad practices of public health communication messages and visual elements applied in the context of Covid-19. The aim was to look at representative samples of good, mixed, bad and ugly official Covid-19 public health message documents, in order to develop recommendations and a toolkit that will guide experts and practitioners to communicate with impact, so that the public understands and supports action on Covid-19. A total of thirty-two documents from seventeen countries were further analysed by researchers individually from October to November 2020.

An inductive detection of the primary themes that emerged in the documents was conducted to determine the themes and major issues explicitly stated to examine deeper themes in Covid-19 public health communication. A series of group discussions among all researchers followed, in order to establish common language and message framing and visual analysis practices and patterns, which in turn led to the development of recommendations.

Table 5.1 Framework Guidelines Employed for Data Analysis

Message and Language Framing	Culture	Does it use words that are familiar and culturally appropriate for the intended readers?
		Are suggestions or instructions specific, realistic and culturally appropriate for the intended readers?
	Inclusivity	Is it gender neutral or inclusive?
		Can readers relate to the health statistics given (do they match as closely as possible to the characteristics of the intended readers and their communities)?
	Language	Is the material/message framed in a friendly/positive way/tone?
		Is the material written in a conversational style, using the active voice?
		Is it keeping sentences simple and relatively short?
		Is it being direct, specific and concrete?
		Is it written as simply as possible, taking into account the reading skills of the intended audience?
		Does it use devices that engage and involve readers, such as stories and quotations, questions and answers?
	Social	Do readers trust the information sources (is it based on information sources the intended audience will trust)?
		Does it emphasize the health impact here and now?
		Does it encourage action now?
	Structure	Is it giving the context first and incorporating definitions into the text?
		Does the material say how to get help or more information?

(*Continued*)

Table 5.1 (Continued)

Visual Design	Colour	Are the colours appealing to the intended readers and free from unwanted connotations or problematic cultural significance?
		Is colour used in a consistent and deliberate way that reinforces the meaning of your messages and enhances their impact?
		Is colour used sparingly (3–5 colour palette)?
		Is text and colour legible?
	Impact	Does the material look appealing at first glance?
		Do the visuals relate directly to the information in the material and reinforce the key messages?
		Are the visuals culturally appropriate for the intended readers?
		Are charts/figures simple and easy to understand?
		Can the visuals evoke affect appropriate for the intended audience?
	Inclusivity	Does the colour take into account that some readers are likely to have diminished or limited colour perception (i.e. colour blind, older people with vivid colour limited perception)?
		Are visuals gender neutral or gender inclusive?
	Structure	Is the size, shape and general look of the material designed with its purpose and users in mind (i.e. more important elements in larger size)?
		Is there a clear and obvious path for the eye to follow through each page?
		Does it have a clear and consistent style and structure?
		Are the visuals clear, uncluttered and consistent in style?

The good, the bad and the ugly

A total of 122 materials from thirty-one countries across five continents (Africa: 7, America: 8, Asia: 9, Europe: 6, Oceania: 1) were examined in the first part of this study. Our findings show that when it comes to the design of Covid-19 public health communication material there are a range of practices (both positive and negative)

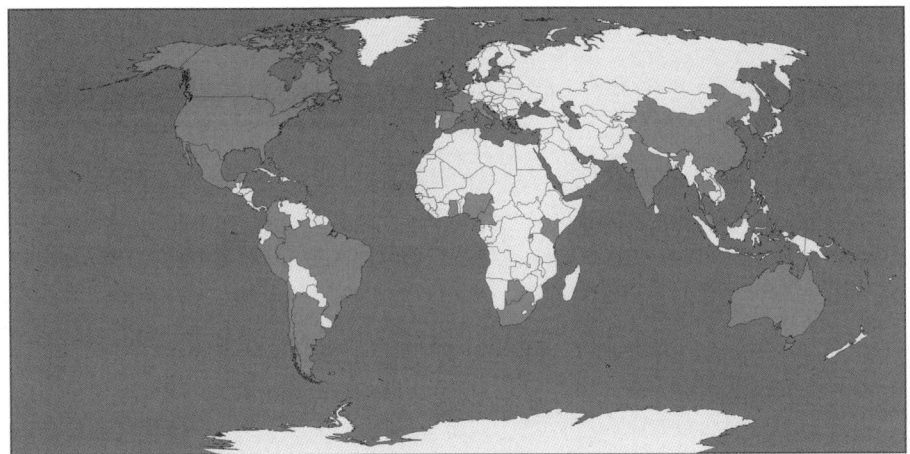

Figure 5.1 Countries analyzed at the first research stage. Image created by Alejandro Moreno Rangel utilizing a free online tool.

found across the material reviewed, irrespective of the country or region they come from. Some are found across most material and countries, some across several and a few in more specific materials and countries (Figure 5.1).

Only about a third of the countries' materials scored consistently for both the message and language framing as well as visual design. Most of these, which scored high for both elements, seem to be countries in North and South America. Also, it becomes clear that most countries did better in terms of language and message framing when compared to their scores in visual design. This highlights opportunities for improvement and the need for more involvement of design researchers and designers in the development of public health communication material for Covid-19.

The analyses by countries show that there is a wide segregation between those countries that performed well and those that did not. More than half (seventeen) of the countries had similar scores between language and message framing and visual design. Nine countries gave a higher importance to language and message framing, while five gave it to visual design.

The general analysis below regards the message and language framing, as well as the visual design.

Language and message framing

The analysis revealed that cultural aspects, such as culturally appropriate words or instructions, of the message were considered as an important aspect while transmitting the message. Whereas the structure aspects, giving the context and details about how to get more help, within the visual communications would require more attention. The most important aspects for a clear language and message framing were considered to be the suggestions or instructions set in the right context and realistic; short and simple sentences; gender inclusivity; and direct, specific and concrete message. While other aspects such as directing for more information and the emphasis of the here and now impacts were not considered as important (Figure 5.2).

Visual design

The analysis revealed that structure aspects, such as clear message framing and consistent and clear structure, of the message were considered as an important aspect while transmitting the message. Whereas the impact aspects, such as making the materials visually appealing and using the appropriate visuals, within the design would require more attention.

According to the reviewed visual examples, the most important aspects for a visual design were considered to be a consistent style and structure, obvious path for the eye to follow and gender neutral or gender inclusive. While other aspects, such as the size of the material and its elements, reader's diminished or limited colour perception, and the text–visuals relation, were the least taken into account (Figure 5.3).

The content analysis below shows specific features of good and bad practices in relation to language and message framing as well as design. Examples were also selected to illustrate good, bad and mixed practices, which we call: *the good*, *the bad*, *the ugly* and *mixed practices*.

The good

The majority of the material reviewed scored high regarding language and message framing. They were written in a gender-inclusive language and provided messages that are appropriate to diverse communication means (e.g. Facebook, Instagram, Twitter) beyond the traditional posters, brochures and leaflets. They kept sentences relatively short with most instructions being direct, specific and concrete. Also, several of the materials employ words that are familiar and culturally appropriate for the intended readers. One example is the leaflet from the Rwanda's Ministry of Health (https://rbc.gov.rw/fileadmin/user_upload/media%20publications/Banner/barrier%20masks%20messages%20english.pdf) about how to use and clean masks properly. They provide clear and short messages on the context of when/how to use, wash and procure masks, as well as on common mistakes to be avoided. Additionally, different ways of getting in touch for further assistance (e.g. phone, email, social media) are provided. A few of these are written in conversational style. Also, most materials made use of sources that are trusted by the readers, coming from authoritative and well-respected national and international bodies.

In terms of the visual design, most materials followed a clear and consistent structure offering and easy path for the eye to follow on the document. Also, that material, which included charts or figures, made good use of these by incorporating ones that are simple and easy to understand. The majority of the materials included legible text and colour, using legible fonts and appropriate contrast of colours. Also, several of them used colour sparingly, employing a maximum of five-colour palette.

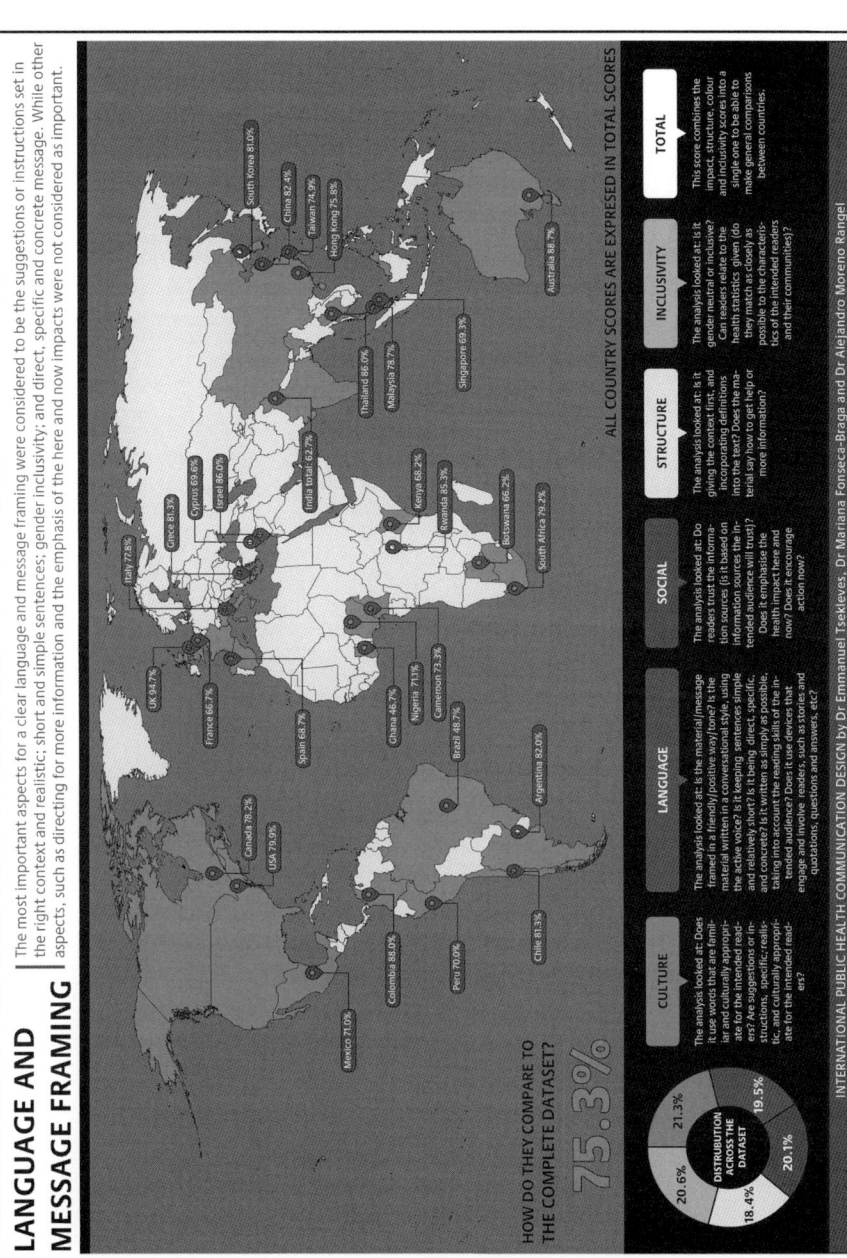

Figure 5.2 Analysis of language and message framing by country. Image created by Alejandro Moreno utilizing a free online tool.

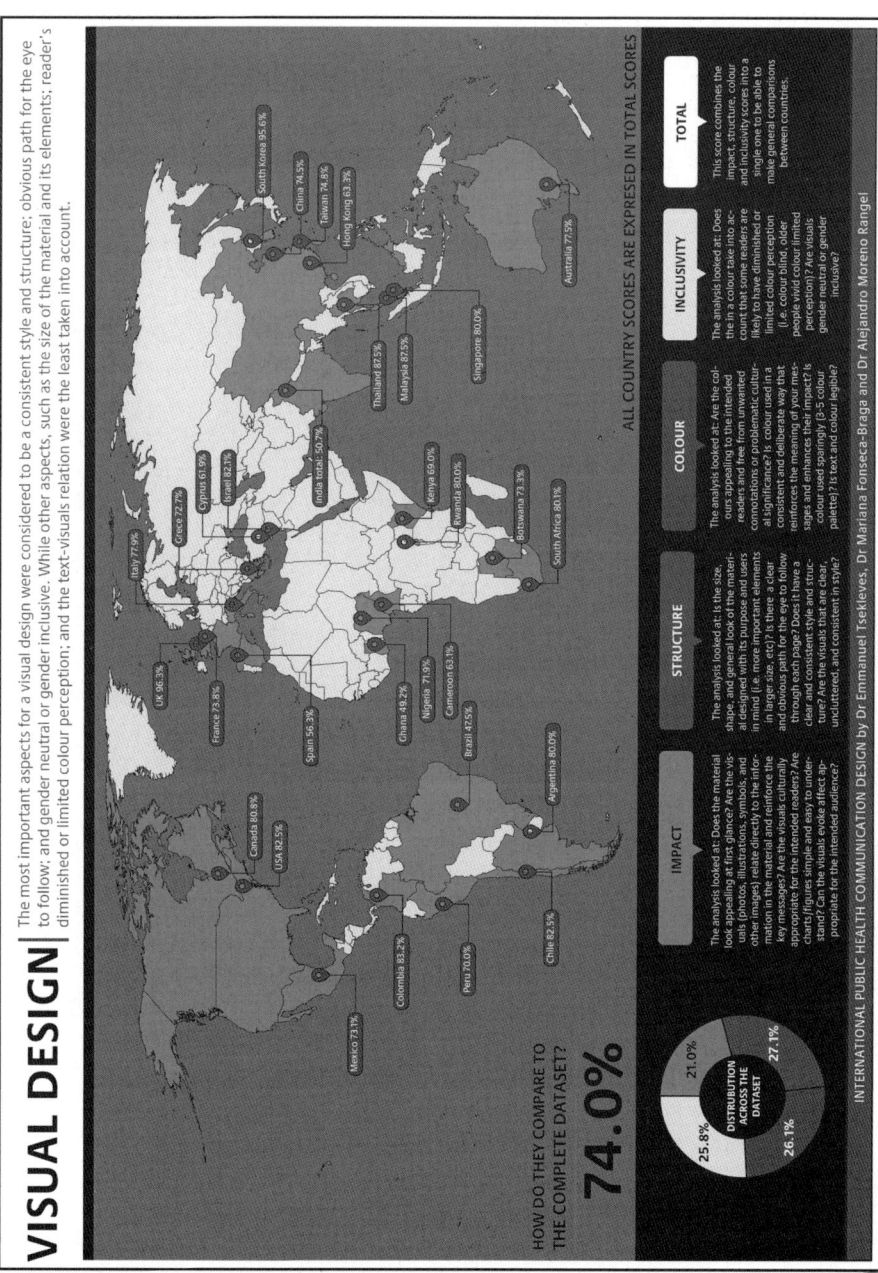

Figure 5.3 Analysis of visual design by country. Image created by Alejandro Moreno Rangel utilizing a free online tool.

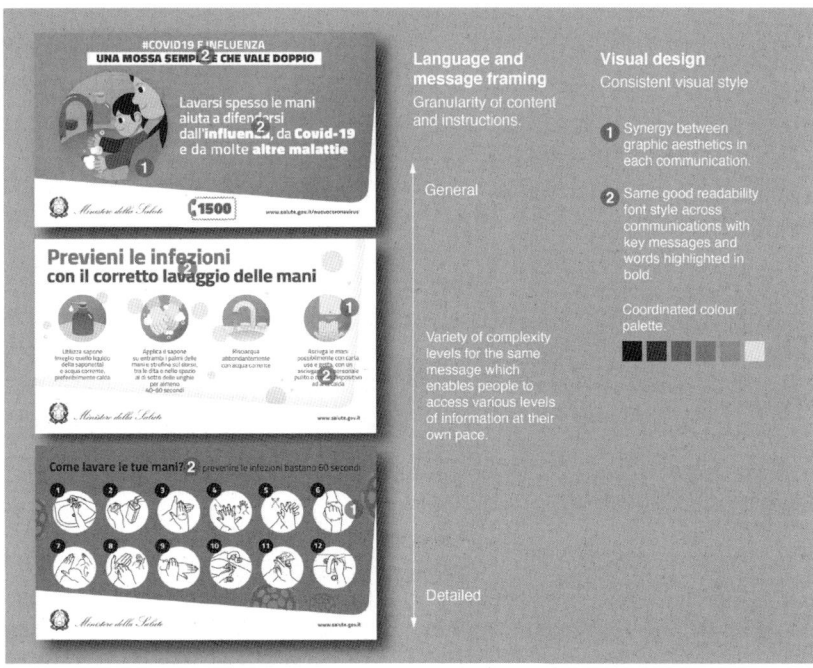

Figure 5.4 Italian Ministry of Health leaflets on handwashing. CC BY 3.0. https://www.salute.gov.it/portale/nuovocoronavirus/homeNuovoCoronavirus.jsp?lingua=english.

The following examples (Figures 5.4 and 5.5) illustrate good practices of language and message framing as well as of visual design (Figures 5.4 and 5.5).

The bad

Structure formed one of the weakest points of the majority of material reviewed. More precisely, many materials did not provide the context first around Covid-19 nor did they explain why it is important that these instructions are followed for the benefit of public health. Some materials lacked accessible further guidance on the measures proposed or guidance on where to get further information if needed.

In terms of language, several of the communication materials may be difficult to understand. These materials use only plain text and adopt a technical language (from medical sciences). These will likely not to be understood especially by disadvantaged communities and people from a low-education background. On top of not considering the reading skills of the information recipients, many of the materials reviewed did not frame the main message in a friendly or positive tone. A few of the materials reviewed did also convey contradicting and misleading messages that neglect cultural aspects. For instance, 'adopt a friendly behaviour without physical contact but always with a smile on your face. . . . The use of masks is recommended everywhere' was included in a material from a Latin American culture. In cultures,

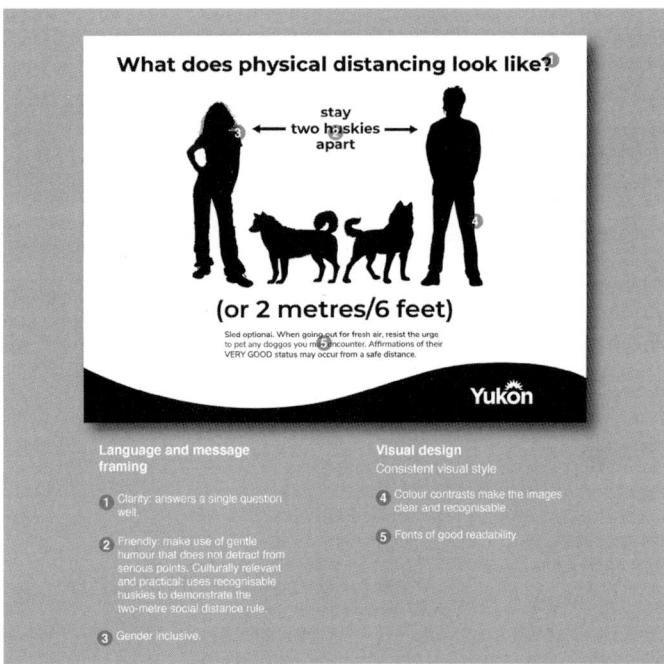

Figure 5.5 Communication material on social distancing by the Yukon regional government in Canada. Copyright Government of Yukon 2023.

such as Latin American ones, in which hugging, kissing and handshakes are used to express a 'friendly behaviour' such messages are confusing and would be worth suggesting safer alternatives.

Furthermore, these plain text messages present authoritative and impersonal instructions when they utilize third-person language and also mix first- and third-person languages, making the message confusing. The communication material by the Ghanaian Ministry of Health on self-quarantine shows examples of these with phrases such as: 'If a person is suspected to have breached the guidelines, they have voluntarily agreed to follow, the surveillance team will work closely with the person to ensure that they understand their obligations.'

Regarding the social impact of the language and message used, some materials failed to emphasize the health impact of Covid-19 here and now. As a result, they did not encourage immediate action to be taken by the intended readers.

One of the least scored areas among the materials analysed was visual design. More precisely, the images used, such as photos, illustrations, did not relate directly to the information and conversely, they did not use effectively the visuals to reinforce the key message. Moreover, the visuals in several cases were not culturally appropriate for the intended readers, as they give instructions that do not make sense or are not possible to be followed in the context as our examples illustrate. As such, the visuals employed in certain cases are neither appropriate nor compelling for the intended audience.

In terms of structure, several materials did not consider the size, shape and general look of the material designed with its purpose and users in mind. Simple visual design practices, such as depicting more important elements in larger size, were ignored. Also, some material included visuals that were unclear, cluttered and inconsistent in style. In most of these cases, the visuals were a direct copy paste from other sources without any editing or processing taking place.

Regarding colour, this was generally well applied, except for circumstances where it was used in an inconsistent and unintentional way (e.g. using colours randomly without a clear purpose such as in drawing attention to a specific message or instruction) diminishing the meaning of their messages and decreasing their impact.

As far as inclusivity, this was not applied universally and often seemed to be an afterthought. For example, many materials did not take into account that some readers are likely to have diminished or limited colour perception (i.e. colour blind, older people with vivid colour limited perception). Gender inclusivity was another issue with several materials, which had made use of visuals, being either gender biased or gender exclusive. The lack of diversity is also noticed regarding social, linguistic and ethnic group backgrounds. This is an element which has been observed in several materials from several countries from the Global South who seem to have copied and pasted messages as well as visuals from Global North countries' material. For instance, the communication material by the Indian Ministry of Health on not overstocking (https://www.mohfw.gov.in/pdf/socialdistancingEnglish.pdf) is neither inclusive nor locally appropriate as characters featured do not represent the country's population demographics, featuring only White people.

The ugly

The 'ugly' examples are unattractive. In some cases, they are too busy, directing attention to irrelevant information; culturally inappropriate and make improper use of visual tools. For instance, the communication material by the South African Department of Health on Covid-19 (https://www.gov.za/sites/default/files/pictures/Mythbuster.pdf) does not signposts where or how to get more information as well as utilizes a distant message such as: 'WHO advise people . . . to . . .' This does not address the population or call for immediate action. Moreover, their visual design is neither inclusive nor locally appropriate as it does not consider ethnic diversity, illustrating predominantly all White family. In addition, there is blurry white text due to the inappropriate application of antialiasing.

Another example is the communication material by the Taiwanese Ministry of Health on handwashing (https://www.cdc.gov.tw/Uploads/Files/3bfcf6db-c2c0-4910-8c8d-f52782e83680.jpg). Their visual design is too busy, presenting an inconsistent style mixing cartoon and real images (photos). It also directs attention to irrelevant information, for instance, the main image which occupies most of the poster is not essential. Furthermore, the text for getting more information and the contact number are too small to be read.

Mixed practices

Some examples analysed presented good features as well as message or visual issues. Our prior work explored these mixed practices (Tsekleves et al., 2021). The poster supporting the fight against Covid-19 by the Kenyan Ministry of Health is an example. On the one hand, it presents good language and message framing. The slogan is culturally relevant and urges people to take action now. It is also available in French and English, both official languages of Kenya. On the other hand, although the main photo utilized is culturally relevant, the visuals also present issues, for instance, with gender-biased visuals. Additionally, the visuals and captions at the bottom of the poster are too small to be seen.

Another example of mixed practices is the communication materials on protecting oneself from Covid-19 by the Peruvian Ministry of Health. It utilizes culturally relevant language and message framing. Posters were available in four Quechua dialects and Ayamara (official languages of Peru), as well as in eight minority native languages. However, the communication is also inappropriate as it is not suitable for or feasible to be followed by indigenous peoples as they often do not have access to running water in their homes.

Discussion and draft recommendations

Health communication materials are intended to solve 'wicked' problems in highly changeable sociocultural, political environments among very diverse people. However, they are often not designed to meet the needs of diverse population groups (Neuhauser and Kreps, 2014). Reaching vulnerable populations, who usually bear the brunt of the effects (financial, health, social) in pandemic situations is very important. Yet, reaching these populations and communicating effectively with them is a critical public health challenge (Neuhauser et al., 2009). Based on the findings and the examples presented above, we propose a set of draft recommendations for the design of public health communication material for Covid-19.

Although there are still some steps to be completed in the development of a full list of recommendations for the public health communication material for Covid-19, our initial analysis reveals some patterns and insights that are emerging. We discuss these as follows (Figure 5.6):

1. Provide the context first and incorporate definitions into the text. As mentioned above, several materials did not provide any context regarding Covid-19 or included any definitions in layman terms. Most critical is the clarification of why should individuals, and the public as a whole, follow the guidelines and instructions offered in the material. This is because, even the most valid and reliable scientific information may be ignored, minimized or processed in a way that results in unanticipated public responses when a communication plan overlooks the reasoning strategies of the audience of the message (Vaughan and Tinker, 2009). Lessons

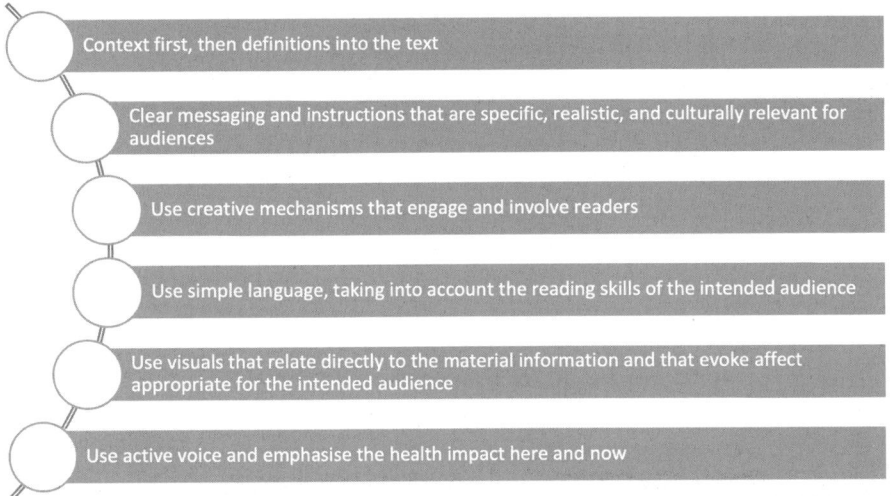

Figure 5.6 Draft recommendations. Image created by Emmanuel Tsekleves.

from past health campaigns demonstrate that these are most successful when communication addresses motivations, emotions and ideas that might contribute to desirable behavioural change but also are compatible with individuals' reasoning strategies (Vaughan and Tinker, 2009).

2. Provide clear messages that consider the cultural aspects and instructions that are specific, realistic and culturally appropriate for the intended readers. Our findings revealed that many materials provided often had instructions which were not culturally appropriate and guidelines, which could not be practically implemented within the targeted socio-economic groups they were targeting. During a pandemic, the way new information is filtered, processed and evaluated is influenced by individuals' daily life circumstances, cultural and psychological risk orientation and traditions regarding health practices. Guidance from socioecological, social cognitive models suggests that health communication is more effective when it is relevant to people's personal and social contexts (Neuhauser et al., 2009). As such, the messages themselves must be compatible with the cultural orientations and socio-economic priorities of affected populations (Vaughan and Tinker, 2009).

3. Use creative mechanisms that engage and involve readers (i.e. stories, quotations, analogies, etc.). Our analysis revealed that this was one of the weakest elements in message and language framing. A handful of material made use of creative devices to engage and involve readers, such as the example form Canada, which used huskies to provide an analogy for physical distance embedding gentle humour. Still, such mechanisms, and especially inclusion of narratives and storytelling, are very powerful and have in the past been employed in health communication (Edgar and Volkman, 2012; Walker, 2019). More precisely, data suggest that narrative message design encourages information sharing as they are perceived as having a story structure and being more understandable and less information overloading, and more transporting (Barbour et al., 2016). Therefore, mechanisms such as storytelling form compelling tools for adding credibility and authenticity (Edgar and Volkman, 2012) to Covid-19 public health messages, especially as they are found to be emotionally evocative and thus more likely for us to act on the message(s) they contain. Furthermore, they provide us with a better understanding about a situation; for instance, the experience of suffering from Covid-19, which in turn helps us understand more about the disease itself.

4. Write them as simply as possible, taking into account the reading skills of the intended audience. Matching readability more closely to users' literacy levels (Neuhauser et al., 2009) is a key component, which several of the materials reviewed did ignore. As already mentioned, some material, especially in Global South contexts, literally translated material into the local languages. This increased the message and language complexity. Instead, linguistic adaptation should be employed to incorporate culturally relevant concepts, and adapt rather than simply translate messages (Neuhauser et al., 2009).

5. Use visuals that relate directly to the information in the material and which reinforce the key messages that evoke affect appropriate for the intended audience. Visuals (photos, illustrations, symbols and other images) and data visualizations can dramatically shape how risks are perceived. Many of the materials analysed did not take that into account, as there were examples, as illustrated in the sections above. In fact, there were cases where language-based content communicated one message about risk, while the visual strategies used communicate a very different message. Effective use of picture is influenced by the context they are used, the level of literacy skills and the extent they are combined with written direction, and the graphic form of the picture whether a line drawing, cartoon, photo, and so on (Walker, 2017). Incorporating culturally relevant visuals (Neuhauser et al., 2009) as well as use of scale and the simplification of images can attract attention, stimulate curiosity (Walker, 2017) and generate affect.

6. Use active voice and emphasize the health impact here and now to encourage action now. Emphasizing the immediate health impact in a way that encourages the intended readers of communication material to take action now is absolutely critical. Pandemics are, ultimately, disasters, and the critical role of immediacy that is central to effective disaster response is also inescapable (Sutton et al., 2020) in the case of Covid-19. Much research indicates that using the active voice makes content livelier and easier to read and understand than the same text written in the passive voice. It can also suggest link with the reader (Walker, 2017; Walker, 2019).

Limitations

Most of our analysis was drawn predominantly on Global North 'standards'. And, as such, has its dominant design influences. Culture plays a critical role in communication. For instance, a Global South reader may consider 'an easy path for the eye' in a different and even opposite way compared to Global North ones.

Conclusion

It is clear from past health epidemics that trust and accurate information can significantly help the public in following public health measures, which help decrease the spread of disease. However, throughout the Covid-19 pandemic we witnessed an 'infodemic', which has confused both the general population and policymakers.

This study presents the positive and negative aspects regarding language and visual design of Covid-19 public messaging in a variety of countries. It also provides draft recommendations on how to effectively plan communication and frame messages that are compelling and actionable to the local audiences considering their social, cultural and economic circumstances.

In the next pandemic, be it now or in the future, the single most important weapon against the disease will be a vaccine. The second most important will be communication (Gesser-Edelsburg et al., 2014). We envisage that this work will contribute to it.

References

Akl, E.A., Oxman, A.D., Herrin, J., Vist, G.E., Terrenato, I., Sperati, F., . . . Schünemann, H. (2011). Framing of health information messages. *Cochrane Database of Systematic Reviews*, 12. https://doi.org/10.1002/14651858.CD006777.pub2.

Barbour, J.B., Doshi, M.J., & Hernández, L.H. (2016). Telling global public health stories: Narrative message design for issues management. *Communication Research*, 43(6), 810–43.

Braun, V., & Clarke, V. (2006). Using thematic analysis in psychology. *Qualitative Research in Psychology*, 3(2), 77–101. https://www.designresearchsociety.org/cpages/sig-global-health.

Brisset-Foucault (2016). *Journalism and Criticism of Power in Africa in Revue Project*, 351(2), 66–72.

Edgar, T., & Volkman, J.E. (2012). Using communication theory for health promotion: Practical guidance on message design and strategy. *Health Promotion Practice*, 13(5), 587–90.

Eysenbach, G. (2020). How to fight an infodemic: The four pillars of infodemic management. *Journal of Medical Internet Research*, 22(6), e21820.

Gagliardone, I. (2016). *The Politics of Technology in Africa*. Cambridge: Cambridge University Press.

Gesser-Edelsburg, A., Mordini, E., James, J.J., Greco, D., & Green, M.S. (2014). Risk communication recommendations and implementation during emerging infectious diseases: A case study of the 2009 H1N1 influenza pandemic. *Disaster Medicine and Public Health Preparedness*, 8(2), 158–69.

Gilmore, B., Ndejjo, R., Tchetchia, A., de Claro, V., Mago, E., Lopes, C., & Bhattacharyya, S. (2020). Community engagement for COVID-19 prevention and control: A rapid evidence synthesis. *BMJ Global Health*, 5(10), e003188.

Lin, L., Savoia, E., Agboola, F., & Viswanath, K. (2014). What have we learned about communication inequalities during the H1N1 pandemic: A systematic review of the literature. *BMC Public Health*, 14(1), 484.

Maunder, R. (2004). The experience of the 2003 SARS outbreak as a traumatic stress among frontline healthcare workers in Toronto: Lessons learned. *Philosophical Transactions of the Royal Society of London Series B: Biological Sciences*, 359(1447), 1117–25.

McGee, J. (2010). The toolkit for making written material clear and effective. *US Centers for Medicare & Medicaid Services*. https://www.cms.gov/Outreach-and-Education/Outreach/WrittenMaterialsToolkit.

Neuhauser, L., & Kreps, G.L. (2014). Integrating design science theory and methods to improve the development and evaluation of health communication programs. *Journal of Health Communication*, 19(12), 1460–71.

Neuhauser, L., Rothschild, B., Graham, C., Ivey, S.L., & Konishi, S. (2009). Participatory design of mass health communication in three languages for seniors and people with disabilities on medicaid. *American Journal of Public Health*, 99(12), 2188–95.

O'Sullivan, G.A., Yonkler, J.A., Morgan, W., & Merritt, A.P. (2003). *A Field Guide to Designing a Health Communication Strategy*. Baltimore: Johns Hopkins Bloomberg School of Public Health/Centre for Communication Programs.

Savoia, E., Lin, L., & Viswanath, K. (2013). Communications in public health emergency preparedness: A systematic review of the literature. *Biosecurity and Bioterrorism: Biodefense Strategy, Practice, and Science*, 11(3), 170–84.

Srinivasan, S., & Lopes, C. A. (2020). *Mediated Sociability: Audience Participation and Convened Citizen Engagement in Interactive Broadcast Shows in Africa*. https://doi.org/10.17863/CAM.52979.

Sutton, J., Renshaw, S.L., & Butts, C.T. (2020). COVID-19: Retransmission of official communications in an emerging pandemic. *PloS one*, 15(9), e0238491.

Tasnim, S., Hossain, M.M., & Mazumder, H. (2020). Impact of rumors and misinformation on COVID-19 in social media. *Journal of Preventive Medicine and Public Health*, 53(3), 171–4.

Tsekleves, E., Fonseca Braga, M., Moreno-Rangel, A., Zhang, L., Salazar, M., Field, H., & Alter, H. (2021). Understanding public health communication design globally during the Covid-19 pandemic: The good, the bad and the ugly. In L. Di Lucchio, L. Imbesi, A. Giambattista, & V. Malakuczi (Eds.), *Design Culture(s) Cumulus Conference Proceedings Roma 2021*. Rome, Italy: Sapienza University of Rome, Cumulus Association, Aalto University, 2569–93.

Van Bavel, J.J., Baicker, K., Boggio, P.S., Capraro, V., Cichocka, A., Cikara, M., . . . Willer, R. (2020). Using social and behavioural science to support COVID-19 pandemic response. *Nature Human Behaviour*, 4(5), 460–71.

Vanderford, M.L., Nastoff, T., Telfer, J.L., & Bonzo, S.E. (2007). Emergency communication challenges in response to Hurricane Katrina: Lessons from the Centers for Disease Control and Prevention. *Journal of Applied Communication Research*, 35(1), 9–25.

Vaughan, E., & Tinker, T. (2009). Effective health risk communication about pandemic influenza for vulnerable populations. *American Journal of Public Health*, 99(S2), S324–S332.

Walker, S. (2017). The contribution of typography and information design to health communication. In E. Tsekleves and R. Cooper (Eds.), *Design for Health*. London: Routledge, 92–109.

Walker, S. (2019). Effective antimicrobial resistance communication: The role of information design. *Palgrave Communications*, 5(1), 24.

Welhausen, C.A. (2015). Visualizing a non-pandemic: Considerations for communicating public health risks in intercultural contexts. *Technical Communication*, 62(4), 244–57.

WHO (2015). *Factors that Contributed to Undetected Spread of the Ebola Virus and Impeded Rapid Containment. One Year into the Ebola Epidemic*. Geneva: World Health Organization.

WHO (2016). *Zika Strategic Response Plan, Revised for July 2016–December 2017 (No. WHO/ZIKV/SRF/16.3)*. World Health Organization. https://www.who.int/emergencies/zika-virus/response/en/.

WHO (2017). *WHO Strategic Communications Framework for Effective Communications*. Geneva: WHO. https://www.who.int/about/communications.

WHO (2020). *Immunizing The Public Against Misinformation*. https://www.who.int/news-room/feature-stories/detail/immunizing-the-public-against-misinformation (accessed 29 September 2020).

6 Design's first line response to the challenges posed by Covid-19 in South America

Chilean and Colombian examples

RICARDO J. HERNANDEZ

Introduction

After the initial surprise and chaos of the Covid-19 pandemic, people around the world started to develop solutions to the challenges placed by the pandemic. These solutions were related to finding new ways to work (George et al., 2021), getting used to studying and living in the same space and developing new alternatives to generate income. Many were linked to the pressure placed on the healthcare system as a result of the large number of patients arriving every day at the hospitals (Atkinson, 2021). Covid-19 was an unknown enemy, and there was no medicine or vaccine at the beginning to fight the evil that took over the world. There was a lot of uncertainty, and lack of data was the first issue people tried to tackle by different means. In terms of the attention of people, it became evident that the medical infrastructure was not prepared. Even in rich and developed countries, there was not enough equipment to treat the patients, much less in countries with significant economic and social deprivations. Doctors and nurses didn't have sufficient protective equipment to do their jobs safely, and the world witnessed probably the worst crisis since the First and Second World Wars.

As people started to develop solutions in the public and private sectors, it was recognized that a multidisciplinary approach was required. We were fighting a very complex issue that needed specialists with different knowledge and expertise. In that context, design as a discipline was crucial for many solutions to the pandemic problems. This chapter presents a particular point of view to classify the contributions design made to those solutions. In general, the examples presented are not an exhaustive list of cases, but the three categories presented are an interesting perspective to understand the ways design created value during the development of the first-line responses to the pandemic: to inform, to protect and to care. These categories can even be used to understand design's contributions at any stage of the pandemic.

Challenges posed by Covid-19

The pandemic caused by Covid-19 changed a lot of things in a very short time. It altered our habits and daily routines, placed limitations and barriers to our productive and recreational activities and put great pressure on the health system (Nundy et al., 2021). If any, Covid-19 made us think about how we were living, and it posed important questions about how we want to live in the future.

Regarding how Covid-19 affected our daily lives, the dynamic of our homes is probably the best indicator to see the profound transformations it caused. In a few months, we moved to work at home and take care of the children full time because the schools were shut down (Mobarak Hossain, 2021), and everyone was locked in their houses for the first time in their lives. Scared by the high chances to get infected by simple contact with other human beings or even by stuff on the shelves at the supermarket, our hygienic and feeding habits also changed. Washing hands constantly, applying the sanitizing gel, cleaning products with alcohol and, probably the most difficult for many, wearing a face mask all day are only a few of many changes we had to implement without any previous preparation.

But the transformations were much further. Covid-19 placed important limitations and barriers to our production activities and also our personal relationships. The way we used to interact with our colleagues changed, moving the work environment into our homes (Gallacher and Hossain, 2020). From one day to the next, we were showing our co-workers the inside of our houses. It stopped at the home offices for a few lucky ones, but for many, it involved showing our kids, our furniture, our bedrooms and even our mess on camera. The daily commuting stopped, the long-distance trips were cancelled and the internet became the most trusted asset in the world. These changes meant, between many consequences, that several small and medium companies went out of the market (Khlystova et al., 2022; Mokter Hossain, 2021) with a huge economic and social impact associated.

Beyond work, personal relationships were heavily disturbed in some cases irreversibly. As everyone was locked in their houses and visits were forbidden, many old members of the families in retirement homes became secluded for their own good with the emotional cost that it produced. Things got worse when people started to fall ill, and many ended at the hospital uncommunicated with their most close ones, and in the sadder cases, dying alone. In modern life, probably only war times were more painful than the last couple of years for many families worldwide.

Perhaps one of the most dramatic vicissitudes we saw during the pandemic was the pressure the Covid-19 placed on the health system (Rabow et al., 2021). Sick people overrun the capacity of hospitals very early in 2020, and this capacity remained insufficient for almost a year before numbers started to show a little relief. Suddenly, there were not enough beds in intensive care units, not enough ventilators to treat critical patients, not even oxygen (Agarwal et al., 2021). There was insufficient personal protective equipment for doctors and nurses to assure safe replacement rates, and the world witnessed the great level of inequality between countries facing all the same evil (Agarwal et al., 2021). Without vaccines and medicine to treat an unknown enemy, health personnel confronted disturbing times with people dying in masses, and more getting infected every day despite the lockdown and the prohibitions. A professional and personal drama mixing helplessness, tiredness and uncertainty (Rabow et al., 2021).

It is not easy to cover all the challenges the Covid-19 placed for humanity in the last two years in just a couple of pages, and the truth is that many of those challenges are far from being resolved. In the coming years, we will still see the consequences of the pandemic, and some of them will remain with us for a long time (Rabow et al., 2021). But in the next section, instead of focusing on those coming years, it will be presented and discussed how design as a discipline became an instrumental tool to respond quickly to many of the transformations mentioned before just at the pandemic's start. It will be impossible to cover all the contributions in which design played an important role. Still, to cover a significant part of them, a classification is proposed according to the nature of the intervention as solutions to inform, solutions to protect and solutions to care. These categories are explained in detail in the following section.

Design response: Examples in South America

Design responses facing the challenges posed by the pandemic produced by the Covid-19 vary in terms of the moment they emerge and the responses' nature. Between the first-line responses, the ones that appear as soon as the problem is recognized as a global issue, it is possible to distinguish between solutions oriented to inform, to protect and to care. This classification aims to cover most of the interventions developed to respond quickly to the challenges placed by the Covid-19 in which design was a fundamental driver and tool, but surely it doesn't cover all. In this sense, this classification aims to organize the design-driven contributions rather than to present an exhaustive list of them.

In practice, the first-line responses in the pandemic came from many different actors. Still, as the Covid-19 took us by surprise, universities were one of the better-suited actors to develop quickly some of the solutions needed. For this reason, the examples shown in the next sections are mainly projects born in academia and then quickly transferred to society through alliances with industry, non-governmental organizations and even implemented directly. An example also came from the public sector as governments were highly active in developing solutions to reduce the negative impacts caused by the pandemic and, in the end, respond to the crisis.

South America is a large, complex and diverse region, and for that, it won't be easy to explore and present solutions developed in all their countries. For this reason, the examples presented are concentrated on initiatives that originated in Chile and Colombia. These two countries have followed different paths facing the challenges placed by the Covid-19. On the one hand, Chile has been recognized probably as the best performer in the region with the fastest vaccination programme and very strict lockdowns. In comparison, Colombia has been more in a middle ground, with early responses in terms of lockdowns and mobility restrictions aiming to stop the spread of the virus, but with high numbers of people infected during 2020 and shortage of beds and equipment to treat patients. The situation evolves every day, right now in 2021, Chile is considered a country with high incidence of the virus and Colombia is in a moderate stage (Centers for Disease Control and Prevention, 2021).

Beyond the successes or failures in each country, the following examples show the commitment, creativity and disposition of many people wanting to help in both countries. They also show the importance of articulated networks between academia, industry, health sector and governmental and non-governmental agencies to tackle the problems placed by the pandemic.

Responses to inform

One of the most traditional fields in design has been graphic and information design (Hernandez et al., 2018). The competencies and skills needed by designers in this field to produce and present data in an attractive, useful and easy to understand way are well known. In the case of the pandemic, data became one of the most important tools to fight the virus and to calculate the risks (So et al., 2020; Zhang et al., 2021). It was clear since the beginning of the pandemic that information was key to stop the spread of the virus; allocate the resources efficiently to treat patients and manage measures like lockdowns, quarantines and mobility restrictions (Bowe et al., 2020; So et al., 2020). In this context, visualizations in official and unofficial websites and platforms to inform people about the numbers of people infected, deceased, hospital occupancy levels, number of people recovered and beds available became crucial (Zhang et al., 2021).

These information systems are, in general, complex arrays of statistical and demographic data than without good design interfaces easily became dense masses of unintelligible numbers. One of those visualizations' purposes was to keep people informed to reduce the levels of uncertainty and show the seriousness of the situation to raise awareness of the importance of complying with the sanitary measures imposed. The way the information was displayed became a crucial aspect in ensuring compliance and good calculation of risks (Bowe et al., 2020; So et al., 2020).

In the following examples it is possible to see the role design played to provide information that was useful and clear for different audiences while keeping the rigour required for the authorities to take actions and decisions around the pandemic's evolution.

Chilean government website

The Chilean government created a dedicated platform to share information about the pandemic (Gobierno de Chile, 2021). This platform includes basic statistical information about the daily number of infected people, people in hospitals and the deceased (see Figure 6.1). As the pandemic was evolving, the platform started to show also historical and accumulative data (see Figure 6.2). It currently shows information by gender, regions in the country and even relationships between symptoms and reported cases (see Figure 6.3). (Data shown correspond to the situation in Chile on 23 October 2021.)

The complexity of the information associated with the pandemic and its implications for particular areas in the country was probably the reason why the traditional tools used to present the data were complemented with better interfaces to show the diversity of what was happening in the whole country. One of these complementary tools that shows the impact design can have on how information is displayed is a territorial viewfinder (see Figure 6.4). In this viewfinder, it is possible to see the number of positive cases confirmed by geographical area in different modes: street, topographic, terrain and imagery, among others (see Figure 6.5).

Figure 6.1 Daily data of cases confirmed, active and recovered – Covid-19 Chile.

Figure 6.2 Evolution of cases confirmed by region – 100,000 habitants – Covid-19 Chile.

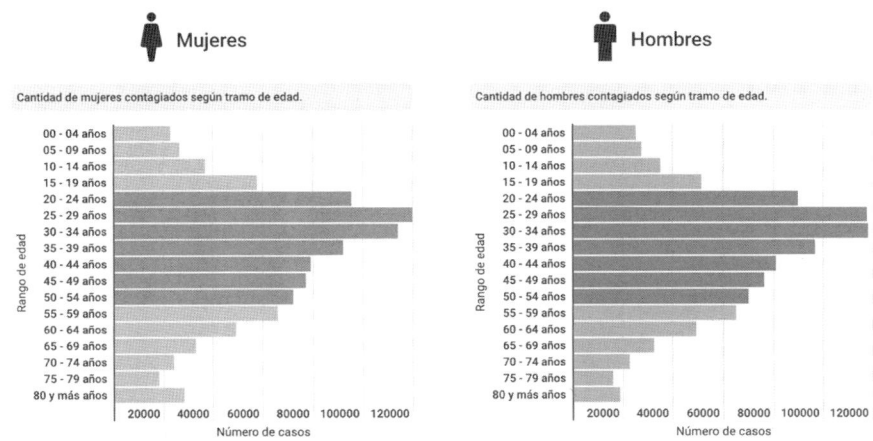

Figure 6.3 Total number of cases confirmed by gender and group of age – Covid-19 Chile.

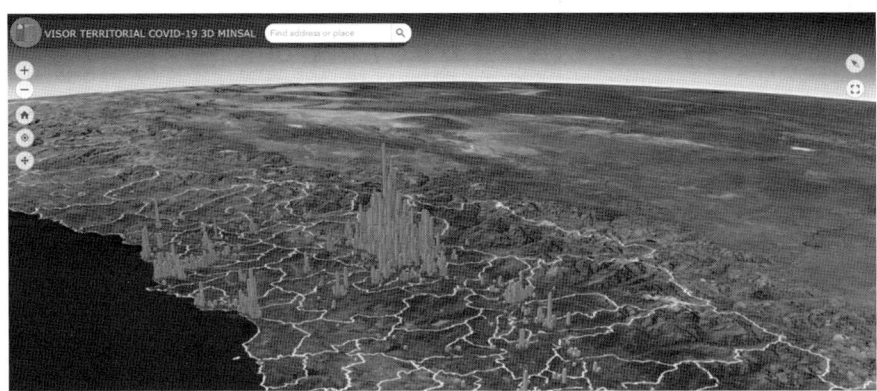

Figure 6.4 Territorial viewfinder – Covid-19 Chile.

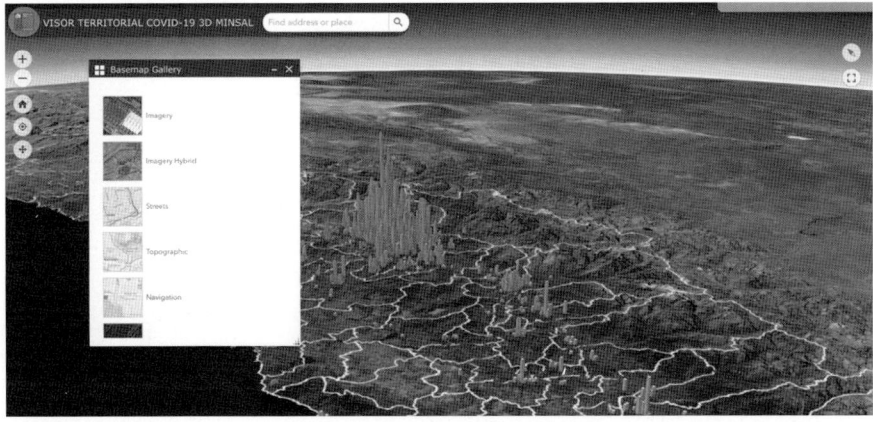

Figure 6.5 Options of visualization territorial viewfinder – Covid-19 Chile.

Research Project COLEV – Universidad de los Andes, Colombia

Another example of how design has an important role in helping to visualize and communicate data associated with the pandemic in a clear and useful way is the research project COLEV (Universidad de los Andes, 2021b). This project developed at the Universidad de Los Andes, Colombia, has different lines of action strongly related to the production and management of data. In their own words, the project aims to 'produce and communicate pertinent evidence that facilitates dialogue between academia and the ones making decisions in public health to give informed answers to covid-19 issues in Colombia' (Universidad de los Andes, 2021b).

In this declaration of purpose, it is clear that one important element beyond the production of evidence is how evidence is communicated. It is a multidisciplinary research project involving academics from engineering, medicine, architecture and design, among other specialities. Among the activities published on the project website that show an interest in how evidence about the Covid-19 is communicated, there is one initiative around the social and cultural aspects that influence the use of data science tools. In this initiative, a multidisciplinary approach is declared to enrich the way data is understood (Universidad de los Andes, 2021b). It is a work in progress and a good example of how design can impact the production and visualization of data linked to the pandemic to different audiences involved in making the decisions.

Another activity in this project where it is possible to see the contribution of design is the 'Museum of Disinformation'. In this initiative, there is declared interest in using design methodologies, among other types of methodologies, to explore and understand the concept of disinformation about the Covid-19 in Colombia during the pandemic (Universidad de los Andes, 2021a). One of the results of this initiative already socialized in the project website is a visualization of fake news about the Covid-19 published and shared in different media in Colombia during one year (see Figure 6.6). These media include social networks, newscasts and text messages. The

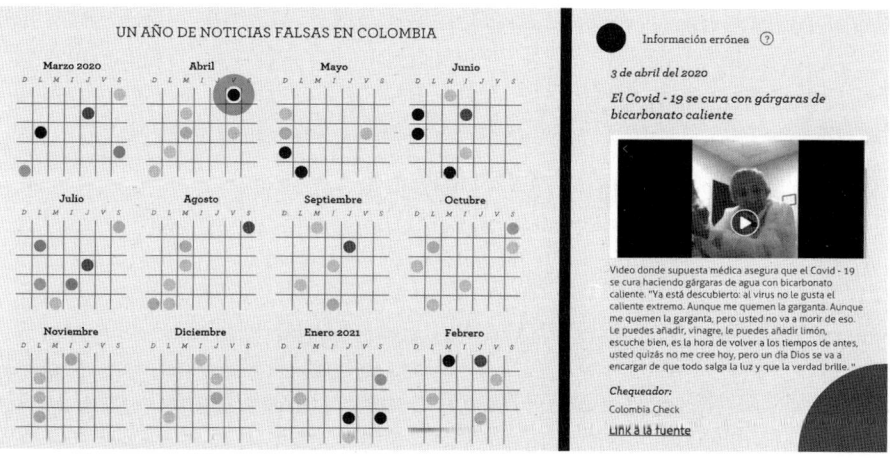

Figure 6.6 Fake news in Columbia – Covid-19 visualization. Project COLEV.

visualization was designed and then programmed to show a historical evolution of this phenomenon of fake news in Colombia about the Covid-19, which surely will inspire interesting debates about the important role of information in the middle of a crisis.

Responses to protect

One area in which design also contributed was developing equipment, tools and strategies to protect people. In the more material sense, design was used in the development of personal protective equipment, important for the people in the streets but vital for the health system personnel fighting the virus at the hospitals (Chao, 2020; Formentini et al., 2021). Something interesting in this category was the active participation of design students involved in projects to design and fabricate that kind of equipment through their courses. In the following examples, it is possible to see two types of projects, both oriented to design personal protective equipment, one supported by a network of students and graduates that participated in the design process and made the equipment at their homes using digital fabrication technologies like 3D printing. The other is a research and development project aspiring to question the current design and need for traditional personal protective equipment to replace them with an ergonomically designed personal ventilator.

Facial shield – Pontificia Universidad Católica de Chile, Chile

This project, led by designer Ángela Decar, integrated a decentralized network of students and graduates to produce a facial shield quickly at the beginning of the pandemic using 3D printing technology and easily accessible materials (Escuela de Ingenieria UC, 2021a). The call came from medical personnel in Chile who needed those shields to treat people infected with Covid-19, making them feel safer and ensuring their health in order to fulfil the needs of a very stressed system.

The shield was designed originally by Prusa, the 3D printer European manufacturer, and then that design was modified in Chile by the Universidad de Chile. The design was formed by a 3D printed support, a sheet of clear and flexible acrylic, and an elastic band to fix the shield to the head (see Figure 6.7). The most interesting feature of this project, beyond the efficient shield's design to be produced quickly and cheap, was the orchestration of people around the crisis to use decentralized machines to produce the shields. In general, the requests received from the health system were managed by the Asociación de Fabricantes por la Emergencia Sanitaria and then distributed to universities and fablabs with the capacity to produce the shields. Students and graduates at the Pontificia Universidad Católica de Chile made available their home 3D printers to produce those shields at the speed needed, and the filament was donated. It was a successful example of collaboration to produce a first-line response to one of the big problems we faced at the pandemic's beginning.

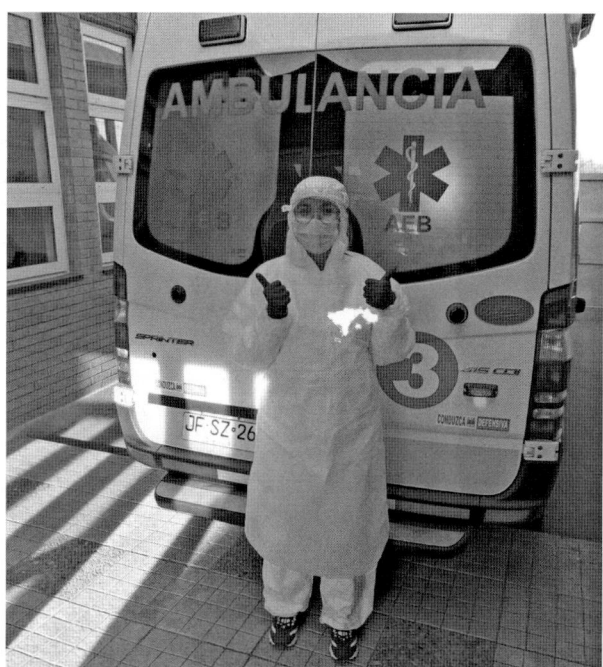

Figure 6.7 Facial shield made at the Pontificia Universidad Católica de Chile, Chile.

Personal ventilator – PersoCO – Universidad de los Andes, Colombia

This project was inspired by the work done by Diana Garay-Baquero, a Colombian scientist at the University of Southampton in the United Kingdom. The project's purpose was to design and develop a personal ventilator for medical personnel that could replace part of the traditional personal protective equipment they use and offer better protection in the fight against Covid-19 (Universidad de los Andes, 2021c). Under the course 'Proyecto Multidisciplinario de Diseño en Ingeniería PMDP', the project involved professors of engineering and design, students from both faculties and called two local companies' attention (Universidad de los Andes, 2021c).

The project aimed to design and develop a personal ventilator that was comfortable to use during very long working hours, with easily accessible materials, locally produced and very efficient in protecting against the virus (Universidad de los Andes, 2021c). Despite that this was a research project and that at the time of writing this chapter the ventilator was not yet produced and in use, it is precious to see how the pandemic created a context where design and engineering students were early involved in a design process in collaboration with the industry. This experience creates essential competencies and highlights the value design has in cooperation with other disciplines to produce solutions taking into account things like

Figure 6.8 Ventilator PersoCO – Universidad de los Andes, Colombia.

usability, ergonomics, aesthetics and mainly the context under which the solutions will be used. The final result shows an exciting design (see Figure 6.8) that beyond the pandemic can become a valuable piece of equipment for the health system in Colombia.

Responses to care

There is another type of first-line response to Covid-19 where design made a great contribution, the design of products and equipment to take care of ill patients at the hospitals. One of the first shocks the world had to face was the shortage of equipment, in particular ventilators, to treat critically ill patients (Agarwal et al., 2021). In general, not all patients with Covid-19 ended at the hospitals. Still, among the many who did, a group of critical patients deteriorated very quickly and had to be treated at intensive care units. For them, ventilators were vital, a real difference between life and death (Agarwal et al., 2021).

The shortage of these machines mobilized efforts from different actors in society to find alternative solutions at the speed they were needed to treat the masses arriving at hospitals every day. Despite the efforts of traditional manufacturers, it was evident very early that those efforts were not enough. For that reason, many projects mainly developed at universities, and manufactures in other industries like cars, started to design and develop different kinds of ventilators to put them in disposition to the health system (Agarwal et al., 2021). Here, one of those projects developed in Colombia is presented.

Beyond the ventilators, there were other necessities associated with the treatment of Covid-19 patients, also covered by university projects. The first case in this section presents the design and development of a face cushion made especially for patients connected to ventilators in the prone position in a hospital in Santiago.

Soporte Facial para Pacientes con Ventilación Mecanica Invasiva (SOFA) – Pontificia Universidad Católica de Chile

As mentioned before, many patients infected with Covid-19 ended in intensive care units connected to ventilators. In those conditions, patients were heavily sedated, and the rotation of their bodies to avoid skin injuries depended entirely on their nurses. Despite the huge efforts made by nurses and personnel at the hospitals, those injuries started to be an important problem. In that context, a doctor from a public hospital in Santiago de Chile approached the design team at DILAB-UC to propose a solution. The task was to design a cushion, mainly for the face, to be used with Covid-19 patients at intensive care units to help the work nurses were doing, trying to avoid skin injuries due to pressure and lack of circulation when patients were in the prone position for days, weeks or even months (Escuela de Ingenieria UC, 2021b).

At DILAB-UC, a team of undergraduate students, designers and academics led by Professor Ricardo J. Hernandez and designer Ángela Decar was formed to tackle this challenge. This was a collaborative process that added more people, including nurses, doctors and intensive care unit specialists, to find the possible solution during the time it was run. After a couple of months from April to June 2020, a face cushion called SOFA was designed, fabricated and delivered to the Hospital de Urgencia Asistencia Publica en Santiago de Chile (see Figures 6.9–6.11) (Escuela de Ingenieria UC, 2021b). The Pontificia Universidad Católica de Chile supported the project, and all the results were made public to be freely used.

This project was a great example of collaboration between academia, industry and the healthcare system. It achieved a great result in a very short period of time that improved the treatment and quality of life of patients with Covid-19 and the work and operation of the hospital involved in the project. A mention of this project in the news can be consulted here: http://www.lanacion.cl/disenan-soporte-facial-para-pacientes-con-covid-19-que-estan-en-posicion-boca-abajo/

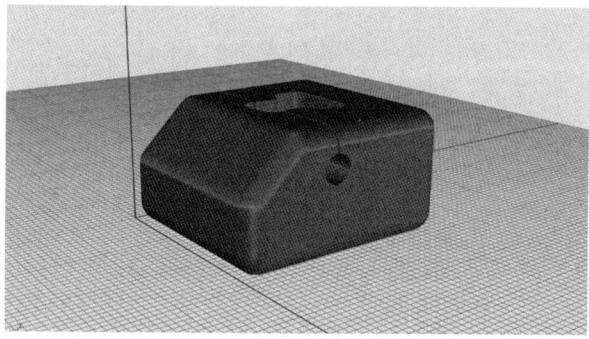

Figure 6.9 SOFA – Project Facial Cushion for Covid-19 Patients – Chile. © Ricardo Hernandez.

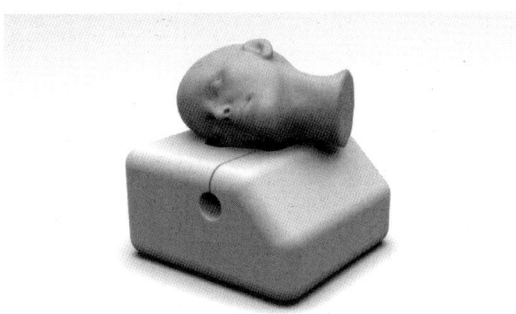

Figure 6.10 SOFA – Project Facial Cushion for Covid-19 Patients – Chile. © Ricardo Hernandez.

Figure 6.11 SOFA – Project Facial Cushion for Covid-19 Patients – Chile. © Ricardo Hernandez.

Ventilator – Universidad Nacional de Colombia Sede Manizales

In Colombia, as in many other countries in the region, universities responded quickly to the shortage of ventilators in public and private hospitals. One of these projects that resulted successfully in an approved ventilator to be used with Covid-19 patients was developed by an academic at the Universidad Nacional de Colombia Sede Manizales. Professor Jorge Estrada designed a small ventilator made to take care of patients suffering from respiratory problems associated with Covid-19 (Ramirez Pineda, 2020). Between its benefits, this ventilator was made widely accessible by its low cost and its easy use compared to the traditional surgical ventilators. The ventilator was also useful to prevent the deterioration of patients before they had to be interned at intensive care units (Ramirez Pineda, 2020).

This ventilator was among many designed and developed early in the pandemic to fight the shortage of medical equipment around the world. Without a strong medical industry, this shortage in countries like Colombia was worsened by lockdowns and flight restrictions that limited importations from Europe and North America, where these ventilators are normally made. This example shows the power and commitment of local researchers and practitioners in the region and the importance of product design as a field of work. Part of the complexity of designing and fabricating a ventilator is linked to the learning curve people have to follow to learn how these machines operate and find the right tuning. For that kind of issue, design can make fundamental contributions to achieve machines that are technologically savvy and user friendly.

Discussion and conclusions

For those of us who work in design, it has been normal to defend our discipline and its contribution beyond its more traditional conceptions and uses (Hernandez et al., 2021). However, as a researcher and academic, I have seen how this situation has changed during the recent years. The expansion of design to new frontiers and work fields has opened the mind of many in the industry and public and private sectors. The value of design has often been considered in relation to product design and graphic design. Today, this value extends to many other areas including public services, innovation, sustainable development, education and health (Hernandez et al., 2018; Sangiorgi and Prendiville, 2014).

Facing the challenges of Covid-19 and the subsequent pandemic, design has been an important part of the tools and knowledge needed to develop quick and effective solutions. As presented in this chapter, first-line responses to the pandemic were crucial to start the fight against an unknown enemy. According to Herbert Simon, design was a crucial means to achieve preferred states in a moment of crisis (Simon, 1996). The examples presented here are far from an exhaustive list of all the contributions design made to the problems linked to the pandemic. There are personal biases towards product design and visualization of data, as they are between my personal areas of interest. For that reason, most important than the examples are the point of view offered to classify and understand the nature of those contributions design made to the first-line responses: to inform, to protect and to care. These three areas cover a wide range of projects in which design took part in helping to develop products, services, digital platforms, infrastructure and strategies in the context of the pandemic. I invite the readers to use these three perspectives to understand and classify the responses they know.

Another interesting exercise I do is to see how first-line responses have evolved through time, and I consciously look to identify how design plays an important role in those responses. An example of this kind of exercise relates, for example, to the visualization of data. In Chile, for example, the platform to inform people about the pandemic has evolved according to the necessities. After the initial confusion, the government launched a lockdown plan that includes phases that, according to the number of cases and the particular situation of an area, define if people could leave their houses, go to work or visit a supermarket. Design played a crucial role to help people to understand those measures and familiarize themselves with the new normality.

The pandemic is not over yet; there are still challenges we will have to face in the future and solutions to come. Something the pandemic has shown us is that to face complex problems, we have to put complex systems in place. It is not the first time that multidisciplinary approaches have to be used to tackle a problem. We have known for several decades that issues like global warming, poverty and management of natural resources are among many topics that require collaborative approaches between multiple disciplines. But the conditions imposed by Covid-19 are unique. In modern times it is the first time we see factories closed around the globe, people lockdown at home, planes on the ground for months, children schooled virtually, malls without people and families connected online for more than a year. Under those special conditions, design has been a crucial discipline to inform, protect and care for people with many different needs. If there is something positive to take out from this pandemic, at least from a very instrumental perspective, it probably will be the fact that we might not need to defend design again. Its value and contribution to society are well proven.

References

Agarwal, K.M., Sharma, P., Bhatia, D., & Mishra, A. (2021). Concept design of the physical structure for ICU ventilators for COVID-19 pandemic. *Sensors International*, 2, 100092. https://doi.org/10.1016/j.sintl.2021.100092.

Atkinson, P. (2021). Global reach. *The Design Journal*, 24(4), 499–502. https://doi.org/10.1080/14606925.2021.1934305.

Bowe, E., Simmons, E., & Mattern, S. (2020). Learning from lines: Critical COVID data visualizations and the quarantine quotidian. *Big Data & Society*, 7(2), 205395172093923. https://doi.org/10.1177/2053951720939236.

Centers for Disease Control and Prevention (2021). COVID-19 travel recommendations by destination. https://www.cdc.gov/coronavirus/2019-ncov/travelers/map-and-travel-notices.html (Retrieved 25 November 2021).

Chao, F.-L. (2020). Face mask designs following novel Coronavirus. *Journal of Public Health Research*, 9(1). https://doi.org/10.4081/jphr.2020.1770.

Escuela de Ingenieria UC (2021a). Escudos Faciales de Protección COVID-19. https://covid19.ing.puc.cl/mascaras-de-proteccion-para-personal-de-la-salud/ (Retrieved 1 October 2021).

Escuela de Ingenieria UC. (2021b). Soporte Facial Para Pacientes con Ventilación Mecanica Invasiva. https://covid19.ing.puc.cl/soporte-facial-para-aliviar-a-pacientes-con-ventilacion-mecanica-invasiva/ (Retrieved 1 October 2021).

Formentini, G., Rodríguez, N.B., Favi, C., & Marconi, M. (2021). Challenging the engineering design process for the development of facial masks in the constraint of the COVID-19 pandemic. *Procedia CIRP*, 100, 660–5. https://doi.org/10.1016/j.procir.2021.05.140.

Gallacher, G., & Hossain, I. (2020). Remote work and employment dynamics under COVID-19: evidence from Canada. *Canadian Public Policy*, 46(S1), S44–S54. https://doi.org/10.3138/cpp.2020-026.

George, T.J., Atwater, L.E., Maneethai, D., & Madera, J.M. (2021). Supporting the productivity and wellbeing of remote workers. *Organizational Dynamics*, 100869. https://doi.org/10.1016/j.orgdyn.2021.100869.

Gobierno de Chile (2021). Cifras Oficiales COVID-19. https://www.gob.cl/coronavirus/cifrasoficiales/ (Retrieved 23 October 2021).

Hernandez, R.J., Cooper, R., Miranda, C., & Goñi, J. (2021). Meanings and uses of design for innovation: Conversations with UK companies. *The Design Journal*, 24(4), 611–30. https://doi.org/10.1080/14606925.2021.1932248.

Hernandez, R.J., Cooper, R., Tether, B., & Murphy, E. (2018). Design, the language of innovation: A review of the design studies literature. *She Ji: The Journal of Design, Economics, and Innovation*, 4(3), 249–74. https://doi.org/10.1016/j.sheji.2018.06.001.

Hossain, Mobarak. (2021). Unequal experience of COVID-induced remote schooling in four developing countries. *International Journal of Educational Development*, 85, 102446. https://doi.org/10.1016/j.ijedudev.2021.102446.

Hossain, Mokter. (2021). The effect of the Covid-19 on sharing economy activities. *Journal of Cleaner Production*, 280, 124782. https://doi.org/10.1016/j.jclepro.2020.124782.

Khlystova, O., Kalyuzhnova, Y., & Belitski, M. (2022). The impact of the COVID-19 pandemic on the creative industries: A literature review and future research agenda. *Journal of Business Research*, 139, 1192–210. https://doi.org/10.1016/j.jbusres.2021.09.062.

Nundy, S., Ghosh, A., Mesloub, A., Albaqawy, G.A., & Alnaim, M.M. (2021). Impact of COVID-19 pandemic on socio-economic, energy-environment and transport sector globally and sustainable development goal (SDG). *Journal of Cleaner Production*, 312, 127705. https://doi.org/10.1016/j.jclepro.2021.127705.

Rabow, M.W., Huang, C.-H.S., White-Hammond, G.E., & Tucker, R.O. (2021). Witnesses and victims both: Healthcare workers and grief in the time of COVID-19. *Journal of Pain and Symptom Management*, 62(3), 647–56. https://doi.org/10.1016/j.jpainsymman.2021.01.139.

Ramirez Pineda, A. (2020). Docente de la Universidad Nacional crea respirador artificial doméstico. https://umcentral.umanizales.edu.co/index.php/docente-de-la-universidad-nacional-crea-respirador-artificial-domestico/ (Retrieved 1 October 2021).

Sangiorgi, D., & Prendiville, A. (2014). A theoretical framework for studying service design practices: First steps to a mature field. *Design Management Journal*, 9(1), 61–73. https://doi.org/10.1111/dmj.12014.

Simon, H. (1996). *The Sciences of the Artificial* (Third Edit). Cambridge, MA: The MIT Press.

So, M.K.P., Tiwari, A., Chu, A.M.Y., Tsang, J.T.Y., & Chan, J.N.L. (2020). Visualizing COVID-19 pandemic risk through network connectedness. *International Journal of Infectious Diseases*, 96, 558–61. https://doi.org/10.1016/j.ijid.2020.05.011.

Universidad de los Andes (2021a). Museo de la desinformación. *Proyecto COLEV*. https://colev.uniandes.edu.co/2-uncategorised/54-objetivo-museo-de-la-desinformacion (Retrieved 1 October 2021).

Universidad de los Andes (2021b). Proyecto COLEV. https://colev.uniandes.edu.co (Retrieved 1 October 2021).

Universidad de los Andes (2021c). Unandinos Diseñan Respirador Cómodo y Eficaz Para Personal Médico. https://ingenieria.uniandes.edu.co/es/noticias/persoco-respirador-covid (Retrieved 1 October 2021).

Zhang, Y., Sun, Y., Padilla, L., Barua, S., Bertini, E., & Parker, A.G. (2021). Mapping the landscape of COVID-19 crisis visualizations. *Proceedings of the 2021 CHI Conference on Human Factors in Computing Systems*, 1–23. https://doi.org/10.1145/3411764.3445381.

7 A team of five million

Tackling the Covid-19 pandemic in New Zealand

TOMÁS GARCIA FERRARI AND CAROLINA SHORT

Introduction: 'Go hard and go early'

The chapter explores key responses taken in New Zealand, including the timeline of the pandemic and official measures taken, the tools used by the government to implement the containment measures which included an information programme to communicate to people what they needed to do. The chapter then summarizes and reflects on design's contribution to the country's strategy and what we can learn from this experience.

The Covid-19 outbreak became evident in February 2020, when New Zealand went into a lockdown after several days of cases increasing. The official response measures were backed by scientific knowledge and experiences from other countries. The government decided to protect the citizens and stop the disease's spread. The message conveyed helped to consolidate the government's approach to controlling Covid-19: first, pursuing an elimination strategy, and later having a minimization and protection procedure. To succeed, the public needed to understand the messages; appreciate their usefulness; and be compliant, becoming a team of five million.

New Zealand's timeline and responses to the pandemic

On 28 February 2020, New Zealand registered its first Covid-19 case. The country was already implementing travel restrictions on foreign nationals from or transiting through mainland China. However, after cases started to increase in Iran, South Korea and Italy, New Zealand was not an exception.

Restrictions on travelling got stricter, and two weeks later, anyone entering the country had to self-isolate for fourteen days – except those arriving from the Pacific Islands. Some days later, borders closed to non-permanent residents, and indoor meetings were cancelled (Figure 7.1).

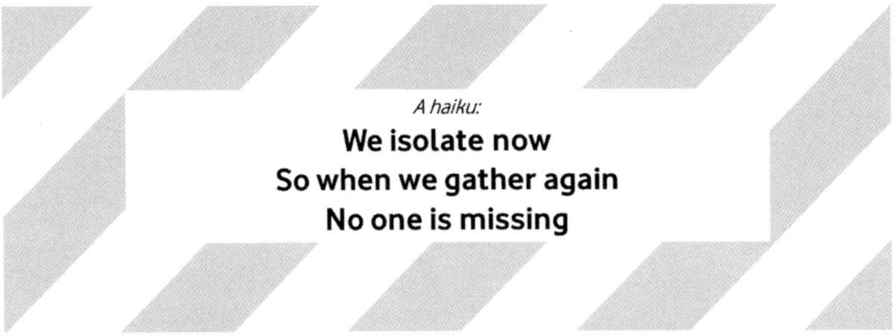

A haiku:
We isolate now
So when we gather again
No one is missing

Figure 7.1 Advertisement on the New Zealand campaign-style based on a haiku by Meria Marom 'We isolate now / So when we gather again / No one is missing'. (A Haiku n.d.).

Measures to guide in times of pandemic

On 21 March 2020, a four-tiered Alert Level system was introduced. The government outlined New Zealand's alert system and specified the public health and social measures to be taken in the fight against Covid-19. These measures are updated based on new scientific knowledge, information about the effectiveness of control measures in New Zealand and overseas. The Alert Level system has helped people understand the current level of risk and the restrictions that legally must be followed (*History of the COVID-19 Alert System*, 2021).

A State of National Emergency was declared on 25 March 2020, and the country went into a lockdown for a month. Ten days later, there were zero Covid-19 cases reported; soon after, there were no more active cases, and life returned to normal for a while. Being the entrance door to New Zealand, Auckland suffered the most restrictions.

Alert Level 4 – Lockdown: Likely the disease is not contained

There is an intense and sustained risk of community transmission of the virus, together with extensive outbreaks. People are instructed to stay in their bubble and not leave their houses other than for essentials; they can do safe recreational exercise nearby. Travel and gatherings are cancelled. Public venues, educational institutions and businesses (except for health and essential services) are closed.

Alert Level 3 – Restrict: High risk, the disease is not contained

There are still multiple cases of community transmission occurring and active clusters in numerous regions. Except for essential personal movement such as going to work, school or local recreation, citizens must remain in their bubbles (open to some exemptions). Low-risk recreation is permitted. When outside, a 2-metre physical distance applies. Work and learning should be done at home when possible; early childhood and primary schools can open with limited numbers. Businesses may open but without customer contact. Flexibility is applied to cases of regional travel and for essential gatherings with social distancing and a limited number of attendees.

Alert Level 2 – Reduce: The disease is contained, but the risk of community transmission remains

There is limited community transmission with some active clusters in more than one region at this level. Social gatherings open for groups of up to hundred. Regular activities open with social distancing when in public spaces. Businesses can be available with tracing and distancing and a limited number of customers. Recreation, sport, educational facilities and other public venues can operate under the same conditions. Face masks are required on public transport.

Alert Level 1 – Prepare: The disease is contained in New Zealand

This alert level remains when Covid-19 is uncontrolled overseas, and the country has sporadic imported cases. Border entry measures apply to minimize the risk of importing Covid-19 cases. Intensive testing for Covid-19 performed, rapid contact tracing of any positive case (self-isolation and quarantine will be required for infected individuals). Schools and workplaces open, no restrictions on personal movement, but people are encouraged to trace places. Gatherings organizers are encouraged to maintain records to enable contact tracing.

The Alert Level system was a strategy that the public could assimilate as it followed the protocolar steps used for risk management. In New Zealand, from a young age, people understand how to behave in an emergency through learning at school about it. Examples would be the tsunami alerts or the NZ Volcanic Alert Level system. Risk management will reduce the likelihood and severity of adverse health and safety outcomes (Figure 7.2).

Vaccinations started early in 2021, and by the end of the year, more than 90 per cent of the eligible population had been fully vaccinated, leading to the implementation of a new protection framework, also known as the traffic lights. The new framework marked the end of the Covid-19 Alert System at 11.59 pm on 2 December 2021.

Containing the outbreak: Contact tracing

New Zealand Public Health System works with different units experienced in managing and controlling illnesses, including those that require tracking and follow-ups. Before Covid-19, the information system employed for outbreaks was not fully connected. Therefore, the Ministry of Health established the 'National Close Contact Service' to coordinate centralized contact tracing. The design of an efficient contact tracing calling system raised the reachability of people. Contact tracing prevents onward transmission by identifying people exposed to a positive or probable infectious case. Effective contact tracing is a decisive ingredient of New Zealand's response to the pandemic, alongside testing and public health risk advice (Allen + Clarke, 2020).

Following the Covid-19 outbreak in New Zealand, Verral (2020) reported how both a quick case detection and contact tracing would provide over 90 per cent efficacy against the pandemic at the population level, making it possible as effective as many vaccines. New Zealand needed to assume a 'new normal' of local transmission and

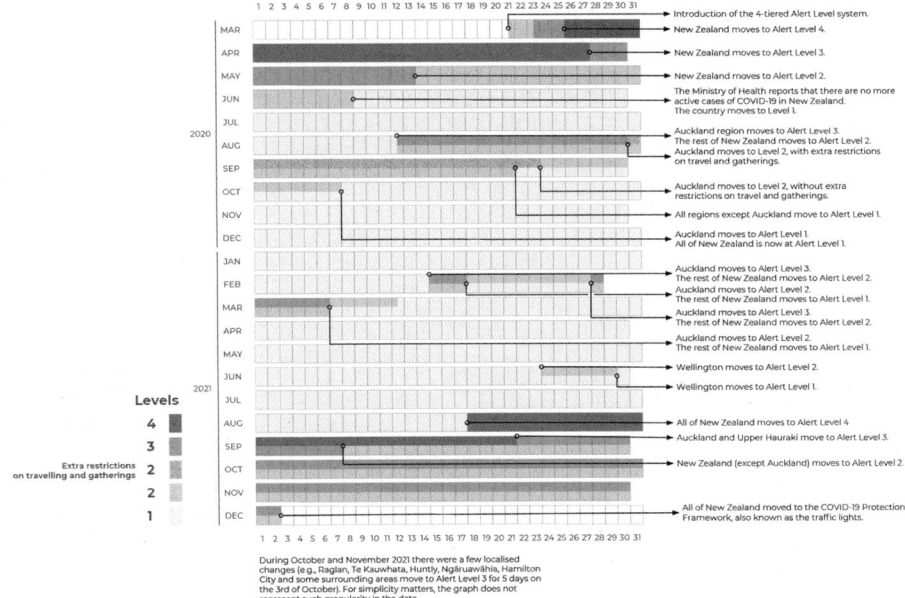

Figure 7.2 The graph shows the Covid-19 Alert System Timeline from 21 March 2020 to 2 December 2021. It is based on graphs done by Vinay Ranchhod and published by RNZ in March 2021, one year into the pandemic (Strongman et al., 2021). Image created by authors.

small clusters without a lockdown (alert level 4), with the potential for one or more extensive outbreaks over the forthcoming two years. The WHO points out public health measures can reverse outbreaks encouraging not to relax general health rules within an imminent upsurge. It has been proved in China, Singapore or South Korea that contact tracing and other measures can control outbreaks. New Zealanders went into another short lockdown only after the Delta outbreak in August 2021, which shows contact tracing was crucial to control the pandemic.

From alert levels to Covid-19 Protection Framework

From 3 December 2021, the New Zealand government brought a new framework for people to follow instructions on minimizing the pandemic's effect and protect themselves and the community against new infection outbreaks and Covid-19 variants. With a significant amount of the population now vaccinated – around 90 per cent of the people with two doses towards the end of 2021 (*Map of COVID-19 Vaccination Rates in New Zealand*, n.d.) – the prospect of having more freedom and the possibility of travelling within the country with a vaccination passport got higher.

The Covid-19 Protection Framework (also known as the traffic lights) highlights the state of the pandemic in the different areas through three settings: Red, Orange and Green (*COVID-19 Protection Framework*, n.d.). It allows more freedom to vaccinated individuals while providing more certainty and protection by minimizing the impact of the pandemic. The new approach is no longer looking into an elimination of the spread but minimizing the hospitalization, assuming there will be cases in the community.

The New Zealand government will carry out a protection strategy through vaccines, control of the infection and public health measures such as contact tracing, case management and testing. If these measures work, the health system will be able to respond effectively to those in need of assistance, reducing the need for widespread lockdowns.

Key components of the Covid-19 Protection Framework are vaccination, social distancing, record keeping and localized lockdown or controls. As vaccinated individuals have less risk of getting Covid-19 or passing it on to others, a high vaccination rate is essential. Businesses and public organizations require workers to be vaccinated. My Vaccine Pass is an official record of the Covid-19 vaccination status. It has become a requisite to participate in certain public events and enter business and public spaces where people cannot avoid close proximity. Besides encouraging 1-metre distancing, capacity limits are implemented to reduce crowding. Record keeping is put into effect mainly by scanning QR codes issued by the government, displayed in workplaces and on public transport to enable contact tracing with the NZ COVID Tracer app. If there are areas with several cases requiring control of the spread, additional restrictions may apply: stay at home, closing of premises or gathering restrictions.

The Covid-19 Protection Framework stages present these characteristics:

Life at Red means there is a need to take action to protect vulnerable communities and prevent failures in the health system. There will be restrictions on numbers for gatherings and events and enforcement in the use of public health measures such as face masks and distancing. The use of My Vaccine Pass to enter places is compulsory (hospitality venues, events, gatherings and gyms). It cannot be asked to access basic needs services, such as supermarkets, public transport and essential health care.

Life at Orange will apply when there is community transmission of Covid-19, which poses a risk to vulnerable communities and pressure on the health system. There is more freedom, and businesses or events can opt to require the vaccination pass, but then limited numbers will apply.

Life at Green stage occurs when there is limited community transmission, and the health system is not compromised. Businesses and venues can choose to open with no restrictions on numbers if requiring the My Vaccine Pass. Otherwise, there will be limitations in numbers.

Communication tools to implement a containment plan

Once the government outlined the measures needed to face the pandemic, it was necessary to establish clear communication with the public, the businesses and the health system. The plan was about containing the outbreak and included prevention of new infections, warning to avoid risky circumstances, support and guidance in case of illness, social behaviour rules, among others. In this section, we describe how the New Zealand plan was supported by a public information programme that included a visual campaign, a mobile app, a website and additional printed matter.

Unite against COVID-19: Human response to a health crisis

The first action to move forward in developing a communication tool that aided New Zealanders in understanding modifications in everyday life was to establish a visual language that will support the different communication platforms. The concept unfolded by a team lead by Mark Dalton at Clemenger BBDO Wellington posed the visual campaign as a human response to a health crisis, portraying the idea of New Zealand as a team that needs to move in coordination. The design system represents the story of how the Kiwis are united and focuses on the people. The campaign is rooted in truth, encouraging a routine that will adjust to a new normal (Figure 7.3).

It required people to believe in what they were asked to follow, as the adjustments demanded compromises. 'Recognisable. Helpful. Empathetic. Kiwi. It encouraged connection and hope. Gave us all reasons to hang on in there. Laughter when we needed it. Reminded us that the sacrifices were all worth it (Figure 7.4). And most importantly, it helped us mourn together, for the ones we lost' (Clemenger BBDO, 2020).

Figure 7.3 *Unite against COVID-19*. Licensed by CC BY-NC 4.0. 'Unite against COVID-19' by New Zealand government/Clemenger BBDO New Zealand CC-BY-NC https://creativecommons.org/licenses/by-nc/4.0/.

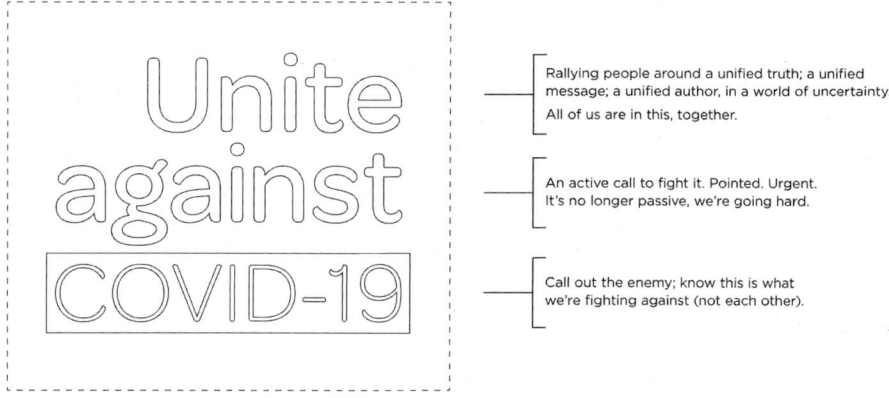

Figure 7.4 Images from the campaign. Clemenger BBDO Wellington.

New Zealand is familiar with the recovery after natural disasters. Earthquakes are one of the frequent natural hazards that put Kiwis into healing circumstances. Dr Sarb Johal, who worked both for the H1N1 influenza outbreak in the UK and community recovery after earthquakes in New Zealand, was consulted and has been of help for the Covid-19 campaign. Empathy in designing a public information campaign is critical to help people understand the right thing to do (Hunt, 2021).

In an interview with *The Guardian*, Clemenger's creative director Mark Dalton explains, 'what we were trying to do was give people a common thing to rally or fight against', the aim was to move people, not through fear but a team spirit. A visual language that presented the yellow stripes on white as team colours supported the team concept. Yellow stripes are well known as warning signs, used together with black in traffic signage and construction sites. The replacement of the black with white lowered the alarm intention into a gentler warning. New Zealand is familiar with this colour combination being used by the Automobile Association. It relates well to the idea of traffic, moving, in opposition to a situation that will paralyse people. The need to keep moving carefully, take action and feel optimistic about a problem that needs collective participation to be solved. The yellow and white stripes served as a unifying symbol of the national response. The agency chose the shade for 'being attention-grabbing without stoking alarm – likewise, the alert tone sounded before each official broadcast' (Hunt, 2021).

Contrasting campaigns based on prohibition or mandate, the encouraging language works well with the New Zealand idiosyncrasy. Examples such as 'washing and drying your hands kill the virus' work as advice promoting individual agency and public response participation.

Iconic illustrations complemented the simple language used in messages for teaching how to proceed in specific circumstances: stay home if sick, respect social distancing, cover with your elbow when coughing and sneezing, be kind to others. The simple black-and-white pictograms promoted inclusivity.

Unite against COVID-19 was based on triggering positive reactions, avoiding guilt and showing support rather than prohibiting actions. Both Director-General of

Health Bloomfield and Prime Minister Ardern regularly addressed the public using encouraging sentences such as 'Stay home, save lives' or 'Act like you have Covid' (NZ Herald, 2020).

Social media worked as customer service channels having government staff answer people's queries and comments. This participation helped the spread of a cohesive message. In addition, institutions and community groups started using the campaign's visual language in their communications, showing genuine assimilation of the visual language. The feeling of ownership of the yellow stripes, the team colours, was the perfect response to Ardern's 'team of five million' (1 News, 2020).

Alongside empathy, the tiered structure used for the Alert Level system served to set order amidst uncertainty. The framework is familiar to New Zealand as it follows the ones used for monitoring natural hazards (earthquakes, volcanos), matching state health criteria to four progressive levels of risk. The steps equip the citizens to face more severe limitations and, at the same time, explain how dangerous the situation is. It provides a roadmap, a plan, that clarifies what and how needs to be done. Johal (2021) emphasized the value of a structure in reducing stress and anxiety within the population.

Impact and success of *Unite against COVID-19* 'Recognising the contribution of the Unite against COVID-19 communications to New Zealand'

Unite against COVID-19 campaign held optimistic numbers according to the agency responsible for its creation: an awareness that reached 97 per cent, an understanding of the tier Alert Levels system of 86 per cent and a trust in government information of 88 per cent (Clemenger BBDO, 2020).

The *Unite against COVID-19* public information programme received recognition from the Designers Institute of New Zealand (DINZ) as design work that makes a significant contribution to the economic, cultural and social growth of Aotearoa New Zealand. DINZ recognizes the campaign as a 'world-class demonstration of the creative power and value that design can bring' (DINZ, 2020).

Heath Lowe, president of DINZ, said that it expressed the impact Covid-19 had on every aspect of people's lives, overpowering alternatives from education and businesses to daily activities. The DINZ prize acknowledges the positive impact a uniform design system such as *Unite against COVID-19* has to support citizens in a crisis.

The campaign achieved three fundamental duties:

1. National union under a recognizable and attainable emblem
2. A sturdy communication platform
3. Clear guidelines for organizations to protect people as they keep running

'If design is the ability to take ambiguity and turn it into clarity, to take the complex and make it simple, then this is design at its best' (DINZ, 2020).

Visual language and details of the campaign

A visual language is a substantial tie a designer can use for an effective communication system, helping to create better first impressions and greater brand recall. Colours, typefaces and imagery are elements that connect a system designed to convey specific messages.

In the *Unite against COVID-19* campaign, the typography aimed to deliver the messages in an objective, reasonable and helpful manner: it had to be legible but warm to feel approachable, human and communicate sensibly (Rawsthorn and Antonelli, 2020). The primary typeface is Omnes, a geometric sans serif with rounded terminals that resemble the nineteenth-century rounded grotesques. Designed by Joshua Darden in 2006, it was conceived as a brand typeface for a national retail chain. Omnes is paired with Baloo by Ek Type, employed for other text in the app, the website and some printed communication. Baloo is an open-source sans serif typeface with a warm feel. Its various weights and generous x-height allow a versatile implementation for diverse text sizes and usage in print and digital media. The colours the agency searched for would need to stand out across different media. The palette had to bear warning but in a friendly tone. An intense yellow (selected considering radioactive leak yellow and hazard yellow) was a good choice without getting into an alarming orange. Black was a logical choice for the text and pictograms, but they were careful not to use bold to avoid being shouty in the 'unite against'. The yellow background is applied to the Covid-19 in a lighter weight (Rawsthorn and Antonelli, 2020). Combining white with yellow worked well, advising people the topic was severe; the yellow stripes are used for warning signage for road signs and hazard signage.

As a narrative expressed through visuals is more effective in a context where people are asked to react and take a particular action, pictograms are used for the different messages of the public information programme. Humans acquire more data through the visual system than using all other senses combined (Lankow et al., 2012). The intended style was to look hand-drawn, to attach the feeling that another human being is telling them what to do, someone trying to help them. The campaign wanted to have an approachable and human feel (Rawsthorn and Antonelli, 2020).

Visual system evolution

As the pandemic continues, new responses are needed to communicate different government containment measures. When the vaccination campaign started in the country, the *Unite against COVID-19* campaign progressed, looking into visual strategies that matched the successful public information system. With the current visual language, the campaign implemented new colours: purple was chosen for all vaccination-related information. Lately, cyan is being used for the Stay safe this summer campaign (summer holidays 2021–2). Other colours have been added for

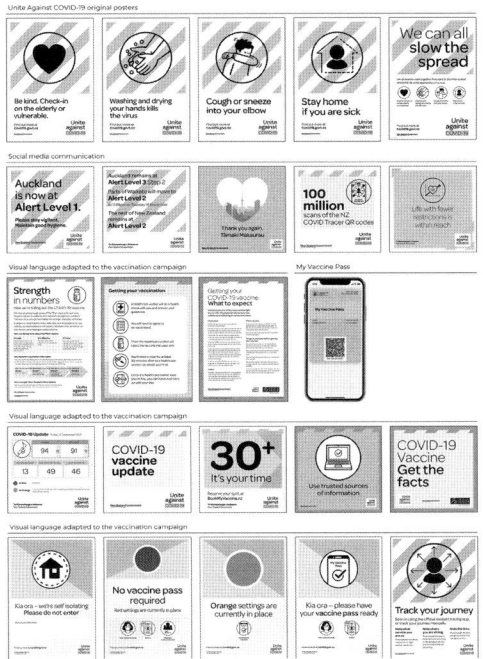

Figure 7.6 A sample of the visual language applied in different media for diverse purposes since first created in 2020 to January 2021.

options (actions to protect yourself and others). Other signs in the form of stickers serve to guide people in large public spaces. Using the Covid-19 website, the government provides an extensive range of tools for businesses to print. These have a consistent visual language and provide an official message which helps communicate a mandate.

Conclusions

When the pandemic started at the beginning of 2020, New Zealand committed to an elimination strategy, focusing on getting to and maintaining 'zero COVID-19'. The strategy was implemented when vaccination was a hope rather than a reality. It has proved effective in preventing deaths (by the end of 2021, fifty-one people have died of Covid-19 in New Zealand), serious illness and a collapse of the national health system. Constraints placed upon movement beyond geographical borders have not stopped social and community life from flourishing, only seen the international businesses sector badly affected.

Almost two years later, the world has several vaccines proven adequate, so the panorama is very different from what we had at the beginning of 2020 when the pandemic started. Vaccination provides both sufficient protection for individuals and the eradication of the pandemic. Therefore, New Zealand moved to a minimization and protection strategy in December 2021. Still, equally important are other measures such as masks wearing, distancing and ventilation, restrictions on gatherings, detection and isolation of cases and contact tracing (Strategic COVID-19 Public Health Advisory Group, 2021).

The communication of those messages plays a crucial role in implementing any strategy. Its success will be completed when people follow these measures and convincingly apply them in the best interest of keeping safe. The role design has played in creating a cohesive communication campaign, easily translated to different platforms and working well in the ecosystem of communication pieces, can be appreciated through these two years of implementation. A good adaptation of the visual language to the new measures shows that the designers had created the original system well. The versatility has made the visual system adjust to the new needs, making it formally and emotionally compelling.

The complex scenario that a global pandemic presents calls for a multidisciplinary perspective. In New Zealand, design had played its role to a high standard, substantially contributing to the country response to the pandemic. The results are worth noting.

References

1 News. (2020). 'We're a team of five million'—Lockdown timeline depends on Kiwis' behaviour, Ardern says. *1 News*, 21 April. https://1news.co.nz/one-news/new-zealand/were-team-five-million-lockdown-timeline-depends-kiwis-behaviour-ardern-says.

A Haiku: 'We Isolate Now / So When We Gather Again / No One is Missing.' (n.d.). https://covid-19archive.org/s/archive/item/17581 (Retrieved 2 September 2021).

Allen + Clarke (2020). *PHU Contact Tracing 'Deep Dive' Summative Rapid Report*. New Zealand: Ministry of Health.

Clemenger BBDO. (2020). Unite against COVID-19. *Clemenger BBDO Website*. https://www.clemengerbbdo.co.nz.

COVID-19 Protection Framework. (n.d.). Unite against COVID-19. https://covid19.govt.nz/traffic-lights/covid-19-protection-framework/ (Retrieved 4 January 2022).

DINZ (2020). *Unite against Covid-19 Campaign*. The Designers Institute of New Zealand. https://designersinstitute.nz/case-study/unite-against-covid-19-campaign/.

Forrester, G. (2020). Coronavirus: Here's my experience using the new Covid-19 tracker app. *Stuff*, 22 May. https://www.stuff.co.nz/national/health/coronavirus/121590753/coronavirus-heres-my-experience-using-the-new-covid19-tracker-app.

History of the COVID-19 Alert System. (2021). Unite against COVID-19, 12 March. https://covid19.govt.nz/about-our-covid-19-response/history-of-the-covid-19-alert-system/.

Howell, B. E. (2020). A tale of two contact-tracing apps: Lessons from Australia and New Zealand. *AEIdeas*, 22 May. https://www.aei.org/technology-and-innovation/a-tale-of-two-contact-tracing-apps-lessons-from-australia-and-new-zealand/.

Hunt, E. (2021). Words matter: How New Zealand's clear messaging helped beat Covid. *The Guardian*, 26 February. https://www.theguardian.com/world/2021/feb/26/words-matter-how-new-zealands-clear-messaging-helped-beat-covid.

Johal, S. (2021). Coronavirus is an existential crisis that comes from an awareness of your own freedoms | Dr Sarb Johal. *The Guardian*, 29 January. http://www.theguardian.com/world/2021/jan/30/covid-is-an-existential-crisis-that-comes-from-an-awareness-of-your-own-freedoms.

Lankow, J., Ritchie, J., & Crooks, R. (2012). *Infographics: The Power of Visual Storytelling*. New York: Wiley.

Map of COVID-19 Vaccination Rates in New Zealand (n.d.). Unite against COVID-19. https://covid19.govt.nz/news-and-data/covid-19-vaccination-rates-around-new-zealand/ (Retrieved 23 December 2021).

Ministry of Health (n.d.). *NZ COVID Tracer App*. Ministry of Health. https://tracing.covid19.govt.nz/.

NZ COVID Tracer App NFC Tags. (n.d.). Ministry of Health NZ. https://www.health.govt.nz/our-work/diseases-and-conditions/covid-19-novel-coronavirus/covid-19-resources-and-tools/nz-covid-tracer-app/using-nz-covid-tracer-app/nz-covid-tracer-app-nfc-tags (Retrieved 4 January 2022).

NZ Herald. (2020). Covid 19 coronavirus lockdown: Jacinda Ardern says Auckland in level 3 at midday; NZ in level 2. *NZ Herald*, 8 December. https://www.nzherald.co.nz/nz/covid-19-coronavirus-lockdown-jacinda-ardern-says-auckland-in-level-3-at-midday-nz-in-level-2/TYGDCTPZDVYRWSKXHELV7PPX3U/.

Rawsthorn, A., & Antonelli, P. (2020). Design emergency. *Wallpaper*, 10 October, 177–9.

Rush (2020). Project: NZ COVID tracer app. *Rush Studios / Work*. https://rush.co.nz/work/nz-covid-tracer-app/.

Strategic COVID-19 Public Health Advisory Group (2021). *Strategy for a Highly Vaccinated New Zealand*. https://covid19.govt.nz/assets/Proactive-Releases/Alert-levels-and-restrictions/10-December-2021/Vaccine-Certificates-and-CPF/COVID-19-Public-Health-Advisory-Group-feedback-letter-from-Sir-David-Skegg.pdf.

Strongman, S., Cooke, M., Davis, R., & Hall, M. (2021). Timeline: The year of Covid-19 in New Zealand. *RNZ*, 28 February. https://www.rnz.co.nz/news/national/437359/timeline-the-year-of-covid-19-in-new-zealand.

Verrall, A. (2020). *Rapid Audit of Contact Tracing for Covid-19 in New Zealand*. Ministry of Health. https://www.health.govt.nz/publication/rapid-audit-contact-tracing-covid-19-new-zealand.

8 Lessons and implications from South Korea's design response to Covid-19

Case studies and analysis of ICT convergence in design

YOORI KOO

Background and purpose of the study

An effective response to global social problems such as Covid-19 can be a good precedent for other countries; this chapter presents a study that systematically analysed Korea's Covid-19 response and has studied its implications in order to contribute to international cooperation for Covid-19 response and offer design solutions to deal with the complex social problems.

In recent years, the idea of design has evolved from result-oriented processes focused on aesthetics to problem-solving processes that consider users, social technologies, cultures and politics. Therefore, these responses have emphasized solving various social problems. In particular, cutting-edge ICTs have been utilized in many areas of the response to Covid-19 outbreak. In this technology-centric approach, integrators with a human-centered design perspective are required to enable the technological convergence of existing solutions to meet users' unmet needs and improve their quality of life. In addition to the need for social innovation and environmental sustainability during Covid-19 outbreak, a 'facilitator' that can effectively engage the socially underprivileged, civic community and industry in the policy decision making is also required. The strategic role of design in solving Covid-19-related social problems has increased in importance, but discussions on the role of design to respond to national disaster situations such as a pandemic, notably the technology–design convergence approach, are in the early stages, and analysis studies based on practical application cases are still lacking.

Therefore, this chapter describes a study that explored implications for the use of designs for various stages of Covid-19 response, along with its strategic purpose and technology convergence through an analysis of Korea's technology–design convergence case analysis in response to the Covid-19 pandemic. Based on the findings, we developed recommendations for strategic directions of technology-convergence and social problem-solving designs to improve capability to respond to national crises.

Research scope and methodology

To clarify the effects of Covid-19 and associated social phenomena, we used the classification proposed by Mullagh et al. (2021) for Covid-19 response (i.e. reaction, adaptation, recovery and resilience). We conducted a literature review on the concepts of 'social innovation' and 'social problem-solving design' to define the role of design as a tool for problem solving. The role and meaning of technology in people's everyday life were also discussed through theoretical considerations on 'design fiction' to derive the implications for the people-centred use of high technologies in every facet of our life.

To analyse technology trends in the post-Covid-19 era, we used nine research and development (R&D) reports published at the national level in 2020 to derive keywords for core technologies. The literature review results were used to synthesize a case analysis framework to analyse the purpose of design use for each stage of Covid-19 response, applications of technology–design convergence and problem-solving methods.

We selected twenty-five cases of high-tech ICT convergence for Covid-19-related social problem-solving design during 2020–1 and analysed them individually using the devised analysis framework. A comprehensive analysis of the cases was performed to determine trends of technology and design convergence and problem-solving methods during each stage of Covid-19 response. Finally, we suggested recommendations for the strategic roles of design and the implications for the technology–design convergence approach, notably in responding effectively to the problems and challenges caused by Covid-19.

Covid-19 and social change

Covid-19 is a respiratory syndrome caused by a viral infection. It was officially reported in China on 31 December 2019 and was declared a global pandemic by the World Health Organization (WHO) on 11 March 2020. Historically, epidemics have continued to emerge in our social and physical environments and have included severe acute respiratory syndrome and Middle East respiratory syndrome. Infectious diseases can spread rapidly due to high urban densities and global connectivity. A global pandemic flow consists of four stages: reaction, adaptation, recovery and resilience (Mullagh, 2021, Table 8.1).

The progress of Covid-19 is progressing through the above stages. Despite a lack of fundamental treatment, at the time of writing it has not progressed to the resilience stage. It is still in transition from the recovery stage, with attempts to recover economically, socially and culturally through vaccinations.

Social problem-solving design

Social innovation

Innovation can be described as creation of new ideas, value addition to ideas, changes in an organization or social phenomena, and expansion of success. The definitions of

Table 8.1 Stages of Pandemic Progression

Reaction	Countries introduce closures or strict tracking systems because of increasing infections. New laws are passed quickly and economy is fundamentally shut down. (Role of direct response – monitoring, control)
Adaptation	Society adapts to the applied systems and becomes accustomed to the 'new normal'. It adapts to new measures like social distancing. People find new ways to connect socially and work remotely. (Response through user communication)
Recovery	Social distancing is still needed, but many industries return to work and schools reopen. Only localized closures are enforced. Economy begins to recover. (Economic and social recovery through the formation, network and participation of culture and art)
Resilience	Lockdown is lifted and social distancing is relaxed to pre-pandemic status. After reflecting upon and examining key issues, we understand what we can learn personally, socially, economically and globally. We use new ways to create well-being for people and the planet. (Creating sustainable economic, social and environmental values)

social innovation share the features of 'new ideas' and 'cooperation between individuals and groups' for solving social problems. Kim (2017) stated that 'social innovation is not entirely new, but the result of a new combination or mixture of existing elements'. In other words, social innovation is not a new idea for solving a social problem, but a paradigm change to solve a problem by changing the existing processes and systems. The second key is cooperation by building relationships to solve local and national social problems. To summarize, social innovation is achieved through cooperation to achieve social goals and by applying new ideas to existing concepts to solve common problems. Therefore, society must recognize the social problems of Covid-19, apply new ideas and new approaches to existing technologies and capital and overcome Covid-19 through cooperation of all members of society.

Definition and role of social problem-solving design

Design plays an important role in the solution of complex and diversified social problems. The literature suggests a variety of perspectives on the role of design to address economic and social challenges (Table 8.2). From the point of view of all designers' efforts for supporting social innovation or solving societal problems, this can be called social innovation design or social problem-solving design.

Cipolla et al. (2016) called social problem-solving design a 'strategic approach to introducing new technologies and knowledge within communities to spread social innovation initiatives'. Extending this connection, Melles et al. (2011) stated that

Table 8.2 Roles of Social Problem-Solving Design

Source	Definition
Manzini (2014)	All that design can do to initiate, facilitate, support, enhance and replicate social innovation.
Cipolla et al. (2016)	Design to disseminate social innovation initiatives as a kind of strategic approach to introducing new skills and knowledge into the community.
Melles et al. (2011)	In a socially responsible project, design empowers users and, as a result, leads to improvements that benefit users. This brings economic benefits to the community.
Hillgren (2013)	Vision, strategy and co-design tools and approaches to develop mature and actionable solutions differentiated from the abstract ideas of existing social innovations.
Akama et al. (2019)	Solving problems and promoting change to achieve specific social goals.

Table 8.3 Promotion of Social Innovation Design (Manzini, 2014)

Direction	Summary
Top-down	Social innovation is promoted by strategic design (government and local government, individual).
Bottom-up	Promotion of social innovation by local communities (individual <–> company).
Hybrid	Early and long-term complex interactions between a variety of initiatives. Measures taken directly by the stakeholders are rapidly disseminated using other interventions provided by institutions, civic groups and companies.

'design should empower users, meet user needs, and provide economic benefits to the community' as a tool for joint design processes with citizens and stakeholders. Design for social innovation leads to change in communities through the introduction of new skills and knowledge, enabling new connections between people. To summarize, social innovation design introduces new technologies and ideas and breaks away from existing abstract social ideas through a variety of design tools and prototyping by visualizing and materializing the ideas to trigger and support social discussions. Design process enables social members to contribute to complex social problem solving. The role of social problem-solving design is to change perceptions and connect people and move them to practical actions to solve social problems.

Social problem-solving designs can be promoted in various ways. Manzini (2014) classified social innovation design into top-down, bottom-up and hybrid methods, based on the direction of promotion (Table 8.3).

Based on these driving directions, the collaborative nature of social innovation becomes apparent. In a top-down approach, the government provides information and guidelines for participation in problem solving to the public. In a bottom-up approach, individuals and groups actively participate in social problem solving within local communities by forming consensus based on common interests. A hybrid approach combines these two methods and represents the integration of society as a whole to solve problems. Social innovation design can solve social problems using these three types of methods to engage in information sharing, meet the needs of local communities and disseminate design solutions.

Our study focused on the role of design as a problem-solving tool and a medium for conveying meaning and investigated the implications of ICT convergence products and services for Covid-19 response. We began by analysing the literature and reports from the post-Covid-19 era to derive keywords in order to analyse the current state of ICT and its applicability.

Analysis of technology trends in the post-Covid-19 era

The advent of Covid-19 led to a rapid increase in digital non-face-to-face services (Fletcher and Griffiths, 2020). This in turn has led to an era of creative digital transformation, where a combination of design and digital has become more important in the daily lives of people. Digital features have widespread applications in knowledge, services and design, and the meaning of 'digital' has expanded as it affects the contents and systems in society.

In line with the digital transformation era, social problem-solving design is achieved through convergence with technology and is also called 'design-R&D convergence'. With the use of the problem-solving methods of design thinking, this is to develop innovative and user-friendly products and services by adding user sensibilities and experiential value to technologies (Kimbell, 2011; Luo et al., 2014). The Fourth Industrial Revolution was first announced at the Davos Forum in 2016; it is being established faster than expected due to the need for non-face-to-face interactions caused by Covid-19. The pandemic has increased interest in core technologies such as telecommuting, remote education and automation.

Therefore, we investigated the technology trends of the post-Covid-19 era based on the application of fourth industrial technologies that have been developed so far. The Future Prediction Brief published by the Korea Institute of Science and Technology Evaluation and Planning announced, 'Future Prospects and Promising Technologies in the Post-Corona Era', including eight areas (health care, education, transportation, logistics, manufacturing, environment, culture and information security) that will experience major changes after Covid-19. It also identified related promising technologies, including digital twins, human augmentation technologies and collaborative robots.

Nine technical reports (since 2020) were analysed:

- Policy measures for industrial technology innovation in the post-Covid-19 era (December 2020 KIAT)
- Future prospects in the smart innovation era and research on science and technology innovation policy (December 2020 KISTEP)
- Analysis of the effect and relationship of technology introduction related to the Fourth Industrial Revolution (October 2020 KIET)
- Promising Technology Report (May 2020 NRF)
- Fourth Industrial Revolution Technology Governance (December 2020 WEF)
- Data Robot is an emerging technology in 2021 (December 2020 NIA)
- Future prospects and promising technologies in the post-corona era (May 2020 KISTEP)
- ICT R&D Technology Roadmap 2025 (December 2020 IITP)
- Major digital issues and ten policy directions for 2021 (December 2020 NIA)

Analysis of these reports revealed the effects of industrial technology in the Covid-19 period. First, it hastens the development of promising technologies and broadens

Table 8.4 Covid-19-Related Technology Keywords

Technology	Definition
Big data	A large dataset that is difficult to process using conventional management methods or analysis systems.
Cloud	Providing virtualized information technology (IT) resources as a service using the internet.
AR/VR	A technology that allows users to indirectly experience situations that cannot be directly experienced in the real world by creating virtual spaces and objects.
Blockchain	Distributed data storage technology that replicates and stores transaction details on multiple computers.
Mobile software	A software application that runs on mobile terminals such as smartphones or tablets.
Autonomous driving	Technology that uses information collected through cameras and various sensors (lidar, radar, ultrasound, etc.) to classify surrounding objects and drive unmanned.
AI	A system that works by reasoning, learning and judging by itself, similar to a human brain.
Robotics	A branch of engineering that deals with robot design, manufacture and operation.
IoT sensor	Technology that connects objects to the internet through various sensors.

their field of application. Second, it leads to data gathering centred on 'personal and social medical care and health' and the convergence of technologies. Lastly, it contributes to the development and improvement with the focus of transforming of every facet of human activities into non-face-to-face activities.

The fourth industry technology key words are therefore derived based on the following criteria: reports that commonly mentioned them and used applied technology that converged with the design. Keywords were derived and summarized (Table 8.4), focusing on technology that converts existing activities to activities that are not conducted face-to-face. Definitions of the technologies were derived from the definitions of nine core technologies of the Fourth Industrial Revolution.

Based on the recent literature it is suggested that society has recently been digitized by converting many areas of daily life into activities that are not conducted face-to-face, and the spread of technology convergence social problem-solving designs is accelerated by the daily use of high and/or new technology. Therefore, it is useful to study how design is used during Covid-19 as a medium between cutting-edge technology and people. In the following section, we conduct case analysis of technology-based design responding to Covid-19, with specific focus on the strategic purpose and type of use of the design for each response step, the method of technology convergence and the approaches to solving the problem. Through this analysis, we intend to draw strategic implications of the role and potential of design in technology-based social problem-solving approaches.

Case analysis

Case selection criteria

The following criteria were used to select Covid-19 response cases in Korea that incorporated design based on fourth industrial technology: (i) development and expansion of Covid-19 response, application and recovery; (ii) cases with a ripple effect related to social issues or policy establishment, and implementation through news reports; (iii) cases of ICT convergence using fourth industrial technology; (iv) design approach or tangible design results. Based on these criteria, twenty-five cases were selected for analysis. Each case was divided into three stages: reaction (A), adaptation (B) and recovery and resilience (C) (Table 8.5).

Analysis framework and method

Analyses of the approaches to social problem solving, the results/design outcomes and convergence of technology and design in the selected cases involved six elements.

First, the basic outline was obtained through the project name and goal. Second, the strategic purpose was analysed by categorizing it based on the Covid-19 response

Table 8.5 List of Selected Cases

Stage	Project name	Year	Agent	Summary	Industry	Source
A-1	Corona 19 website	2020	Centers for Disease Control	Provision of information on the number of infected people and the stage of Covid-19 throughout Korea	Medical treatment	Corona Virus Infectious Disease website: 1 paper; 2 news press releases http://ncov.mohw.go.kr/
A-2	Mask app	2020	Civic Hacker	Mask stock status information application	Medical treatment	3 news press releases and the Ministry of Science and ICT
A-3	Corona 100m alert app	2020	Tina-3D	Notification service app that alerts when approaching the area visited by a confirmed patient	Medical treatment	Tina-3D develops Kobaek Plus related to Covid-19: 2 news releases from JoongAng news
A-4	Toss Emergency Disaster Subsidy	2020	Toss	App service to check emergency disaster fund usage	Finance	Emergency disaster relief funds can be applied for and managed through Toss: toss feed
A-5	QR code electronic access list	2020	Ministry of Health and Welfare	Identification of the route of infection and prevention of group infections	Medical treatment	4 news press releases, including KBS NEWS, Naver and Kakao
A-6	Covid-19 check-up	2020	Heo Jun-nyeong	Confirmation through self-diagnosis of Covid-19	Medical treatment	'Corona 19 Check-up' app listed as WHO Corona 19 solution: 2 news press releases and Herald Economy; 'Corona 19 Check-up' application

(Continued)

Table 8.5 (Continued)

Stage	Project name	Year	Agent	Summary	Industry	Source
A-7	MEDIP PRO COVID19	2020	Medical IP	Covid-19 confirmation	Medical treatment	Medical IP distributes 'MEDIP COVID19' worldwide for free: 2 news releases and health news
B-1	Seocho-gu Untact Screening Clinic	2020	Seocho-gu, Seoul	Covid-19 screening clinic space design	Medical treatment	A study on spatial planning of screening clinics for respiratory infectious disease (Covid-19) Establishment of a screening clinic in Seocho-gu
B-2	KAIST negative pressure mobile ward	2020	KAIST	Negative pressure mobile ward for the convenience of patients and medical staff	Medical treatment	3 cases of Naver design, news materials and the homepage for the KAIST negative pressure ward mcm.kaist.ac.kr
B-3	'A mask is the answer'	2020	Suwon	Citizen participation campaign in Suwon city	Living	Suwon city's 'Mask is the answer' campaign spread online and offline: News1 and 4 news press releases; Suwon City website
B-4	Seoul Corona Exhibition	2020	Graphica	Corona-themed online exhibition	Culture Art	2020 Seoul Corona Exhibition website and 2 news press releases https://www.seoul-corona.com/

B-5	30 Second Song Soap Campaign	2020	Cultural sports; Ministry of Tourism	Improving handwashing habits in children soap dispenser	Medical treatment	Ministry of Culture, Sports, and Tourism provided 'Baby Shark 30 Second Song Soap' to museums and art galleries: 2 news press releases including YTN; YouTube
B-6	LG U+ Elementary School Country	2020	LG U+	Non-face-to-face education system	Education	LG U+ launched 'U+ Elementary Country' to help homeschool elementary school students: 2 news press releases and energy economy; U+ Elementary Country
B-7	Jibmusil	2020	Alicon	Telecommuting workspace design	Living	Naver design and jibmusil website https://www.jibmusil.com/
B-8	2020 Busan Biennale	2020	Busan Biennale	An online exhibition that allows exhibition hall viewing in 3D	Culture Art	2020 Busan Biennale online website and 2 news press releases http://www.busanbiennale.org/kr/index.php?pCode=bienn01
C-1	Soonchunhyang University Metaverse entrance ceremony	2021	SK	Non-face-to-face entrance ceremony; Metaverse space	Education	Competition for global Metaverse leadership: 3 news press releases including the Maeil Ilbo
C-2	Hyundai Uncommon Store	2021	Hyundai	Non-face-to-face store payment service	Distribution/Logistics	The Korean version of 'Amazon Go' in The Hyundai Seoul: 4 news press releases including electronic newspapers; The Hyundai Seoul website

(Continued)

Table 8.5 (Continued)

Stage	Project name	Year	Agent	Summary	Industry	Source
C-3	Coov electronic vaccine	2021	Korea Centers for Disease Control and Prevention	Vaccination verification system	Medical treatment	2 news press releases and the Coov website https://www.coov.kr/
C-4	Deli plate	2021	Baemin	Autonomous serving robot	Restaurant business	2 news releases and Baemin Deli Plate website https://robot.baemin.com/
C-5	Medihere	2021	Medihere	Telemedicine service	Medical treatment	3 news press releases and the Medihere website https://www.medihere.com/
C-6	ZEPETO	2021	Naver	VR platform using AR and AI technology	Culture Art	3 news materials and the ZEPETO website https://www.naverz-corp.com
C-7	Drug Control Center	2021	Vitcon	Real-time monitoring of vaccines and pharmaceuticals	Medical treatment	IoT solution company Vitcon built a safe vaccine storage 'medicine control center': Farm News and 2 news press releases
C-8	Smart IoT Air Shower	2021	Gyeyang-gu, Yongin-si	Improving air quality by disinfecting building entrances and exits	Medical treatment	Incheon Gyeyang-gu installed 'Smart IOT Air Shower' to stop fine dust and virus particles: 2 news press releases including security news

C-9	Kimmi Robot	2021	Ministry of Health and Welfare	In-hospital non-face-to-face care service	Medical treatment	SKT, commercialization of 5G-based complex quarantine robot 'Kimi': 3 news press releases including information and communication newspapers
C-10	AIDBOT	2021	KAIST	Non-contact quarantine robot	Medical treatment	A quarantine robot that detects movements of confirmed cases and uses UV light and disinfectant sprays: 2 news press releases including the Seoul Shimbun

stage. Strategic purposes of design to solve social problems were categorized using the five objectives of the Seoul Basic Plan for Social Problem-Solving Design (Seoul Metropolitan Government, 2020) (i.e. awareness improvement type, information transfer and action induction type, network construction type, problem discovery and R&D type) and Koo and Lee's (2017) public service/policy field consumer interactivity and classification based on the category of problem-solving participation (i.e. information delivery/policy publicity type, behaviour conversion type, policy activity participation type, internal training type, public service creation type). These strategic purposes were divided into four types: (i) information delivery (informs society of the seriousness and social problems), (ii) action induction (behaviour change through active citizen participation by providing social innovation design solutions), (iii) network construction (improves problem-solving potential and continuity by creating an environment for communication and collaboration) and (iv) problem-solving R&D type (creates strategic value for user experience through technological research based on design methodology).

Third, the type of final design results was determined based on a literature analysis (Seoul Metropolitan Government, 2020) of domestic and foreign social problem-solving design cases. They included (a) branding and promotion, (b) information design, (c) product and kit design, (d) digital content, (e) spatial/environmental design, (f) governance capacity building and (g) core R&D solutions.

Fourth, we analysed ten fourth industrial technologies derived from the above analysis of industrial technology trends in the Covid-19 era (see Table 8.6). If the case used a complex technique, all relevant techniques were analysed.

Fifth, based on Manzini's (2014) classification of the design approaches to social innovation, the problem-solving methods were classified as top-down (central and local governments are the main actors), bottom-up (promotion by companies and individuals) or hybrid (collaborative upper and lower relationships from the planning stage).

Finally, pandemic stages (Table 8.6) were analysed based on the time of occurrence, strategic purpose and problem-solving approach. Recovery and resilience phases are currently in transition, so they were further divided into three phases to clarify the application flow of cases.

Taking 'Corona 19 homepage(A-1)' (Table 8.6) as an example, the Korea Centers for Disease Control and Prevention created a webpage dedicated to Covid-19 and related updates. This is a case of visualizing information so that people could see the infection status in each region at a glance. The information was delivered to the public from the early days of the Covid-19 outbreak in a top-down format. Transparent collection and delivery of information through big data resulted in precise Covid-19 trends and government response guidelines. Digital content, including text, graphs, charts, maps and images, was displayed on a single screen to allow systematic understanding of large amounts of data. The Corona 19 website was an example of the reaction stage response that led to isolation of infected individuals using strict GPS-based tracking systems.

Table 8.6 Example of a Case Study Framework

Analysis Element	Contents
Project name	Corona 19 Homepage (Medical)
Objective	Provision of Covid-19 infection status and related information
Strategic purpose of design use	i) Information delivery (status of infected individuals)
Types of design utilization	b) information design; d) digital content (dashboard and map user interface)
Applications of technology	Big data (location tracking), mobile/software
Approaches to problem solving	Top-down (Government → People)
Corona response stage	Reaction

All cases were classified and analysed using the same format. Through the framework analysis we were able to identify the strategic purposes and types of designs, the applications of technology and design convergence to solve social problems and the approaches of problem solving. Based on the findings, we developed suggestions for effective countermeasures against Covid-19 through the implementation of social innovation design, as well as directions for future use of design to solve social problems.

Individual case analysis

1. Synthetic analysis of reaction stage cases

In the reaction stage, user interfaces (UIs), such as dashboards and maps, were actively used to deliver information regarding closure of social activities. The strategic purpose of information delivery was to educate the public about the seriousness of Covid-19, its countermeasures and related social problems.

Early in the Covid-19 outbreak, data collected through location tracking were visualized using UIs, and applications and platforms were actively used to deliver information about Covid-19. Examples of information delivery using map UI designs include 'Corona 19 Homepage(A-1)', 'Mask App(A-2)' and 'Corona 100m Alert App(A-3)'. Users could check the infection status and trends, and distance by region through the entire map of Korea using the 'Corona 19 Homepage' dashboard (Figure 8.1(a)). The 'Mask App' and 'Corona 100m Alert App' used map UI designs to detect the user's location and provide information within a certain distance. They also showed the current status of mask stock and the locations of infected individuals.

In addition, problem-solving R&D type design cases include 'Toss Emergency Disaster Fund(A-4)', 'QR Code Electronic Access List(A-5)' and 'Corona 19

Checkup(A-6)', which provided services by supplementing the problems arising from government policies related to Covid-19. These services are user-centred solutions for the effective implementation of government policies and are designed to allow users to participate in relevant government policies without social contact or visiting public institutions and medical facilities by prioritizing the user's convenience (Figure 8.1(b)–(d)).

'MEDIP PRO COVID19(A-7)' is also a problem-solving R&D type application that allows 3D visualization of limitations of current medical technology through AR/VR. In this case, doctors and medical personnel are the users. Social problem-solving methods were provided by the Korea Centers for Disease Control and Prevention in the early stages of Covid-19 outbreak, by delivering information and implementing policies. Hybrid forms were also observed, in which platform-related companies participated as mediums to increase user access to information and policies (Table 8.7).

2. Synthetic analysis of adaptation stage cases

With exponential increase in the number of infections, a simple shutdown was not enough to prevent the spread of Covid-19. Korean society adapted to this situation by applying new measures such as step-by-step social distancing, non-face-to-face interactions, remote work and novel ways for education. In the adaptation stage, strategic objectives of action induction and problem-solving R&D types used more diversified technologies compared to the reaction stage. 'Suwon City Mask is the Answer campaign(B-3)' and '30 Second Song Soap Campaign(B-5)' are examples of this. The Suwon City 'Mask is the Answer Campaign' aimed to make wearing masks mandatory for citizens, while the '30 Second Song Soap Campaign' aimed to improve handwashing habits among children. The technology used and the results achieved were different, but the Suwon mascot and Pinkfong's baby shark character were both used to induce familiarity and pleasure among users. These were produced as image and video content on SNS and YouTube channels to enhance the promotional effect. Social problem-solving design using characters was shown to be effective in enabling emotional sympathy between users and technological products and services, while inducing interest and continuous action among users (Figure 8.2(a) and (b)).

Network-building and problem-solving R&D type solutions were mainly used to ensure social distancing in industrial spaces. The 'Seocho-gu Untact Screening Clinic(B-1)' and 'KAIST Negative Pressure Mobile Ward(B-2)' cases changed the space in wards and hospitals with high incidence of contact infections. These were carried out using design processes in collaboration with medical industry experts and design teams. Medical spaces were designed for infection prevention and psychological stability, taking into account the medical service users and providers.

The Seocho-gu Untact Screening Clinic used a sign system design to separate confirmed cases from patient movement lines. The KAIST negative pressure mobile

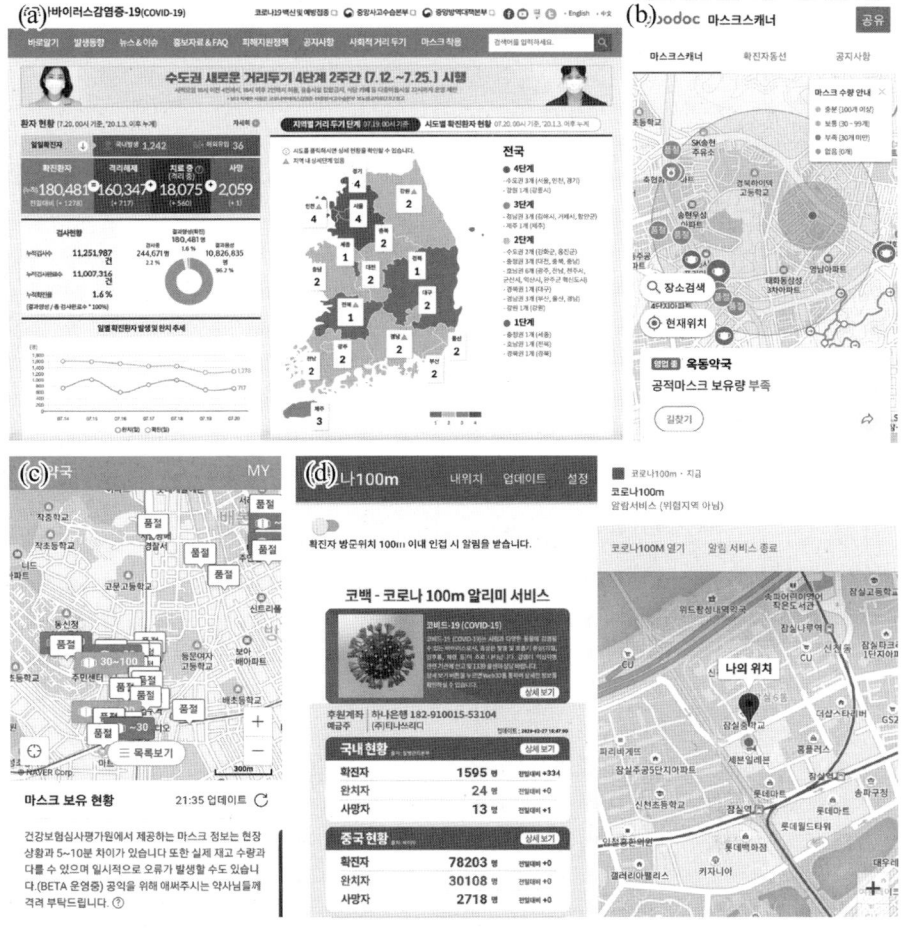

Figure 8.1 (a) 'Map UI information design application in the reaction stage: (A-1) "Coronavirus Infectious Disease-19" Homepage Screen in 2020'. © Korea Disease Control and Prevention Agency (KDCA) All rights reserved. (KDCA's public work is used according to KOGL and was used as the homepage screen of https://ncov.kdca.go.kr in 2020.) (b) Map UI information design application in the reaction stage: (A-2) Goodoc mask scanner app*. (*This is a healthcare super app providing users with various functions in line with the pandemic, including a corona mask scanner, a cost comparison service for Covid-19 testing and non-face-to-face treatment.) © Goodoc All rights reserved. (c) Map UI information design application in the reaction stage: (A-2) 'NAVER app place service indicating mask holding status'. © NAVER Corp. All rights reserved. (d) Map UI information design application in the reaction stage: (A-3) Corona 100m Alert App*. (*This is a self-developed app created by Tina3D for the purpose of visualizing information about coronavirus in 3D and providing a notification service to prevent the spread of corona. Its main function is to induce a detour by sending a notification when a confirmed person approaches within 100 m of the current location.) © TiNA3D All rights reserved.

Table 8.7 Synthetic Analysis of Reaction Stage Cases

	Objective	Strategic Purpose of Design Use	Design Usage Type	Technology Used	Approach to Problem Solving
A-1	Sharing infection status and personal hygiene information	i) information delivery (Trends of infected persons)	b) information design and d) digital content (dashboards, national map UIs)	Big data (location tracking), mobile software	Top-down (Government → Citizens)
A-2	Providing mask stock status	i) information delivery (mask stock)	b) information design and d) digital content (Map UIs based on location)	Big data (location tracking), mobile software	Hybrid (Government ↔ Civic Hacker)
A-3	Notification service when approaching areas visited by confirmed patients	i) information delivery (patient location)	b) information design, d) digital content (Map UIs based on location)	Big data (location tracking), mobile software, AI	Hybrid (Government ↔ Tina 3D)
A-4	Convenience of emergency disaster subsidy	Iv) problem-solving R&D type (Status of Disaster Fund Usage)	d) digital content (User-friendly UI)	Mobile software	Hybrid (Government ↔ Toss)
A-5	Identification of the route of infection and prevention of group infections	iv) problem-solving R&D type	d) digital content (User-friendly recognition systems and UIs)	Big data (location tracking), mobile software	Hybrid (Government ↔ Platform enterprise)
A-6	Confirmation of Covid-19 self-diagnosis	iv) problem-solving R&D type	d) digital content (User-friendly UIs)	Big data (location tracking), mobile software, AI	Bottom-up (Individuals → Citizens)
A-7	Covid-19 confirmation	iv) problem-solving R&D type	d) digital content (Image 3D conversion, admin UIs)	Big data, AI, AR/VR	Bottom-up (Medical IP → Medical)

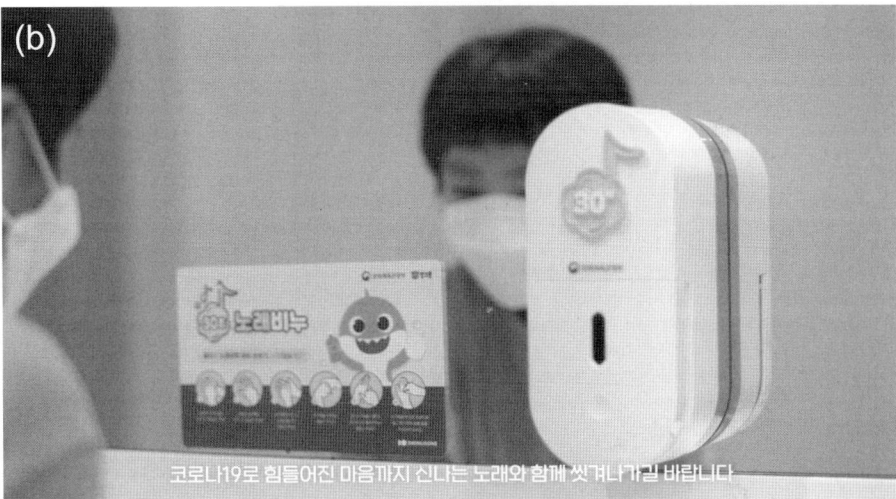

Figure 8.2 (a) Cases of action induction using PR campaign and character design in the adaptation stage: (B-3) Citizen participatory advertisement as part of the 'Mask is the answer!' campaign. © Suwon City Local Government All rights reserved. (Suwon City's public work is used according to KOGL and can be found at https://www.suwon.go.kr.) (b) Cases of action induction using PR campaign and character design in the adaptation stage: (B-5) '30 Second Song Soap' promotion using the Baby Shark character. © Ministry of Culture, Sports and Tourism (MCST) All rights reserved. (MCST's public work is used according to KOGL and can be found at https://www.mcst.go.kr.)

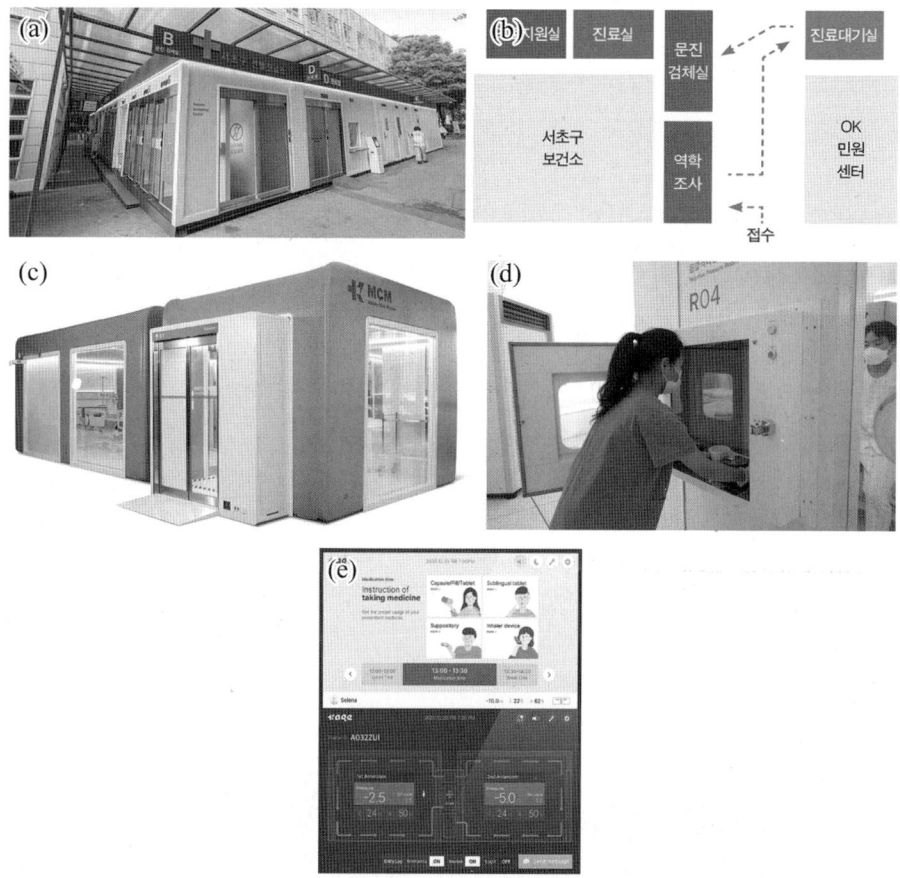

Figure 8.3 Cases of the healthcare environment and user experience design in the adaptation stage: (B-1) (a) Untact screening clinic in Seocho-gu; (b) it's moving line plan*. (*The entire process, from epidemiological investigations to specimens, is a non-contact walk-through with patients, allowing medical staff to work in a safe and pleasant environment without protective clothing.) © SEOCHO SEOUL KOREA, All rights reserved. (Seocho local government's public work is used according to KOGL and can be found at http://seocho.newstool.co.kr.) Cases of the healthcare environment and user experience design in the adaptation stage: (B-2) (c) Mobile Clinic Module (MCM)* developed by the Korea Aid for Respiratory Epidemic initiative at KAIST; (d) contactless meal delivery to patients; (e) negative pressure ward UI for patients. (*MCM wins Best of the Best at 2021 Red Dot Design Award, simultaneously in the Product Design and Brand & Communication Design categories. Related information will be continuously updated on mcm.kaist.ac.kr.) © Professor Tek-Jin Nam and Associates, CIDR Lab., Department of Industrial Design, KAIST. All rights reserved.

ward was designed as a lightweight mobile ward through prototyping using 3D programmes. KAIST negative pressure mobile ward used a display UI for patients and managers, configured inside the negative pressure frame facility, to improve usability, and provided emotional stability for users and service providers using indirect lighting. Both medical environments successfully lowered the Covid-19 infection rates through spatial/environmental design, ensuring smooth functioning of the hospital (Figure 8.3(a)–(e)).

The '2020 Seoul Corona Exhibition(B-4)' and '2020 Busan Biennale Exhibition(B-8)' were cases that allowed access using web space instead of material space as it became impossible for citizens to visit the field of culture and art. The 2020 Seoul Corona Exhibition established a website allowing domestic designers to produce and display their works with the theme of Corona. The 2020 Busan Biennale exhibition used VR/AR for a 3D exhibition and displayed the description and location of each exhibition piece in an easy-to-see manner, giving visitors a sense of actually viewing the works in an exhibition hall (Figure 8.4).

The cases of 'LG U+ Elementary School Country(B-6)' and 'jibmusil(B-7)' had a common goal of minimizing contact between people and maximizing the efficiency of non-face-to-face work and education due to changes in their respective environments. 'jibmusil' created a non-face-to-face office space for workers who could not separate their work and personal lives for reasons such as housework or childcare. The furniture designs in the space were divided into three modules, considering the user's preferences and work type. An unmanned system of applications was used to minimize contact with managers. 'LG U+ Elementary Country' provided learning content in VR/AR using various characters to enhance the learning in non-face-to-face educational environments. The use of animation effects to encourage voluntary participation made learning lively and stimulating.

Figure 8.4 A case of online-based exhibition design in the adaptation stage: (B-8) Busan Biennale 2020 Online Exhibition* 3D viewing room. (*Biennale in the era of non-face-to-face aims to maximize the three-dimensional effect and synesthetic experience the audience feels when meeting on-site work by utilizing the latest IT technologies, such as 3D stereoscopic images and virtual reality (VR).) © Busan Biennale Organizing Committee All rights reserved.

In the adaptation stage, central and local governments led action-inducing campaigns in a top-down problem-solving approach. Problem-solving R&D cases, in contrast, used a bottom-up approach with voluntary involvement of companies to solve industrial problems and provide products and services. Compared to the reaction stage, the services provided in these cases focused on social and individual value creation, and the subject of service operation is gradually led by private companies as well as public institutions at the national level, and thus applied to more diverse fields.

3. Synthetic analysis of recovery and resilience stage cases

Daily life in Korea is recovering with the spread of vaccination. Return to a pre-Covid-19 state will require sustainable solutions to social problems, and these will foster economic and social recovery. Unlike the reaction and adaptation stages, the recovery and resilience stage involved use of Metaverse space cases with the strategic purpose of networking, and problem-solving R&D type robots and devices (Figure 8.5(a) and (b)).

The non-face-to-face online Metaverse environments created by 'Soonchunhyang University Metaverse Entrance Ceremony(C-1)' and 'ZEPETO(C-6)' are examples of systems that allow users to design their own unique characters and communicate freely within a virtual space (Table 8.8). ZEPETO provided a network space that allowed users to communicate freely within and outside Korea. In the absence of cultural events and travel, it helped overseas industrial exchanges and K-Pop revitalization.

'Deliplate(C-4)', 'Kimi Robot(C-9)' and 'Aidbo(C-10) t' maximized the advantages of non-face-to-face services using robots with IoT/sensor, autonomous driving and AI functions. The robots provide a friendly and unique experience to users by showing facial expressions through a display and can be managed by an administrator through a convenient interface.

The 'Smart IoT Air Shower(C-8)' and 'vitcon-medicine control center(C-7)' cases also involved use of IoT/sensors for recognizing human entry and exit, sterilization and safe transportation and storage of medicines. Relevant information can also be visualized, monitored and managed through a display. Traditionally, functionality of robots and devices was emphasized, with design being a part of the post-processing. However, the focus has now shifted to meticulous body movement designs, sounds and content, and external design for emotional communication. The control systems of these robots and devices utilize dashboard-type UIs designed for administrators (Figure 8.6(a)–(d)).

In the recovery and resilience stage, problem-solving methods were generally based on the company's interests, for example, 'Deliplate(C-4)', 'Hyundai Uncommon Store(C-2)' and 'ZEPETO(C-6)'. Some methods involved related companies and the government cooperating to provide services from the planning stage, for example,

Figure 8.5 (a) Cases of design for social communication using Metaverse in the recovery and resilience stage: a. (C-1) Soonchunhyang University entrance ceremony based on Metaverse platform*. (*Students created their own avatars and participated in the campus playground of a three-dimensional virtual world where the boundary between reality and virtuality disappeared.) © Soonchunhyang University. All rights reserved. (b) Cases of design for social communication using Metaverse in the recovery and resilience stage: b. (C-6) Metaverse community platform 'ZEPETO' with its unique avatar worldview. © NAVER Z Corp. All rights reserved.

'Kimi Robot(C-9)' and 'Coov Electronic Vaccine(C-3)'. Local governments also directly participated in social problem solving by installing products such as 'Smart IoT Air Shower(C-8)'. All three of these forms are seen in this stage, indicating that Korean society, as a whole, is actively participating in resolving Covid-19-related problems (Table 8.9).

Table 8.8 Synthetic Analysis of Cases in the Adaptation Stage

	Objective	Strategic Purpose	Design Usage Type	Technology Used	Problem-Solving Method
B-1	Prevention of hospital-acquired infections	iv) problem-solving R&D type	e) space/Environment design and g) core R&D solutions (non-contact medical space design)	IoT/Sensors	Top-down (Government → Citizens)
B-2	Prevention of hospital-acquired infections	iv) problem-solving R&D type	e) Space/Environment design and g) core R&D solutions (Negative pressure ward space design)	3D Printing, IoT/Sensors	Bottom-up (KAIST → Citizens)
B-3	Mandatory wearing of masks	ii) action induction	a) branding and promotion, and d) digital content (SNS promotional content using characters)	Mobile software	Top-down (Government → Citizens)
B-4	Domestic designer exhibition platform production	iii) network construction	d) digital content and f) governance capacity building (Web exhibition space design)	Cloud	Bottom-up (Graphica → Designers + Visitors)
B-5	Improving children's hand washing habits	ii) action induction	a) branding and promotion, and c) product and kit design (Character-based video promotional content)	IoT/Sensors	Top-down (Government → Citizens)
B-6	Non-face-to-face learning	iv) problem-solving R&D type	d) digital content (non-face-to-face learning content)	VR/AR	Bottom-up (LG → Students)
B-7	Non-face-to-face office space	iv) problem-solving R&D type	e) space/Environment design and g) core R&D solutions (non-face-to-face workspace design)	Mobile software	Bottom-up (Alicon → Office workers)
B-8	Non-face-to-face exhibition space	iv) problem-solving R&D type	d) digital content (Web exhibition space design)	VR/AR	Bottom-up (Busan Biennale → Visitors)

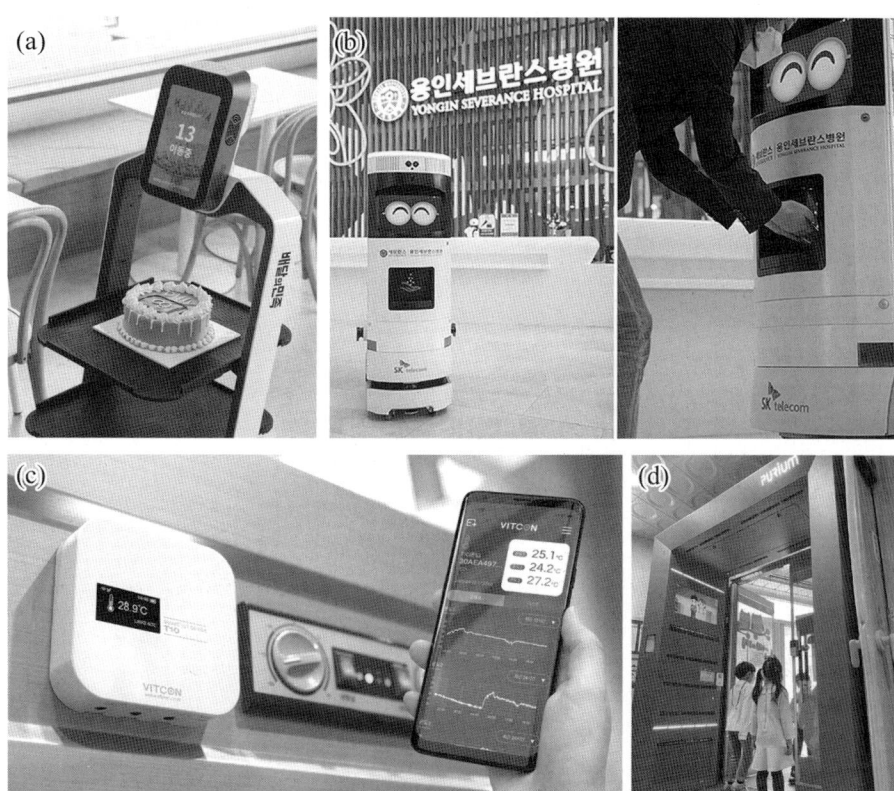

Figure 8.6 (a) Cases of design of user interaction with robots and IoT devices in the recovery and resilience stage: a. (C-4) Food-delivery app Baemin's serving robot 'Dilly plate'. © Woowa Brothers Corp. All rights reserved. (b) Cases of design of user interaction with robots and IoT devices in the recovery and resilience stage: b. (C-9) Non-face-to-face care service robot, 'Kimi' that combines the roles of a guidance robot and a quarantine robot. © SK TELECOM Co., Ltd. All rights reserved. (This image was produced by SK Telecom Newsroom and can be found at https://news.sktelecom.com.) (c) Cases of design of user interaction with robots and IoT devices in the recovery and resilience stage: c. (C-7) Smart medicine refrigerator temperature management system UI by VITCON. © VITCON Co., Ltd. All rights reserved. (d) Cases of design of user interaction with robots and IoT devices in the recovery and resilience stage: d. (C-8) Smart IoT air shower installed at a day care centre in Gyeyang-gu, Incheon. © Gyeyang-gu District Incheon Metropolitan City. All rights reserved. G87 can be found at https://www.gyeyang.go.kr.

Analysis synthesis

Implications for the use of design to solve problems in each stage of Covid-19 response were derived through the analysis of twenty-five technology–design convergence cases. Design utilization was assessed in terms of each stage of Covid-19 response, approach to problem solving, type of design used based on the strategic purpose and scope of technology utilization (Figure 8.7).

Table 8.9 Synthetic Analysis of Cases in the Recovery and Resilience Stage

	Objective	Strategic Purpose	Design Usage Type	Technology Used	Problem-Solving Method
C-1	Provision of online space for non-face-to-face entrance ceremony	iii) network construction	d) digital content and building governance (Metaverse space and character design)	VR/AR	Bottom-up (SK → Citizens)
C-2	Non-face-to-face store payment service	iv) problem-solving R&D type	e) space/environment design (Unmanned store design)	AI	Bottom-up (Hyundai → Citizens)
C-3	Vaccination verification system	iv) problem-solving R&D type	d) digital content (Information provision setting UIs)	Blockchain	Hybrid (Centers for Disease Control + Blockchain Labs)
C-4	Serving food with minimal contact	iv) problem-solving R&D type	c) product and kit design, and g) core R&D solutions (non-face-to-face serving robot)	Autonomous driving, Robotics, IoT/Sensors	Bottom-up (Baemin → Citizens)
C-5	Telemedicine service	iv) problem-solving R&D type	d) digital content (Telemedicine UI)	AI, Mobile software	Bottom-up (Medihere → Citizens)
C-6	Non-face-to-face networking	iii) network construction	d) digital content and building governance (Metaverse space and character design)	VR/AR, AI, Mobile software	Bottom-up (Naver → Citizens)
C-7	Real-time drug monitoring	iv) problem-solving R&D type	d) digital content (monitoring UIs for administrators)	IoT/Sensors, Mobile software	Bottom-up (Enterprise → Citizens)

C-8	Improving air quality by disinfecting building entrances and exits	iv) problem-solving R&D type	c) product and kit design, and g) core R&D solutions (dashboard UIs for admins)	IoT/Sensors, AI	Top-down (Government → Citizens)
C-9	Minimal-contact in-hospital patient care	iv) problem-solving R&D type	c) product and kit design, and g) core R&D solutions (in-hospital guidance robot)	IoT/Sensors, Autonomous Driving, Robotics, AI	Hybrid (SKT + Yongin Severance Hospital)
C-10	Non-contact quarantine	v) problem-solving R&D type	c) product and kit design, and g) core R&D solutions (autonomous driving quarantine robot)	IoT/Sensors, AI, Autonomous Driving, Robotics	Bottom-up (KAIST → Citizens)

First, the strategic purpose varied with the Covid-19 response stage. In the reaction stage, information-delivery and problem-solving R&D types were more common (Figure 8.7). The information-delivery type used UI designs to visually deliver information on infection status (A-1, 2, 3). This encouraged the public to wear masks and avoid social contact. The problem-solving R&D type provided services by detecting problems in public policies created at the beginning of the Covid-19 period. The adaptation and recovery and resilience stages involved action induction, network construction and problem-solving R&D types. During these stages, the problem-solving R&D type helped identify problems in various industries, instead of improving the national response. Non-face-to-face platforms were created for art galleries and museums (B-4, 8). Robots were introduced to reduce contact infections in places where face-to-face interaction is essential, such as hospitals and restaurants (C-4, 9). Meanwhile, network construction created a virtual Metaverse space (C-1, 6) to allow domestic and international communication, as well as facilitated recovery of overseas cultural exchange such as K-pop. Using this non-face-to-face approach, the world can be reconnected within a virtual space.

Second, the longitudinal axes of top-down, bottom-up and hybrid problem-solving methods remained uniform in each step of the cases, indicating that social problems were solved through public–private governance (Figure 8.8). Characteristics of Covid-19 responses were divided into stages and analysed as follows. In the initial reaction stage, the Korea Centers for Disease Control and Prevention provided nationally collected information and implemented policies (A-1), while platform-related companies served as mediums to deliver the information and policies to the public. Bottom-up problem-solving methods increased in the adaptation and recovery and resilience stages. Cases in the recovery and resilience stage involved initiatives taken by companies to solve user-contact problems that could not be achieved using a state-led approach. This suggests that the companies adapted to systems that generate profits while actively participating in social problem solving (Figure 8.8).

Lastly, the types of designs used and the characteristics of these diverse technologies were classified based on their strategic purposes. Comparing area (A) of the reaction stage in Figure 8.8 with areas (B) and (C), it can be seen that the technologies used in the service diversified as the steps progressed. This reflects the important role of digital transformation in Covid-19-related social situations, with industries introducing various technologies. Technology convergence for strategic purposes and design utilization was achieved as follows.

Information-delivery type designs, such as 'Corona 19 Website(A-1)', 'Mask App(A-2)' and 'Corona 100m Alert App(A-3)', of the Korea Centers for Disease Control and Prevention used digital content apps. These were created on the web and visualized as UIs in the form of maps or dashboards using infrastructure technologies, such as big data. Information was displayed on maps as infographics so that anyone, regardless of age or gender, could understand the information and take action on their own.

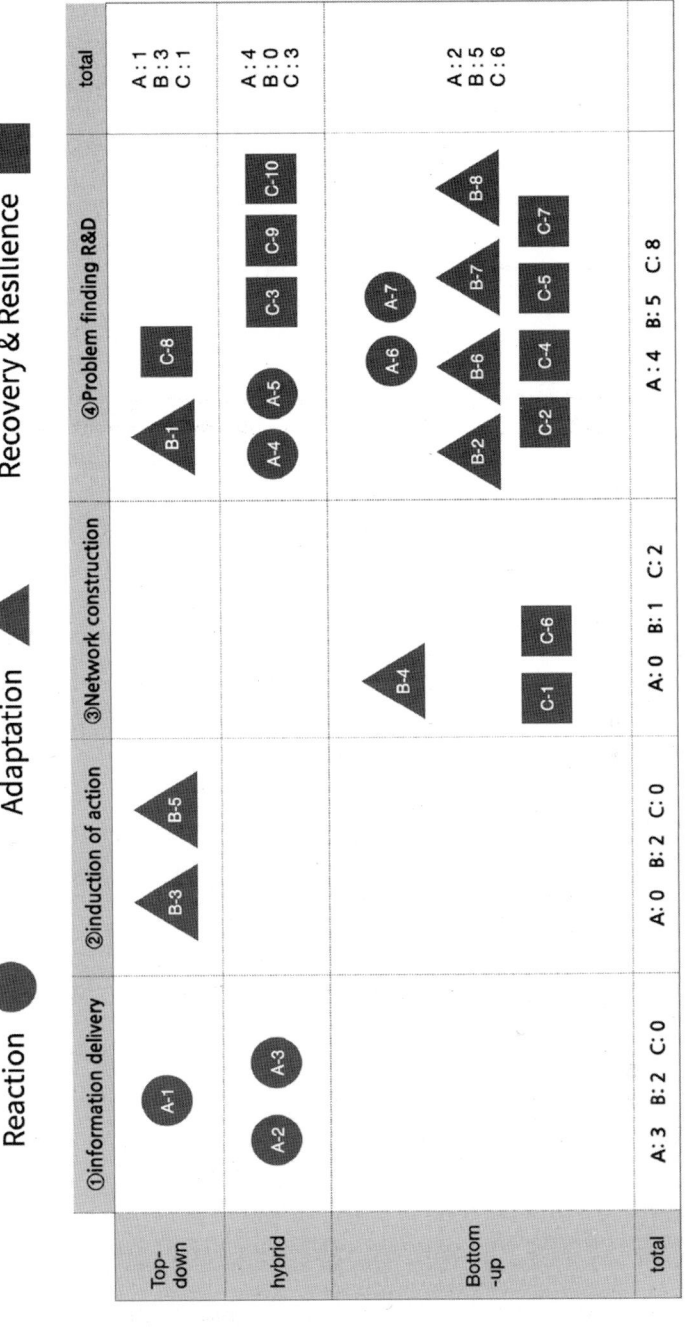

Figure 8.7 Analysis of problem-solving methods and strategic goals for Covid-19 response stage. © Yoori Koo.

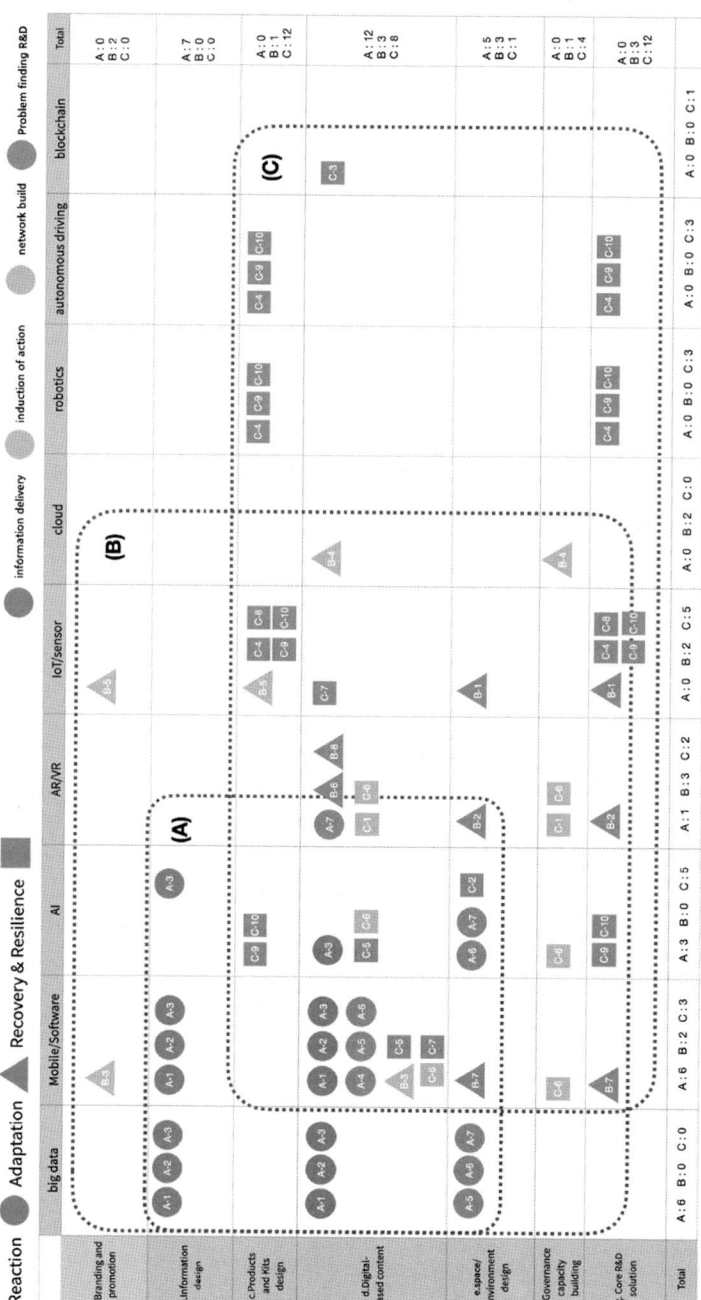

Figure 8.8 Comprehensive analysis of design and technology use according to strategic purposes. © Yoori Koo.

The 'Suwon Mask Campaign(B-3)' and the '30-Second Song Soap Campaign(B-5)' were action-inducing campaigns that used branding and public relations designs to convey information and encourage participation. Characters and SNS videos were used in these campaigns. The use of character design within the industry enables emotional communication because users are familiar with the products and services. Visual delivery of social solution designs using characters was effective in inducing interest and behaviour modification.

Network construction was used to design individual avatars with AR/VR in Metaverse spaces, such as 'ZEPETO'. The company designed a virtual space allowing people to visit and enjoy the place indirectly. Covid-19 led to social disconnect, and the Metaverse space allowed users to design online personas and express their thoughts and emotions.

Problem-solving R&D types used space/environment designs to block transmission of infections by configuring the space to control movements in hospitals. Sign systems and indirect lighting were also used to improve user accessibility and psychological stability. The design process, monitoring system UIs and the environments were created for the convenience of not only users but also service providers, that is hospital medical staff. Meanwhile, in other industries, unmanned systems reduced contact infections and promoted use of applications to simplify services. Products and kits design was mainly related to robotics and included autonomous driving and IoT sensor technologies. Focus on the appearance and interface design of robots led to the creation of a more intimate experience for users and increased convenience.

Suggestions and implications

Based on the study described above, we developed suggestions and implications for future directions in social problem-solving designs.

First, collaboration for problem solving should proceed as a user-centred process. Our case analyses revealed various directions of problem-solving methods, indicating the necessity to establish a network of various participants, such as the government, companies and citizens, and to encourage collaboration among stakeholders. The information-delivery and problem-solving R&D types involved outstanding public–private collaborations. The example of the 'mask app (A-2)' shows how citizen developers, known as 'Civic Hackers' were granted access by the state to public data. Furthermore, application programming interfaces and web/app environments were provided by companies in response to the shortage of masks. The government has provided public data to develop effective methods, customized for the public, through collaboration between citizens and businesses (A-2, 5).

Companies such as Jibmusil (B-7) and Hyundai Uncommon Store (C-2) have created social products and services to meet the potential needs of users for preventing Covid-19 and maintaining daily life (B-4, 6, 7; C-2, 5, 6, 7). These products and services were used in accordance with government policy to overcome the Covid-19 crisis.

Second, the designs should consider not only the results but also the processes involved in solving social problems. Designs should be used as tools for user-centred problem discovery and collaboration, and application of technologies should be developed in an everyday context. However, there are still difficulties as design is considered in terms of post-processing instead of internal structure. The Seocho-gu Untact Screening Clinic (B-1) and the KAIST negative pressure mobile ward (B-2) are examples of process application, where the design teams took the initiative in planning and proposed a problem-solving process that is similar to those used in scientific research and engineering. This illustrates the role of design as an integrator and coordinator. The KAIST negative pressure mobile ward did not limit users to patients, but provided a positive atmosphere for medical personnel, patients and managers by using a specialized UI for each. In other words, design can be a medium for grasping and sharing knowledge in various fields to provide effective services to multiple users. It can allow various stakeholders to jointly participate in solving problems that cannot be solved without collaboration. It has the potential to define problems in a new light and to find solutions through visualization (Steen, 2013). As integrated coordinators, post-Covid-19 era designs should meet social and economic objectives and create shared value by connecting various stakeholders, including service providers and consumers.

Third, social problem-solving designs should consider future effects on technology and services. The location-tracking apps (A-1, 2, 3) and QR code electronic access list (A-5) create a conflict between personal privacy and public safety. Although large-scale spread of Covid-19 or any other infections may be prevented by tracking the location of infected individuals, this form of 'monitoring' has the potential for misuse. Therefore, instead of interpreting the results of technology application piecemeal, its influence should be considered in the context of the relationship between technology, people and society. Designers should try to predict social, cultural and ethical changes during the planning stages of products and services using design fiction. Care must be taken to avoid causing harm to the community through design.

Fourth, with daily life applications of design through a combination of various technologies, it is necessary to connect people with technologies, rather than merely introducing new technologies. Industrial environments, such as Metaverse, have been developed to allow users to freely consume desired content, regardless of time and place (C-1, 6). Design convergence contents are also being developed along with various technologies, such as VR/AR, AI and robotics, as can be seen in 'LG U+ Elementary Country(B-6)' and 'Deliplate(C-4)'. Korean society will continue to adapt to ensure social, economic and cultural exchanges. Interaction designs with unmanned systems for customized user experience were emphasized, and sound and content design and external design were required for emotional communication with robots. Therefore, designers must have high receptivity and understanding of various technologies, non-face-to-face services and problem-solving abilities. A greater focus on the emotional connection between technology and people is required to increase the value of future products and services.

The study described in this chapter has the limitation that quantitative impact of each element of experience could not be demonstrated, as a limited number of cases were qualitatively analysed. However, it demonstrated the direction of design utilization based on the stages of Covid-19 response and the characteristics of design elements and technology convergence. It also illustrates how necessary it is to expand design-centred problem-solving R&D. It is still necessary, however, to raise awareness about the value of design as a medium for technology utilization and for solving social problems. It is also necessary to nurture designers who can think comprehensively using both technical and social analysis. Furthermore, systematic research is needed to understand, evaluate the use of design during the Covid-19 and post Covid-19 era, to ensure we can increase social and economic value through design going forward.

References

Akama, Y., Yee, J., Hill, R., & Tjahja, C. (2019). Impact and evaluation in designing social innovation: Insights from the DESIAP KL workshop and symposium.

Cipolla, C., Joly, M.P., Watanabe, B., Zanela, F., & Tavares, M. (2016, May). Service design for social innovation: The promotion of active aging in Rio De Janeiro. In *Service Design Geographies: Proceedings of the ServDes. 2016 Conference* (No. 125). Linköping University Electronic Press, 365–75.

Fletcher, G., & Griffiths, M. (2020). Digital transformation during a lockdown. *International Journal of Information Management*, 55, 102185.

Hillgren, P.A. (2013). Participatory design for social and public innovation: Living labs as spaces for agonistic experiments and friendly hacking. Public and collaborative: Exploring the intersection of design. *Social Innovation and Public Policy*, 75–88.

Kim, K.G. (2017). Meaning of social innovation and recent trends. Gwangju Jeonnam Research Institute. No. 7, Special 01, 1–30.

Kim, W.D. (2020). [KSME opinion] science and technology in the new normal era after Corona 19. *Mechanical Journal*, 60(8), 4–5.

Kimbell, L. (2011). Rethinking design thinking: Part I. *Design and Culture*, 3(3), 285–306.

Koo, Y.R., & Lee, S.M. (2017). Developing UX design strategies for the better engagement of the public through the use of gamification in the public service and policy sector. *Archives of Design Research*, 30(4), 87–106.

Luo, J., Olechowski, A.L., & Magee, C.L. (2014). Technology-based design and sustainable economic growth. *Technovation*, 34(11), 663–77.

Manzini, E. (2014). Making things happen: Social innovation and design. *Design Issues*, 30(1), 57–66. https://doi.org/10.1162/DESI_a_00248.

Melles, G., de Vere, I., & Misic, V. (2011). Socially responsible design: Thinking beyond the triple bottom line to socially responsive and sustainable product design. *CoDesign*, 7(3–4), 143–54.

Mullagh, L., Cooper, R., Thomas, L., Sacks, J., Jones, P.L., & Jacobs, N. (2021). Designing for a pandemic: Towards recovery and resilience. *Strategic Design Research Journal*, 14(1), 161–74.

Steen, M. (2013). Co-design as a process of joint inquiry and imagination. *Design Issues*, 29(2), 16–28.

Seoul Metropolitan Government (2020). Seoul social problem solving design basic plan 108–109p.

PART III Recovery and Resilience
Building for the Future

Chapters in this section offer examples of design interventions, design principles and design tools from which we can learn to navigate design research and practice to create the digital, the physical and hybrid worlds of the future. We reflect upon lessons learned during the pandemic to responsibly consider how design can be used in building the future.

9 Here to stay

Design-led recovery from Covid-19 in New York

MARIANA AMATULLO AND ISABELLA GADY

Introduction

The generative role of design in addressing some of society's most intractable challenges to effect positive change is part of an evolving argument about its increasing agency in public and private sectors alike. In this chapter, we probe the effectiveness of design's agency in the context of the Covid-19 outbreak in the United States and, more specifically, in New York City, one of the world's epicentres of the pandemic during the first quarter of 2020. We examine two design case studies that address some of the disparities the pandemic brought into full view: *Family Pockets by Sour* (working title), a design service conceived by SOUR architecture for the HeyMama membership network to support working mothers and families juggling child-care, and *South Bronx Community Gardens Activation*, a public space reactivation project of the NeighborhoodsNow initiative facilitated by the Urban Design Forum and the Van Alen Institute. Two overarching research questions underpin our examination of these projects: (1) What can we learn about the unique agency of design from two projects that sought to create sustainable strategies for recovery? and (2) How did the pandemic's shelter in place mandates impact the design research methods and participatory design practices of these projects?

Crises lay bare society's faults. A crisis of unprecedented scale and scope with a fountain of issues and competing priorities and no response playbook attached (Leonard et al., 2020), Covid-19 threw the world into a state of trauma first heralded as an equalizer event that quickly revealed wide disparities, disproportionately affecting vulnerable groups across race, gender and socio-economic status (JungHo, 2021). In the United States, the pandemic compounded many systemic axes of inequality with long-term secondary health, psychological and socio-economic impacts for individuals and families – all of which are yet to be fully assessed (Perry et al., 2021).

While the precarity unleashed is unquestionable, this chapter argues that design interventions aspiring to positively impact the downstream consequences of Covid-19, such as *Family Pockets by Sour* and *South Bronx Community Gardens Activation*, present a source of optimism, pointing to design's capacity to help communities adapt to profound disruption, recover from devastating circumstances and ultimately build resilience.

Methods

Research design of the study

Given the empirical nature of this research, we adopted case study methodology (Yin, 2009) and combined it with a grounded theory approach (Charmaz, 2006; Strauss and Corbin, 1997). Since research designs with multiple cases tend to produce stronger validity and reliability, we followed this logic, selecting two cases to explore the world of theory and the experience of practice simultaneously. We strove to discern patterns and contrasts and extend these into emerging theory (Yin, 2009). Our approach was both explanatory – we wanted to understand *why* decisions were made and *how* they were executed, and exploratory – we sought to understand *what* design research processes teams adapted to accommodate the constraints imposed by the pandemic and *what* were the resulting outcomes.

Sample, data collection and data analysis approach

We followed a deliberate sampling plan to select cases which present 'transparently observable' phenomena correlated to our research questions (Eisenhardt, 1989). To narrow down our scope in this sampling, we applied the following four criteria:

1. **A design-led approach:** a 'designerly' mode (Nigel, 1982) as a core driver of the interventions proposed.
2. **Co-creation ethos:** a participatory research approach with diverse stakeholders.
3. **Fourth-order design outcomes:** We searched for projects seeking systemic solutions, following Buchanan's classic framework (Buchanan, 1992).
4. **Long-term implications from Covid-19:** We looked for projects that presented a sustained and holistic approach to intervention.

Data collection occurred between early June and the end of July 2021. We designed a two-stage process of semi-structured Zoom interviews with project and design leaders followed by a second round of written interview questions to probe key areas of interest after initial coding. Secondary desk research and artefacts provided by the project teams rounded up our inputs. Our data analysis included a constant comparison method and an iterative coding process with memo writing to advance from open, descriptive codes to a progressive level of higher conceptual codes that shaped our interpretations and theorizing (Strauss & Corbin, 1997).

Case one: *Family Pockets by Sour*

In early March 2020, right before the pandemic turned the world upside down, Pinar Guvenc, partner at the architecture and design firm SOUR, and Katya Libin, co-founder and CEO of HeyMama, a private membership community 'for career-driven mothers', first met in New York to start exploring avenues for potential collaboration between their organizations. Their initial discussion was fast-tracked a few weeks later, as the onslaught of the pandemic shut down schools and day care centres and closed companies' offices, forcing an unprecedented remote work experiment that became especially challenging for working parents. Suddenly, the urgent need to support families in their new blended home lives, especially working mothers homeschooling young children, emerged as an extremely worthwhile focus for collaboration.

With the *Family Pockets by Sour*, (Table 9.1) Guvenc and Libin set out to undertake a joint project that would rely on a robust co-creation logic that could leverage both the design expertise and inclusive research methods of SOUR, and the established ecosystem of knowledge from the membership network of HeyMama. A driving aspiration of their vision was to shape long-term solutions for working mothers, beyond the unique context of the pandemic:

> We were looking at the challenges of this new work situation and asking ourselves how these might impact families in the long term. It became clear that besides the official site, this new reality requires us to rethink the homesite, and especially what this new situation means for working moms.
> (Guvenc in an interview with authors, June 2021)

The project's objective to make an impact downstream is especially relevant given that in the United States, the Covid-19 crisis crystallized a set of pre-existing and systematic factors including affordable access to childcare, which have long impacted working families, with a disproportionate share of the burden borne by women.

Since the launch of the research phase of the project in April 2020, the *Family Pockets* toolkit has undergone multiple rounds of iteration and prototyping. It is shaping up as a service design project with an innovative kit of parts that include engaging activities for the whole family. An overarching goal is to address stressful family dynamics and leverage the experiences from the blurring of boundaries between work–life and home–life of the crisis with purposeful tools: for example, children feeling excluded or shunned when parents cannot give them focused attention while working and a sense of 'guilt' from multitasking, time-starved parents:

> Each intervention comes with a certain activity or prompt for the family to help create collaboration, communication or bonding opportunities; we are hoping that they become routines/habits in the household and therefore have lasting effects way beyond physical intervention.
> (Guvenc, July 2021)

A prototype example is the 'Askin Napkin' activity (Figures 9.1 and 9.2) designed to create a communication and bonding opportunity for families. The prompts are

Table 9.1 Family Pockets by Sour

Project Name	'Family Pockets by Sour' (working title)
Summary	The collaboration between HeyMama and SOUR intends to help families balance a new 'work-life' blend that emerged with Covid-19 through a kit of activities.
Project Start and Timeline	April 2020 launch with 8-month-long research/concept stage, followed by the start of physical prototyping in July 2021.
Project Partners:	• SOUR, an architecture and design studio addressing social and urban problems: https://www.sour.studio/ • HeyMama, a US-based private social and professional network created to propel mothers forward in work and life: https://heymama.co/about-heymama/
Target Audience	Primary: • Working mothers: either self-employed, freelancers or working for companies • Children aged 4 to 13 Secondary • Parents as a whole and families.
Project Team Size and Roles:	Design team of seven plus subject matter experts at key junctures. Approximately 100 mothers and their families have participated throughout research and prototyping phases. Design and expert roles include: • Industrial Designers • Design Strategists • Designer Researchers • Architects • Communication Designers • Therapists
Project Anticipated Outcomes	An Activity Toolkit integrating household everyday objects to foster family connection and support working parents. The kit is meant to be disseminated through the HeyMama network and via targeted corporate partnerships as a value add to new hybrid workplace demands in the post-Covid-19 transition.
Design Disciplines	• Service Design • Product Design

(*Continued*)

Table 9.1 (Continued)

Project Name	'Family Pockets by Sour' (working title)
Design Methods Applied	• Net ethnography of 'working moms' via TikTok and Instagram • A week-long diary study via WhatsApp in collaboration with Openbox • User Testing Session • Prototyping • User Survey • User Interviews • Expert Interviews • Desk Research (popular media scan, reports)
The Covid-19 Factor	The project team worked entirely in a virtual mode with no in-person sessions The design process and methods had to be adapted for the digital space.

Figure 9.1 Prototype of the 'Askin Napkin' activity during family meals. SOUR.

designed to create intentional interaction moments during mealtimes and solicit empathic dialogue and connection.

Table 9.1 provides a summary of the project at glance.

Case two: *South Bronx Community Gardens Activation*

In a city with the bustling humanity and population density of New York, public spaces are 'the life between buildings' (Gehl, 2011). They extend small living spaces, serve

Figure 9.2 Storyboard for the 'Askin Napkin' activity during family meals. SOUR.

as a forum for residents to connect and are at the core of the city's thriving economic activity and desirability. For socially vulnerable residents, public spaces such as parks and community gardens are significant sites for community cohesion (Anguelovski et al., 2020). They are also much less common in poorer neighbourhoods than in high-income areas (Trust for Public Land Report, May 2021). *South Bronx Community Gardens Activation* (Table 9.2) emerged as part of the renewed urgency to increase access to public space that Covid-19 catalysed:

> These gardens are relatively Covid-safe spaces; they are key hubs for gatherings and community service delivery, yet underutilized. Ian and other organizers of Banana Kelly felt a renewed sense of urgency to activate those spaces as it became clear Covid wasn't going to go away immediately, and these gardens would provide a safe place for gatherings and community organizing.
> (Oliver Oglesby, Michael Van Valkenburgh Associates, Inc., July 2021)

Launched as part of the larger *NeighborhoodsNow* initiative by New York-based non-profits Urban Design Forum and Van Alen Institute to channel pro bono resources from New York-based design firms, the project aims to revitalize the use of community gardens managed by the grassroots organization Banana Kelly, which has served South Bronx residents for the past forty years through the development of affordable housing, community services and advocacy. In addition to reimagining community gardens as critical service distribution hubs, the project aims to respond to racial–ethnic disparities this marginalized community has long suffered. As the testimonials below point out, this racial reckoning, which became all the more pronounced with the Black Lives Matter rallies that followed the May 2020, George Floyd killing in the United States, cannot be underestimated. It was an important factor in activating this project in particular and informing more generally design approaches for recovery from the pandemic that characterized many other community-based efforts in New York:

> Many professions, design included, recognized the ways we need to do better to support our community-based organizations, underinvested communities, and our black and brown neighbors.
> (Martha Snow, Urban Design Forum, July 2021)

Table 9.2 South Bronx Community Gardens Activation

Project name	South Bronx Community Gardens Activation
Summary	South Bronx Community Gardens Activation is part of NeighborhoodsNow, a rapid-response initiative to channel pro-bono resources from New York-based design firms into community-driven recovery strategies. The project aims to revitalize Banana Kelly's four garden sites (Longwood, Hunts Point, Morrisania and Mott Haven), allowing access to public space and services for area residents.
Project Start and Timeline	The project is part of a September 2020 seed grant RFP from the NeighborhoodsNow initiative. Launched in February 2021, the project's implementation is slated for completion by September 2021.
Project Partners	Project Conveners: • Urban Design Forum, New York City-based independent membership organization advancing solutions to urban challenges: https://urbandesignforum.org/ • Van Alen Institute, New York City-based independent nonprofit architectural organization that works in the public realm: https://www.vanalen.org/Community Partner: • Banana Kelly, South Bronx-based community improvement association (BKCIA): https://www.bkcianyc.org/ NeighborhoodsNow: https://neighborhoodsnow.nyc/ Working Group of design and subject matter experts: • Michael Van Valkenburgh Associates • The Greenest Fern • BD Feliz • Fried Frank Law • Silman Engineering • Neighbourhood Residents
Target Audience	Banana Kelly community members, gardeners; and South Bronx residents.

Project Team, Size and Roles	Core group of approximately fourteen people across the following constituencies
	
	Project Conveners:
	- Urban Design Forum
	- Van Alen Institute
	
	Community Partner:
	- Banana Kelly
	  - Garden Leaders
	  - Lead Organizers
	  - Youth Organizers
	  - Garden Stewards
	
	NeighborhoodsNow Working Group:
	Michael Van Valkenburgh Associates (MVVA), Brooklyn-based landscape architecture and planning firm (team of 5)
	- The Greenest Fern, Bronx-based sustainable designer and planner(1)
	- BD Feliz, South Bronx based graphic designer and artist (1)
	- Fried Frank, Supporting Law Firm (1)
	- Silman, Structural Engineer (1)

Project Anticipated Outcomes	Design infrastructure improvements and new community services for the four gardens and a vacant lot in the neighborhood. Supported by seed funding ($10,000), outcomes include the following: Adopt-a-Bucket program; Banana Kelly's first community newspaper *The Peel* and several 'Community Walls' to keep the community informed about news and garden activities.
Design Disciplines	- Service Design - Landscape Design - Communication Design

(Continued)

Table 9.2 (Continued)

Project name	South Bronx Community Gardens Activation
Design Methods Applied	- Prototyping (by building mock-ups) - Site visits and analysis - Conversations with Banana Kelly residents and community members - Community Surveys - Neighbourhood/tenant canvassing - Community meetings - Community clean-up days and other in-person events - Materials research, and horticultural research - Construction detailing - Hand drawing - Collaging/rendering - Diagramming - Mapping - Collaborative brainstorming (via Miro Board).
The Covid-19 Factor	- Strong interest of the design and creative community – partially due to collision of Covid-19 and the social justice uprising in the US in 2020 - Blended outreach strategy: virtual and in-person

Figure 9.3 Proposal for a vacant lot on East 163rd Street recreates the classic New York City stoop as hub to engage neighbours with play and programming and invites the community to shape the long-term vision of the space. Photomontage courtesy of BD FELIZ, and photograph courtesy of Urban Design Forum and Van Alen Institute.

The outcomes of the *South Bronx Community Gardens Activation* project include the implementation of a comprehensive reimagining of the physical environment and use of Banana Kelly's gardens to support efforts to build social infrastructure through community organizing and other services including communication campaigns for the area's residents (see Figures 9.3 to 9.5). Table 9.2 presents the project at a glance.

Findings

The two cases we discuss in this chapter add to an evolving body of research that aims to capture the design community's response to the mid- to long-term strategies for a post-pandemic world (Rossi et al., 2020). This section presents insights from the salient themes that emerge from our analyses across both projects. We connect our insights with the literature and theorize about a few considerations that have generalizable lessons for the design community as we move past the crisis.

Design agency and the design for social innovation lens

Design has always been a way of engaging with the world around us. With the global shutdown in 2020, the concept of design agency as a form of action connecting

Figure 9.4 April 2021 clean-up day led by Banana Kelly community organizers to prepare a recently acquired vacant lot as a participatory stage for temporary design interventions and neighbourhood programming. Photograph courtesy of Banana Kelly Community Improvement Association, and poster design courtesy of BD FELIZ.

to the core of our social lives suddenly took on a new purpose. As these cases highlight, design's capacity to foster social cohesion within the unfolding experience of the pandemic in New York can be characterized less as solutionism but as a more expansive notion of design considered as 'social sensitivity (. . .) and a proposition of tangible values and aspirations' (Adams et al., 2021, p. 1).

The *Family Pockets by Sour* and *South Bronx Community Gardens Activation* projects applied highly dynamic co-design processes and consensus-building methodologies (see Table 9.4). In this sense, they both attempt to intervene with tangible artefacts and services in complex social dynamics to shape conversations about 'making things happen' (Manzini, 2014). As a result and from a theoretical perspective, we situate both projects in the design for social innovation field, a maturing constellation of relational design practices that are oriented towards

Figure 9.5 Vibrant mural designs bring colour to the College Avenue Garden and a visual identity that unites all Banana Kelly's community gardens, activating existing wall and ground planes while featuring designated space for youth to leave their mark. Photomontage courtesy of BD FELIZ, and photograph courtesy of Urban Design Forum and Van Alen Institute.

processes of social change (Bund et al., 2013; Manzini, 2014; Amatullo et al., 2016, 2021). Within this framework, three sub-themes surface from the cases' interviews, which point to manifestations of design agency that are not necessarily novel but seem to have arisen with renewed force and consequential implications.

Making the abstract tangible

As the testimonials culled from our interviews demonstrate (Table 9.3), the ability designers have to conceive, envision and plan by turning ideas into material and tangible outputs through tried and true techniques such as visualization and prototyping (Valentine, 2013), and communicate among diverse stakeholders (Björgvinsson et al., 2012), emerge as particularly valuable forms of agency in both projects. Bearing witness to the many real-time transformations the pandemic forced upon everyone, with a particular toll on marginalized populations, gave the design teams in these projects a front-row seat 'to put things together and bring new things into being' (Schön, 1983) and amplify reflexive practices within the newfound constraints of working in remote circumstances. The ability to listen and mediate with

Table 9.3 Design Agency and the Design for Social Innovation Lens

Sub-themes	Family Pockets	South Bronx Community Gardens
Making the abstract tangible	'design has the ability to turn [insights] into something tangible by creating a three dimensional response. (…) this ability manifests through the careful folding in of insights (…) into prototypes' (project lead)	'here is real know how (…) about these very technical design questions, (…) that makes it possible to go from having an idea (…) to actually know what to buy and how to build it' (project convener)
	'Designers have this power to create something that can be perceived and used by the masses. It was crucial for us to create something physical as we found ourselves in an increasingly digital world' (project lead)	'The Miro board the design team had put together, its beautiful organisation and the visualization of strategy really moves these kinds of projects forward in a way that adds value' (project convener)
Designers as catalysts	'The power of design lies in both the digital and the physical. Designers can quickly sketch and illustrate ideas, providing a user with an image of what a solution might look like. That is very powerful' (project lead)	'The goal was for design to take up a catalytic role in the reactivation of these spaces by bringing together technical design expertise with Banana Kelly's community organizing work' (designer)
	'User and co-ideation sessions allow us to gain immediate feedback. In that sense, designers have a great power through creating different mediums of communication' (project lead)	'Design can't do everything. (…) But it is good at synthesising and providing the glue between things' (designer)
	'the delivery of the research prompts and the content we gathered were all visual and leaned on design to communicate and convey' (design researcher)	'Design as a coordinating medium bringing together all sorts of different factors, different disciplines, different perspectives and opinions, and different kinds of expertise' (designer)

Design and power dynamics	'Quotes received in interviews/discussions throughout the diary studies were very insightful for the design decisions. Executing it through WhatsApp enabled moms to respond to prompts whenever it works best for them' (project lead)	'Banana Kelly's central goal for the Neighborhoods Now project was to use the process of design to connect and engage residents and build power; a key word here being "process"' (designer)
	'We underestimate children's capacity to collaborate, when properly communicated, children have shown tremendous understanding of family needs and were very willing to collaborate' (project lead)	'Our work was focused on using the process of design to build up both physical and social infrastructures that will support community organizing, build power, and reactivate programming' (designer)
	'Sometimes digital platforms can be even more inclusive in terms of reaching more geographies and including participants who might otherwise be hesitant to get involved' (design researcher)	

tangible outputs the community-led visions that arose through the different phases of research and prototyping with mothers and children in the case of *Family Pockets*, and with the residents of the South Bronx in the case of the *Community Gardens Activation* project, evidence an important dimension of design agency that appears to have been leveraged successfully in both projects.

Designers as catalysts

Both cases confirm designers' capacity to propel change and act as catalysts to help communities see new possibilities in concrete ways (see Table 9.3); this is an important sub-theme and manifestation of design agency that emerges from these projects. The design research probes and prototypes deployed by the design teams sparked creativity and created forward momentum for community-led innovation. As examples of 'fourth-order' design (Buchanan, 1992), both projects also showcase the experience of designers who are primarily acting as facilitators of organizational processes and asking questions of value and principle, working to identify challenges, meet social needs and create new social relations for positive transformation.

Design and power dynamics

The final dimension of design agency that stands out in both cases is the notion of how power dynamics played out in the context of remote design research and virtual interactions (see Table 3). At the heart of the definition of power is one's ability to influence an outcome or an action. A fundamental aspect of design and participation is relational: it is about building relationships of mutual respect – and trust – with stakeholders, 'making power' in solidarity (Blomberg and Karasti, 2012; Costanza-Chock, 2018). On-the-ground work with communities is how designers typically engage in co-design processes. The shift to remote was, in this sense, quite foreign and unexpected at first. As the testimonials from the designers in these projects attest, many barriers to participation and access were never overcome, especially with some of the more marginalized communities in the *South Bronx Community Gardens Activation* project. That said, the remote circumstances also contributed at times to make more visible, ever-present power-laden dynamics that can often go unnoticed in design for social innovation projects when designers descend into a community as the 'experts'. The blended media techniques used in *Family Pockets* proved an effective source for experimentation that amplified participation (e.g. giving users the chance to make their voices heard asynchronously on their own time). These and other examples reveal the silver lining of the going remote situation: the generation of a sense of heightened trust among the designers versus non-designer relationships (see Table.3), which in some cases resulted in increased stakeholder participation.

Impact of Covid-19 on design research and co-design processes

Community-led modes of research and engagement

Overnight, the pandemic impacted the work of design professionals at all levels of their knowledge production – from research, ideation to prototyping and testing. The crisis forced everyone to flex, adapt and stand up to new working modes to meet the new demands.

At times, this meant adopting a digital-first approach, for example as with *Family Pockets*, where the team opted for digital ethnography conducted via WhatsApp instead of onsite research. Other times, it required adapting existing methods to a virtual context: for example, shifting onsite meetings to Zoom and revisiting analogue research methods for the new virtual environment.

The co-design ethos and participatory design research techniques that highlight the creativity of designers and people not trained in design working together in the design development process (Sanders et al., 2008) are core to both of our projects (Table 9.4). The circumstances of Covid-19 pushed designers to think hard about stakeholder participation and effective engagement in the design process. Perhaps one of the most promising learnings post-pandemic will be to assess how much of the virtual environment became a constraining force in terms of access to participation as opposed to how it may have unlocked new spaces for imagining and realizing empowering processes of collaboration that put communities in the driver's seat of influence and decision making. Some of our insights from the *South Bronx Community Gardens Activation* project highlight the latter dimension of empowerment, one that emerged out of the pandemic's adversity. Specifically, Michael Van Valkenburgh Associates's (MVVA) intention to plan and publicize their community meetings to engage constituencies in design through various digital modes pretty much failed, with poor stakeholder turnout. MVVA had to pivot with a 'train the trainers model'. By purposely designing capacity-building tools for community organizers to lead visioning and outreach exercises within their residents, instead of designing new and separate activities they would have controlled as the experts, MVVA made their participants lead the process and leveraged existing community engagement programmes from Banana Kelly to cull insights.

The digital as barrier

While digital technologies had already dramatically reshaped the design industry pre-pandemic, the sudden necessity to implement projects from start to finish in an all-remote manner surfaced new challenges, particularly concerning access. A number of factors such as 'Zoom Fatigue', the increased reliance and time spent on videoconferencing and poor digital literacy posed inclusion challenges (Bailenson,

Table 9.4 Impact of Covid-19 on Design Research and Co-design Processes

	HeyMama	South Bronx Community Gardens
The digital as co-design innovation source	'diary studies gave great insight into families day-to-day; through the daily prompts we have shared with them via WhatsApp, and by capturing responses or activities via photos and videos, we were able to gather on the spot/authentic feedback' (project lead)	'when traditional in-person outreach was less viable, our team had to be creative both in how we worked with each other and in how we involved the community' (designer)
	'digital platforms can be even more inclusive in terms of reaching more geographies and including participants who might otherwise be hesitant to get involved' (design researcher)	'Moving between mediums allowed us to be safe and acknowledges the different ways COVID affected the way we communicate and engage with one another. (. . .) while we are used to running community meetings, these changed conditions led to a huge learning process on our ends' (designer)
	'working with blended media to learn and gain insights was very helpful' (project lead)	
The digital as barrier	'we had to make all our methodologies digital and the implementation remote. (. . .) with children in mind, we needed to ensure that the language in implementing our methodologies was accessible' (project lead)	'We followed a mostly virtual engagement strategy throughout, (. . .) it became more challenging to reach and hear back from people as everyone seemed to experience Zoom fatigue' (designer)
	'There wasn't the same opportunity to just hang out with people in a less unstructured way and gain trust' (design researcher)	'What [Banana Kelly] found to be most successful in reaching people and generating excitement and participation was door-to-door contact, direct calls, and in-person (COVID-safe) community events whenever possible' (designer)

Community-led research and engagement	'[Moms and their children] interviewed each other. First, mom's interviewed their children, then the other way around; they recorded themselves and sent it to us, which I think led to more genuine responses from the children. I'm sure they felt more comfortable with their moms than us' (project lead)	'Early disappointment [with our engagement strategy] led us to pivot and develop tools that would equip Banana Kelly organizers to safely lead visioning and outreach exercises within their own community' (designer)
	'Moms and kids gave feedback that the research prompts they received felt fun, rewarding, and even helped them de-stress and enjoy their days better' (design researcher)	'I think that's part of what we tried to do with the programme was to really to like, build momentum and build capacity for community based partners' (project convener)
	'We used private WhatsApp messages (. . .) so that the moms and kids could participate asynchronously and contribute their content whenever was most convenient to them' (design researcher)	'The engagement provided a push, training, design thinking and all other things necessary to make [this work] happen for a while, far into the future' (designer)

2021). This was the case in *South Bronx Community Gardens Activation* project, where the digital barrier raised ethical and equity-oriented questions (Roberts et al., 2021) that in some instances, only the return to in-person activities in Covid-19-safe environments seem to have alleviated. This is a cautionary tale about the limitations of the virtual environment and is also illustrative of material and literacy barriers that are especially problematic in settings where designers work with socially vulnerable communities.

The digital as co-design innovation source

The empirical insights from these projects highlight a new frontier of co-design innovation happening in the virtual environment that the pandemic nurtured, undoubtedly one of the silver linings of the crisis. As mounting research confirms, the design community embraced digital modes of communication and socializing under Covid-19 that may represent opportunities and important learnings moving forward (Li et al., 2020; Roberts et al., 2021).

The *Family Pockets* project team chose to experiment with a blended-media approach from the start, harnessing the innovative potential of digitally facilitated co-design and research. Hoping to elicit explicit and tacit knowledge that would allow the design team to gain a thorough understanding of the everyday reality of working moms, they opted for digitally facilitated diary studies integrating different media formats. These included written communication formats, sketching and drawing exercises and video recordings. The pandemic gave the team no choice but to integrate these tools given the sheer impossibility of conducting in-person research at users' homes face-to-face. Surprisingly, the design team's agility and improvisation in expanding their repertoire of methods generated new flexibility for participants vis-à-vis their schedules, increasing the engagement rate, with, for example, mothers enlisting their children in the design process with strong results (Table 9.4).

Limitations/further directions for future research

One area we have touched only in passing but which merits future research resides in inquiry about the long-term, transformational impact the pandemic may have in our design, use and perception of space (Honey-Rosés et al., 2020). One key potentiality that both cases in this chapter foreground is the opportunity of interrogating space as a consequence of Covid-19, and how the pandemic's lessons may be further leveraged to design more equitable, greener and healthier cities. A second front for ongoing study relates to the nested social questions that emerge from the disparity that the pandemic has laid bare and the responsibility designers have to contribute to inclusive and systemic solutions for community building and well-being.

Conclusion

The window that Covid-19 has pried open in the United States presents an opportunity to reflect anew about the agency of designers in society and their capacity to contribute long-term recovery solutions that may alleviate structural disparities that have arisen over many decades. The two cases we present in this chapter point to outcomes underway that make evident successful recovery will require systemic approaches, actionable execution plans and multi-stakeholder expertise along with design agency. Both projects give us reason to hope that designers will take the lessons from the barriers they have overcome and the opportunities they have seized during these extremely trying times and ensure they are 'here to stay' enabling services and environments that will help us build healthier and more equitable communities for all.

References

Adams, B., Marenko, B., & Traganou, J. (2021). Design in the pandemic: Dispatches from the early months. *Design and Culture*, 13(1), 1–8.

Amatullo, M., Boyer, B., Danzico, L, May, J., & Shea, A (eds) (2016). *Leap Dialogues: Career Pathways in Design for Social Innovation*. Pasadena, CA: Designmatters at ArtCenter College of Design.

Amatullo, M., Boyer, B., May, J., & Shea, A., (eds) (2021). *Design for Social Innovation: Case Studies from Around the World*. Abingdon, Oxfordshire: Routledge.

Bailenson, J. (2021). Nonverbal overload: A theoretical argument for the causes of zoom fatigue. *Technology, Mind, and Behavior*, 2(1).

Blomberg, D.J., & Karasti, H. (2012). Ethnography: Positioning ethnography within participatory design. In *Routledge International Handbook of Participatory Design*. Abingdon, Oxfordshire: Routledge, 106–36.

Bund, E., Hubrich, D.K., Schmitz, B., Mildenberger, G., & Krlev, G (2013). Blueprint of Social Innovation Metrics: Contributions to an Understanding of Opportunities and Challenges of Social Innovation Measurement. A deliverable of the project: "The theoretical, empirical, and policy foundations for building social innovation in Europe" (TEPSI). European Commission 7th Framework Programme, Brussels: European Commission, DG Research.

Björgvinsson, E., Pelle, E., & Hillgren, P.A. (2012). Design things and design thinking: Contemporary participatory design challenges. *Design Issues*, 28(3), 101–16.

Buchanan, R. (1992). Wicked problems in design thinking. *Design Issues*, 8(2), 7–35.

Charmaz, K.C. (2006). *Constructing Grounded Theory: A Practical Guide Through Qualitative Analysis*. Thousand Oaks, CA: Sage.

Costanza-Chock, S. (2018). Design Justice: towards an intersectional feminist framework for design theory and practice. In C, Storni, K. Leahy, M. McMahon, P. Lloyd, & E. Bohemia (Eds.), *Design as a Catalyst for Change - DRS International Conference 2018*, 25-28 June, Limerick, Ireland. https://doi.org/ 10.21606/drs.2018.679.

Cross, N. (1982). Designerly ways of knowing. *Design Studies*, 3(4), 221–7.

Eisenhardt, K.M. (1989). Building theories from case study research. *The Academy of Management Review*, 14(4), 532–50.

Gehl, J. (2011). *Life Between Buildings: Using Public Space*. Washington, DC: Island Press.

Honey-Rosés, J., Anguelovski, I., Chireh, V.K., Daher, C., Konijnendijk van den Bosch, C., Litt, J.S., Mawani, V., McCall, M.K., Orellana, A., Oscilowicz, E., Sánchez, U., Senbel, M., Tan, X., Villagomez, E., Zapata, O., & Nieuwenhuijsen, M.J. (2020). The impact of COVID-19 on public space: An early review of the emerging questions – Design, perceptions and inequities. *Cities & Health*, S263–S279.

JungHo, P. (2021). Who is hardest hit by a pandemic? Racial disparities in COVID-19 hardship in the U.S. *International Journal of Urban Sciences*, 25(2), 149–77.

Leonard, H.B., Howitt, A.M., & Giles, D.W. (2020). Crisis Management for Leaders Coping with COVID-19. Boston: Harvard Kennedy School. https://www.hks.harvard.edu/sites/default/files/centers/research-initiatives/crisisleadership/files/PCL_Crisis-Management-for-COVID_Web20200428.pdf (accessed 28 July 2021).

Li, J., Ghosh, R., & Nachmias, S. (2020). In a time of COVID-19 pandemic, stay healthy, connected, productive, and learning: Words from the editorial team of HRDI. *Human Resource Development International*, 23(3), 199–207.

Manzini, E. (2014). Making things happen: Social innovation and design. *Design Issues*, 30(1): 57–66.

Perry, B.L., Aronson, B., & Pescosolido, B.A. (2021). Pandemic precarity: COVID-19 is exposing and exacerbating inequalities in the American heartland. *Proceedings of the National Academy of Sciences*, 118(8). https://www.pnas.org/doi/epdf/10.1073/pnas.2020685118.

Roberts, J., Kessa, P., Alexandra, E., & Richards, M.P. (2021). It's more complicated than it seems: Virtual qualitative research in the COVID-19 Era. *International Journal of Qualitative Methods*. https://www.tandfonline.com/doi/epdf/10.1080/23748834.2020.1780074?needAccess=true&role=button.

Rossi, E., Di Nicolantonio, M., Ceschin, F., Mincolelli, G., dos Santos, A., Kohtala, C., Jacques, E, Cipolla, C., & Manzini, E. (2020). Design contributions for the COVID-19 global emergency (part 1): Empirical approaches and first solutions. *Strategic Design Research Journal*, 13(3), 294–311.

Rossi, E., Di Nicolantonio, M., Ceschin, F., Mincolelli, G., dos Santos, A., Kohtala, C., Jacques, E., Cipolla, C., & Manzini, E. (2020). Design contributions for the COVID-19 global emergency (part 2): Methodological reflections and future visions. *Strategic Design Research Journal*, 14(1), 2021.

Sanders, E.B.N., & Stappers, P.J. (2008). Co-creation and the new landscapes of design. *CoDesign*, 4(1), 5–18.

Schön, D.A. (1983). *The Reflective Practitioner: How Professionals Think in Action*. New York City: Basic Books.

Strauss, A., & Corbin, J.M. (1997). *Grounded Theory in Practice.* Thousand Oaks, CA: Sage.

Valentine, L. (2013). *Prototype: Design and Craft in the 21st Century*. London: Bloomsbury.

Yin, R.K. (2009). *Case Study Research: Design and Methods*. (4th Ed.). Thousand Oaks, CA: Sage.

10 Design for a post-pandemic world

Embedding business resilience through design

BOYEUN LEE, ELISAVET CHRISTOU AND DAVID HANDS

The impact of Covid-19 to traditional business structures

The contemporary business environment is witnessing considerable change and uncertainty and as a result, organizations – regardless of size and market activity – have become increasingly vulnerable to external forces and market disruptions. Furthermore, set against the backdrop of Covid-19 and the massive challenges that it has presented to organizations and society, a radical reappraisal of established business models and organizational systems is urgently required. Organizations and governments around the world have realized that they were not adequately prepared for a global pandemic and that they had to reactively improvise their crisis response strategies due to their crisis response capabilities being too rigid and inflexible. Alongside this unprecedented event, globalization and the deregulation of trade and global markets have equalized organizational competitive environments in terms of access to human resource, information and technological expertise (however, some industry sectors have been disproportionately affected, such as hospitality and aviation). In order to remain competitive in these unpredictable times, organizations have had to continually reinvent themselves through reappraising their structures, systems and strategic objectives. Organizational agility and resilience is the new mantra influencing boardroom decision-making activities, where contingency and adaptability need to be woven into the fabric of the organization. As we move into an era of extreme uncertainty, organizations are operating in extremely turbulent and dynamic market forces – many of which are beyond their control.

We are witnessing an increasing pace of technological and market developments, coupled with increased customer demands and expectations. In today's ever increasingly crowded marketplaces, organizations (regardless of size) cannot afford to be complacent in the delivery of their products and services – competitiveness and agility are now a commercial imperative and a prerequisite for long-term survival. It is widely acknowledged that the best route to commercial success is offering consumers products and services that exceed their expectations, and at the heart of this is the creation and delivery of value-added products driven by innovation. These value-added products and services are the end result of a set of complex and interrelated processes intelligently managed by the organization. In turbulent environments, in which organizations are currently functioning – and undoubtedly will be functioning for the foreseeable future – design remains a crucial value opportunity for the inspiration of creativity and the ability to formulate quick responses to latent market challenges. Central to the issue of organizational agility to respond to unforeseen market dynamics is that of size and organizational structure that may hinder the ability to respond to unforeseen external forces. At one end of the spectrum, SMEs can usually function with a single manager at the top, directing resource and vision in response to shifting market demands. At the opposite side of the spectrum are large multinational organizations whereby the divisions of functions and human resource sit beneath many layers of hierarchy and decision making. Consequently, senior managers and decision makers in large organizations are often far removed from the point of delivery – be it a product or a service; or frequently, both. Furthermore, they are likely to have limited understanding of day-to-day operational issues, customer needs and quality difficulties, unless they make a specific point of gaining first-hand experience of customer interactions.

This public health crisis has led to abrupt changes not only in daily routines and livelihoods but also in the way organizations in all sectors do business around the globe. The organizations have been affected in nearly every aspect of business activity: how companies engage and interact with their customers, how supply chains deliver products and services, how the employer/employee relationship and the business ecosystem are reconfigured and how customers choose and purchase them. In some countries where the vaccination roll-out has progressed faster, the phases of the Covid-19 pandemic have been progressing from reaction, adaptation and recovery to resilience. In each phase, organizations have made distinctive strategic decisions to bring on recommencing future state. Some of the reaction-related activities have been to keep employees safe and prioritize operating essential business functions. During the adaptation and recovery phases, companies have considered transforming their business process and strategy for the new normal from the perspective of business longevity. Change is inevitable and as such, organizations need to be proactive and agile in order to respond to unforeseen challenges that may lie ahead. In stable, predictable market environments, change is incremental and can be accommodated for; however, 2020 witnessed a seismic change that fundamentally transformed the business landscape – the global pandemic Covid-19. Widespread shutdowns of commercial enterprises, restrictions in the movement of people both within and beyond national borders have affected virtually every sector of organizational and industrial life. Established business models and organizational practices have undergone dramatic reappraisal in how we work, consume and lead our daily lives. Emerging from the ongoing chaos of Covid-19 has necessitated innovations in the development, delivery and consumption of products and services.

Anderson et al. (2021) based in the influential Pew Research Center, USA, undertook a research study to anticipate life following Covid-19, to consider what life will be like in 2025 in the wake of the outbreak of the global pandemic and other crises in 2020. Some 915 innovators, developers, business and policy leaders, researchers and activists responded. Their broad and nearly universal view is that people's relationship with technology will deepen as larger segments of the population come to rely more on digital connections for work, education, health care, daily commercial transactions and essential social interactions.

While most organizations across industries have struggled from a long term and far-reaching negative impact of the pandemic, this crisis has ironically shed new light on the values of embracing digital solutions and creating a landscape of encouraging continuous innovation. In addition to global pandemics, there are more subtle and discrete changes that are continually arising (for some these are opportunities, for others – distinct threats), namely that of the rise of Big data, IoT and AI that are transforming established marketplaces. Many leading companies have developed and strengthened their business models over many decades, but the shift to IoT is often more challenging for them. From tennis rackets to coffee machines, IoT has the potential to create endless disruptive innovations, often in a plethora of unforeseen business segments. Tony Shakib, Global IoT business acceleration leader at Microsoft Azure, believes that we are at an inflection point where some companies are taking investment in IoT infrastructure seriously, allowing them to capture meaningful data, and integrate it into their workflow management systems. He points out: 'Gradually we're crossing from the experimental phase to mass adoption.' He explains, 'Once we get there, we'll see real change. Once you start connecting devices and using data intelligently, the amount of innovation you can do becomes exponential' (IoT Business News, 2020). History can provide us with many examples of organizations and commercial enterprises that had failed to keep pace with market developments, the same could happen again to organizations that fail to embrace the digital revolution. Emerging technologies can prove beneficial to any organization, regardless of their expertise, prestige and heritage, as it provides companies with the tools to shift away from traditional manufacturing and traditional business models to a fertile landscape of interconnected devices, services and holistic systems. According to several business reports, the use of digital enablers and disruptive technologies has become a top business priority. Sixty-seven per cent of the surveyed companies participating in KPMG's 2020 global survey have accelerated their digital transformation strategy as a result of Covid-19 (KPMG, 2020).

The coronavirus crisis and subsequent national lockdowns have led to the majority of the customers having to move to online channels where nearly everything has become 'untact (no contact)' or 'ontact (contact online)'.

Historically, designers (and indeed, enlightened commissioners of design) have played an important role in creating innovative solutions when barriers and challenging circumstances are present. They are equipped with skills and mindset through which they could develop and deliver distinctive value propositions to their customers. The only difference since the outbreak of the pandemic is that we need more focus on the touchpoints in the digital instead of the physical world.

The following two sections discuss business cases of embracing digital tools and technologies, specifically data, AI and robots, along with their benefits and challenges.

The authors also discuss the role and value of designers in accelerating recovery and business prosperity during periods of extreme complexity and uncertainty. The authors' aspiration for this chapter is for it to act as a guide for designers and businesses who are working to overcome the crisis and to also help them build resilience for potential future threats.

Business transformations: The move to online virtual spaces

Businesses fostering digital transformation

Over the last decades, businesses have leveraged emerging technologies, which have played a critical role in carrying innovation. For example, the construction toys company, LEGO, has been known as an inspiring example of successful digital transformation. LEGO has been focusing for a long time on physical toys and has been hesitant to embrace new technologies until the company started to struggle with attracting customers with a growing interest in computer games. After coming close to bankruptcy in 2004, the company restructured its business by launching new digital-based products such as movies, mobile games and mobile applications. Now LEGO has its own crowdsourcing platform where customers can upload their ideas for physical products that can be launched commercially. In addition, LEGO has launched a new series of kits called 'Mindstorm' that includes sensors with which customers can build a structure and code software to develop their own robots. To support customers create their own robots, LEGO has expanded their business to 'Lego Education'.

The process of digital transformation of society, economy and culture has been taking place for almost two decades now. The Covid-19-related lockdowns have resulted in organizations competitively shifting their business activities to digital spaces or delivering new digital services, which align with their specialities. This can be viewed as one bright side to the pandemic as businesses have shown outstanding creativity to thrive by transforming themselves unexpectedly during times of crisis. The following sections discuss several business cases that have successfully utilized digital tools, from simply providing the same value proposition online to more actively leveraging big data, AI and robots in their business.

Digital transformations

A number of small- and medium-sized businesses in the northwest UK area have gone digital to adapt to Covid-19-related changes. Temple Yoga is one local business in Lancaster, UK that pivoted to an online model due to Covid-19. The company could not safely offer in-person yoga class, but the customers believed that yoga will help maintain their physical and mental well-being while dealing with the lockdown's uncertainty and isolation. Thus, they started to provide Zoom classes which enables the company to keep its services to existing customers while shifting its business to a subscription model. The entertainment industry has also been disrupted, being encouraged to shift towards virtual environments. For example, Emeraude Escape, a Paris-based escape room company, created online escape rooms, which can be customized and are offered in five different formats of design. Digital tools allow the company to deliver their service in a new way that is still relevant to their offerings and target audience. Companies that moved to online business models can run more efficiently and they can reach more customers without physical restrictions. As we can see from the two cases, institutions and organizations of all types try digital platforms; the fitness industry now provides virtual sessions on streaming services, both live and pre-recorded, and the entertainment industry created new game products in a digital space. Shifting to an online business model can be the first step forward towards digital transformation, but some companies in finance, retail and food industries move forward even further.

Traditionally, people who use bank services have been relying on physical visits to local branches for financial advice and support. However, as a number of bank branches had to close for health safety reasons during the Covid-19 lockdowns, there has been a steep increase in customers using online banking. TSB bank, a retail and commercial bank in the United Kingdom, has added a 'Smart Agent' feature to their website during the Covid-19 pandemic. A combination of a chatbot and live agent helps customers to ask questions and receive answers 'live' from the personnel. Through this new function, TBS bank is better connected to and continues to help their customers and free up the bank's employees, offering customers in-branch interactions with the duty of care to keep them safe. TSB has accelerated the digital transformation of business activities in direct response to the coronavirus pandemic, transforming a large number of offline forms into electronic forms. It ensures customers' safety while making the service accessible at home. Adobe XD, a prototyping tool for user experience and interaction design, played a significant role for the company to create seamless and intuitive end-to-end journeys for bank employees and customers. This advanced design tool enabled TBS not only to launch a number of vital forms online in under a week, but also to deliver a great digital experience for business customers in the long term. The European bank is another case in the financial industry that has digitized their core service offerings within eight weeks since the pandemic outbreak.

During lockdowns, it was easy to see the warning signs at the high street shop windows (Figure 10.1). The traditional security industry business models have been disrupted by Covid-19 and have been switched to novel business models with a strong emphasis on embracing digital technology. One example is the Keyholding Company (KHC), the UK's alarm-response specialist. While there has been a national and regional lockdown over the UK, the business has been pushed to be less reliable for keeping the clients' property secure based on physical interactions. This is because with many businesses closed, the company no longer needed to lock and unlock buildings on behalf of the personnel. However, the clients were

Figure 10.1 Most stores put burglary warnings at the windows when they have to shut.

still concerned about whether empty properties could stay locked and secured. As such, the KHC offered data-driven security solutions, including touch-free entrances, remote building management systems, an app-based keyless solution and smart locks. Based on the digitally driven access control systems, KHC can analyse data on potential risks. While the pandemic has been challenging for all businesses it has also highlighted many opportunities in digital technology adoption for maximum quality of service. The key to accelerating digital transformation is through driving a better consumer experience using a flexible digital platform while making being agile, a priority.

Increasing prevalence of non-human interactions and use of robots/AI

Leveraging AI has been transforming the brand experience with customers being more connected and satisfied. The travel industry has been particularly affected by the pandemic. EasyJet, a British airline group, tried to minimize the blow by launching trials of 'Epax'. Epax is a new inflight digital retail solution, developed by Gategroup, an airline retail and catering specialist, in partnership with Black Swan Data who specialized in AI. It allows inflight customers to browse, order and buy from inflight retail ranges while minimizing physical contact with equipment or material onboard. Using machine learning algorithms and data on customers, offerings that are more relevant are being recommended to them. While the flight attendants have more difficulties handling travelling in Covid-19, the platform minimizes the cabin crew contact with passengers and provides passengers with an improved travel experience (Inflight, 2020).

Retail is another industry that struggled to make a breakthrough during the lockdown period. Levi Strauss & Co., a leading American denim brand, has implemented artificial intelligence, machine learning and data science to improve customer experience and help. The Covid-19 pandemic accelerated a data-driven approach and AI to enhance operational efficiencies over a creative and imaginative design process. The AI team helps designers and planners by using product images to predict demand for new products based on computer vision. It can predict the demand for the new products based on comparing similarities between specific designs sold in the past and new designs that have never been sold. For a company with significant brand power like Levi's, AI technology does not only predict demand, but it also sets trends. For example, the balloon jeans designed using AI became the post-pandemic trend. Moreover, AI enables Levi's to enhance and expand customer experience even further, deepening the connections with them and improving the existing loyalty programme 'RedTab'. Until recently, the company only knew about its customers through information collected during the transaction process. However, with more data available, Levi's now creates customers' profiles and predicts specific benefits in a very personalized way for the members of the RedTab loyalty programme.

One way to revitalize retail businesses is to leverage AI by replacing business activities in physical space to digital channels; the supplementary approach for the businesses to get back to a 'new normal' is to deploy a fully automated machine, a robot. Amidst negating personal contact to avoid the spread of the virus, the physical space remains significant for many businesses, like airlines. British Airways invested in trials of the fully autonomous service robots at Heathrow Terminal 5 to help passengers navigate through the airport (Forbes, 2019). *Bo* and *Mim* were designed and developed by BotsAndUs, a London-based technology company specializing in robotics and artificial intelligence, as a way to enhance customer services in real and public spaces. Both robots work as a unison interacting with customers in multiple different languages. These commercial robots in physical public spaces ensure customers are satisfied and safe from the public health crisis.

The cases described here are only a few among many, but beyond the conditions under the pandemic, investing in robotics and machine learning technology may be considered strategically as it can offer several benefits to many industries: faster work performance with fewer mistakes, having human capital resources for the higher value tasks and identifying and addressing unforeseen areas of waste.

Tensions and challenges of adopting new technologically oriented practices

The pandemic has forced every company from start-ups to enterprises, to prioritize embracing digital tools. Amidst ongoing disruption, change is essential for companies to keep up with shifting trends, which might be changing the conventional business activities permanently. Digital technologies will be continuously evolving, deployed by companies to create innovative breakthroughs. One of the critical benefits that we observed through the cases that adopted digital technologies is the potential to create novel value through being connected to their customers more closely. Companies undergoing new technologically oriented practices have better access to the insight they need because not only life and work has moved online but also the availability of data on varying consumer behaviour and market changes has escalated. While the adoption of digital technologies presents great opportunities, it also presents distinct challenges for businesses. Many businesses have been reluctant to embrace a digital transformation as they would have to face key obstacles, including translating the data into an actionable state; having to invest in the internal capability related to digital transformation and various issues on the system and data privacy, security, ethics and trust. As there are a number of challenges, unsurprisingly, 70 per cent of digital transformations fail (Forbes, 2019). Digital transformation means thorough change in business processes, activities and competencies to fully engage with customers at each touchpoint in the customer experience. This is where the businesses' strategic approach is required, to help overcome challenges and issues based on a user-centred mindset. Design has been always good at solving issues with a designerly way of thinking and doing.

Business resilience: Embedding a design-intense strategy

Return to the basics (design principles similarly applied to digital spaces)

The impact of the pandemic has proven that the organizations going digital strive to deliver the brand experience for their customers and work experience for their employees as expected as before pandemic times. To build business resilience beyond the Covid-19 pandemic, adopting emerging technologies and data-driven innovation is considered more significant than ever before, and this is where designers can contribute as they are equipped with skills to address problems in innovative ways. Designers often critically question and explore a problem area and then fully imagine reaching to creative solutions. Designers' contributions towards accelerating innovation are evident, statistically proved by Design Council (2007) and McKinsey (2018). To prepare for these challenges and the move to the next normal, a set of design principles should be considered not only at the tactical level but also at the strategic level. Through reflecting on the designerly way of thinking and doing can help build business resilience, bring about innovative solutions in adopting emerging technologies, and generate new cultures and processes for collaboration through the crisis. Over the last ten years, design thinking has attracted the attention of senior management professionals, as indicated by the burgeoning amount of journal articles in management circles. Olsen, Cooper and Slater (2000) argue that design can be translated into competitive advantage through the creation of customer value. Dunne (2011) lends further support to this sentiment by adding 'Designers seek to empathize with users and understand how the user experience appears from their perspective.' Kumar and Whitney (2007) concur by suggesting 'in doing so, they hope to create innovations that appeal to unarticulated needs and can become a source of competitive advantage'. Design as a problem-solving process could be introduced within the organization, being deployed as an alternative means of competitive advantage where traditional methodologies and tools are insufficient in turbulent fast paced markets. Furthermore, where data is either non-existent or insufficient, a design thinking approach to new market opportunities could yield significant results to the company. Management activities and routines in less turbulent markets are often, detailed, analytical and stable, characterized with predictable outcomes – outcomes that frequently cannot satisfy ever demanding market audiences. With strong emphasis on gleaning detailed user insights, design thinking for new business contexts could provide richer criteria for user-centred innovation. Firstly, the vast array of design's ethnographic tools could be applied to the ideation process, supported with input from other business functions, thus fostering a strong multidisciplinary approach to innovation. Often, such ethnographic data collection activities could lead to a 'shift' in perspectives from those taking part, moving from a place of 'judgement' to a place of endless 'possibilities'.

Primarily, building business resilience must be based on customer-centric value creation. Designers must understand the digital literacy of their customers and design the solution accordingly, as it is critically interrelated to digital service adoption and acceptability. The visual languages and interactions should be designed to be intuitive and straightforward in order to be more inclusive for users not familiar with using digital services. The entire customer journey, every step the customers go through in engaging with the service, must be thoroughly considered to deliver a coherent customer experience. Thus, all the online touchpoints should be identical to their physical touchpoints in terms of brand identity. Customer experience should be adopted as a more holistic approach, aligning organizations' strategy, process and cultures around it.

Another critical principle observed by the companies that adopted digital transformation successfully within a short period of time is moving boldly and failing fast, one of the designerly ways of doing and thinking. As digital disruption requires a business to experiment and take risks, Design Sprints could be one tactic to be used as a process of focusing on a specific problem, creating multiple solutions, building prototypes and getting rapid feedback within a short period of time. Digital infrastructure should be built rapidly, connecting front, middle and back offices, incorporating user insights from the first idea until long after the final launch. The primary concepts characterizing the digital platform will be refined while being tested with end-users. Designers' ability is much appreciated here to create a digital product, whether it be a visual representation or working prototypes to the final design. The practice of iterating, testing and learning rapidly should be encouraged across business activities. Consequently, the willingness to experiment and shift business models becomes no longer the most significant barrier for companies responding to chronic digital disruption.

The business process and culture must be prepared to be more collaborative, open and flexible than ever in post-pandemic times. A global pandemic puts enormous stress on embedding digital transformation and shifting business models on organizations regardless of industry and size. Change for a short time may burden the organizations due to the shortage of internal capabilities. Moreover, the problems we face are more complicated with the barriers caused by the virus, so building partnerships and collaborating with governments, stakeholders and competitors is recommended. To nurture a co-creation culture, a top-down approach could be helpful, such as empowering designers to lead the team and train employees to a design mindset. Deploying digital tools and strengthening digital capabilities may also encourage collaboration and open working processes and cultures through digitally being connected with stakeholders and customers.

Now, more than ever, businesses need designers to support and assist in navigating through challenges and complexities and to achieve innovative business solutions. However, there are emergent issues that designers must consider.

Strategic level of intervention instead of tactic level (fourth order design)

One of the best advantages of firms moving forward to digital transformation is to harness big data in terms of business recovering and flourishing. In post-Covid-19 times, market dynamics will be rapidly reshaped throughout the uncertain future and customers' behaviours may not return to before Covid-19 patterns. However, with data automatically collected from their digital platforms, companies can anticipate customers' needs relatively more easily than before. Big data on customers can be automatically collected and then monitored to improve existing services, guide marketing and sales resources towards the right customers and uncover emerging customer needs. This has the potential to bring meaningful value to companies: by meaningful value here we mean, satisfying customers through interpreting data into insights for the products or services. However, there are a number of challenges designers have to consider when creating data-driven digital platforms.

The proliferation of cyber security threats is one of the critical challenges that businesses should be prepared for and build resilience in the current environment. Trust, privacy, security and ethics are key priorities for organizations to create value when adopting emerging technologies. Customers share their personal data with companies to gain benefits while using their services. However, if there is an issue of cyber security, the companies might not only lose customers and their trust, but also lose part of the market share. The Facebook–Cambridge Analytica data scandal is one of the biggest globally known data breach cases. Facebook failed to protect millions of users' personal data, which was used for advertising during the presidential election in 2016. They apologized and informed users which apps had accessed their data and agreed to pay £4 billion to the UK's Information Commissioner's Office (BBC, 2019) (Figure 10.2).

There are design tactics and strategies that could help to prevent these cyber security issues. First, when different devices are interconnected in which users' data is likely to be shared by the companies between the platforms, designers can entitle the way of controlling data privacy to the users. For example, 'Orbit Privacy App' is designed to explore how users configure their privacy settings (Lindley et al., 2018). Although it is a conceptual design through design fiction approach, it triggers businesses and designers to consider how users could deal with data issues (Figure 10.3).

Second, designers can also build trust through providing users with transparent and legible information on the AI. Through the Uncanny AI project led by ImaginationLancaster, design researchers seek how trust can be engendered in

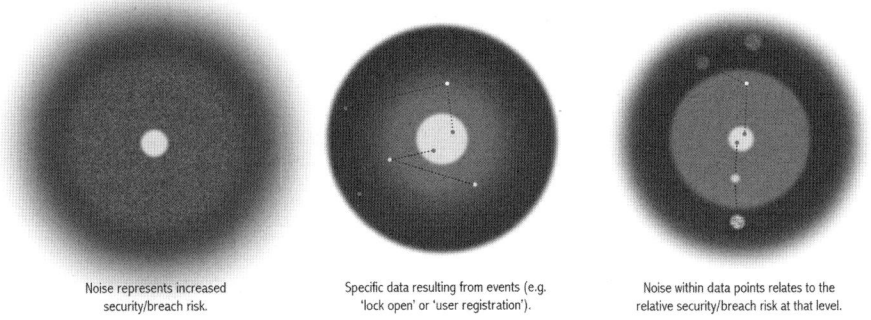

Figure 10.2 Prototype designs extending the core Orbit concept to communicate richer information.

Figure 10.3 A set of icons for legible AI is being tested in a co-creation workshop.

users when Artificial Intelligence is used. To make AI legible, a set of icons is designed with a hope of helping users to better understand and trust the decisions made by AI. As businesses become dependent on data and connectivity, designers need to ensure that 'trust by design' becomes a central component of business activities. The design sector crucially needs to establish design knowledge and implication in deploying data, AI and robotics, helping organizations and value chain actors to meet the market and changing business requirements.

Conclusions

Within a state of extreme uncertainty and constant challenges, organizations are beginning to realize that the old solutions put forward by management consultants are no longer sufficient in order to prosper in the post-pandemic world. In the new market economy where consumers hold considerable purchasing power, the creation of meaningful value is at the forefront of business activities, and businesses are turning towards the design profession for their design thinking skills to foster transformative change. At the beginning of this chapter, the authors introduced the many differing forces that are impacting upon businesses, in particular Covid-19 and the financial devastation that lies in its aftermath; not only to organizations, but to individuals and society as a whole. Turbulent times and uncertainty are placing new challenging demands upon how we act, think and organize our daily lives – this is no different to the organization, regardless of size and areas of operation. We will see tremendous changes in the post-Covid-19 world. Organizations will be keen on creative support, in not only new product and service development but also business transformation. Designers will empower the recovery by supporting the development of distinctive solutions, demonstrating improvements, developing new systems and experiences. Designers should proactively uphold these opportunities to drive business resilience beyond the 'new normal'. The key is continuing to experiment and innovate with customers and other stakeholders. With the design approach, companies may become more agile, more open and more customer centric than before.

References

Anderson, J., Rainie, L., & Vogels, E. (2021). Experts say the 'new normal' in 2025 will be far more tech-driven, presenting more big challenges. Pew Research Center. https://www.pewresearch.org/internet/2021/02/18/experts-say-the-new-normal-in-2025-will-be-far-more-tech-driven-presenting-more-big-challenges/ (accessed 5 March 2021).

BBC (2019). Facebook to be fined $5bn over Cambridge analytica scandal. https://www.bbc.co.uk/news/world-us-canada-48972327.

Design Council (2007). The value of design Factfinder report. https://www.designcouncil.org.uk/fileadmin/uploads/dc/Documents/TheValueOfDesignFactfinder_Design_Council.pdf.

Dunne, D. (2011). User-centred design and design centred business schools. In R. Cooper, S. Junginger, & T. Lockwood (Eds.), *The Handbook of Design Management*. Oxford: Berg, 128–43.

Earle, C (2020) Limitless possibilities: Delivering disruption with IoT, IoT Business News https://iotbusinessnews.com/2020/09/25/98414-limitless-possibilities-delivering-disruption-with-iot/.

Forbes (2019). *The Top Digital Trends for 2019*. Top 10 Digital Transformation Trends For 2019Forbeshttps://www.forbes.com › danielnewman › 2018/09/11.

KPMG International (2020). Going digital, faster. https://emeraude-escape.co.uk/digital-escape-room/.

Kumar, V., & Whitney, P. (2007). Daily life, not markets: Customer-centered design. *Journal of Business Strategy*, 28(4), 46–58.

Lindley, J., Coulton, P., & Akmal, H. (2018). Turning philosophy with a speculative lathe: Object-oriented ontology, carpentry, and design fiction. In C, Storni, K. Leahy, M. McMahon, P. Lloyd, & E. Bohemia (Eds.), *Design as a Catalyst for Change - DRS International Conference 2018*, 25-28 June, Limerick, Ireland. https://doi.org/10.21606/drs.2018.327.

McKinsey & Company (2018). The business value of design. https://www.mckinsey.com/capabilities/mckinsey-design/our-insights/the-business-value-of-design.

Olson, E. M., Slater, S., & Cooper, R. (2000). Managing design for competitive advantage: A process approach. *DMI Journal*, 11(4), 10–17.

Preston, A. (2020). easyJet trials Epax to improve onboard hospitality. Inflight. https://www.inflight-online.com/easyjet-trials-epax-to-improve-onboard-hospitality/.

Further Reading

https://www.internetsociety.org/resources/doc/2019/trust-opportunity-exploring-consumer-attitudes-to-iot/.

https://www.juniperresearch.com/press/retail-spend-on-iot-to-reach-2-5bn-by-2020.

https://imagination.lancaster.ac.uk/project/uncanny-ai/.

11 Moving with the music

Co-designing Jalisco's post-pandemic cultural policy through orchestration

BAS RAIJMAKERS AND MEGAN ANDERSON

Innovation for culture

Joined by various other partners and coordinators, including the British Council Mexico, Aura, Birds of Paradise and advisors from the Policy Lab and Design Council (both in the UK), STBY concluded an ambitious and novel project in the summer of 2021 to encourage a more open and accessible form of cultural policy making in a post-pandemic Jalisco, a coastal state which lies on the Pacific Ocean. Jalisco is one of the thirty-two federal entities of Mexico. We used and experimented with a combination of various co-design methods, including dozens of interviews, community polling, stakeholder mapping, policy timelining and various activities with a group of twenty-five 'ambassadors' – like collaborative workshops, auto-ethnography and speculative fiction. The main deliverables of the project included a set of policy recommendations, crafted with the cultural community of Jalisco and a toolkit-like resource to help others learn from the process and methodology.

In the face of Jalisco's lockdown restrictions, creativity seeped online and the government provided support where it could. As in many other countries, however, the cultural sector in Jalisco was hit particularly hard by Covid-19. The crisis nevertheless acted as a catalyst for cultural institutions and agents to rethink an already struggling sector more strategically. How could things be restructured and reimagined to not simply address the short-term challenges of Covid-19, but also to favour the economic reactivation of a sector that has always been undervalued? Many actors mobilized to address these questions, including those in academia and civil society. Jalisco's government department for culture, Cultura Jalisco, was among these actors and sought to address this question in the most participatory and inclusive way possible. In such unprecedented times, governments are increasingly open to exploring more creative and speculative approaches to policy making (Kimbell and Vesnić-Alujević, 2020). The impact of Covid-19 on the cultural sector thus provided a window of opportunity and sense of urgency to reimagine the future of the sector using a design approach. This is how the *Innovation for Culture* programme was born.

Facilitating a policy co-design programme in the Covid-19 context did not come without its challenges. Participatory design methods in a public sector context usually involve significant amounts of physical, face-to-face interaction. As a Design Research agency, STBY is used to embracing co-design principles like putting people first, communicating visually and inclusively, collaborating, co-creating and iterating, in very physical and tangible contexts (Design Council, DATE). Activities like workshops, community forums and citizen panels are more easily done in physical settings as there are low barriers to technology. Physical settings also provide for higher levels of engagement, trust and empathy building, which are highly valued elements of policy co-design (Bason and Austin, 2019).

Lockdown restrictions made all of this impossible. We were forced to adapt our usual approaches to overcome the barriers presented by Covid-19. While our adaptations came with a number of risks and downsides, we also experimented with and discovered a way of doing policy co-design that has benefits and implications for how this type of work is done in the future, even in non-Covid-19 contexts. Being forced to adapt helped us think about what a blended form of policy co-design might look like and the tools, methods and mindsets needed to involve people in a more designerly way.

There were obvious adaptations that we had to make. Namely, there was a complete shift to online interaction. Communication and collaboration with all stakeholders had to be done virtually. This forced us to upskill in terms of using and adapting new digital collaboration tools to support our work together. Although a struggle at times, the technology itself was relatively easily adaptable and adapted to. The main challenge came in keeping all stakeholders aligned, engaged and harmonious in light of the complexities and uncertainties of the programme and the wider context of a prolonged pandemic. Facilitating a networked policy design process requires not only an adaptation of tools, skills and process, but also one of overall mindset and facilitation style. Over the course of the project, we found it helpful to liken our approach to that of an orchestra. Together, we had to work towards everyone moving with the music.

Orchestration

Design's application to the policy process is 'slowly coming into focus in an unmapped frontier' (Amatullo, 2014). While designers and governments have been applying design principles to public sector services since the 1960s (Sanders and Stappers, 2008; Puttick et al., 2014), the application of design to public policy has only gained momentum since the late 1990s (Bason, 2014; Howlett, 2014). Significant knowledge exists on 'policy' and 'design' as separate concepts but a limited (yet growing) body of literature exists where the two concepts intersect: 'design for policy' or 'policy design' (Bason, 2014; Mintrom and Luetjens, 2016; Blomkamp, 2018). Alongside this gap, there is little guidance from practice in the form of case studies covering aspects like how to facilitate and oversee policy co-design processes. We therefore had to borrow and combine concepts, frameworks and guidance from various disciplines to inform our own approach. Throughout and in reflection upon our own process, we found the concept of orchestration a helpful way to understand how we managed the overall flow of the policy design process and how a diverse group of stakeholders can collectively band and move along to craft policy recommendations.

The concept of orchestration emerged in the literature as a set of activities aimed at the development, management and coordination of actors that are intended to create or extract value from a network of often loosely tied actors (Dhanaraj and Parke, 2006). Orchestration is thus a fundamentally dynamic and uncertain activity, where participation is voluntary and coordination resembles enabling leadership rather than strict management (Ritala et al., 2012). Such coordination respects the specific identities of each actor and tries to ensure that they continue to collaborate fruitfully (Parmentier and Mangematin, 2014). The origin of the concept of orchestration refers to loosely coupled systems (Orton and Weick, 1990) and differs from traditional coordination models due to the lack of an imperative hierarchy (Toigo et al., 2021).

We found orchestration a particularly relevant way to understand and negotiate the complex dynamics of our own policy co-design process. Co-design requires agile, flexible, iterative and networked ways of working and managing that traditional management and leadership models struggle to account for. Furthermore, working at the nexus of policy and design is a constant balancing act. Design is a creative, user-centred approach to problem solving (Christiansen and Bunt, 2014) while policy is a rational approach to problem solving (Junginger, 2014). The ability to understand, negotiate and balance these dynamics is what orchestration is all about.

Orchestration transcends processes and disciplines

Orchestration has become a term to help understand activities which align collaborators, to achieve and maintain harmony between them and to sustain this 'while the music plays' in order to respond to whatever happens in the orchestra or the world around it (Raijmakers et al., 2015). These activities are particularly important when facilitating innovation processes in contexts where many external factors are beyond one's control. The political climate of Jalisco in combination with the Covid-19 context at the time of our project is a case in point.

The nature of the activities that, together, constitute orchestration prevent us from describing it as a design process or innovation model in itself (Raijmakers et al., 2015). There are many models and frameworks that already exist for these. The Design Council's Double Diamond model is perhaps the most known model, which illustrates the diverging and converging design methodology that stakeholders go

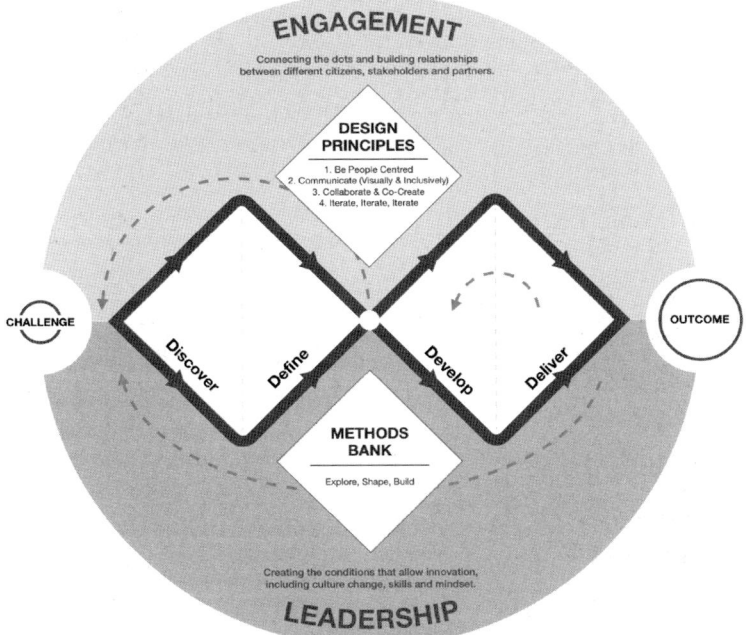

Figure 11.1 As well as highlighting the design process, Design Council's framework for innovation also includes the key principles and design methods that designers and non-designers need to take, and the ideal working culture needed, to achieve significant and long-lasting positive change. We see orchestration as the activity that keeps all of these elements flowing together. Image copyright Design Council 2019.

through to achieve a design outcome (Design Council) (Figure 11.1). The latest iteration of the Double Diamond, the Framework for Innovation, goes beyond this process and also includes the key principles, design methods and working culture that transcend this methodology.

As well as highlighting the design process, Design Council's framework for innovation also includes the key principles and design methods that designers and non-designers need to take, and the ideal working culture needed, to achieve significant and long-lasting positive change. We see orchestration as the activity that keeps all of these elements flowing together.

We see the activities that happen 'between and around' stages like those highlighted in the Double Diamond as orchestration activities. We shy away from using terms like 'management' and 'leadership', specifically in networked and participatory innovation projects where the aim is to distribute power and decision making as much as possible. While leadership and management skills are no doubt needed and valued in these contexts, they do not capture the attitude and mindset that a term like orchestration implies. As such, orchestration also does not bind itself to a specific discipline. In this sense, as an activity, orchestration can be done by people from different backgrounds, and different disciplines can contribute to successful orchestration. As such, orchestration lives between disciplines, rather than being part of a single discipline. Orchestration is as much beyond a discipline as it is beyond process.

Orchestration is a balancing activity

Orchestration has proven to be a very fruitful term to use when we try to understand networked collaboration. This is also true for the complex opportunities and wicked problems, like Covid-19, that our economies and societies are faced with today. But it is not an easy term to use. It is not a clear process that can be explained in a diagram – orchestration is an activity and overarching mindset that consists of several other, related activities that together make innovation projects flow and fly along a non-predefined path.

Design has a key role to play in orchestration. Networked innovation can only be achieved by many disciplines working together, and design has a distinctive, strategic value to offer in this mix. Creating harmony and aligning networks of people and organization are elements of orchestration that happen more easily and with better results when design skills like storytelling, visualizing, speculating and prototyping are used to build common ground and involvement. Typical design activities such as creative workshops clearly help to navigate towards successful outcomes.

Orchestration involves a number of principles that often need to be addressed simultaneously. To keep projects in harmony and flow often feels like a balancing act. Balancing focus on the bigger picture and the smaller details alongside the stakeholders and the content requires an understanding and attunement of four connected, complementary principles of orchestration (Raijmakers et al., 2015):

- Steering processes
- Navigating
- Building common ground
- Building involvement

These principles do not happen in any particular order; they are not steps and nor are they mutually exclusive. They happen simultaneously and are often mutually reinforcing. These are all activities in themselves and orchestration is the activity that keeps these other four moving, connected and in balance. Orchestration is a perpetual movement in addressing complex problems with many stakeholders. Orchestration helps to progress towards a collaborative result that is delivered and can be used, but is not necessarily finished and can evolve over time. This can be visualized as a continuous movement. The remainder of this chapter uses these four principles as a way to reflect on the *Innovation for Culture* project. Finally, we conclude with the introduction of a policy co-design 'playbook' that brings the practices and lessons of the *Innovation for Culture* project together in a format that allows others to benefit from what we learned and try out these evolving practices themselves, in new contexts.

Steering processes

A complex project like *Innovation for Culture* is not predictable and every step that needs to be taken cannot be prescribed. The pandemic further exacerbated that. The best way to respond is to be flexible and agile in managing the project. A major danger that remains is lack of progress. Things like programming events and organizing collaboration help to keep the ball rolling for everyone involved and connect micro-steps into a shared journey. The steering of these kinds of processes is needed to achieve short-term development goals especially when long-term goals are perhaps clear but still broadly defined. At the start of *Innovation for Culture* it was unclear how exactly we would be able to achieve our project goals in the end, more than six months ahead. Steering is focused on short-term goals that are clearer and more precise, for instance when the aim is to create a bit more common ground by investigating a certain issue together. Steering processes can range from facilitating and supporting to directing, depending on the partners involved, the initiatives they have taken already and how far they have progressed in the project, for instance.

Several types of steering are possible and needed. *Innovation for Culture* provided several examples from the way we described our process to participants, to the ways in which we reminded everyone of the progress we were making and how we made our continuous evaluations actionable.

> **A SQUIGGLY FIVE-STAGE PROCESS HELPED US ALL MOVE IN THE SAME DIRECTION TOGETHER**
>
> Five main steps framed the overall journey of the *Innovation for Culture* project: Understanding, Engaging, Exploring issues and opportunities, Validating and prioritizing and finally, Recommending policy. We developed these stages early on in the project, when the need for them became clear as a communication tool rather than a project management tool. The stages were quite fluid, and there was often some overlap between them. Some activities even continued throughout all of the stages, such as 1–1 interviews. While there were blurry lines and some continuous activities throughout, it helped to have a shared overall journey that kept everyone on track. Even though it felt overly simple at times, it helped keep everyone on the same page and proved an essential sense-making tool when things got a bit complex. The visual representation of clear steps and boxes in addition to a squiggly line helped balance the desire for structure and certainty and flexibility amidst uncertainty and was an excellent communication tool (Figure 11.2).

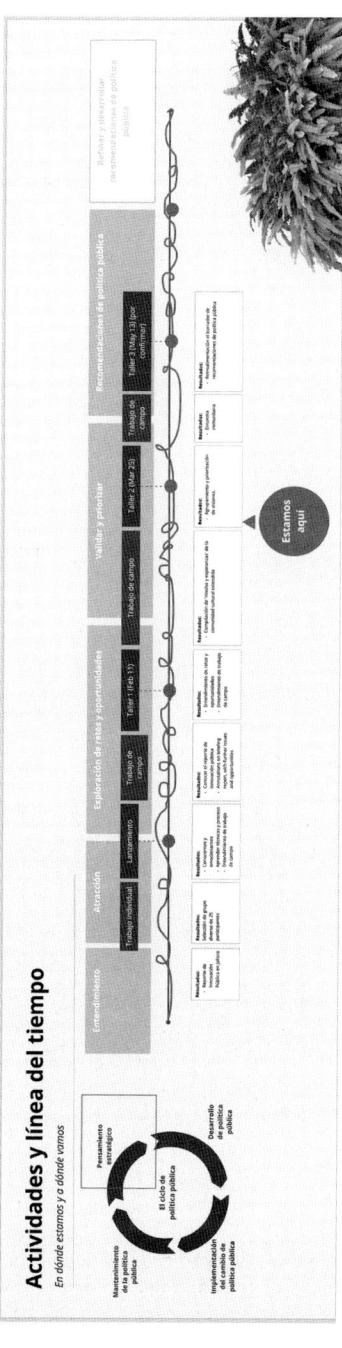

Figure 11.2 Timeline of about four months, describing the five main stages in light blue, and all activities in dark blue. Results are outlined in the white boxes below and the red squiggly line suggests the process is not as linear and boxed-in as it may seem. Image British Council Creative Commons Licence CC-BY-NC-SA 4.0.

WEEKLY CORE-STAKEHOLDER MEETINGS AND REGULAR GROUP WORKSHOPS HELPED KEEP THE PACE

Though project stakeholders could not meet physically due to Covid-19, we met frequently online throughout the project. We met weekly for more than half a year, with a 'core' group of about ten stakeholders to discuss very specific agenda items concerning next steps of the projects. Virtual participatory workshops provided a regular way to discuss both the project trajectory and project content (i.e. policy issues and objectives) with our wider participant group. We devoted at least 15 minutes per workshop to provide for a 'steering' conversation, reminding everyone how far we had progressed on our timeline and what was still to come while allowing time for questions too. Upon reflection, there were moments when the time between workshops felt a bit too long (5–6 weeks) and we were therefore unable to have a steering moment when it was perhaps needed. To correct for this, it would have been wise to adjust the pace of the project to allow for more collective steering with participants (Figure 11.3).

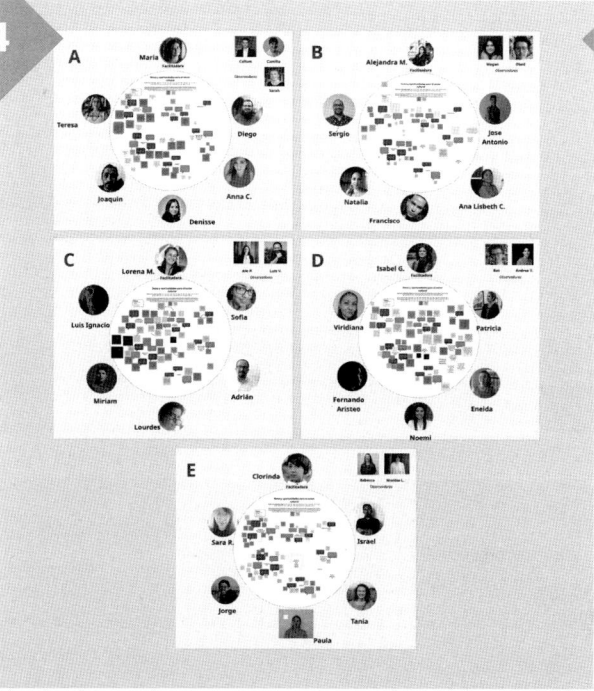

Figure 11.3 Example of a gathering on a virtual whiteboard (we used Miro) during one of the online workshops where we worked around five virtual tables in Zoom and Miro at the same time, with five participants, a facilitator and two observers at each table. Image British Council Creative Commons Licence CC-BY-NC-SA 4.0.

> **EVALUATION WAS FREQUENT BUT LIGHT-TOUCH AND ACTIONABLE**
>
> We used a mix of surveys and 1–1 interviews to get feedback after each session. We also assigned 'observer' roles for each session and had them take notes according to a simple, structured format that related to the surveys. We tried to keep the surveys as light-touch as possible, so as not to burden participants and ensure we were able to quickly integrate their feedback into the planning of future sessions and activities. We were particularly keen to learn about the experiences of those with accessibility requirements and checked-in often to make sure they felt comfortable and supported. While repeated surveys are more efficient and good to keep an overview of general trends, 1–1 conversations are more personal and constructive. Feedback from evaluation activities allowed us to course-correct when needed and make small adjustments in terms of process, content and communication.

Navigating

While steering aptly describes how we supported and guided project activities on a more micro-level and short-term basis, we were well aware that this needed to be balanced with a focus on the bigger picture and overarching objectives of *Innovation for Culture* in the long term. We wanted to avoid that the activities by themselves ran well, but would not amount to any meaningful policy recommendations in the end. Striking this balance was made more difficult by the attention required to adapt many activities that normally would take place in face-to-face settings and rooms with physical materials to working from home during the pandemic. Not seeing the forest from the trees is a bigger risk in a policy co-design context that is more uncertain due to the novelty of the activities and the collaborations. Setting goals and key performance indicators (KPIs) at the start of policy co-design, as we did for *Innovation for Culture*, is not enough to avoid this risk. Constant attention to goals and KPIs during the project is needed as many dynamics, events or stakeholders can easily lead the project off course. Navigation is a crucial activity in an ever-changing and complex environment to get to that dot on the horizon that is the shared goal of a network.

Navigating to a dot on the horizon need not be an abstract activity that we learned during *Innovation for Culture*. Activities we did in workshops, such as envisioning, imagining, prototyping and making, all helped to reiterate our dot on the horizon and make it concrete. Regular consultations of an advisory group we had set up, working with the KPIs and co-creating the public image of *Innovation for Culture* contributed to actively navigating towards our goals as well.

REITERATING THE DOT ON THE HORIZON

Throughout the project, we had to constantly remind ourselves and all stakeholders involved of the overarching objective of the project: to develop a set of policy recommendations for Jalisco's cultural sector using a methodology that was as participatory and open as possible. It was easy to lose sight of these objectives as we dove into the details of the project. Constantly revisiting this dot on the horizon helped frame all of our more detailed activities. At the beginning of each workshop we revisited a process map which provided a visual overview of the main steps of our journey. The final stage was 'develop policy recommendations' and it was clear that this remained our objective throughout. At the same time, we emphasized that the journey to that final outcome might not always be smooth or direct; there would be possible loops or backtracks along the way as we collectively tried to figure things out. We also were transparent about not knowing exactly how to reach that goal step by step at the start. Despite potential detours, this objective remained our dot on the horizon and helped everyone move in the same direction, one activity at a time (Figure 11.4).

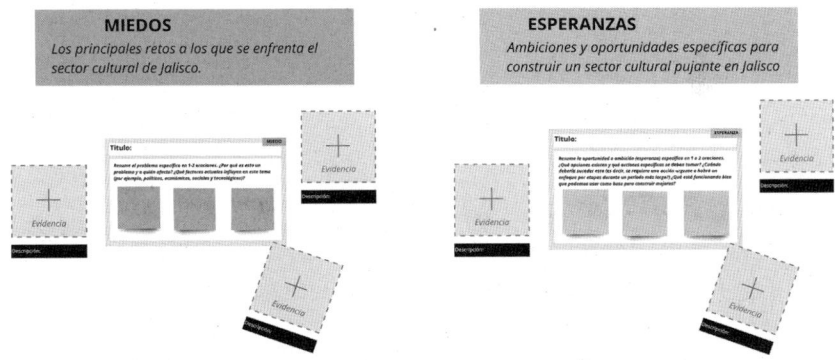

Figure 11.4 One of the activities we designed focused on the hopes (esperanzas) and fears (miedos) of the twenty-five participants for the future of the cultural sector in Jalisco. This required them to look ahead and create 'dots on the horizon' that the policy recommendations we wanted to develop jointly would have to respond to. Image British Council Creative Commons Licence CC-BY-NC-SA 4.0.

CONSULTING AN ADVISORY GROUP TO HELP SEE THE FOREST FROM THE TREES

Sometimes it helps to have a pair of expert fresh eyes to consult throughout a project of this nature. For the *Innovation for Culture* project we had various stakeholders advise us monthly throughout the project. They helped us evaluate the participatory activities to ensure they were helping us meet our objectives in terms of content, methodology and inclusion aspects. They also sat-in on the various workshops as observers. With an understanding of our objectives without the distraction of the messy details, they were able to provide invaluable feedback with regard to the direction we were heading. When situations became tense and overcomplicated, they were able to help us to step-back by providing a bigger-picture perspective. In this way, they held a strong navigating role. We used this approach to identify, and later slightly adjust, the five stages of our journey, for instance, when it became clear we all needed something simplified like that to hold on to during our entire journey.

SETTING KPIS FROM THE GET-GO HELPS TO PRIORITIZE MEANS AND OBJECTIVES

The process of creating KPIs at the beginning of the project helped us define our final destination and the journey there at a level that was not too prescriptive. While the frequent evaluation of these KPIs through surveys and observations helped to steer the project in the right direction in the short term, their sheer presence throughout the project acted as a sort of navigational map to make sure we were constantly revisiting the bigger picture. In 1–1 interviews, we checked the confidence among our participants that their efforts would be noted and make a difference in the end. Subsequent surveys after each major activity also allowed us to see that participants' confidence was indeed growing as we progressed and strong at the end of the project. It is hard for everyone to do this kind of thinking and revisiting, especially those who are deeply involved in building community and involvement. As a result, we had a separate semi-devoted monitoring and evaluation role to make sure the overall objectives remained present in everyone's minds.

MONITORING PUBLIC RESPONSES AND ENGAGING IN THE PUBLIC DEBATE TO CO-CREATE A PUBLIC IMAGE

The cultural sector as a whole, outside our group of participants, needed to be kept on board as well though. *Innovation for Culture* was a very visible and also political project. Cultura Jalisco (Jalisco's ministry of culture) and British

> Council were constantly monitoring responses to *Innovation for Culture* in the media to see if our long-term goals were resonating with the public or needed clarification through an intervention we could make like offering an interview to a newspaper. The Culture Minister who championed the project was replaced halfway through our journey, and we needed to get the new minister on-board with our goals to secure attention and follow-up at the end of our project. At the end of the project British Council organized a two-day online conference with a range of panels and presentations to publicly reflect on the project and frame its activities and results in relation to the original goals.

Building involvement

A crucial activity in policy co-design is building involvement among the participants and even beyond in the cultural sector, in the case of *Innovation for Culture*. The people we selected for our sessions partly represented larger organizations, and others who were participating on a more individual basis often felt they needed to represent others like themselves. Since the pandemic was isolating everyone to a certain extent, working from home and seeing less of colleagues or peers than previously, we had to give some extra attention to building and maintaining these relationships. Successful collaboration relies on personal relationships and on the trust between them. Where no such relationship exists, orchestration can help build these relationships and get the stakeholders that are needed on board. Two levels of trust must exist: level 1 between the individual participants in the network and level 2 between each participant and their organization or peer group, which after all has to deliver on the promises of their representative in the collaborative network. We designed the programme in such a way that between the online workshops via Zoom and Miro, we provided time and activities that all twenty-five participants were asked to do not just themselves but also with their organization or peer group. We called this their 'fieldwork' that allowed all of us to build a wider involvement.

Building involvement was a constant effort during *Innovation for Culture*, from finding the twenty-five participants that acted as 'ambassadors' to putting Equality, Diversity and Inclusion (EDI) at the core, to designing a robust yet intimate online environment, up to creating ownership of policy recommendations towards the end.

> **BUILDING COMMUNITY AND CONFIDENCE NEEDED CONSTANT EFFORT THROUGHOUT**
>
> The people involved in policy co-design make all the difference. Inviting and selecting people requires much attention and is rarely a smooth process along a set path. To get a grip on how we could achieve our goals regarding a di-

versity of unique perspectives of the people involved, and being as inclusive as possible, we made an engagement plan and carefully considered our approach to incentivizing and retaining participants. Offering reasonable payment for the time spent was central to this. Equally important was managing expectations regarding results and change carefully, to build confidence with the group that their efforts would not be in vain. For twenty-five places in the working group (similar to Citizen Advisory Groups) we received about ten times as many applications. This required extensive campaigning and encouragement of people from groups who rarely self apply. Once selected we put considerable effort into creating community by giving ample time for conversation in the (online) sessions. Where the connections between people would emerge quite naturally if we would have been able to bring them into one room, we now had to design the interactions and introductions because all contact was virtual. On the virtual whiteboard that supported all our workshops, we designed a virtual museum where everyone introduced themselves (see Figure 11.5).

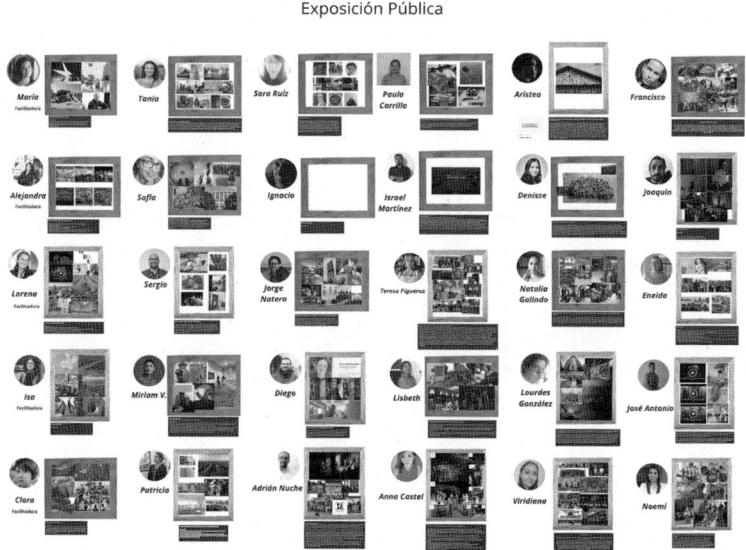

Figure 11.5 The diversity of unique perspectives that the participants brought to the *Innovation for Culture* programme was crucial to its success. We needed to communicate the extent of this diversity to the participants, who largely did not know each other yet. We achieved this by inviting everyone to introduce themselves in a virtual museum (on a virtual whiteboard) where we created an empty frame for each participant to fill with images and a caption that represented what culture in Jalisco looks like and feels like to them. Image British Council Creative Commons Licence CC-BY-NC-SA 4.0.

EDI WERE AT THE CORE OF THE PROGRAMME

Our participant group of twenty-five included people with various disabilities, including visual impairment and learning disabilities. We had a dedicated EDI lead in our team who constantly had us reflecting on how to make our process and activities accessible to all. We also worked with an external party, Birds of Paradise, with significant EDI experience in the cultural sector in particular, as advisors along the way. All activities were designed with EDI in mind and there was a budget dedicated to this from the get-go. This did not mean everything went well. If we learned one lesson, it was that you need to be prepared in many different ways. We always put much effort in being inclusive, by allocating a generous budget first and then asking participants for their needs and finding tailored solutions. Creating the right adaptations for people with disabilities was, however, not very different in principle from creating the adaptations that were needed for all of us in response to the pandemic (Figure 11.6).

Figure 11.6 To put EDI at the core of *Innovation for Culture*, we had to improvise and improve. This ranged from 'translating' visual, virtual whiteboards into word docs that screen readers can work with, to sign language interpreters on Zoom calls who later were. Image British Council Creative Commons Licence CC-BY-NC-SA 4.0.

ZOOM AND MIRO ENABLED VIRTUAL COLLABORATION WITH TWENTY-FIVE 'AMBASSADORS', ALONG WITH ROBUST TECH SUPPORT AND FACILITATION

The biggest adaptation we had to make in response to the pandemic was that *Innovation for Culture* had to take place completely virtually. We had to get creative in terms of creating a safe, hospitable and warm environment. We factored in a lot of core values in the design of our collaborative workspace on Miro, a virtual whiteboard which we used throughout the project, in combination with Zoom. This reliance upon technology in delivering the project, consisting of 3 hour events with around 50 participants, required solid technical support to make sure things worked. A separate organization was hired to support us, including live spoken interpretation between English and Spanish due to the international aspect of the programme. Having people's faces on the board helped things feeling more personal in this technical environment. When we split into breakout rooms on Zoom, we also split into separate tables on Miro, with profile photos and name tags for each seat. We added some plants to the board, which also made things feel more informal. While these little things take more time and effort, it is worth it in the end. Participants said it added a lot in terms of making them feel more welcome. It created a more intimate and safe space for having the conversations we were aiming for, which fitted well with the more intimate spaces that everyone was calling in from: our homes instead the professional environments of our offices, theatres and studios (Figure 11.7).

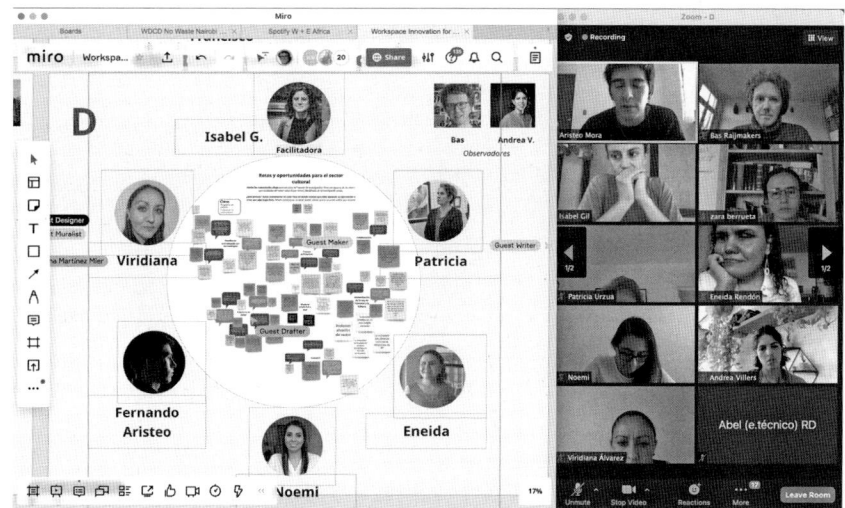

Figure 11.7 A more intimate space for conversation, in a Zoom breakout room and around a table on the Miro board, with the participants visible around the table as well as on the Zoom tiles. Image British Council Creative Commons Licence CC-BY-NC-SA 4.0.

> **CREATING OWNERSHIP OF POLICY RECOMMENDATIONS AND LEARNINGS**
>
> One of the biggest challenges throughout the project was assuring people that something would happen with the resulting policy recommendations. From previous experiences, some participants feared that this process would be tokenistic and lack follow-through and commitment. This is a recurring challenge for many participatory initiatives, as there are so many factors beyond the control of project stakeholders that inhibit implementation, like budget, broader policy agendas and leadership capacity. It was therefore very important for us to accept this reality, but nevertheless emphasize our efforts to keep the ball rolling beyond the official end of the project. Our government champion within the Cultura Jalisco ministry really helped with sharing and advocating for the process and its results throughout the ministry. They are currently seeking more budget to start acting upon some of the recommendations. A website, which showcases the entire programme, acts as a public hub to showcase the project and our learnings, but also create excitement, public accountability and collective ownership. Programmes like *Innovation for Culture* require a considerable communications effort throughout to create ownership way beyond the people involved in the project directly and the communications skills and capacity of British Council were crucial to achieve this.

Building common ground

Building involvement alone is not enough for policy co-design. After all, the result we were aiming for with *Innovation for Culture* was policy recommendations co-created by the cultural sector in Jalisco. To achieve this we also needed to build common ground, the fourth orchestration activity that focuses on content rather than people. This activity is often overlooked or hurried through. When results are due and there is still a lot of development work left to do, it seems a waste of resources to spend time and energy on building common ground between the participants in the network. We aligned all stakeholders through sharing prior research (e.g. the Policy Timeline and Stakeholder Map in the Briefing Report) and unique perspectives (through the conversations in the workshops) to establish common ground as the basis for fruitful collaboration. This approach remained valuable throughout the project. Domain knowledge needs to be built, and everyone's values, contributions and expectations need to be made explicit. Due to the permanent shared workspace we had on Miro, where all materials could be found 24/7, and regular meetings that we organized in that space, this was perhaps the easiest adaptation to the pandemic we had to make. When sharing documents in addition to meeting in person in a physical space, just a few times, the continuity of a shared work and meeting space that our virtual whiteboard on Miro offered is not present.

We used our virtual shared space to create a solid shared knowledge basis at the start, and then gradually crafted common ground through visual storytelling and conversations. Constant communication helped keep everyone on the same page and avoid scope creep amidst complex stakeholders. We co-created policy priorities and pathways, and eventually proposed a spectrum of actions formatted as policy recommendations.

KICK-STARTING THE PROJECT BY GETTING THE LAY OF THE LAND

Policy co-design never starts with a blank slate. For *Innovation for Culture*, we started with learning about the history of cultural policy making in Jalisco and who is involved in the cultural sector at the moment. Mexican creative studio Aura did the necessary research through expert interviews and desk research to create a Stakeholder Map and a Policy Timeline to communicate results in a written report. These are all well-used tools that do not require extensive training, but they do require conversation and discussion to make sure that the many different perspectives that all stakeholders have are present in the results. It is inevitable that new perspectives and stakeholders will present themselves as the policy co-design develops. Therefore Aura kept interviewing people as the next stages evolved and updated the initial Briefing Report they created for all participants as we went along. It was crucial that Aura also helped to facilitate the workshops and analyse their results, as they also created the report with the policy recommendations at the end of the project (Figure 11.8).

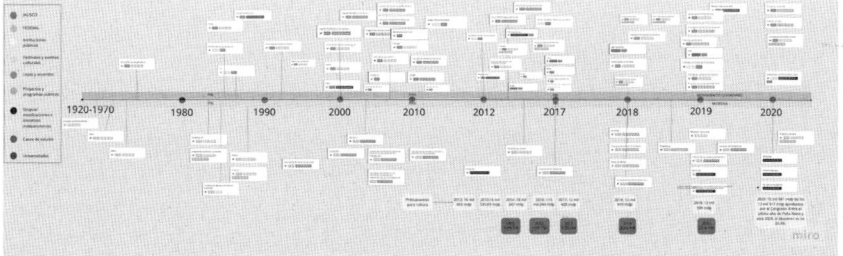

Figure 11.8 Interactive timeline of cultural policy in Jalisco, Mexico for the past hundred years, with detailed stories about each element of the timeline that pop up when the item is clicked. When building common ground, it is important to know the ground that you are standing on, with all its sensibilities as well as possibilities. Maps of the past like these offer a shared reference (even if it is contested) for discussions about possible policy futures. Image British Council Creative Commons Licence CC-BY-NC-SA 4.0.

CRAFTING POLICY GOALS THROUGH CONVERSATIONS AND VISUAL STORYTELLING

Conversations were our key ways to bring participants together, and sometimes connect them to experts as well. These group dialogues were strongly supported in a number of ways with online tools that were adapted from tools and materials normally used in a room with people sitting around a table or standing at a wall. We found that with some adjustments, meeting in virtual spaces using online versions of the same tools worked just as well. Deliberative Mapping really helped to show how spoken words from the conversations were noted and organized into overviews, insights and eventually policy goals, which were expressed as Future Headlines in a speculative magazine from 2024 about the cultural sector in Jalisco, eventually. To develop these using all diverse perspectives present, we asked participants to share their own Hopes and Fears and those of some of their peers, using Appreciative Inquiry in one of the fieldwork tasks for participants that they performed in between the Group Dialogue sessions. The Miro virtual whiteboard was used by participants in between workshops as well to report on their fieldwork, making this an exercise that was visible to each participant as it unfolded, allowing them to respond to each other with their fieldwork (Figure 11.9).

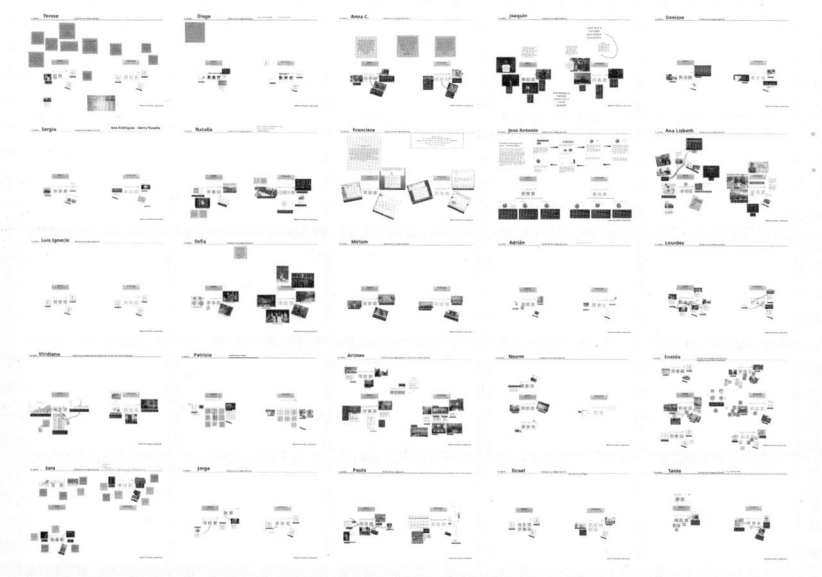

Figure 11.9 Hopes and Fears of twenty-five participants and their peers on the virtual whiteboard, an exercise that developed over the course of several weeks in between two workshop sessions. Image British Council Creative Commons Licence CC-BY-NC-SA 4.0.

CONSTANT COMMUNICATION HELPED KEEP EVERYONE ON THE SAME PAGE AND AVOID SCOPE CREEP AMIDST COMPLEX STAKEHOLDERS

Our team included a mix of expertise in terms of policy making and cultural policy, policy research, participatory innovation management, inclusion and diversity, branding and communication design and event management. We were constantly learning from each other, and coaching on the go was the norm from day one. Roles and responsibilities were fixed at the beginning of the project, but these became a bit fluid throughout. This was sometimes a positive and sometimes a negative thing. On the plus side, it allowed us to be flexible and adaptive and spot and respond quickly to unmatching interpretations and expectations. In other cases, it led to a bit of confusion and 'scope creep'. Weekly team meetings helped us stay aligned in terms of who was doing what, but even so we sometimes dropped the ball amidst the complexities of the project. Being open and understanding towards one another, and the trust we had built from the beginning despite never meeting in person, were always crucial to getting things back on track. Meeting weekly for 45 minutes to an hour is a huge investment, but it was needed to build the trust we needed to be able to rely on each other in the core team, which consisted of some twenty people across seven organizations with people coming in and out during the project as well.

CO-CREATING POLICY PRIORITIES AND PATHWAYS

We collected many policy issues along the way that were important to various actors in the cultural sector. This resulted in many topics and issue areas to address going forward. We knew we did not have the time to detail every single policy area and potential recommendation, so we had to create some focus. Prioritization is always tricky and the response to 'who gets to decide?' is never easy. We organized multiple activities to get a sense of which recommendations should receive the most attention and effort going forward, and which could be given less focus for now. In a workshop we split into groups after doing a round of dot voting on the 'headlines of the future' to see where participant priorities lie. We discussed these chosen headlines in more depth to flesh out possible actions towards these goals. Informed by these discussions, we created a set of goals and actions per theme and built a community survey to validate our work and discover knowledge gaps (Figures 11.10 and 11.11).

Figure 11.10 Dot Voting on the headlines of the future speculative magazine from 2024, which contained articles created from analysis of the Hopes and Fears exercise the participants did in an earlier workshop and fieldwork with their peers. Here, participants are adding post it notes with their names to articles they strongly support. Image British Council Creative Commons Licence CC-BY-NC-SA 4.0.

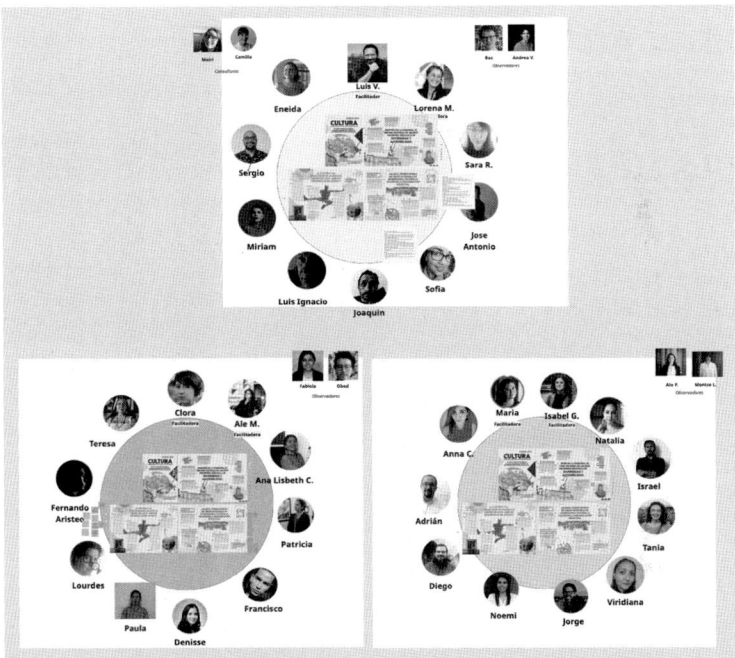

Figure 11.11 The magazine from the future with votes from participants to prioritize certain future situations and ambitions was consequently used to steer conversations in three groups, at three virtual round tables. Image British Council Creative Commons Licence CC-BY-NC-SA 4.0.

PROPOSING AND DISCUSSING A SPECTRUM OF ACTIONS

It is difficult to define where exactly this stage begins and ends, as there were a few iterations of what finally became 'final' recommendations. We used the government as a System tool, developed by Policy Lab, as we moved from general aims and actions crafted with participants, to more honed and specific recommendations. It helped us to consider different forms of action available to governments, ranging from powers of control that we often associate with authorities such as licensing, regulating, assurance and enforcement, to different forms of influence such as advising, agenda setting, role modelling and scrutinizing. Once we were happy with the level of granularity, we created a draft version of the policy recommendations for final feedback from our participant group. We discussed this feedback in a collaborative workshop and arranged an expert panel, inspired by a Citizen's Assembly approach to foster further critical discussion of our drafted recommendations (Figure 11.12).

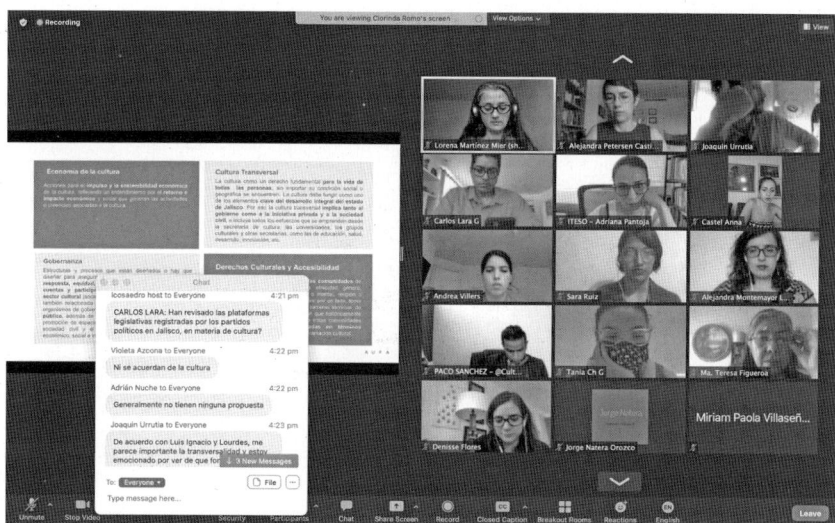

Figure 11.12 Discussing an early version of the policy recommendations with the participants in a Zoom breakout room, using screen share and the chat channel. External experts were involved in the discussions to offer suggestions on, for instance, the feasibility of policy directions that the participants desired. Image British Council Creative Commons Licence CC-BY-NC-SA 4.0.

Conclusion

The *Innovation for Culture* programme required an approach that recognized the various perspectives and attitudes of many different stakeholders that needed to be held in balance to keep all of the moving parts flowing through uncertainty. The 'normal' uncertainty of an evolving field like policy co-design was further exacerbated by the need to adapt to the Covid-19 pandemic. In that sense, we were confronted with some more uncertainty, rather than facing sudden uncertainty where before there was none. Many of the approaches we normally take to face the uncertainty of the situations we work in as design researchers and policy co-designers also helped us to face the new uncertainties of the pandemic. The four aspects of orchestration describe the fundamentals of this approach well by not focusing simply on the stages and project tasks, but on the connected movements and activities that surround and flow through them.

Nevertheless, this was perhaps one of the more complex projects STBY engaged in as a Design Research agency. The extreme nature of this context – with all of its uncertainties – pushed the boundaries of our practice and there are elements we can take away, even in non-Covid-19 contexts. The ways in which we typically build involvement and common ground had to be completely adapted to a virtual environment. But as everyone adapted to online settings and ways of staying connected, we saw benefits of this way of working beyond Covid-19 contexts. Online collaboration tools like Zoom and Miro helped all stakeholders stay connected and own a shared working space together, also in between sessions. Distance was no longer an issue and everyone could participate relatively equally. Though visually impaired participants and those with lower digital literacy required more support, this experience forced us to provide that support in ways that everyone benefited from and all stakeholders can take with them beyond this project. In the future, we see a way of facilitating policy co-design processes that combines the best of the physical and virtual.

This project was a learning goldmine, and we realized early on that this creates a responsibility to share our lessons. STBY developed a Playbook towards the end of the project, by reflecting upon our experience and translating what we learned into future practice for the participants and wider stakeholder group of the cultural sector in Jalisco. The Playbook is also intended for those who were not involved in this project to help inspire and guide their own future participatory design projects. Standing on the shoulders of others who have done such great work in this space, we made our own adaptations to existing tools and methods in order to suit our own objectives in *Innovation for Culture* and the complex environment that Covid-19 presented. Richly illustrated with examples of how we adapted and combined tools that others before us designed and piloted, the Policy co-design Playbook is now publicly available via the British Council for everyone who wants to get their hands dirty and adapt our approach to their own context.

References

Amatullo, M. (2014). The Branchekode.dk Project: Designing with purpose and across emergent organizational culture. In C. Bason (Ed.), *Design for Policy*. Farnham: Gower Publishing, 152.

Bason, C. (2014). Introduction: The design for policy Nexis. In C. Bason (Ed.), *Design for Policy*. Farnham: Gower Publishing, 3.

Bason, C., & Austin, R. (2019, March–April). The right way to lead design thinking. *Harvard Business Review*, 82–91. https://hbr.org/2019/03/the-right-way-to-lead-design-thinking.

Blomkamp, E. (2018). The promise of co-design for public policy. *Australian Journal of Public Administration*, 77(4), 729–43.

Christiansen, J., & Bunt, L. (2014). Innovating public policy: Allowing for social complexity and uncertainty in the design of public outcomes. In C. Bason (Ed.), *Design for Policy*. Farnham: Gower Publishing, 41.

Design Council (DATE). Framework for innovation. https://www.designcouncil.org.uk/news-opinion/what-framework-innovation-design-councils-evolved-double-diamond.

Dhanaraj, C., & Parkhe, A. (2006). Orchestrating innovation networks. *Academy of Management Review*, 31(3), 659–69.

Howlett, M. (2014). From the 'old' to the 'new' policy design: Design thinking beyond markets and collaborative governance. *Policy Science*, 47, 199.

Junginger, S. (2014). Towards policymaking as designing: Policymaking beyond problem-solving and decision-making. In C. Bason (Ed.), *Design for Policy*. Farnham: Gower Publishing, 57.

Kimbell, L., & Vesnić-Alujević, L. (2020). After the toolkit: Anticipatory logics and the future of government. *Policy Design and Practice*. https://doi.org/10.1080/25741292.2020.1763545

Mintrom, M., & Luetjens, J. (2016). Design thinking in policy making processes: Opportunities and challenges. *Australian Journal of Public Administration*, 75(3), 391–402.

Orton, J.D., Douglas, J., & Weick, K. (1990). Loosely coupled systems: A reconceptualization. *Academy of Management Review*, 15, 203–23. https://doi.org/10.2307/258154.

Parmentier, G., & Mangematin, V. (2014). Orchestrating innovation with user communities in the creative industries. *Technological Forecasting and Social Change*, 83(C), 40–53.

Puttick, R., Baeck, P., & Colligan, P. (2014). *i-teams: The Teams and Funds Making Innovation Happen in Governments Around the World*, Nesta and Bloomberg Philanthropies report, London, 13

Raijmakers, B., Vervloed, J., & Wierda, K. (2015). One design under a groove. *CRISP Magazine*, 1(5), 24–30. https://www.stby.eu/wp/wpcontent/uploads/2015/07/CRISPmagazine5_Orchestration.pdf.

Ritala, P., Hurmelinna-Laukkanen, P., & Nätti, S. (2012). Coordination in innovation-generating business networks–the case of Finnish mobile TV development. *Journal of Business & Industrial Marketing*, 27(4), 324–34. https://doi.org/10.1108/08858621211221698.

Sanders, E., & Stappers, P.J. (2008). Co-creation and the new landscapes of design. *Co-Design*, 4(1), 3.

Toigo, T., Wegner, D., Silva, S.B.D., & Zarpelon, F.D.M. (2021). Capabilities and skills to orchestrate innovation networks. *Innovation & Management Review*, 18(2), 129–44. https://doi.org/10.1108/INMR-10-2019-012.

12 Designing resilient cities post-Covid-19
CHRISTOPHER BOYKO AND RACHEL COOPER

Cities and their urban populations have been affected severely by the Covid-19 pandemic. During the height of lockdown in cities across the world there was a change in patterns of use, more use of green space, less use of transport systems and less footfall in city centres, with decline in activity in the retailing and leisure sectors.

The health and well-being of urban populations always has been a matter of concern ever since humans congregated together in communities and specific places. Public health and the impact of the environment were taken seriously in the UK during the mid-nineteenth century by a number of advocates for public health and environmental change. For example, Dr William Duncan illustrated the role of poor living conditions and the spread of infectious disease in Liverpool and became the first Medical Officer of Health (Grace, 2021). He was in post during an epidemic of cholera and approached it by looking at behaviour change and improving the state of the urban environment.

In urban design there is a plethora of literature concerning the way in which we design homes, neighbourhoods and cities and the consequent impact on health and well-being. Well-known design recommendations resulting from the theories and practice insights are summarized in Cooper et al. (2014):

Designing for health objectives:

1. *Promoting physical activity and healthy diets* by incorporating traffic calming devices (e.g. curving streets, sharp bends, chicanes, narrow roads, changes in surface to signify pedestrian priority); providing interconnected street layouts and short blocks; ensuring footways are wide and smooth; incorporating greenery, especially to provide a buffer zone between pedestrians and traffic; ensuring good links to nearby facilities and amenities, especially food stores; creating mixed-use development, particularly through the inclusion of shops and restaurants/cafes in residential areas and providing space for growing fruit and vegetables.
2. *Combatting respiratory illnesses and allergies* by ensuring homes have good air quality through adequate ventilation; maximizing the use of natural materials in the home; using greenery to combat effects of traffic on air quality outside the home and reducing traffic overall.

3. *Reducing the likelihood of injuries* by ensuring the design of stairs, windows, balconies and heat sources in the home do not create unnecessary risks; reducing the speed of traffic on the street and ensuring the infrastructure is maintained and safe.
4. *Mitigating the health impacts of climate change* by ensuring homes can be kept warm in winter (cheaply) and cool in summer (without the need for air conditioning); using passive design principles where possible (e.g. passive solar gain, cross-ventilation); ensuring homes are flood resistant and mitigating the urban heat island effect through use of reflective surfaces and greenery.

Designing for well-being objectives:

1. *Facilitating successful childhood development* by ensuring adequate space and privacy in the home and between rooms (e.g. through good sound insulation); allowing space for homework; ensuring good sound insulation from external noise; ensuring good air quality and warm homes; providing a high level of natural daylighting; providing houses rather than flats for families; ensuring the street is safe for children to play in, by calming traffic, including crossings and facilitating surveillance from inside homes (e.g. windows facing the street); optimizing the amount of greenery in the environment; incorporating features – especially natural ones, such as shallow water features, stones and logs – that encourage informal play; providing parks and open spaces, including play areas with natural elements, such as trees, water and rocks that stimulate creativity and designing dedicated spaces in neighbourhoods for teenagers to 'hang out'.
2. *Enabling independence in older age* by incorporating Lifetime Homes standards and dementia-friendly design features; providing a range of house types including assisted living developments, retirement villages and co-housing schemes; providing a hierarchy of streets from busier, main streets to quieter, residential ones; ensuring footways are smooth, plain and wide to incorporate seating; providing buffer zones (e.g. grass verge) between the footway and road and providing adequate toilet facilities and incorporating landmarks and wayfinding cues (e.g. trees, postboxes, clocks, towers) in buildings and neighbourhoods.
3. *Reducing stress* in the home by ensuring good sound insulation between rooms and from the outside and optimizing natural daylight; optimizing the amount of greenery to provide views from inside and to absorb sound; providing quiet, natural spaces that offer opportunities for rest and retreat and; providing clear signage, obvious entrances and wayfinding cues to reduce anxiety and stress alongside a similar approach to providing a user-centred, flexible public transport system.

4. *Promoting positive mood/emotions* by providing homes where people can feel private and where they can experience peace and quiet and including interesting features that are human scale, such as flower boxes and balconies in flats while optimizing greenery and views of it.
5. *Facilitating good relationships* by providing adequate privacy as well as opportunities for social interaction; providing good sound insulation between rooms, ensuring enough spaces for different activities to take place; designing space for families to eat together; creating a buffer zone between the private realm of the home and public realm of the street (e.g. through small front gardens); maximizing opportunities for interaction with neighbours (e.g. through front doors facing the street; inclusion of porches, terraces/balconies and lower level boundaries to allow 'chatting over the fence'); designing a connected, walkable street network that includes retail, services and amenities in residential areas and providing an efficient, effective public transport system that can facilitate people's ability to get out and about and meet others.
6. *Enabling people to concentrate* and be productive when working by providing good sound insulation and natural daylight with views of greenery and ensuring good air quality and designing workspaces that are controllable, adaptable and personalizable.
7. *Helping make people feel safe from crime* by ensuring clear demarcation of private and public space and ensuring entrances to homes face the street; providing good surveillance of public spaces and adequate street lighting and making sure that places and spaces are easy to maintain.

During the Covid-19 pandemic, one issue came to the fore in relation to urban design: the density of urban form in the context of the spread of Covid-19 and our perceptions of well-being and safety from the virus. There was a general feeling of people leaving cities for more space in rural or suburban environments, and that people were concerned about the density of the city, their access to green space and clean outdoor environments. Therefore, the next section considers density and urban form and asks whether we need to reconsider density in relation to designing resilient, post-Covid-19 cities.

The relationship between density and urban form

Spatially speaking, density refers to the number of units in a given area (Boyko and Cooper, 2011). Within a city, the types of unit are inestimable and include physical things that are either stationary or travelling, and natural or humanmade, such as trees, lamp posts, buses, office blocks and people. The area within which the units may be found also can vary, often depending on who is measuring density, their reasons for doing so and the scale at which they wish to measure density. For example, architects may wish to create a mixed-used housing project and consider total floor area (Johnny Winter, Edward Cullinan Architects, personal communication, 6 June 2011); local authority planners may be adhering to policy around space standards and talk about dwelling densities (DETR, 1998) and developers may be seeking to fit the most housing on a plot of land and discuss parcel densities (Forsyth, 2003).

Connected with density is an important term to distinguish, particularly in the context of Covid-19 in cities (see 'How Covid-19 is changing perspectives on density in cities' section): crowding. Whereas density is perceived by many to be an objective concept, crowding is related more to an individual's subjective experience of a space and consequent social situation. In this case, crowding typically is negative and may be affected by environmental (i.e. perception of too little space), interpersonal (i.e. perception of too many people in a space) or intrapersonal factors (Churchman, 1999; see also Mandel et al., 1980). While cities often are designed and planned with density in mind using objective measures, it is important to acknowledge – and attempt to design out – the negative influences of crowding that are experienced by residents, where possible.

As a concept, then, density is fundamental to the planning, architecture and urban design of cities (Rapoport, 1975). By examining density, local authorities and other stakeholders can describe, predict and control how urban land is used (Berghauser Pont and Haupt, 2007; DETR, 1998). Doing so undoubtedly has an impact on the urban form of cities and subsequent policies, which have been linked to notions of sustainability (City of Vancouver, 2008; DETR, 1998; Haughey, 2005; Jenks and Dempsey, 2005) and climate change (Williams et al., 2010).

The form of low and high urban density

Much research and debate on the impacts of density on urban form has been devoted to either end of the density spectrum: sprawl (low density) or compactness (high density). In cases of sprawl, estate or subdivision-style residential development involving single-family homes with private gardens at the periphery of metropolitan areas dominates (the pattern of development may be scattered, leapfrog or take the form of strips or ribbons; Ewing, 1997). Non-residential development in these settings mainly comprises stand-alone shops and services. There also is significant road construction as well as water and sewer infrastructure (Burchell and Mukherji, 2003).

While desirable for some to live away from the 'hustle and bustle' of the urban core on private parcels of land, there is a price to pay. Sprawling developments typically have poor accessibility among related land uses, making it difficult to go through or bypass these areas for other areas. Functional open space also is in short supply, as most developable land is adopted for private use (Ewing, 1997). Furthermore, government costs tend to increase when growth spreads outward and costs for new development can be higher compared with more compact developments (Burchell and Mukherji, 2003). Finally, when combined with high deprivation, low-density neighbourhoods have greater incidences of individual ill-being in comparison with low- or high-deprivation neighbourhoods that also are high in density (Boyko et al., 2020).

In contrast to urban sprawl, compact or high-density developments often attempt to maximize land by 'building up', via tower blocks or skyscrapers, thus saving land, in principle, for other uses (e.g. agriculture, green space). More recently, architects and planners have been endorsing gentle, hidden or invisible densities (City of Vancouver, 2008); repairing and refurbishing low-density housing to increase densities (Roaf, 2010) and designing for high density, rather than high rise (Whitehead, 2012). In addition, high-density cities tend to focus on creating sustainable public transportation infrastructure and services (Shin, 2010), maximizing development on brownfield land (Burton, 1999; Shin, 2010) and around public transport nodes and promoting mixed use (Breheny, 1997).

As with sprawl, there also are disadvantages to higher urban densities:

- Exacerbating traffic congestion and parking problems (Breheny, 1992; De Roo and Miller, 2000; Rydin, 1992).
- Creating congestion at public transportation facilities, such as train stations (Ruback and Pandey, 1992).
- Intensifying pollution due to the lack of space for trees and shrubs that would cool and purify the air (Breheny, 1992; De Roo and Miller, 2000; Williams et al., 2000).
- Living in crowded, cramped conditions (DETR, 1998).
- Losing privacy and increasing proximity to noise and nuisance (De Roo and Miller, 2000; DETR, 1998).
- Obstructing views and causing overshadowing (Hitchcock, 1994).
- Increasing relative prices for dwellings, land and goods and services (Alexander, 1993; LSE, 2006).
- Using more energy in the construction of buildings (Rydin, 1992).

One additional disadvantage of high-density living worth noting is the detriment to individual and collective well-being. Particularly when coupled with poor-quality housing and neighbourhoods, poor access to infrastructure and services and potential issues relating to isolation and 'urban anonymity', high-density development can increase mental health problems (e.g. anxiety, depression, stress, distress). High density also is related to increased physical illness, including headaches, muscle pain and itchy skin (see Cooper et al., 2008, for additional references).

How Covid-19 is changing perspectives on density in cities

Since March 2019, epidemiologists alongside other scholars and practitioners have been keeping a close watch on Covid-19 infection rates, hospitalizations and deaths.

Some have suggested that cities across the globe have been at the epicentre of disease transmission, with density playing a fundamental role (Coşkun et al., 2021; Imdad et al., 2021; Jamshidi et al., 2020; Kodera et al., 2020; Mansour et al., 2021; Salama, 2020). In the Global South, where policies around compact cities and densification often are applied without detailed consideration of the local context (Harrison et al., 2021; Watson, 2002; Zapata Campos et al., 2021), researchers have found that neighbourhood population density mediates the spread of infectious disease in cities (Sahasranaman and Jensen, 2021). Researchers also discovered a moderate association between population density and Covid-19 transmission in India; a positive relationship between density, virus spread and wind speed in Turkey (Coşkun et al., 2021) and a strong connection between the density of older people in cities in Iran and Covid-19 morbidity and mortality rates (Khavarian-Garmsir et al., 2021). In the Global North, where densities tend to be lower and comparatively more compact city policies exist, the number of studies indicating an explicit link between density and Covid-19 is fewer (see Bliss and Capps, 2020). However, there are some suggestions that high-population cities in Italy have experienced greater transmission rates (Cartenì et al., 2020) and that American metropolitan population significantly predicts infection rates (Hamidi et al., 2020).

In opposition to the above, there has been research in both the Global North and South, showing no association between different types of density in cities and Covid-19 transmission rates (Bhadra et al., 2020; Boterman, 2020; Carozzi et al., 2020; Federgruen and Naha, 2021; Hamidi et al., 2020; Pafka, 2020; Perone, 2021; Sun et al., 2020). Rather, such studies have indicated that other factors may be mediating or moderating this relationship (Khavarian-Garmsir et al., 2021), including extensive use of face coverings and enforcement of social distancing measures (Novakovic, 2020), overcrowding (Khavarian-Garmsir et al., 2021), migration to urban centres (Khavarian-Garmsir et al., 2021) and connectivity to other places through airports and open borders (Bliss and Capps, 2020; Hamidi et al., 2020). In fact, some researchers have suggested that cities are safer against catching Covid-19, compared with rural areas, especially if social distancing is enforced and mass gatherings are minimized (Bliss and Capps, 2020; Kotkin, 2020; Novakovic, 2020). They argue that cities – especially large ones – possess the resources to help during pandemics, such as healthcare facilities (Novakovic, 2020), stadiums to create makeshift hospitals and grocery stores within walking distance.

Post-pandemic refocusing

Whether or not there is a positive association between density in cities and Covid-19, many policymakers and practitioners have been looking ahead to the future to consider how density in its different forms can be employed to reduce incidences of communicable disease transmission in future. For example, some local authority planners have stated that the future of cities during pandemics should be about finding the balance between densification/integration and compartmentalization/separation in different parts of the city (Crosbie, 2020; Salama, 2020). This might be through temporary, micro-scale efforts, such as designing in effective social distancing measures, or through more permanent, urban-scale attempts, like creating healthy neighbourhoods that prioritize safety and walkability (Khavarian-Garmsir et al., 2021; Salama, 2020).

Creating more public spaces within the dense, urban fabric of the city is another approach that some policymakers and practitioners are considering in the fight against Covid-19. An increase in public open spaces per capita may help to achieve notions of sustainability and liveability in urban areas affected by communicable disease (Afrin et al., 2021; Bolleter et al., 2021; Chang, 2020; Novakovic, 2020). Public spaces should be flexible (Sepe, 2021) and of sufficient quality to help reduce the risk of community transmission and enhance public health (Novakovic, 2020), particularly among the most vulnerable residents living in high-density areas (Afrin et al., 2021). The establishment of networked green spaces also should be prioritized, as they can connect between dense urban and natural areas (Eltarabily and Elgheznawy, 2020). Respondents to a survey further suggest improving access to private open spaces for residents to use when needing 'somewhere to escape other than a balcony' (Bolleter et al., 2021, p. 12). In Sendra and Sennett's (2020) words, the design of cities needs to work like an accordion so that people can spread out when needed and then come back together, creating multiple, flexible, networked public spaces of sufficient quality that can reinforce this idea.

In connection with having more public spaces, policymakers and practitioners also saw transport infrastructure being overhauled in the future. Megahed and Ghoneim (2021) suggested that dense cities of the future might need fewer parking spaces and roads, which could be converted into safe cycling and walking networks. Less space devoted to private vehicles and traffic, and more investment in public health safety on public transport (Khavarian-Garmsir et al., 2021), also could lead to an enhanced public realm that is suitable for social distancing (Novakovic, 2020). At the district or neighbourhood scale, designing developments that are more neighbourhood oriented could support residents in walking or cycling more and help them to accomplish more in one trip through the available mix of services nearby (Khavarian-Garmsir et al., 2021).

In terms of exploring new ideas for how housing design can support reductions in communicable diseases in dense cities, the response tended to focus on lower-density solutions. For some, the answer was to design more detached housing, complete with adequate gardens, which would allow for more light, air and nature alongside better facilities for social distancing and food production (Megahed and Ghoneim, 2020). Others believed in a slightly higher-density option, with more three-storey flats needing to be built – high-rise buildings would require lifts, which might mean crowding in a confined space – and policies created around minimum dwelling sizes that had common circulation spaces. The main issue, according to respondents of Bolleter et al.'s (2021) survey, is the number of residents in a room or interior corridor, which more easily could transmit Covid-19.

From a policy perspective, some scholars have suggested that clear guidance be developed for describing public spaces in relation to physical distancing, particularly in high-density areas, that can be communicated to, and implemented easily by, residents (Eltarabily and Elgheznawy, 2020; Sahasranaman and Jensen, 2021). Policymakers also should be focusing on density-related issues when designing and maintaining neighbourhoods, such as improving self-sufficiency in connection with jobs, food production, education, health and energy (Bolleter et al., 2021). Whatever the policy, though, it is imperative that local authorities adopt measures that are tailored to community needs and micro-morphologies to ensure that solutions to prevent disease transmission are reduced (Hamidi et al., 2020; Kamalipour and Peimani, 2021; Khavarian-Garmsir et al., 2021).

Finally, technological solutions have been discussed as contributing towards the minimization of Covid-19 transmission rates, albeit not necessarily in dense cities. Automated, touchless technologies, including voice-activated lifts, hands-free lighting, ventilation systems to remove air pollution and antibacterial surfaces, have been mooted as ideas for architects and designers to implement in homes, offices and healthcare environments (Chang, 2020). Other technological approaches could be introduced to better manage future pandemics and reduce misinformation on social networking sites, such as creating forecasting programmes using GIS to identify and communicate outbreak details (Afrin et al., 2021). Integral to these approaches is the development and maintenance of informal technical networks (Lee, 2020a, 2020b).

Don't panic: Principles for designing resilient and healthy places

From these early studies of Covid-19, density and urban design, one might summarize the findings and recommendations as turbo boosting pre-Covid-19 research and guidance. The jury is still out so far as the relationship between density and the prevalence of Covid-19 infection, but what is clear is that in the Global South and in those cities with high levels of substandard living, Covid-19 did take a hold (Sahasranaman and Jensen, 2021). This is, of course, related to crowded conditions, lack of good quality shelter, access to water and poor sanitation. So we are back to the basic principles of urban design for public health and are looking to achieve UN-Habitat Target 11.1: By 2030, ensure access for all to adequate, safe and affordable housing and basic services and upgrade slums (UN-Habitat, 2018). More specifically all people should have access to:

- Improved water;
- Improved sanitary facilities (e.g. private toilets);
- Sufficient space/living area;
- Durable, permanent and protective housing;
- Security of tenure.

- Promotes positive mood/emotions
- Reduces Stress
- Designs the neighborhood for children
- Enables independence in older age
- Promotes physical activity & healthy diet
- Makes moving about easy
- Facilitates good relationships
- Helps make people feel safe from crime
- Reduces the sense of crowding
- Durable, permanent, protective Housing
- Sufficient space
- Access to water
- Access to sanatory facilities (private toilet)
- Security of tenure

Design cities that are 'easy on the eye', green, clean, accessible, friendly, courteous, affordable, resilient and sustainable

Figure 12.1 Basic requirements to improve general levels of health and well-being in cities. Adapted from Cooper et al. (2014).

The UN Economic and Social Council (2021) report suggests that

> Before the pandemic, cities had rising numbers of slum dwellers, worsening air pollution, minimal open public spaces and limited convenient access to public transport. The direct and indirect impacts of the COVID-19 pandemic are making it even more unlikely that this Goal (Goal 11. Make cities and human settlements inclusive, safe, resilient and sustainable) will be achieved, with more people forced to live in slums, where quality of life is deteriorating and vulnerability increasing.

Coming back to cities that, by and large, have achieved these basic requirements, there is still much-needed work to improve general levels of health and well-being, as summarized in Figure 12.1 and drawn from the previous research described above.

However, the recent Covid-19 studies, and our own experience of 2020 and 2021, suggest that, in addressing these requirements, urban designers, planners, developers, ethical investors and policymakers should additionally focus on:

Urban form

Think more carefully about planning and look for a balance between densification/integration and compartmentalization/separation in different parts of the city. Indeed, earlier work on mixed-use developments has illustrated the challenges and benefits, stating that a 'more comprehensive understanding of the mix and scales' is required (Evans et al., 2009, p. 215) and a more comprehensive and sensitive assessment of neighbourhoods from multiple perspectives (e.g. neighbourhoods that offer local working and access to a mix of services nearby, especially good quality food and social connections).

Also, in terms of the connectedness of places, it is important to reduce the reliance on cars, continuing to develop public transport systems, while 'designing-in' public health safety on public transport, to encourage people out of the 'safety' of their own mobility space, back onto public transport.

Public spaces and places

Increase public open spaces per capita, to improve sustainability and liveability generally. Also, make public spaces flexible, creating more permanent, multiple, flexible, networked public spaces of a quality that enable people to come together, yet spread out (enabling social distancing), when necessary. Suggestions include establishing networks of green spaces through dense areas, connecting quickly between built form and natural form. Changing the nature of dense cities in this way may include fewer parking spaces and roads, converting them into green infrastructure for safe cycling and walking.

Neighbourhood and community

Covid-19 has illustrated the importance of neighbourhood-scale support and community engagement; therefore, it is critical that measures developed are done with communities and tailored to meet their needs. This is important in all situations, whether that is substandard housing, an inner-city site or a suburb. Health, well-being and resilient urban form must work for both population and planet and are more likely to be successful if the future is co-created and owned by the majority of the residents.

Homes and housing

Being locked down, confined to our homes, raised so many concerns related to crowding, density and also isolation. Already, there is a call for more open spaces for residents to use when needing 'somewhere to escape other than a balcony'. Indeed, a balcony was a benefit for residents who wanted to get into the fresh air and communicate with neighbours. Homes that allow for more light, air and access to nature are now a priority, as well as access to facilities for food production. Common circulation spaces also should be designed to reduce crowding and enable social distancing.

Urban technology

The affordance of technologies used in cities has illustrated the benefits of automated, touchless technologies, including voice-activated lifts, hands-free lighting, ventilation systems to remove air pollution and antibacterial surfaces. Also, sensor systems and digital media can enable us to continue to work, learn and travel safely. However, these need to be designed for everyone: inclusivity, access and universality must be designed to ensure they benefit everyone, while maintaining principles of privacy and trust.

None of these principles are new: they build on our knowledge of designing future cities for the well-being of people and the environment. However, they are not simple to execute; they require an approach that considers cities as complex systems, with multiple interdependencies. They require many disciplines, professions and communities to work together, to translate data and to make decisions that can be understood through a theory of change. We would argue that designers are skilled in coordinating this complexity, by drawing together the various perspectives and knowledges and visualizing the complexity. Making material the vision helps everyone see a tangible way forward. A final recommendation is that we don't panic, but train more designers to develop these skills and help to design better cities and neighbourhoods, post-Covid-19!

References

Afrin, S., Chowdhury, F.J., & Rahman, M.M. (2021). COVID-19 pandemic: Rethinking strategies for resilient urban design, perceptions, and planning. *Frontiers in Sustainable Cities*, 3, 668263.

Alexander, E.R. (1993). Density measures: A review and analysis. *Journal of Architectural and Planning Research*, 10(3), 181–202.

Berghauser Pont, M., & Haupt, P. (2007). The relation between urban form and density. *Viewpoints*, 11(1). http://www.urbanform.org/journal/viewpoints/viewpoints0107.html.

Bhadra, A., Mukherjee, A., & Sarkar, K. (2021). Impact of population density on COVID-19 infected and mortality rate in India. *Modeling Earth Systems and Environment*, 7, 623–9.

Bliss, L., & Capps, K. (2020, 13 March). Are suburbs safer from coronavirus? Probably not. *CityLab*. https://www.bloomberg.com/news/articles/2020-03-13/are-suburbs-safer-from-coronavirus-probably-not.

Bolleter et al. (2021). Implications of the COVID-19 pandemic: Canvassing opinion from planning professionals. *Planning Practice & Research*. https://www.tandfonline.com/doi/full/10.1080/02697459.2021.1905991.

Boterman, W.R. (2020). Urban-rural polarisation in times of the corona outbreak? The early demographic and geographic patterns of the SARS-CoV-2 epidemic in the Netherlands. *Tijdschrift Voor Economische En Sociale Geografie*, 111(3), 513–29.

Boyko, C.T., & Cooper, R. (2011). Clarifying and re-conceptualising density. *Progress in Planning*, 76, 1–61.

Boyko, C.T., Cooper, R., Coulton, C., & Hale, J.D. (2020). Health, wellbeing and urban design. In C.T. Boyko, R. Cooper, & N. Dunn (Eds.), *Designing future cities for wellbeing*. New York: Routledge, 158–70.

Breheny, M. (1992). *Sustainable Development and Urban Form*. London: Pion.

Breheny, M. (1997). Urban compaction: Feasible and acceptable? *Cities*, 14(4), 209–17.

Burchell, R.W., & Mukherji, S. (2003). Conventional development versus managed growth: The costs of sprawl. *American Journal of Public Health*, 93(9), 1534–40.

Burton, E. (1999). The compact city: Just or just compact? *Urban Studies*, 37(11), 1969–2001.

Carozzi, F., Provenzano, S., & Roth, S. (2020). Urban density and COVID-19. Discussion paper series (DP No. 13440). Bonn, Germany: IZA Institute of Labor Economics.

Cartenì, A., Di Francesco, L., & Martino, M. (2020). How mobility habits influenced the spread of the COVID-19 pandemic: Results from the Italian case study. *Science of the Total Environment*, 74, 140489.

Chang, V. (2020, 19 April). The post-pandemic style. *Slate*. https://slate.com/business/2020/04/coronavirus-architecture-1918-flu-cholera-modernism.html.

Churchman, A. (1999). Disentangling the concept of density. *Journal of Planning Literature*, 13(4), 389–411.

City of Vancouver (2008). *EcoDensity Charter*. Vancouver: City of Vancouver.

Cooper, R., Boyko C., & Codinhoto, R. (2008). The effect of the physical environment on mental wellbeing. State-of-science review: SR-DR2. In *Foresight Mental Capital and Wellbeing Project*. London: The Government Office for Science.

Cooper, R., Burton, E., & Cooper, C.L. (eds) (2014). *Wellbeing and the Environment*. Oxford: Wiley Blackwell, 661–63.

Coşkun, H., Yilidirim, N., & Gűndűz, S. (2021). The spread of COVID-19 virus through population density and wind in Turkey cities. *Science of the Total Environment*, 751, 141663.

Crosbie, M.J. (2020). How might the COVID-19 change architecture and urban design? *CommonEdge*. https://commonedge.org/how-might-the-COVID-19-pandemic-change-architecture-and-urban-design/.

De Roo, G., & Miller, D. (2000). *Compact Cities and Sustainable Urban Development*. Aldershot: Ashgate.

Department of the Environment, Transport and the Regions (DETR) (1998). *Planning Research Programme: The Use of Density in Urban Planning*. London: TSO.

Eltarabily, S., & Elgheznawy, D. (2020). Post-pandemic cities - The impact of COVID-19 on cities and urban design. *Architectural Research*, 10(3), 75–84.

Ewing, R. (1997). Is Los Angeles-style sprawl desirable? *Journal of the American Planning Association*, 63(1), 107–26.

Evans, G., Aiesha, R., & Foord, J. (2009). Urban sustainability: Mixed-use or mixed messages? In R. Cooper, G. Evans, & C. Boyko (Eds.), *Designing Sustainable Cities*. Oxford: Wiley-Blackwell, 190–217.

Federgruen, A., & Naha, S. (2021). Crowding effects dominate demographic attributes in COVID-19 cases. *International Journal of Infectious Diseases*, 102, 509–16.

Forsyth, A. (2003). Measuring density: Working definitions for residential density and building intensity. Design brief, 8. Minneapolis: Design Center for American Urban Landscape, University of Minnesota.

Grace, J. (2021). Liverpool's Dr Duncan - Britain's first medical officer of health. *Culture Liverpool*. https://www.cultureliverpool.co.uk/liverpools-dr-duncan-britains-first-medical-officer-of-health/.

Hamidi, S., Sabouri, S., & Ewing, R. (2020). Does density aggregate the COVID-19 pandemic? *Journal of the American Planning Association*, 86(4), 495–509.

Harrison, P., Klein, G., & Todes, A. (2021). Scholarship and policy on urban densification: Perspectives from city experiences. *International Development Planning Review*, 43(2), 151–73.

Haughey, R.M. (2005). *High-Density Development: Myth and Fact*. Washington, DC: Urban Land Institute.

Hitchcock, J. (1994). A primer on the use of density in land use planning. Papers on Planning and Design no. 41. Toronto, Canada: Program in Planning, University of Toronto.

Imdad, K., Sahana, M., Rana, M.J., Haque, I., Patel, P.P., & Pramanik, M. (2021). A district-level susceptibility and vulnerability assessment of the COVID-19 pandemic's footprint in India. *Spatial and Spatio-Temporal Epidemiology*, 36, 100390.

Jamshidi, S., Baniasad, M., & Niyogi, D. (2020). Global to USA county scale analysis of weather, urban density, mobility, homestay, and mask use on COVID-19. *International Journal of Environmental Research and Public Health*, 17(21), 7847.

Jenks, M., & Dempsey, N. (eds) (2005). The language and meaning of density. In *Future Forms and Design for Sustainable Cities*. Oxford: Architectural Press, 287–309.

Kamalipour, H., & Peimani, N. (2021). Informal urbanism in the state of uncertainty: Forms of informality and urban health emergencies. *Urban Design International*, 26, 122–34.

Khavarian-Garmsir, A.R., Shafiri, A., & Moradpour, N. (2021). Are high-density districts more vulnerable to the COVID-19 pandemic? *Sustainable Cities and Society*, 70, 102911.

Kodera, S., Rashed, E.A., & Hirata, A. (2020). Correlation between COVID-19 morbidity and mortality rates in Japan and local population density, temperature, and absolute humidity. *International Journal of Environmental Research and Public Health*, 17(15), 5477.

Kotkin, J. (2020, 20 March). Not-so-mass transit. *The Washington Post*. https://www.washingtonpost.com/outlook/2020/03/20/what-will-have-changed-forever-after-coronavirus-abates/?arc404=true#KOTKIN.

Lee, V.J., Aguilera, X., Heymann, D., Wilder-Smith, A., Lee, V.J., & Heymann, D.L. (2020a). Preparedness for emerging epidemic threats: A lancet infectious diseases commission. *The Lancet Infectious Diseases*, 20(1), 17–19.

Lee, V.J., Ho, M., Kai, C.W., Aguilera, X., Heymann, D., & Wilder-Smith, A. (2020b). Epidemic preparedness in urban settings: New challenges and opportunities. *The Lancet Infectious Diseases*, 20(5), 527–29.

LSE (2006). *Density- A Debate about the Best Way to House a Growing Population*. London: LSE.

Mandel, D.R., Baron, R.M., & Fisher, J.D. (1980). Room utilization and dimensions of density. *Environment and Behavior*, 12(3), 308–19.

Mansour, S., Al Kindi, A., Al-Said, A., Al-Said, A., & Atkinson, P. (2021). Sociodemographic determinants of COVID-19 incidence rates in Oman: Geospatial modelling using multiscale geographically weighted regression (MGWR). *Sustainable Cities and Society*, 65, 102627.

Megahed, N.A., & Ghoneim, E.M. (2020). Anti-virus built environment: Lessons learned from COVID-19 pandemic. *Sustainable Cities and Society*, 61, 102350.

Megahed, N.A., & Ghoneim, E.M. (2021). Indoor Air Quality: Rethinking rules of building design strategies in post-pandemic architecture. Environmental Research, 193, https://doi.org/10.1016/j.envres.2020.110471.

Novakovic, S. (2020, 29 March). Will COVID-19 spell the end of urban density? Don't bet on it. *Azure*. https://www.azuremagazine.com/article/will-COVID-19-spell-the-end-of-urban-density-dont-bet-on-it/.

Pafka, E. (2020, 12 May). As coronavirus forces us to keep our distance, city density matters less than internal density. *The Conversation*. https://theconversation.com/as-coronavirus-forces-us-to-keep-our-distance-city-density-matters-less-than-internal-density-137790.

Perone, G. (2021). The determinants of COVID-19 case fatality rate (CFR) in the Italian regions and provinces: An analysis of environmental, demographic, and healthcare factors. *Science of the Total Environment*, 755, 142523.

Rapoport, A. (1975). Toward a redefinition of density. *Environment and Behavior*, 7(2), 133–58.

Roaf, S. (2010). The sustainability of high density. In E. Ng (Ed.), *Designing High-Density Cities for Social and Environmental Sustainability*. London: Earthscan, 27–39.

Ruback, R.B., & Pandey, J. (1992). Very hot and really crowded: Quasi experimental investigations of Indian 'tempos'. *Environment and Behavior*, 24(4), 527–4.

Rydin, Y. (1992). Environmental dimensions of residential development and the implications for local planning practice. *Journal of Environmental Planning and Management*, 35(1), 43–61.

Sahasranaman, A., & Jensen, H.J. (2021). Spread of COVID-19 in urban neighbourhoods and slums of the developing world. *Journal of the Royal Society Interface*, 18, 20200599.

Salama, A.M. (2020). Coronavirus questions that will not go away: Interrogating urban and socio-spatial implications of COVID-19 measures. *Emerald Open Research*. https://emeraldopenresearch.s3.amazonaws.com/manuscripts/14632/c1f07818-059b-4ad1-8337-1dec710f3cf5_13561_-_ashraf_salama.pdf?doi=10.35241/emeraldopenres.13561.1&numberOfBrowsableCollections=6&numberOfBrowsableInstitutionalCollections=0&numberOfBrowsableGateways=6.

Sendra, P., & Sennett, R. (2020). *Designing Disorder. Experiments and Disruptions in the City*. London: Verso.

Sepe, M. (2021). COVID-19 pandemic and public spaces: Improving quality and flexibility for healthier places. *Urban Design International*, 26, 159–73.

Shin, S.W. (2010). Sustainable compact cities and high-rise buildings. In E. Ng (Ed.), *Designing High-Density Cities for Social and Environmental Sustainability*. London: Earthscan, 293–308.

Sun, Z., Zhang, H., Yang, Y., Wan, H., & Wang, Y. (2020). Impacts of geographic factors and population density on the COVID-19 spreading under the lockdown policies of China. *Science of the Total Environment*, 746, 141347.

UN-Habitat (2018). *SDG Indicator 11.1.1 Training Module: Adequate Housing and Slum Upgrading*. Nairobi: United Nations Human Settlement Programme (UN-Habitat).

UN Economic and Social Council (2021). *Progress towards the Sustainable Development Goals*. https://unstats.un.org/sdgs/files/report/2021/secretary-general-sdg-report-2021--EN.pdf.

Watson, V. (2002). The usefulness of normative planning theories in the context of Sub-Saharan Africa. *Planning Theory*, 1(1), 27–52.

Whitehead, C.M.E. (2012). *The Density Debate: A Personal View*. http://eprints.lse.ac.uk/63375/1/whitehead_the_density_debate_author.pdf.

Williams, K. (2000). Does intensifying cities make them more sustainable? In K. Williams, E. Burton, & M. Jenks (Eds.), *Achieving Sustainable Urban Form*. London: E & FN Spon, 30–45.

Williams, K., Joynt, J.L.R., & Hopkins, D. (2010). Adapting to climate change in the compact city: The suburban challenge. *Built Environment*, 36(1), 105–15.

Zapata Campos, M.J., Kain, J.-H., Oloko, M., Stenberg, J., & Zapata, P. (2021). Urban qualities and residents' strategies in compact global south cities: The case of Havana. *Journal of Housing and the Built Environment*, 37, 529–51.

13 Reimagining the use of outdoor learning environments in secondary education

ANA RUTE COSTA

Introduction

The potential of the use of outdoor learning environments (OLE) for the promotion of better teaching and learning in secondary education has not yet been fully understood (Blackmore et al., 2011). Despite some historical experience with open-air schooling (Meckel, 1996), the context of the Covid-19 pandemic has highlighted the timeliness of further design research in this field and the value of OLE to promote health and well-being.

The benefits of OLE for children, especially in early years and primary education, are well known (Khan et al., 2018). However, there is a lack of evidence, as well as a dearth of practice, relating to the design and use of OLE in secondary education. Over the last twenty-five years, governments around the world have invested huge amounts of money in school infrastructure. However, most of these interventions focused mainly on the internal learning environments and OLE were overlooked.

We need to bring designers, researchers, educational practitioners, pupils and policymakers around the same table and reimagine the future of OLE (Armitage, 2006). More than playgrounds, the OLE can be places for exchange, expand, challenge and supersede our knowledge and understanding of the world.

This chapter reflects on the previous uses of OLE, considers the Covid-19 pandemic experience and reflects on possible future uses of OLE in secondary education. This chapter concludes by highlighting how design research can inform the future of OLE in the fields of Policy, Educational Practice and Architectural Design and ways of collaboration.

The value of OLE

The advantage of OLE is well known in younger ages (Blanchet-Cohen and Elliot, 2011; Wishart and Rouse, 2019) and rapidly growing and gaining support with a bigger number of forest nurseries and schools that provide outdoor learning opportunities (Bates, 2020; Cudworth and Lumber, 2021). Research shows that young people are more motivated to learn when outside, often developing different relationships and skills (Woolner and Triplady, 2019). The Natural Connections Demonstration Project

(Waite et al., 2016) shows great evidence of the benefit of outdoor learning activities for young people, staff and schools and establishes links with different areas: mental health, physical activity, physiological health. According to Merewether (2015), outdoor learning spaces are important for children because they are able to pretend, move, observe and be social.

Various governments have been reviewing their policies and encouraging the use of OLE, especially providing advice and guidance for the Early Years Foundation (The Scottish Government, 2018). Despite the growing interest in nursery and primary school settings (Little et al., 2017), within secondary education and further educations the OLE has received little policy, practice or research attention and does not appear to be central to future school interventions. According to Edwards-Jones et al. (2018), some of the challenges to integrate outdoor learning into school practices and strategies are related to policy-, people-, place-, and resource-related issues.

Across the world, there has been a movement from traditional teacher-led learning environments supported by conventional school building design to 'learner-centred' approaches supported by engaging learning environments (Blyth et al., 2019). These flexible learning spaces that support a wide array of teaching and learning possibilities are often called by 'Innovative Learning Environments' (French et al., 2020). However, most of these interventions focus on the internal learning environments. In 2003, the Building Schools for the Future programme was initiated with a plan to invest £45 billion over fifteen years to rebuild every school building in England with an aim to create inspirational learning environments for both students and staff so that they feel valued and encouraged; however, the focus was again mainly on the internal space of the school building (Duthilleul et al., 2021).

The Innovative Learning Environments and Teacher Change project suggests blurring the border between internal and external learning spaces and having the possibility to extend learning activities to outdoors, for example outdoor decks, terraces adjacent to indoor learning spaces (Young et al., 2020). The school learning spaces should be seen as a continuous learning environment from interior to exterior without defining a mental border between these two physical spaces. OLE designed for teaching and learning can improve children's attainment and their perceived well-being (Khan et al., 2019); however, these studies are limited to primary school environments. There is a lack of evidence on how outdoor spaces can support innovative pedagogical approaches in secondary schools, and no reason why their power should be limited to primary age students. We need to keep providing outdoor environmental experiences that are developmentally appropriated for secondary students, an OLE rich in sensory experiences that help students retain and retrieve what they have learned. OLE that can promote formal and informal learning opportunities, problem-based learning, collaborative team-based activities, individual learning outside of the school buildings.

Considering the recognized value of outdoor learning we can look back to the previous experiences and analyse the use of OLE throughout history to help us reimagine the future.

OLE and Pandemics

The open-air schools started in Germany, in the beginning of twentieth century. Purpose-built schools were designed to combat the widespread rise of tuberculosis (Greene, 1912). By 1908, the open-air school's typology was implemented in different countries across Europe and America. These spaces, conceived for children physically debilitated, provided open-air therapy, fresh air, good ventilation, exposure to outdoor environments and would improve children's health.

The classrooms provided wide access to the outdoors with large windows and cross ventilated spaces. In some cases, the classroom would be located outdoors and explore the benefits of learning outside of the box, with no walls or roof (MessiNessi, 2016). After the First World War the open-air school movement became organized. The first international congress took place in Paris in 1922, and it was followed by four more: Belgium 1931, Germany 1936, Italy 1949 and Switzerland 1956 (Châtelet et al., 2003). Most of the open-air schools created during this period replicated the formal indoor classroom environment outdoors, without any changes of furniture organization neither adjustments to the natural environment. However, in some schools, there was an exploration of the OLE to empower different types of teaching and learning approaches. After the Second World War, with the introduction of antibiotics and the improvement of living conditions, the open-air schools lost their popularity but some other concepts generated during this period, for example the forest school, are still in use today.

There are several examples of forest schools worldwide, especially associated to the early year's foundation stage and primary curriculum. These schools have arisen from the need to enhance the naturalistic and environmental learning approach (Waite et al., 2014).

In this sense, most of the schools that offer open-air teaching nowadays are focused on environmental learning. One of the contemporary example school is IslandWood School, in Washington State, United States (IslandWood School, 2021). This school provides a complete outdoor classroom and a complementary learning programme with six distinct ecosystems, including a forest, cattail marsh, bog, stream, pond and a marine estuary. IslandWood School offers an experiential environmental science programme for young people and for the community and the school buildings are carefully conceived to support this approach.

The environmental global issues that we are facing worldwide are not a pandemic but they can cause several if we don't take care of our planet. Hands-on experiences in an engaging OLE are powerful strategies that can empower young people to implement sustainable practices. Every school is located in a particular place and the design of the OLE can enhance these characteristics.

Covid-19 pandemic experience

According to various studies, the risk of Covid-19 transmission is lower outdoors (Bulfone et al., 2020; Rowe et al., 2021; Weed and Foad, 2020). This fact empowered people to meet outside during Covid-19 pandemic and to recognize the value of outdoor environments (Quay et al., 2020). This happened across our society, especially in schools, where outdoor learning opportunities enable learners to connect with nature and provide access to these meaningful places and experiences (Collins et al., 2020). Outdoor learning was seen as a potential response for the reopening of schools amidst the pandemic (Sheikh et al., 2020; Spiteri, 2020).

The open-air school movement was referenced to deal with a pandemic, providing design solutions that can be adapted to different types of buildings and natural environments (Blei, 2020). However, the return of the open-air school solution during Covid-19 in some cases was dismissed and considered too difficult, before it's even tried (Khazar, 2020). Denmark was one of the first countries reopening their schools during Covid-19 and hold classes outside so children and young people could be outside as much as possible (Gargiulo, 2020). Several schools across the world reported the increased use of OLE to mitigate the risk of Covid-19 transmission (Melnick and Darling-Hammond, 2020) and provide greater opportunities for collaborating with classmates under social distancing measures (Hamilton and Wood, 2020).

Considering the Covid-19 experience and looking at the future use of OLE, young people reported the will of integrating outdoor spaces into learning beyond Covid-19 pandemic. The research project, Spaces and Tools for Learning during Pandemic, developed in two schools in Lancashire during Covid-19 pandemic (Costa, 2021) reveals that young people (16–18 years old) are willing to move to a blended learning approach with a more diverse set of learning spaces outdoors (e.g. quiet study areas, teamwork areas). Young people would like to make the most of their school's outdoor areas and have access to covered external areas and glass houses.

Another study with young Scots from Edinburgh, Aberdeenshire and Glasgow during onset of the pandemic revealed that young people wanted more opportunities for teaching and learning outdoors (Hamilton and Wood, 2020). Therefore, there is a need to characterize and collaboratively rethink the current and future use and design of OLE in secondary education to enhance teaching and learning experiences.

As a response to Covid-19 pandemic, Rosan Bosch Studio and IDOM have designed a school where teaching takes place both indoors and outdoors, blending the space between internal and external spaces and creating permanent connections between them. According to Bosch, cited in (Crook, 2021), 'The architectural structure brings nature in and out of the building, while it invites students to constantly move between inside and outside areas, supporting more sustainable and activating learning experience.' The school building is conceived to promote a continuous learning environment that activates learning potentials and minimizes health risks.

The design and use of OLE can also go beyond the school domain. According to the report presented by the Trust for Public Land (2020), the renovation of the schoolyards in America can improve student education and health outcomes and solve the problem of park inequity experienced during Covid-19 pandemic by allowing the community to use the space when the school is closed. The Trust for Public Land claims the transformation of schoolyards into community parks, with multi-use recreation fields. This strategy would enable more people to have access to a playground in a walking distance from their houses and create an intergenerational learning area when the school is closed – not only during Covid-19 pandemic but always. The investment in building outdoor spaces can enhance learning now and well into the future and support educators to get kids outside, Covid-19 or not (The Trust for Public Land, 2020).

There are plenty of opportunities for alternative pedagogical approaches outside of the classroom and to explore rich experiential qualities of OLE (Waite, 2011) within the school and broader community.

The use of OLE in secondary education

Creating OLE where young people can develop different activities affords learning opportunities that can't be replicated in the indoor school environment. The use of OLE for teaching and learning activities is related to the space available and to the school practices. In most of the cases, teachers are the ones that can promote the use of OLE in their instructional practices. According to Bloom et al. (2010), secondary teachers have identified far more obstacles and challenges than elementary teachers. When a teacher enters a classroom with traditional desks and a board, they know exactly how to teach and approach pupils. By encouraging the use of OLE for teaching and learning might be challenging because it would require teachers to leave their comfort zone, but at the same time it will generate critical thinking and promote creative teaching and learning approaches.

'An adult will lose concentration after 25 to 30 minutes (. . .) a child in elementary school will lose concentration after 5 or, at the most 10 minutes, and an adolescent after 15 to 20 minutes' (Breithecker, 2010). In this sense, why are we asking pupils to sit for 6–10 hours a day and moving for less 1 hour a day? If we can change the location of regular teaching and learning activities, young people will be able to explore new surroundings with their minds and bodies and associate learning to a specific place and/or activity.

The OLE can engage young people with their imaginations (Schoolyards, 2021); the way spaces are designed and conceived can create endless opportunities to play and discover. Young people don't play in the same way as children do but they can certainly enjoy the richness of living organism, exploring nature or simply being surrounded by it (Mau, 2010). The learning context becomes important on the teaching and learning activities that are designed and delivered.

According to Staples (2015), the concept of contextualized mobile learning can be described by three different types of learning: (1) learning through context, (2) learning in context and (3) learning about context. If we apply these concepts to OLE, we can promote learning through outdoor context, where learner experiences the outdoor context and the available learning tools do satisfy their learning goals. We can promote learning in an outdoor context where the environment provides a specific setting to support an interpretation. And we can learn about the outdoor context, where the natural surroundings are the object of learning.

The Bloom's revised taxonomy (Anderson and Krathwohl, 2001) distinguishes different levels of human cognition and different levels of thinking. Remembering, Understanding and Applying are considered lower-level cognition skills and Analysing, Evaluating and Creating are higher-level thinking skills. At OLE we can promote all the thinking skills. However, being in a different and stimulating context we might be able to give a bigger emphasis to higher-level thinking skills and promote hands-on meaningful learning experiences.

All these learning approaches can be promoted through an informal and/or formal teaching and learning approach and according to their user's needs. OLE are also an excellent context to promote interdisciplinary approaches and integrated learning strategies. 'Learning outside the classroom in real-life environments calls for designing comprehensive integrated learning activities, in which the focus is on a complex real-life phenomenon or a problem requiring different levels of knowledge and skills from various disciplines for solving it' (Mettis and Valjataga, 2021, p. 499). OLE can provide the perfect environment to bring different subjects together and provide cross-disciplinary work. This is an excellent way to promote creativity and stimulate cooperation and knowledge exchange.

One of interdisciplinary outdoor learning activities examples is the Edible schoolyard, a programme created at Berkeley's Martin Luther King Jr. Middle School. 'Teaching young people how to feed themselves and how-to live-in community responsibly is the centre of an education' (Waters, 2021). The Edible schoolyard curriculum includes a science, nutrition and nature for the creation of fresh and healthy delicious food.

Other examples of interdisciplinary outdoor learning activities are part of bigger festivals and school events – a science fair, a woodland trail, a sports day. These are special opportunities that bring community together outdoors and help to develop meaningful learning experiences.

If governments invest on the OLE to promote different teaching and learning opportunities across the school community, these spaces can also be opened to the community and expand the outdoor learning opportunities to all.

Several governments across the world promote the use of school's OLE by the community when the school is closed. The Scottish government has launched in 2016 the Scotland's Play Strategy, a toolkit for using school grounds for playing out of teaching hours (The Scottish Government, 2016). The Boston Schoolyard Initiative (2021) between 1995 and 2013 has converted asphalt playgrounds into dynamic centres for recreation, learning and community life. Most of the schools in Norway, Denmark, Finland and Sweden have their OLE open over the weekends when the schools are closed. The Trust for Public Land (2021) has been promoting access to nature and the outdoors for the last fifty years and they have helped to covert and upgrade several OLE and ensure that everyone in the United States has access to a high-quality park close to home.

Learning is not a contained process and the OLE does not need to stop within school borders. The commute routes from home to school can provide a pleasant learning journey. Walking paths and bicycle trails connecting a school with the homes can generate peer learning opportunities and extend the social relationships developed at school. More than buildings, the school is the community that inhabits that space and specific architectural affordances can bring this community together.

Allowing young people to share their school with wider community provides endless learning opportunities and promotes intergenerational dialogue. With a lifelong learning perspective, being able to go back to school and share the learning environment is essential. The OLE is the best place to start this relationship; this transitional space between the school and the city is where the natural exchange can take place.

In this era of lifelong learning, the young people who make up this new learning generation need to be able to go back to school to keep on learning. More than schools we need learning centres open to the community. We may not go back to the Hellenic and Roman periods where there were no formal schools and the learning spaces were determined by the teacher's location. However, we can get some inspiration from the outdoor community spaces in ancient Greek and Roman periods and shape the future of OLE opened to all.

Inspired by Greek and Roman cities: Spaces and uses of the OLE – a possible framework

The OLE in a school should be seen as learning city that connects all the school buildings, brings the learning community together and engages with further audiences outdoors. Teaching and learning interactions would take place outdoors in the open air (Nasir et al., 2014). If we take as reference the Greek (Morris and Knodell, 2015) and Roman (Sewell, 2015) city structures, the outdoor public space was composed of different structures: theatre, forum, colonnaded courtyard, palaestra, agora and seating areas. Each of these structures did have a specific form and function and would provide different learning opportunities to their users. Considering the original form and function of these spaces in ancient Greek and Roman cities, we will reflect how this may relate and inspire the present and future OLE in schools.

Palaestra

The palaestra did have different designs according to the site context and constraints in Greek and Roman cities. However, most of the time, it was a rectangular court surrounded by colonnades with adjacent rooms, the gymnasium. Most of the OLE in secondary schools have a palaestra, the gymnasium/sports centre and sports fields where young people can practice different individual and team sports. The main difference between the designs of these spaces in ancient cites and school's sports facilities is the relationship between these two indoor and outdoor areas. In most of the schools, the sports centre and the sports fields are independent spaces, without any transition areas. In ancient cities, the colonnade would establish the transitions between indoor and outdoor and create a covered external area for athletes to decompress, socialize and get ready for the next activity. These areas are important to promote peer learning social interactions between sports activities and generate the school culture.

Physical education, in particular through the use of sports halls, has an important role to play in the promotion of health and well-being environments. These spaces need to be accessible and visible as permanent invitation to be used and appropriated. We need more than a sports field but exciting and inspiring places to be, to exercise and to develop social relationships.

Agora/forum

Agora and forum were two public plazas in Greek and Roman cities, respectively. Both the agora and the forum refer to the centre of public space, the centre of day-to-day life, the place for meetings and public discussions. These spaces were designed primarily as a marketplace and were surrounded by shops. Furthermore, many of the important structures of the ancient cities were located on or near the agora/forum and the space was used for different events, for example public speeches, processions, elections, any important public event. Similarly, to ancient Greek and Roman cities, every school needs an agora/forum, the most celebrated meeting place, the heart of the school community. The place for welcome week, market place, science fairs, parades and strikes, the space to see and to been seen. The outdoor learning space that brings the community together and generates a vibrant learning environment.

Colonnaded courtyard

The colonnaded courtyards, also known as peristyle in Greek architecture, were a continuous porch formed by a row of columns surrounding a courtyard, a garden or the perimeter of a building. This typology was used in private and public buildings and would provide a transition between interior and exterior. Later the peristyle typology was adopted by Christian cloisters where the external covered area was used as a meditation and contemplation space. Cities across the world also use similar structural principle; external arcades are designed to provide sheltered areas for pedestrians in a city.

There are several schools that have colonnaded areas, cloisters and arcades. These external covered spaces establish the relationship between interior and exterior areas and are useful OLE. The use of these spaces can be enhanced by adding different urban elements according to the environment pretended, for example flowers, fountains, benches, sculptures, fish ponds. If a school does not have any arcade, these elements can be added and can enhance the use of OLE.

By creating a strong relationship between indoors and outdoors, we can bring the outside inside and establish direct relationships between where we are and what surround us. These transitional spaces (indoor/outdoor) can provide outdoor stimulation, views, vistas and outdoor supervised spaces. OLEs associated with classrooms that are outdoors and covered, are an excellent extension of the indoor learning environments and a way of disrupting the learning and teaching approach and help young people to be focused for longer periods.

Theatre, benches and urban elements

The use of mobile technologies in outdoor learning in both formal (for instance Burden and Kearney, 2016; Kärki et al., 2018) and informal environments (for instance Land and Zimmerman, 2015; Zimmerman et al., 2019) are important to consider. These studies demonstrate that it is possible to create meaningful mobile outdoor learning events, which show positive results on student learning.

The Greek theatres were integrated in the landscape, normally on a hillside to use the natural slope of the terrain to create the space for the audience. The Roman theatres were generally built upon their own foundations as independent structures.

The topography of an OLE can support different types of amphitheatres and create spaces for small/big audiences to perform, exchange, observe, present, criticize in a scenic environment. These spaces can be intrinsically related to the site context or be additional/stand-alone elements. Places to seat, to meet, to gather different scale groups and audiences are essential to invite people to use the OLE. These places allow us to slow the pace and create individual/group outdoor learning experiences in mindful places for pause, reflection and knowledge assimilation.

The use of OLE in secondary education: Design research to inform policy, educational practice and architectural practice

The future design research has the potential to explore the design and uses of OLE in secondary education, characterize the existing OLE (spaces and uses) in secondary education settings and rethink the design and use of OLE in secondary education.

By bringing teachers, students, governors and community together in a participatory design research we would be able to envision the future of OLE. From forest schools, to outdoor classrooms and tailored outdoor learning activities, there is a wide range of possibilities to map and discover. Design research has the potential to produce a series of visuals and reflections about the design and use of OLE. These would enable us to provoke and engage with a wider audience (e.g. parents to policy makers and governmental bodies) and generate a discussion about the future of OLE and the potential of teaching 'outside the box'.

Engage in meaningful conversations about changing the OLE. Students, parents, teachers, teaching assistants, principals, community members and politicians are important stakeholders to shape the future of OLE and create spaces suitable for all. We need to ask ourselves why do we like to be in some places and not other places? Why do we emotionally like to be in some OLE and not in others? Design research can find the answer to these questions and shape the OLE accordingly.

Policy

- Prioritize the refurbishment/upgrading of OLE parallel to school building's interventions.
- Playgrounds and a wood/park are essential structures for a school and for a neighbourhood. Why not sharing them? Policy making can have a big impact on how OLE are used and maintained.

Educational practice

- OLE can provide sensory experiences that students will retain and retrieve throughout their life. By exploring sound, smell, taste, touch and movement on OLE, we will be able to provide transformative learning experiences.
- You can start a project in school that has impact on the whole neighbourhood/community. Take inspiration from the work developed by Erin Gruwell (1999). The OLE will be the perfect place to bring everyone together.
- The use of OLE can offer learning opportunities beyond normal teaching and learning activities and explore different settings. Some examples can be found on the Boston Schoolyard Initiative (2021).

Architectural design

- The design of furniture and OLE can be related to pedagogies and learning (Architects, OWP/P, Furniture, VS, Design, Bruce Mau, 2010) and that can have an impact on student's outcomes (Blackmore et al., 2011).
- Young people are the most imaginative partner. Visualize the future of OLE with young people; their poignant perspective may give the essential insights needed. If young people get enthusiastic when they are asked to participate in a design fiction exercise, imagine when they co-design their future school!
- OLE does not need to be at the ground level. We can design different OLE across the school, providing different spaces linked with different internal areas; we can make them more accessible and promote different types of uses.
- OLE need to be accessible as permanent invitation to be used and appropriated.

References

Anderson, L.W., & Krathwohl, D.R. (2001). *A Taxonomy for Learning, Teaching and Assessing: A Revision of Bloom's Taxonomy of Educational Objectives: Complete Edition*. New York: Longman.

Architects, OWP/P, Furniture, VS, Design, Bruce Mau. (2010). *The Third Teacher*. New York: Abrams.

Armitage, M. (2006). The influence of school architecture and design on the outdoor play experience within the primary school. *International Journal of the History of Education*, 535–53. https://doi.org/10.1080/00309230500165734.

Bates, C. (2020). Rewilding education? Exploring an imagined and experienced outdoor learning space. *Children's Geographies*, 3(18), 364–74. https://doi.org/10.1080/14733285.2019.1673880.

Blackmore, J., Bateman, D., Loughlin, J., O'Mara, J., & Aranda, G. (2011). *Research into the Connection between Built Learning Spaces and Student Outcomes*. East Melbourne: Department of Education and Early Childhood Development.

Blanchet-Cohen, N., & Elliot, E. (2011). Young children and educators engagement and learning outdoors: A basis for rights-based programming. *Early Education & Development*, 757–77. https://doi.org/10.1080/10409289.2011.596460.

Blei, D. (2020, 1 September). When tuberculosis struck the world, schools went outside. *Smith Sonian Magazine*. https://www.smithsonianmag.com/history/history-outdoor-schooling-180975696/.

Bloom, M.A., Holden, M., Sawey, A.T., & Weinburgh, M.H. (2010). Promoting the use of outdoor learning spaces by K-12 inservice science teachers through an outdoor professional development experience. In A. Bodzin, B.S. Klein, & S. Weaver (Eds.), *The Inclusion of Environmental Education in Science Teacher Education*. Dordrecht: Springer, 97–110. https://doi.org/10.1007/978-90-481-9222-9_7.

Blyth, A., Velissaratou, J., & Caddy, J. (2019, January). Analytical framework for case study collection: Effective learning environments. In OECD (Ed.), *Directorate for Education and Skills Education Policy Committee*. https://www.oecd.org/education/effective-learning-environments/Analytical-Framework-for-Case-Study-Collection.pdf.

Boston Schoolyear Initiative. (2021, 23 August). *School Yards*. Retrieved from Boston Schoolyear Initiative: http://www.schoolyards.org/index.html.

Breithecker, D. (2010). The body-brain connection. In O. Architects & B. M. VS Furniture (Eds.), *The Third Teacher*. New York: Abrams, 82–4.

Bulfone, T.C., Malekinejad, M., Rutherford, G.W., & Razani, N. (2020). Outdoor transmission of SARS-CoV-2 and other respiratory viruses: A systematic review. *The Journal of Infectious Diseases*, 223(4), 550–61. https://doi.org/10.1093/infdis/jiaa742.

Châtelet, A.-M., Lerch, D., & Luc, J.-N. (2003). *L'école de plein air. Une expérience pédagogique et architecturale dans l'Europe du XXe siècle*. Paris: Éditions Recherches. https://doi.org/10.4000/histoire-education.1122.

Collins, M., Dorph, R., Foreman, J., Pande, A., Strang, C., & Young, A. (2020). *Policy Brief: A Field at Risk: The impact of COVID-19 on Environmental and Outdoor Science Education*. Berkeley: University of California.

Costa, A.R. (2021). Homing into school. The best of two worlds, reflections from COVID-19 Pandemic. *Environments By Design: Health, Wellbeing and Place*. AMPS.

Crook, L. (2021, 14 April). *Dezeen*. Retrieved from Dezeen.com: https://www.dezeen.com/2021/04/14/markham-college-lower-school-peru-rosan-bosch-studio-idom/.

Cudworth, D., & Lumber, R. (2021). The importance of Forest School and the Pathways to nature connection. *Journal of Outdoor and Environmental Education*. https://doi.org/10.1007/s42322-021-00074-x.

Duthilleul, Y., Woolner, P., & Whelan, A. (2021). *Constructing Education: An Opportunity Not to Be Missed*. Thematic Review Series. Paris: Council of Europe Development Bank.

Edwards-Jones, A., Waite, S., & Passy, R. (2018). Falling into LINE: School strategies for overcoming challenges associated with learning in natural environments (LINE). *Education 3-13*, 46(1), 49–63. https://doi.org/10.1080/03004279.2016.1176066.

French, R., Imms, W., & Mahat, M. (2020). Case studies on the transition from traditional classrooms to innovative learning environments: Emerging strategies for success. *Improving Schools*, 175–89. https://doi.org/10.1177/1365480219894408.

Gargiulo, S. (2020, 17 April). Denmark's return to school gives glimpse of what classrooms will look like post-lockdown. *CNN*. https://edition.cnn.com/2020/04/17/europe/denmark-coronavirus-first-school-intl/index.html.

Greene, A.J. (1912). The open air school movement, 1904–1912. *The Public Health Journal*, 3(10), 547–52. http://www.jstor.org/stable/41997320.

Gruwell, E. (1999). *The Freedom Writers Diary*. New York: Broadway Books.

Hamilton, J., & Wood, J. (2020). *Scot Youth and COVID*. A Place in Childhood. http://aplaceinchildhood.org/wp-content/uploads/2020/07/ScotYouthandCOVID-report-Jul-2020.pdf.

IslandWood School. (2021, 20 August). IslandWood School. Islandwood.org: https://islandwood.org/.

Khan, M., McGeown, S.P., & Islam, M.Z. (2018). 'There is no better way to study science than to collect and analyse data in your own yard': Outdoor classrooms and primary school children in Bangladesh. *Children's Geographies*. https://doi.org/10.1080/14733285.2018.1490007.

Khan, M., McGeown, S., & Bell, S. (2019). Can an outdoor learning environment improve children's academic attainment? A quasi-experimental mixed methods study in Bangladesh. *Environment and Behaviour*, 1–26. https://doi.org/10.1177/0013916519860868.

Khazar, O. (2020, 28 July). Why can't we just have class outside? It might be the answer to America's school-reopening problem. https://www.theatlantic.com/health/archive/2020/07/outdoor-schools-coronavirus/614680/.

Little, H., Elliott, S., & Wyver, S. (2017). *Outdoor Learning Environments. Spaces for Exploration, Discovery and Risk-taking in the Early Years*. London: Routledge. https://doi.org/10.4324/9781003116660.

Mau, B. (2010). Naturalize play spaces. In O. Architects, V. Furniture, & B. M. Design (Eds.), *The Third Teacher*. New York: Abrams, 96.

Meckel, R.A. (1996). Open-air school and the Tuberculosis child in early 20th-century America. *Archives of Pediatrics and Adolescent Medicine*, 150(1), 91–6. https://doi.org/10.1001/archpedi.1996.02170260095016.

Melnick, H., & Darling-Hammond, L. (2020). Reopening schools in the context of COVID-19: Health and safety guidelines from other countries. Policy Brief. Learning Policy Institute.

Merewether, J. (2015, February). Young children's perspectives of outdoor learning spaces: What matters? *Australasian Journal of Early Childhood*, 40(1). https://doi.org/10.1177/1836939115040001.

MessiNessi. (2016). *MessiNessi*. Retrieved from messinessichic: https://www.messynessychic.com/2016/03/15/classrooms-without-walls-a-forgotten-age-of-open-air-schools/.

Mettis, K., & Valjataga, T. (2021). Designing learning experiences for outdoor hybrid learning spaces. *British Journal of Educational Technology*, 52(1), 498–513. https://doi.org/10.1111/bjet.13034.

Morris, I., & Knodell, A.R. (2015). Greek cities in the first millennium BCE. In *The Cambridge World History: Volume III Early Cities in Comparative Perspective, 4000BCE-1200CE*. Cambridge University Press, 343–63. https://doi.org/10.1017/CHO9781139035606.021

Nasir, N.H., Salim, F., & Yaman, M. (2014). The potential of outdoor space utilization for learning interaction. *Fostering Ecosphere in Built Environment*. International Islamic University Malaysia. https://d1wqtxts1xzle7.cloudfront.net/38807289/THE_POTENTIAL_OF_OUTDOOR_SPACE_UTILIZATION_FOR_LEARNING_INTERACTION-with-cover-page-v2.pdf?Expires=1636304693&Signature=FSSjuTbzexhKZW7FD-BpqxO1sVlOm5le9TAVpcNaBo9rh5cZsV4GTwSMWO1luCA0orPsVAhBc6h9d3Vyh2ic6vvl.

Quay, J., Gray, T., Thomas, G., Allen-Craig, S., Asfeldt, M., Andkjaer, S., . . . Pedersen, K. (2020). What future/s for outdoor and environmental education in a world that has contended with COVID-19? *Journal of Outdoor and Environmental Education*, 93–117. https://doi.org/10.1007/s42322-020-00059-2.

Rowe, B.R., Canosa, A., Drouffle, J.M., & Mitchell, J.B. (2021). Simple quantitative assessment of the outdoor versus indoor airborne transmission of viruses and COVID-19. *Environmental Research*, 198. https://doi.org/10.1016/j.envres.2021.111189.

Schoolyards. (2021, 15 September). *Schoolyards Learning Resources*. Retrieved from Schoolyards: http://www.schoolyards.org/teaching.resources.html

Sewell, J. (2015). Urban planning, Roman. In C. Smith (Ed.), *Encyclopedia of Global Archaeology*. New York: Springer. https://doi.org/10.1007/978-1-4419-0465-2_1488.

Sharples, M. (2015). Making sense of context for mobile learning. In J. Traxler & A. Kukulska-Hulme (Eds.), *Mobile Learning: The Next Generation*. Abingdon: Routledge, 140–53.

Sheikh, A., Sheikh, A., Sheikh, Z., & Dhami, S. (2020). Reopening schools after the COVID-19 lockdown. *Journal of Global Health*, 10(1). https://doi.org/10.7189/jogh.10.010376.

Spiteri, J. (2020). Assessing the usefulness of outdoor learning in the early years during the COVID-19 pandemic in Malta. *Malta Review of Educational Research*, 14(1), 141–61.

The Scottish Government. (2018). *Out to Play – Creating Outdoor Play Experiences for Children: Practical Guidance*. The Scottish Government. ISBN 9781787814448 https://www.gov.scot/publications/out-play-practical-guidance-creating-outdoor-play-experiences-children/.

The Scottish Government. (2016). *Scotland's Play Strategy, Valuing Play, Every Day*. Edinburgh: The Scottish Government. www.gov.scot.

The Trust for Public Land. (2021, 10 September). *tpl*. Retrieved from The Trust for Public Land: tpl.org.

The Trust for Public Land. (2020). *School's Out: In a Time of Compounding Crises, America's Schoolyards are Packed with Potential.* https://www.tpl.org/sites/default/files/Schools-Out_A-Trust-for-Public-Land-Special-Report.pdf.

Waite, S. (2011). Teaching and learning outside the classroom: Personal values, alternative pedagogies and standards. *Education*, 65–82. https://doi.org/10.1080/03004270903206141.

Waite, S., Passy, R., Gilchrist, M., Hunt, A., & Blackwell, I. (2016). *Natural Connections Demonstration Project, 2012–2016: Final Report.* Natural England Commissioned Reports.

Waitep, S., Bolling, M., & Bentsen, P. (2014). Comparing apples and pears?: A conceptual framework for understanding forms of outdoor learning through comparison of English Forest Schools and Danish udeskole. *Environmental Education Research*, 868–92. https://doi.org/10.1080/13504622.2015.1075193.

Waters, A. (2021). *Our Edible Schoolyard.* Retrieved from our edible schoolyard: https://www.ourediblescoolyard.org/.

Weed, M., & Foad, A. (2020). Rapid scoping review of evidence of outdoor transmission of COVID-19. *medRxiv.* https://doi.org/10.1101/2020.09.04.20188417.

Wishart, L., & Rouse, E. (2019). Pedagogies of outdoor spaces: An early childhood educator professional learning journey. *Early Child Development and Care*, 189(14), 2284–98. https://doi.org/10.1080/03004430.2018.1450250.

Woolner, P., & Triplady, L. (2019). Enhancing wellbeing through broadening the primary curriculum in the UK with open futures. In H. Hughes, J. Franz, & J. Willis (Eds.), *School Spaces for Student Wellbeing and Learning: Insights from Research and Practice.* Singapore: Springer, 157–75.

Young, F., Cleveland, B., & Imms, W. (2020). The affordances of innovative learning environments for deep learning: Educators' and architects' perceptions. *The Australian Educational Researcher*, 693–720. https://doi.org/10.1007/s13384-019-+4-y.

14 Resilient digital technologies

NAOMI JACOBS, ZACH MASON, DAVID PEREZ, ROSENDY GALABO, DAVID GREEN, JOSEPH LINDLEY, PETER J. CRAIGON, STEVE BENFORD, DIMITRIOS DARZENTAS AND HANNE G. WAGNER

Introduction

For many people, the Covid-19 pandemic meant that a great deal of work and personal socialization could not be carried out in physical proximity and had to be relocated into the virtual spaces afforded by digital collaboration technologies such as videoconferencing (Okabe-Miyamoto et al., 2021; Anh et al., 2022).

For those with access to them, applications like Zoom and Microsoft Teams rapidly replaced existing communication structures. The detailed and tangible three-dimensional spaces we previously inhabited were, overnight, collapsed into walls of interrupting faces discourteously mediated by the unavoidable latency of the internet (Garg et al., 2022).

While there are many benefits to the opportunities this digital pivoting enables, there are also limitations. 'Zoom fatigue' (Wiederhold, 2020) rapidly became a familiar concept. Bailenson (2021) has theorized that this is due to several factors such as excessive amounts of close-up eye gaze, cognitive load, increased self-evaluation from staring at video of oneself and constraints on physical mobility. There are also social challenges posed by lack of physical presence in a shared space (Kilteni et al., 2012) and lack of opportunities for the serendipity which is a key factor for creative collaboration (Woods, 2014).

For design researchers and practitioners, there are additional challenges which arise from the physicality of much of design as an activity. Talking about design education, but applicable to the wider field, Hill (2021) notes that design 'requires physical interaction – with each other, and with things, infrastructures and environments – in order to understand or imagine how the intangible qualities of culture might be embodied in tangible things and experiences'. In the absence of access to these physical spaces due to the pandemic, rapid adaptation to the digital milieu had to take place. This transition often required, in effect, rapid prototyping combined with live testing, as lessons were learned from early implementations and taken forward into subsequent activities.

In this chapter, the authors have come together to describe three case studies of how design researchers and practitioners explored ways to continue interactive collaboration despite the inability to meet in person, with a view to how this flexible approach to traditional physical interactions enabled a resilient response to pandemic restrictions and gave rise to learnings which may feed into improved practice going forward.

Case study 1: Distributed co-design approaches

This case study presents how the co-design knowledge in physical environments supports the adaptation of online and distributed approaches to co-design. The design-led research lab ImaginationLancaster has co-design as part of its philosophy and has large experience in conducting co-design processes in a variety of physical settings before Covid-19 (Cooper et al., 2018). Co-design involves a process of three layers of practice (Galabo and Cruickshank, 2021) and the pre-Covid-19 approach to each of these was as follows:

1. Planning activities before physical events involves considering the vision (what we want to achieve) with the reality (how we are going to achieve it) of a co-design process. The vision implies the definition of a desirable and meaningful outcome for all the participants. The reality involves the creative consolidation of the conditions and resources available into a sequence of planned human interactions. Each interaction is a stage of the co-design process which involves the definition of the engagement activities and the use of physical spaces and materials.

2. Facilitating human interactions involves implementing the plan in a physical space, where a facilitator uses methods, techniques and tools to enable creative dialogues between participants in order to achieve an agreed objective and desired outcomes. The job of facilitation involves understanding and adapting the paralanguage used in the physical setting (e.g. intonation, pitch and speed of speaking, hesitation noises, gesture and facial expression) to make sure everyone can understand and contribute to the design and decision-making processes.

3. Doing engagement activities involves participants sharing specific work or life experiences in a creative manner that are often supported by paper-based tools provided in a physical space. In these activities, participants make, enact, and tell their stories and ideas to co-design physical outputs such as artefacts and spaces, as well as intangible outputs such as processes and strategies. Tools give participants the ability to visualize and create things in a creative way, enabling them to externalize their ideas, and imagine and act out possible futures in engagement activities.

Due to the Covid-19 pandemic, the co-design process had to be adapted to ensure completion of existing and future projects. Although videoconferencing and digital platforms for collaboration became increasingly available, the co-design knowledge acquired through practice cannot be replicated in online settings. The main challenges of running co-design workshops online are the loss of part of the paralanguage and limitations to responses caused by the absence of physical presence. To understand the design language of online settings, the technological limitations and how to address these challenges, the research team ran a pilot study called DisCO (Distributed Co-design) in April 2020. The aim of the study was to explore the use of digital platforms in collaborative research initiatives. This pilot project allowed us to develop a new set of principles for designing and running online workshops (Galabo et al., 2020) which have been further refined through a series of events. In the following sections, we describe two of these co-design projects that were conducted online and provide some preliminary insights on the adaptation of the co-design process in distributed online environments.

Designing research ecosystems at Design Research Society (DRS) conference 2020

In August 2020, a group of researchers of ImaginationLancaster delivered an online workshop about innovation ecosystems at the DRS2020 conference. The workshop was initially designed to be physically delivered at the conference in Australia. However, the conference was held online due to the Covid-19 pandemic. The workshop aimed at enhancing the understanding of ecosystems through a co-design workshop using a paper-based tool developed and tested for mapping innovation ecosystems (Nthubu et al., 2019).

The initial plan involved using the paper-based tool in a two-part session of 105 minutes total, as a co-design framework enabling the participants to agree on criteria for successful ecosystems, identify contacts, draw insights and discuss how to activate and sustain these insights (Figure 14.1). This was redesigned into a 1-hour workshop delivered using online platforms (Galabo et al., 2020). The research team chose Miro whiteboard, a popular tool used in design practice, since participants were delegates of a design research conference. The icebreaker was redesigned to pick any 'thing' around their workspace and nominate another participant to do the same with the aim to understand basic network concepts, such as connections. The other tasks involved working around the framework to enhance the understanding of research ecosystems.

A pre-recorded video presentation instructed participants how to use the digital tools and graphic elements to interact in the workshop. These interactions were supported by a technical producer with expertise in using the mediating technology. The technical producer assisted the main facilitator, who was less familiar with the design language of online environments (e.g. breakout rooms, reactions, emojis), in adapting his approach into online environments.

Designing digital resources to enable participants to exchange ideas in online environments involved keeping interactions simple and minimizing the cognitive load in the tasks. This was done by breaking down the tasks into four design spaces to

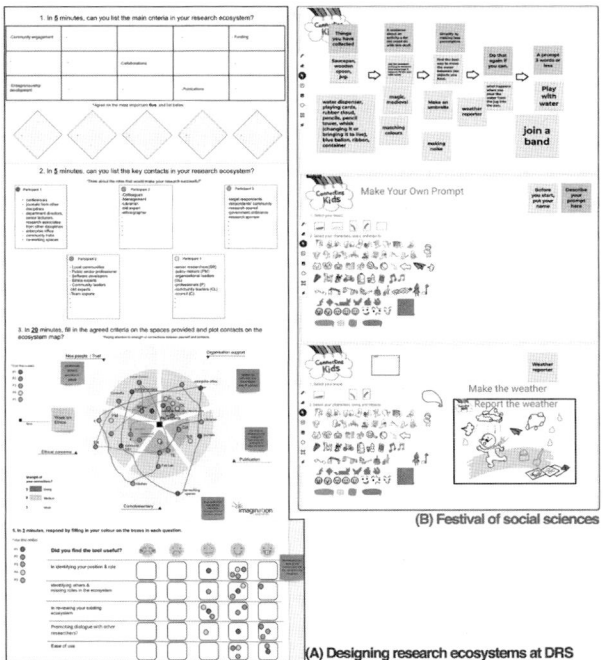

Figure 14.1 Digital resources produced for the (a) designing research ecosystems at DRS and (b) festival of social sciences workshops. Images supplied by project teams.

enable participants to lessen the need of high digital literacy and make the tasks easy to complete. Participants' interactions included clicking on text fields and typing their information, copying and pasting and drawing connections using line tools available in the platforms.

Festival of social sciences

The Covid-19 pandemic exacerbated the inequalities in education in vulnerable sectors. Children with no access to an internet connection found themselves isolated at home and disengaged from their schools. A group of researchers from Lancaster University delivered a co-design project that aimed to create educational materials for these children. The project, called 'project in a box', would deliver a collection of objects, stationery materials and 'prompt' posters that invite six-year-old children to explore, build, tell and test. This co-design approach was disseminated during the 2020 version of the ESRC Festival of Social Sciences.

Ten people assisted in an interactive co-design workshop that focused on creating playful 'prompts' for children. The intent was to explore what the sensorial stimuli of objects and artefacts that were easily found at home could mean to children. The facilitation challenge was in how to enable participants to think, feel and experience these stimuli while taking part in an online digital workshop. The workshop followed a *hybrid approach* in which physical and digital resources and platforms were used.

First, participants were asked to explore their homes wearing an imaginary pair of 'six-year-old glasses' that allow them to see their spaces and artefacts differently. Once participants discovered objects that caught their attention, they were asked to share their 'discovery' with the rest of the participants. Thus, pieces of rope turned into snakes, wooden spoons into magic wands and ribbons into rivers. From this point they were asked to describe in three words or less a prompt activity to children. Some of the ideas that emerged included 'join a band', 'play with water', 'build a home' and 'connect'. The next activity was to turn these ideas into prompt posters on Google Jamboard. Graphic assets created for the co-design project were used as resources to develop the posters, allowing participants to turn their experiences into attractive graphic representations of their ideas.

Online co-design insights

Considering that co-design processes use familiar mechanisms to enable people to be creative in their own way (Galabo, 2020), both cases provide some insights on how to successfully design and run online workshops that are described within the three co-design layers of practice below.

(1) *Planning*: Two main elements were considered when planning the online workshops – using hybrid activities to engage participants and easing the accessibility to digital platforms. Activities such as the exploration from the perspective of six-year-olds were planned to enable participants to spark their creativity, have fun and engage with the activity. Similarly, exploring the workplace to find connections and learn network concepts provided a first understanding of what the DRS workshop was about. To ease the accessibility to the platforms, the activities were broken down into small and easy tasks to reduce information workload. Thus, participants could draw connections and create digital prototypes in a quick and straightforward way. The preparation of digital tools allowed participants to engage with the activities, collaborate and achieve the outcomes of the workshops in less than 2 hours.

(2) *Facilitating*: These distributed approaches enabled the delivery of online workshops that were geographically separated, but which physically engaged participants beyond the computer screen through a hybrid approach. Although there is a loss of part of the paralanguage, this was compensated by making use of participants' work/home spaces and the digital resources such as tools and graphic assets that enable people to express and facilitate creative conversations. Understanding how the chosen digital platforms work enables the blending of physical facilitation skills and the technical layer into co-design processes.

(3) *Doing*: When designing interactions, simple graphics and basic actions lessen the need for high digital literacy. The use of stickers, sharpies and pro formas in physical workshops were adapted to enable participants to co-design

ecosystems or playful prompts for children in online environments. These workshop materials were analogous to the resources available in digital formats in the chosen online platforms, such as graphic assets, templates and basic drawing tools. Although participants were instructed to use these resources, participants were not restricted to them. They could also draw or add images from external sources. This was one of the benefits of working online as the number of resources is almost unlimited.

Case study 2: Tangible tools in a virtual context

Card-based tools are well established in helping stimulate, structure and inspire thinking in design settings (Peters et al., 2020, Roy and Warren, 2019, Wolfel and Merritt, 2013). The Cardographer project is developing a platform to support the creation and use of such card-based tools, to enable longitudinal reflection on their use through the capture of design data and its analysis through interactive visualizations of the card and design spaces (Darzentas et al., 2019).

Several card sets have been developed in connection with the Cardographer project. The design and function of the cards range from ideation cards for mixed reality games (Wetzel et al., 2017) and museum and gallery visitor experiences (visitorbox.org n.d.) to sets to aid engagement with 'ethics by design' of technology (Urquhart and Craigon, 2021). Sets relating to the ethics of research and research policy impact are also in development. These cards are typically physical cards, similar to playing cards, to be used in co-located face-to-face sessions where cards are selected and arranged to stimulate and structure discussion (Figure 14.2).

With the onset of the Covid-19 pandemic, physical face-to-face workshops using card-based tools became impossible. The immediate challenge was to digitize the cards and processes of use (e.g. see the process in Urquhart and Craigon, 2021) so that they could be conducted in an online distributed way with

Figure 14.2 Example physical card sets from left to right, Visitor Box, Mixed Reality Game Cards and Moral-IT cards. Images supplied by project teams.

as little detriment to the ideation, learning, reflection and engagement process as possible.

Cardographer and trialling existing systems

Cardographer had been envisioned to include an end-to-end platform that would support virtual card workshops for remote sessions. This aspect therefore became a priority in the pandemic. Developing this bespoke system in time would not have been possible, so to respond rapidly we trialled several third-party platforms (typically used for online games or collaboration) to help meet the immediate need for online card sessions. These ranged from Virtual Tabletop (VTTs), such as Tabletop Simulator, Tabletopia and PlayingCards.io, to online collaboration platforms such as Miro and Mural. This diverse selection of software helped support online card sessions and the project refined its design requirements for Cardographer.

These systems were trialled during a series of teaching and research activities using different sets of cards, including the Moral-IT cards (Urquhart and Craigon, 2021) and Mixed Reality Game Cards (Wetzel et al., 2017; Darzentas et al., 2019). Our reflections on these trials form the basis of the observations reported here. They were not used in isolation, typically paired with online meeting software such as Microsoft Teams or Zoom to allow for communication and supported by the functionality they offer.

Physical to digital: Barriers to entry and vital backup

From our experience and as shown in prior work (e.g. Urquhart and Craigon, 2021) the physicality of cards is important in how they operate as engagement and ideation tools. We therefore initially set out to replicate physical card sessions as far as possible in an online context. Several elements, however, resulted in unforeseen 'hoops to jump through' and barriers to entry which necessitated deployment of backup solutions and alternative approaches to allow the sessions to meet their goals.

How easily a user could access and use a piece of software was crucial to how, or even if, it could be trialled. For example, despite its sophistication, Tabletop Simulator was never tried with participants as it requires individual paid licenses. Tabletopia enables access to a similar 3D tabletop space via a browser and is free via guest access. It however proved inaccessible in one instance where distributed participants were unable to access the session that had been prepared for them. In other cases, it proved computationally resource intensive for participants with varied connectivity and devices and, although operational, frustrated some users due to lag and delay causing them to prefer a backup. The backup was a PDF of the cards and a shared notes sheet to be completed collaboratively either through Microsoft Teams or Google documents. This allowed the session to continue and the learning to be achieved by browsing the PDF and choosing cards, discussing them as a group and making notes on the sheet provided (e.g. for the Moral-IT card process board, see

Urquhart and Craigon, 2021). The success of this relatively unsophisticated method then became a reliable starting point and backup to avoid the potential for technical problems to disrupt or derail future workshops.

Having said this, when a task was introduced as solely using a PDF of the cards and notes sheet, one group requested to manipulate images of the cards on a PowerPoint slide indicating a desire to manipulate the cards 'physically' and visually, analogously to how it would be done in a face-to-face session.

Capturing discussion

While manipulating virtual cards was revealed as *not* being critical to the success of a session, holding discussion and making notes *was*, as facilitated by the structured notes sheet. This demonstrated the necessity of recording notes and annotations alongside the cards (not available through Tabletopia for example). Easy note taking and annotation (to underpin and go alongside virtual card manipulation) was therefore central to the value of Miro, an online collaborative whiteboard, for immediately supporting online card sessions. From our experience, Miro was also more easily accessed, through free educational accounts for the project team with participants simply clicking on a link to access the shared workspace. The lower barriers to entry of Miro and annotation functionality led to a greater confidence that sessions could be conducted as intended in a multi-user setting using the cards and same process board from previous face-to-face sessions.

Understanding cards more than the process

One key difference of Miro is that the cards are treated as one-sided 2D images without any of the functional paradigms of playing cards, such as flipping, stacking, drawing or having a hand of cards. The users still, however, engaged with the images as 'cards' with the information importantly presented in card form. A tacit familiarity with cards as a 'thing' and concept helped people to understand what they were required to do in choosing or discussing a 'card'. The widely understood concept of 'a card', as well as how they present information, meant that the task could be more easily communicated and engaged with in the online environment.

By contrast the process, or how to use the cards, was less intuitive. The role of boards (whose structure was replicated in notes sheets) as visual guides to the process to be followed (supported by instructions and examples) of where to place cards was therefore important. While cards may be familiar, the process to engage with ethics or design mixed reality game experiences was less so, requiring clear instructions.

Translating card *process*, not simply cards

Translating the use of card-based tools to an online context, as briefly described here, has revealed insights into the nature of card use and process key to their resilience, with wider relevance. To summarize, this rests on translating the *process* not solely the *cards* (or other artefacts used within the process being moved online) and doing so as technologically simply as possible. Sessions were successful when simple and accessible with the lowest barriers to entry. The initial backup option of a basic notes sheet (representing the process board) to capture discussion with reference to a PDF of the cards was foundational to meeting the same aim as a face-to-face session supported by a clearly explained and structured process. Card sessions were therefore conducted successfully online and the process forms the foundation for the requirements of the bespoke Cardographer VTT in development. Having said this, however, the value of being able to manipulate the cards online as images or physicalized cards remains, to be built upon this foundation. Drawing from the observations sketched here, notes and process boards will be combined with 'physicalized' virtual cards to produce a more faithful and comparable online representation of card sessions to complement and augment face-to-face sessions when their possibility returns.

Case study 3: Virtual co-presence and experimental digital spaces

While workshops and tool-based activities are structured, and last a finite amount of time, this is only one type of interaction which needed to be adjusted for new online circumstances. Challenges to more *ad hoc* interactions are driven by a variety of factors including a lack of differentiation between the spaces we work and relax in, constant delays in conversation which reduce the flow of discussion, and – perhaps – misinterpretations of why face-to-face interactions are important. One response to these issues is the video game inspired conferencing space Gather Town, and our experiments with Gather Town are the topic of this section of the chapter.

Game spaces – by which we mean the virtual spaces inside video games – are generally designed to be enjoyable, and the spectrum of video games also represents a huge diversity of digitally mediated interaction. Gather Town aims to capitalize on these by positioning itself at the intersection between a dynamic game world and videoconferencing. While conference calls are like shouting across a concert hall to fulfil many different types of social interaction, Gather Town is built from the ground up for each varying use case. Users choose avatars which are placed within a top-down two-dimensional space, and a heuristic of proximity allows users, via their avatars, to initiate videoconferences dynamically. These spaces are designed by the managers of the space, enabling attendees to feel separation between the different Gather Town spaces they connect to due to their unique configurations, replicating the movement between physical spaces. The two-dimensional format of Gather Town is extremely flexible allowing Gather Town spaces to vary significantly, from copies of familiar building structures to futuristic spaceships and pseudo-psychedelic labyrinths to be unravelled through exploration.

The imperfect nature of videoconference calling is self-evident to everyone who partakes in it, with interactions closer to telephone calls than in-person meetings. In contrast, Gather Town draws its design from games, leveraging metaphors for space and proximity by creating digital copies of physical spaces, and designing entirely new abstract spaces, allowing for richer immersive experiences. We describe some of our experiments using Gather Town in this way below.

At the beginning of the pandemic, we created a Lancaster Design Studios Gather Town space, which simulated an existing space (Jacobs and Lindley, 2021). This familiarity enabled it to stay populated for longer, with users mimicking their spatial attitudes from physical space. Sections of the space could then push out of reality to portray spaceships, remaining relatable due to the original grounding.

However, we also explored the use of Gather Town beyond recreations of existing concepts of space. *The Egg* was the first of these experimental forays into using Gather Town. We elected to submit a link to a Gather Town space in response to a call for papers at a conference. In other words, the Gather Town space *is* the paper (which is titled *This is not a paper*) (Lindley et al., 2021). Unearthing an ability to create non-linear narratives through stories enabled participants to get lost in a visual journey. It took a paper and exploded it, enabling traversal from introduction to end where each section was self-contained so interaction with others was less likely, akin to choose your own adventure game. Commenting on the shortcomings of videoconferencing, it invited its users into a playful metaphor-riddled expanse where they might chance across others lost within its rooms. At points *The Egg* was deliberately hard to navigate, with many hidden elements and routes echoing the 'Easter Egg' aesthetic of game culture where the players find secrets.

Ways of Seeing is another Gather Town-based research paper-like environment which simultaneously aims to increase the size and complexity, but also to make the space easier to navigate for participants. Iconification was considered here as a way to create a language for the users to navigate the space with familiarity, akin to the notion that the 'confusing streets of Venice become traversable after one or two experiences, since they are rich in distinctive details, which are soon sequentially organized' (Lynch, 1960). Simple circles were chosen to represent portals which could be used to navigate within the space, allowing users to communicate with each other where they might go within the paper spatially, for example 'shall we go and meet at the introduction?' Focusing around a large central space conceptually changed the way interaction occurred. Due to its increased transparency, the experience became more shared, similar to a collaborative adventure map (Figure 14.3).

Our most recent experiment with Gather Town is an exhibition space showcasing the work of ImaginationLancaster. With this space, we elected to simplify portals and movement between sections. This gave users the option to hold a single button to be led through most of the content sequentially or navigate themselves through the use of three icons. Aiming to combine the spatial language of *The Egg* and *Ways of Seeing*, navigation could be linear or explorative, with an intent to increase the accessibility of the space, while giving users opportunities to converse with others.

Figure 14.3 Gather Town: Four instances of experimental spaces. Top to bottom: Imagination Exhibition Space, *The Egg*, *Ways of Seeing*, the Lancaster Design Studio. Images supplied by project teams.

While this is unarguably the most accessible space of the three, this potentially rendered it devoid of character; 'there is some value in mystification, labyrinth, or surprise in the environment'. While 'there must be no danger of losing basic form or orientation, of never coming out', confusion and exploration created inviting and intriguing spaces. The 'surprise must occur in an over-all framework' (Lynch, 1960, p. 5) in order to ground its delights, but without risk or reward, a user may feel unmotivated to endeavour further within an environment after too long.

The notion of reading a room is something which has been lost since remote working began. Breakout rooms, cameras or even concepts like Teams Together Mode all fail to alleviate the inescapable feeling of being talked at. Gather Town breaks free from the flatness of web conferencing as a format by making dimensional space the primary experience, alongside video calls which react within the space. The way users engage with such spaces is to be carefully considered. With our earlier iterations of Gather Town space experiments, the navigation methods were less linear, allowing more room for exploration and Easter eggs. While those who have played games find navigating Gather Town (with its art style inspired by retro video game graphics) easier and more inviting, this led to confusion for those not versed in video game norms, finding difficulty noticing the subtle symbols which indicate portals between sections of the space.

The avatars also lend themselves to the gamification of the experience, connecting the user to the space they're in. Being encouraged to move around the space to reveal different sections of the image reinforces this feeling, as well as only being able to talk to others by being close to them within the environment. Like story-based games, there is nothing designed to make you come back to the spaces, so with the prospect of archiving in mind, you may be preserving the research paper, but not the experience, as the footfall will rapidly decline after any virtual event. This creates events which mimic those in the real world, creating urgency to attend interactive experiences, as opposed to watching a pre-rehearsed or recorded videoconference. Gather Town spaces created to emulate offices may share similar issues, but this is dependent on their initial uptake.

In terms of a response to the pandemic, if video calls were a popup tent in a car park to fulfil Covid-19 testing at a moment's notice, experiences like Gather Town are the vaccination programme. Planning with each user group in mind creates a rigid structure that, while taking longer to reach fruition, facilitates enjoyable and varied interactions through digital spaces, as long as the users are willing to engage in the game-like interactions. The diverse options provided through its systems are challenging to use effectively. But with proper consideration for the types of user who are attending a given space, it can simulate alternative spaces which are far richer in interaction, variety and engagement than any traditional videoconferencing experience could be stretched to afford.

Conclusion: Implications for the future of collaboration

Taking these three cases together, we can demonstrate that during the pandemic there were many opportunities for technology to step in and provide solutions for the restrictions to in-person interaction and design activities. However, unexpected barriers and new findings were encountered in each context, and we can conclude that translating traditionally physical activities to online contexts is not straightforward. It is particularly difficult to blend physical expectations (such as cards which can be manipulated) with digital affordances. An exploratory and flexible approach is necessary, where alternative strategies are tried and iterated.

An interesting commonality between these cases is the adaptation, appropriation and use in each of existing platforms and services, rather than the creation of bespoke software. For example, the use of Gather Town as a conference paper and novel format. These uses may have been outside those intended or imagined by the designers of the platforms, and therefore creative solutions had to be found to features that might be limitations to these particular uses. The process of collaborative design and interaction is the key concern in these case studies, not the tools, therefore resilience requires allowing multiple options for participating.

Accessibility is also key concern highlighted by these cases. Not everyone is as familiar with digital spaces, has access to computers that can run sophisticated graphics or a strong internet connection to support high upload/download capacities. Having alternative methods in mind which have lower bandwidth requirements and less sophisticated methods, such as was the case with the co-design activities, can be particularly valuable.

For future practice, it will be important to build upon these learnings and create hybrid interactional spaces and tools which make use of the best available processes, not restricted to the purely digital or physical. 'Only when digital and physical come together can meaningful transformation happen, and design is a practice for understanding and shaping these interactions, as well as integrating and connecting with others' (Hill, 2021). By bringing the most successful aspects of these adaptations into our practice, we can be resilient in the face of not just potential future pandemics and other crises, but also add benefit in other contexts. For example, allowing remote participation brings greater inclusion for those who cannot physically take part in events or who wish to limit their long-distance travel given the sustainability impacts.

References

Anh, L.T., Whelan, E., & Umair, A. (2022). 'You're still on mute'. A study of video conferencing fatigue during the COVID-19 pandemic from a technostress perspective. *Behaviour & Information Technology*, 1–15. doi:10.1080/0144929X.2022.2095304.

Bailenson, J.N. (2021). Nonverbal overload: A theoretical argument for the causes of Zoom fatigue. *Technology, Mind, and Behavior*, 2(1). https://doi.org/10.1037/tmb0000030.

Cooper, R., Dunn, R., Coulton, P., Walker,S., Rodgers, P., Cruikshank, L., Tsekleves, E. et al. (2018). Imagination Lancaster: Open-ended, anti-disciplinary, diverse. *She Ji: The Journal of Design, Economics, and Innovation*, 4(4), 307–41. https://doi.org/10.1016/j.sheji.2018.11.001.

Darzentas, D., Velt, R., Wetzel, R., Craigon, P.J., Wagner, H.D., Urquhart, L.D., & Benford, S. (2019). Card mapper: Enabling data-driven reflections on ideation cards. In *Proceedings of the 2019 CHI Conference on Human Factors in Computing Systems*. New York: Association for Computing Machinery, Paper 571, 1–15. https://doi.org/10.1145/3290605.3300801

Galabo, R. (2020). A framework for improving knowledge exchange tools. PhD thesis, Lancaster University.

Galabo, R., & Cruickshank, L. (2021). Making it better together: A framework for improving creative engagement tools. *CoDesign*, 1–23. https://doi.org/10.1080/15710882.2021.1912777.

Galabo, R., Nthubu, B., Cruickshank, L., & Perez, D. (2020). Redesigning a workshop from physical to digital: Principles for designing distributed co-design approaches. In Tatiana Rivchun & Liudmila Aliabieva (Eds.), *Design: Vertical & Horizontal Growth*, 64–70.

Garg, S., Srivastava, A., Glencross, M., & Sharma, O. (2022, April). A study of the effects of network latency on visual task performance in video conferencing. In *Extended Abstracts of the 2022 CHI Conference on Human Factors in Computing Systems (CHI EA '22). Association for Computing Machinery.* , New York, Article 213, 1–7. https://doi.org/10.1145/3491101.3519678.

Hill, D. (2021) Design education needs physical space. https://medium.com/a-chair-in-a-room/design-education-needs-physical-space-35bd49f39549 (accessed 19 July 2021).

Jacobs, N., & Lindley, J. (2021) Room for improvement in the video conferencing 'space'. *AoIR Selected Papers of Internet Research* (forthcoming).

Kilteni, K., Groten, R., & Slater, M. (2012). The sense of embodiment in virtual reality. *Presence: Teleoperators and Virtual Environments*, 21(4), 373–87.

Lindley, J., Sturdee, M., Philip Green, D., & Alter, H. (2021). This is not a paper. In *2021 CHI Conference on Human Factors in Computing Systems: Making Waves, Combining Strengths*, CHI EA 2021.

Lynch, K. (1960). *The Image of the City*, Vol. 11. Cambridge, MA: MIT Press.

Nthubu, B., Richards, D., & Cruickshank, L. (2019). Disruptive innovation ecosystems: Reconceptualising innovation ecosystems. *Conference Proceedings of the Academy for Design Innovation Management*, 2(1), 629–44. https://doi.org/10.33114/adim.2019.09.318.

Okabe-Miyamoto, K., Durnell, E., Howell, R.T., & Zizi, M. (2021). Did zoom bomb? Negative video conferencing meetings during COVID-19 undermined worker subjective productivity. *Human Behavior and Emerging Technologies*, 3(5), 1067–83.

Peters, D., Loke, L., & Ahmadpour, A. (2020). Toolkits, cards and games – A review of analogue tools for collaborative ideation. *CoDesign*. https://doi.org/10.1080/15710882.2020.1715444.

Roy, R., & Warren, J.P. (2019). Card-based design tools: A review and analysis of 155 card decks for designers and designing. *Design Studies*, 63, 125–54. https://doi.org/10.1016/j.destud.2019.04.002.

Urquhart, L.D., & Craigon, P.J. (2021). The Moral-IT deck: A tool for ethics by design. *Journal of Responsible Innovation*, 8(1), 94–126. https://doi.org/10.1080/23299460.2021.1880112.

Visitorbox. https://visitorbox.org/ (accessed 15 July 2021).

Wetzel, R., Rodden, T., & Benford, S. (2017). Developing ideation cards for mixed reality game design. *Transactions of the Digital Games Research Association*, 3(2), 175–21.

Wiederhold, B.K. (2020). Connecting through technology during the coronavirus disease 2019 pandemic: Avoiding "Zoom Fatigue". *Cyberpsychology, Behaviour and Social Networking*, 23(7), 437–8.

Wölfel, C., & Merritt, T. (2013). Method card design dimensions: A survey of card-based design tools. In P. Kotzé, G. Marsden, G. Lindgaard, J. Wesson, & M. Winckler (Eds.), *Human-Computer Interaction – INTERACT 2013*. Lecture Notes in Computer Science, Vol. 8117. Berlin, Heidelberg: Springer. https://doi.org/10.1007/978-3-642-40483-2_34

Woods, M. (2014). Serendipity in practice: A social state. In Alison Williams, Derek Jones, & Judy Robertson (Eds.), *Bite: Recipes for Remarkable Research*. Leiden, Netherlands: Brill Sense. http://www.jstor.org/stable/10.1163/j.ctv2gjwn0p.

15 Conclusion

Principles for resilience

As we write this concluding chapter in the UK, we are continuing to experience the challenges posed by a new Covid-19 variant and have passed the sad milestone of 150,000 deaths in the UK alone. While seemingly not as dangerous as the previous Covid-19 variants, these new variants highlight the need for societies to remain adaptable while developing greater resilience for the future. However, we need to reflect upon our collective experience in order to draw out lessons and ensure that governments and citizens globally are as prepared as possible for the next pandemic (or indeed any sudden global challenge), in stark contrast to the lack of preparedness witnessed in many countries in early 2020.

The contributions in this volume not only offer insights into how we might learn from the ways in which design has been deployed, to varying degrees of success, over the last two years, but also how we might use design to embed this learning in our future endeavours. We asked authors to respond to the four stages identified: reaction, adaptation, recovery and resilience, and to use the database we created as a starting point to their responses. The responses we received highlight the myriad ways in which design has been used at all levels of society around the world. The chapters explore a diverse array of contexts and scales, from the mundane and personal to the national, and even global. The authors have covered the rapid deployment of technologies, both in the personal work and education settings, including the design of contact tracing applications; the need for clear and engaging graphic visual communication and the value of seeing it as a problem that can be tackled together; the need for design to be a work in progress, where it is 'imperfect'; design at a strategic level in the context of the UK; the impacts of Covid-19 upon our built environments; and case studies at a national level from locations that were considered to have dealt with the crisis successfully.

From these experiences and explorations, we can draw out key principles and learning that might form part of a call to action from the world of design and beyond. This is vital to maintain the momentum that accumulated in the early days of adaptation, where national governments and international NGOs called for a complete re-evaluation of societies and a universal tackling of inequalities that were highlighted at all stages of the pandemic.

Resilience, agility and 'less than perfect' design

Throughout the pandemic we have seen governments and global agencies call for societies to 'build back better' (HM Treasury, 2021; OECD, 2020; UN, 2020). These calls also refer to resilience and the perils of returning to 'business as usual'. Furthermore, major global issues including sustainability and reduction of health inequalities have been embedded into these calls, to use the experiences and momentum in public policy created over the last two years for greater public good.

While we use the term 'resilience' as a key stage of this pandemic and of building our resilience for the future, this term is contested and sometimes problematic. One of the key components of resilience is the notion of 'bouncing back', the return of a system to its natural state or to recover from disasters (Holling, 1973; Paton, 2001; Coles, 2004). However, the two key issues that have emerged during the pandemic have been the realization that we cannot and should not return to the state we were in prior to Covid-19, and that calls for resilience often place responsibility with communities to think about how we use this crisis as momentum for change for the better now and in the future, so better work/life balance, better environments, better infrastructure, better healthcare systems can crucially save us from increasing climate change.

The nature of Covid-19 is 'transboundary' (Bryce et al., 2020), which has presented unprecedented pressures on organization, personal and community resilience. Furthermore, Covid-19 sits within the constellation of wicked, complex and systemic problems (Ritter and Webber, 1973; Hill, 2012) that require strategic and innovative design approaches and the careful design of policies to tackle them (McCartney et al., 2020), as we saw in Chapters 3 and 10.

In this volume we see communities building their own resilience, of 'bottom-up' resourcefulness (MacKinnon and Derickson, 2013), through the design of PPE and ventilators to the creation of mutual aid groups and the development of online communities. By understanding design as a process that does not always have to lead to perfect products or systems, the authors in Chapter 2 suggest that design as a 'work in progress' will always be 'wholly useful'.

Agility has been vital, whether this leads to imperfect, rapidly produced designs (e.g. PPE equipment made at home, some communication design and development and deployment of contact tracing apps) or more considered, but still responsive, such as the generative social distancing measures. Some of these designs will not be required again because they have served their purpose. For example, the production of home-made masks and PPE equipment filled a gap in supply that has since been filled by government intervention. If lessons from Covid-19 are taken on board, then should future pandemics occur, these issues should not be faced again. As discussed in Chapters 1 and 2, these designs, often produced by amateurs or 'non-designers', were often 'imperfect'. However, they served a purpose, both in terms of enabling producers to occupy their time during lockdowns and to bring about a sense of agency when many people felt helpless. These designs also embody a sense of care, that through making the simple designs, the makers demonstrated the importance of not only producing masks (both hand-sewn and 3D printed) to protect themselves, but also to protect those working on the frontline, where supplies were inadequate.

We have seen that some more mature design responses presented here, such as the rapid introduction of social distancing measures, and the generative social distancing designs, as explored in Chapter 4, will be of great use and should be part of any plans for emergency response in the future. It is also vital that supply chains, procurement process and governance systems are adequately designed for future pandemic scenarios, as we saw issues with ventilators and companies rapidly producing products with government backing that were not used due to the design brief being inadequate (Chapter 1).

The increased convergency of the digital and physical worlds, of responsiveness and agility might be less than perfect, but were 'good enough'

The convergence of the digital and physical space occurred early in the pandemic, with organizations at global, national and local levels forced to rapidly move online or change their business models. The impacts of these moves, as explored in Chapter 10, demonstrate that while opportunities exist in this space, organizations should think carefully about how design is deployed, both in the development of new products and in the design of new, hybrid, business models.

The authors of Chapter 14 presented a range of case studies representing the rapid move to digital technologies that had huge implications upon education, work and social interactions. While this move afforded opportunities for participation for those who had previously been excluded physically or geographically, digital exclusion was highlighted along economic and social fault-lines. It is vital that the deployment of technologies in future pandemics takes such exclusion into account and ensures that access is offered, whether through the design of systems and software requiring lower specification hardware or internet access that is not high speed.

We also saw the need for redesigning our physical world, from education provision to ensuring safe and healthy spaces and cities. During lockdowns access to public green spaces became vital for those without their own. However, unlike previous public health crises that have resulted in grand public architecture, more responsive approaches, such as the generative social distancing designs of Chapter 4, must be considered for future crises. Agility must be embedded into our cities, to enable rapid yet clearly understood signage systems for future pandemics, in addition to ensuring health in urban spaces.

Education everywhere has been of particular concern, in particular, the delivery of education at all levels highlighted the potential for blended learning, of new modes of delivery but it also highlighted the inequalities in provision of equipment and infrastructure, and the need to consider the very places in which education occurs

(Chapter 13). The physical design of the spaces in which we and work in have been very prevalent throughout the pandemic, for both our mental and physical health. This will no doubt continue and design has a significant role to play going forward, building on the momentum for change while being cognisant of the behaviour response in society and organizations. Adaptation and flexibility have become a watchword in terms of learning, working and life in general; the role of design to help decision making in organization, governments, communities is significant and the case can be made that design can do this.

One obvious recognition was that the pandemic increased significantly the adoption of technologies. Thus, design research and the design profession must embrace technological change, be ready for rapid adoption, understand the implications on society and the environment, such as behaviour change, inclusivity, accessibility, security and privacy concerns as well as the energy and environment challenges digital technologies generate. These rapid technological adaptations require agility, and sometimes a less than perfect solution that solves with challenges, with care.

Questioning the role of the designer

Throughout the pandemic the wide range of roles fulfilled by designers has been highlighted, from the strategic (as seen in Chapter 3), to the material (e.g. the design of new spaces, products and services), problem framing and problem solving (e.g. in government policy design). By bringing these examples to the fore, the contributions in this book demonstrate the nature of design as a technical social bridge.

We saw the role of the designer transformed around the world. Individuals and communities emerged to address the gaps left by policymakers, particularly responding to the lack of PPE equipment in the early stages, as outlined in the first two parts of the book. As Chapter 3 highlights, the bulk of the design work that has taken place during [the pandemic] is at the level of the 'everyday' where, as Manzini argues, widespread disruptions now mean that 'more subjects must learn to design their own lives' (Manzini, 2015, p. 31). However, in order to do so people require agency and resources. We saw people redesigning their lives rapidly, whether to engage in home-schooling, or working from home, which worked for some, but often meant women were disadvantaged (Independent Panel for Pandemic Preparedness, 2021).

Chapter 8 highlighted a range of design interventions from South Korea, a country considered to have dealt more successfully with the outbreak than countries such as the United States and UK. The examples in this chapter demonstrate the importance of collaboration for problem solving, but that should proceed as a user-centred process. The authors argue that it is necessary to establish a network of various participants, including governments, companies and citizens and to encourage collaboration among stakeholders. The authors also argue, based on the studies they present, that designs should consider not only the results but also the processes involved in solving social problems. Designs should be used as tools for user-centred problem discovery and collaboration, and application of technologies should be developed in an everyday context. Post-Covid-19, designs should meet social and economic objectives and create shared value by connecting various stakeholders, including service providers and consumers. Indeed this is something that has been promoted for many years by those who advocate the role of design in industry and academia; however, the evidence from the pandemic in this volume and elsewhere has illustrated further how design can and should meet current and future social, economic and environmental challenges.

It is clear from past health epidemics that trust and accurate information can significantly help the public in following public health measures, which help decrease the spread of disease. However, throughout the Covid-19 pandemic, we witnessed an 'infodemic', which confused the general population and policymakers. It is vital that clear and trustworthy information is provided and that it is communicated clearly to non-experts and experts alike. Chapter 5 offers draft recommendations on how to effectively plan communication and frame messages that are compelling and actionable to local audiences considering their social, cultural and economic circumstances.

So for design academics and design professionals there are some fundamental facets of design that remain: (1) products, places and messages always need considerable design expertise; (2) designers tend to be skilled integrators, coordinators and orchestrators of people, processes and knowledge, which must be embedded in their education and developed in the profession; (3) creative thinking and making skills come to the fore in a crisis, these underline a profession, that has expanded beyond designing things, to designing services and policies, and this will be essential to address future, immediate (e.g. pandemic) and long-term (e.g. climate change) crises.

Critical collaborations and power dynamics

The reflections in this volume point towards the vital contributions of collaborations throughout the pandemic in myriad ways. We saw technology companies work together in the development of contact tracing applications (Chapter 1). Collaborations between large organizations, such as Apple and Microsoft, in developing contact tracing applications and in the production of ventilators. This highlights the potential for collaboration to engage in global challenges and ensure we address wider values than those of a profit or financial motive. The authors of Chapter 12 point towards collaboration between a range of disciplines as being fundamental to designing healthy and resilient cities post-Covid-19. However, we must bear in mind the potential power dynamics that exist during 'non-crises' times. During the pandemic these dynamics were often put aside, in favour of rapid collaboration for the common good. We also saw the rise of 'bottom-up' approaches of mutual aid groups and individuals as a result of power vacuums, where governments were dealing with large-scale policy design and implementation. In addition, we saw the dispensing of 'red tape' and bureaucracy within governments to ensure the rapid awarding of contracts, although this was also littered with challenges (as with the UK Government, for example, Lacobucci, 2021).

Reflections

The responses in this volume offer personal insights at a moment in time that are, in some cases, responsive and emergent, covering a range of international perspectives. As a record of immediate design responses around the world, we hope this volume offers valuable insights that can be reflected upon as we begin to emerge from the pandemic. The responses highlight design as it has occurred at all levels of society throughout the pandemic, and that the act of designing and making was as important socially as it was at a wider, more professional level. As an act of care, in which everyone is a designer, but that there are professional designers who are trained to design, facilitate design and provide the framework for everyone to be part of that process. We must now reconsider how we understand and deploy design within the multiple global crises that exist, including climate change, biodiversity loss and hunger (Nature, 2020). What this volume has illustrated is that design that works in a crisis is collaborative, agile, both specific and strategic, action oriented and must be inclusive and sustainable.

References

Bryce, C., Ring, P., Ashby, S., & Wardman, J.K. (2020). Resilience in the face of uncertainty: Early lessons from the COVID-19 pandemic. *Journal of Risk Research*, 23(7–8), 880–887.

Coles, E.B.P. (2004). Developing community resilience as a foundation for disaster recovery. *Australian Journal of Emergency Management*, 19, 6–15.

Hill, D. (2012). *Dark Matter and Trojan Horses: A Strategic Design Vocabulary*. London: Strelka Press.

HM Treasury (2021). *Build Back Better: Our Plan for Growth*. London: HM Government. https://www.gov.uk/government/publications/build-back-better-our-plan-for-growth. ISBN 978-1-5286-2415-2.

Holling, C. (1973). Resilience and stability of ecological systems. *Annual Review of Ecology and Systematics*, 4, 1–23.

Iacobucci, G. (2021). Covid-19: Ministers told to reveal names of companies in "VIP lane" for PPE contracts, *BMJ*, 375, 2554.

Independent Panel for Pandemic Preparedness and Response (2021). *COVID-19: Make it the Last Pandemic* (Report).

MacKinnon, D., & Derickson, K.D. (2013). From resilience to resourcefulness: A critique of resilience policy and activism. *Progress in Human Geography*, 37(2), 253–270.

McCartney, G., Fenton, L., Morris, G., & Mackie, P. (2020). "Superpolicies" and "policy-omnishambles". *Public Health in Practice*, 1, 100003.

Manzini (2015). *Design, When Everybody Designs: An Introduction to Design for Social Innovation*, Cambridge, Massachusetts: MIT Press

Nature (2020). Sustainability at the Crossroads. *The International Journal of Science*, 23/30 December 2020. https://media.nature.com/original/magazine-assets/d41586-021-03781-z/d41586-021-03781-z.pdf.

OECD (2020). *Building Back Better: A Sustainable, Resilient Recovery After COVID-19*. https://www.oecd.org/coronavirus/policy-responses/building-back-better-a-sustainable-resilient-recovery-after-covid-19-52b869f5/.

Paton, D.J.D. (2001). Disasters and communities: Vulnerability, resilience, and preparedness. *Disaster Prevention and Management*, 10, 270–277.

Rittel, H.W.J., & Webber, M.M. (1973). Dilemmas in a general theory of planning. *Policy Sciences*, 4(2), 155–169.

United Nations (2020). *Covid-19 Inequalities and Building Back Better*. https://www.un.org/development/desa/dspd/2020/10/covid-19-inequalities-and-building-back-better/.

Index

'1m+' social distancing rule 66–7
3D printing technology 105
30 Second Song Soap Campaign 144

adaptation stage of pandemics 12
   cities and public space 24
   data visualization 19–21
   graphic design and communication 19
   PPE 23
   technology design and use 17
   ventilators 23–4
Adobe XD 191
aerosol/droplet spread 65, 67, 71
agility 267–8
agora/forum 245
AI; see artificial intelligence (AI)
Alert Level System, New Zealand 115–16
   lockdown (alert level 4) 115
   prepare (alert level 1) 116
   reduce (alert level 2) 116
   restrict (alert level 3) 115
   timeline 117
Alphabet Inc. 15
Anderson, J. 188
Apple watch 17
aprons 21, 22
artificial intelligence (AI) 135, 140, 146, 150, 154–5, 160, 189–90, 192–4, 196–7
AR/VR 135, 144, 146, 159
'Askin Napkin' activity 167, 169–70
Audi 18–19
AutoCAD building plan 71–2
autonomous driving 135, 150, 154, 155, 159

Bailenson, J. N. 252
Bailey, J. 53
balloon jeans 193
bands 17

Banerjee, B. 52–3
Bañón, C. 71
Bañón, L. 71
bar charts 19–20
basic healthcare 1
Belgium 17
benches 246
Berardi, Franco 'Bifo' 43
Big data 135, 142, 143, 146, 156, 189–90, 196
biometric monitoring 17
Black Swan Data 192
Blauvelt, Andrew 36
Blees, G. J. 69
Blockchain 135, 154
Bloom, M.A. 242–3
Bloom's revised taxonomy 243
Bo and Mim 193
boosters 11
Boston Dynamics 16
BotsAndUs 193
Boyer, B. 54
bracelets 17
Branzi, Andrea 35
Braun, V. 81–2
Buchanan, C. 52
building common ground 215–20
building involvement 211–15
Bulgaria 17
Burberry and Barbour 22
business, Covid-19 impact to
   resilience 194–7
     design principles to digital space 194–6
     fourth order design 196–7
   structures 187–90
   transformations 190–4
     digital transformation 190–2
     non-human interactions, increasing prevalence of 192–4
     robots/AI, use of 192–4

card-based tools 257–60
Cardographer project 257–8
cards 259–60
care 34–5
Centers for Disease Control and Prevention (CDC) 19
Chan, A. H. S. 69
Chilean response to Covid-19
 challenges 100–5
 facial shield 105
 government website 101–5
 SOFA 108–9
China
 PPE equipment 21
 robots use in pandemic 16
 Shenzhen Smart Drone UAV 15
choropleth maps 19–20
Cipolla, C. 132
cities and public space
 adaptation stage of 24–5
 reaction stage of 24
cities design 223–33
 Covid-19 changing perspectives on density in 227–8
 density and urban form, relationship between 225–6
 for health objectives 223–4
 homes/housing 232
 low/high urban density 226–7
 neighbourhood/community 232
 post-pandemic refocusing 228–30
 principles for 230–1
 public spaces and places 232
 urban form 231–2
 urban technology 232–3
 for well-being objectives 224–5
Civic Hackers 159
Clarke, V. 81–2
clear communication 18
climate change 12
Cloud 135, 152
co-design
 distributed approaches to 253–4
 knowledge 253–4
 online, insights 256–7
Cohen, A. K. 9
COLEV research project, Colombia 104–5
Colombian response to Covid-19
 challenges 100–1
 COLEV research project 104–5
 personal ventilator, PersoCO 106–7
 ventilator 109–10
colonnaded courtyards 245–6
Comarch Life Wristbands 17
community 232
community transmission 118
contact tracing mobile applications, in pandemic 13–14
Cooper, R. 194
Covid-19 pandemic 1–3, 37–40, 79
 challenges 99–100
 design, use of 9
 design responses to 35–40, 100–11
 effects 1–2, 9
 international public health communication design in 79–95
 need for design research and 2
 New York's design response to 165–84
 in New Zealand 114–28
 NHS mobile application 13–14
 risk information 81
 and social change 131
 South American first line response to 98–111
 South Korea's design response to 130–61
 stages of progression 11–12, 132
 as transboundary crisis 9
Cromwell, J. R. 9
cyber security threats 196

Dalton, Mark 119–20
Darden, Joshua 122
dashboards 143
data collection 37–40
data science 104, 193
data visualization, in pandemics 2, 19–21, 26
 adaptation stage 19–21
 in New Zealand 20
 reaction stage 19–21
 in UK 20
Decar, Ángela 105, 108
Decoding Spaces 2D Isovist 73
Denmark 241
design 50
 agency 174–8
 agility 27
 and care 34–5
 categories 40

cities post-Covid-19   223–33
contexts for   50
contingent/boundaried/conditional solutions, multiplicity of   36
Covid-19 pandemic, responses to   35–40
disciplines   10
early insights, review of   40–3
fields   50
forms, multiplicity of   36
fundamental element to   36
imperfect, usefulness of   48
international public health communication   79–95
interventions   37–42, 44–7
of large-scale transformations   52
meanings/interpretations, multiplicity of   36
needs of research   2–3
New York's Covid-19 response   165–84
New Zealand's Covid-19 response   114–28
of/with/for community   26
of policy   53–4
for post-pandemic world   187–98
and power dynamics   179
R&D convergence   134
reactions   9–28
research   2–3
social distancing   65–76
for social innovation lens   174–8
South America's Covid-19 response   98–111
South Korea's Covid-19 response   130–61
speed   27
strategic   50–9
of technologies   26
waves of   36
Designers Institute of New Zealand (DINZ)   121
Design History of the Covid-19 Virus, A   37
designing collaboratively   26–7
designing sustainably   27
Design Sprints   195
digital divide   12
digital platforms   1, 191–2, 195–6, 253–6
digital technologies   26, 252–64
collaboration, implications for   263–4
designing research ecosystems   254–7

festival of social sciences   255–6
online co-design insights   256–7
distributed co-design approaches (case study)   253–4
tangible tools in virtual context   257–60
virtual co-presence and experimental digital spaces (case study)   260–3
digital transformation   190–2
digital work   59
DINZ; *see* Designers Institute of New Zealand (DINZ)
Disability Unit   57–8
DisCO (Distributed Co-design) study   254
dog robots   16–17
drones, use in pandemic   14–16
DRS2020 conference   254–7
Dubey, R. K.   71, 75
Duncan, William   233
Dunne, Anthony   36
Dunne, D.   194
Dyson   24

Ebola outbreak, West Africa   80
EDI; *see* Equality, Diversity and Inclusion (EDI)
Edible schoolyard   243
Edwards-Jones, A.   239
electronic bands   17
Emeraude Escape   191
emergency signage   68–9
Epax, inflight digital retail solution   192
Equality, Diversity and Inclusion (EDI)   211, 213
Estrada, Jorge   109
European bank   191

Facebook   23
Facebook-Cambridge Analytica data scandal   196
facial shields   21–2, 105
Family Pockets by Sour project   165–9, 175, 177–83
festival of social sciences   255–6
fifth-order design   52
Fischetti, M.   71
Fitbit   17
fitness trackers   17
floor markings   25

Index   275

Flugge, C. 65
fourth-order design   52, 179, 196–7
Fry, T. 3, 28
future pandemics, threats of 9

game spaces 260
Garay-Baquero, Diana 106
Gategroup 192
Gather Town 260–3
   The Egg 261–2
   ImaginationLancaster 261–2
   Ways of Seeing 261–2
global branding, Covid-19-related campaigns 18–19
'Global Call out to Creatives' competition (WHO) 18
gloves 21
government communications 18
government public health campaigns 2
graphic communication 25–6
graphic design/communication, in pandemics
   adaptation stage 19
   reaction stage 18
      global branding 18–19
      government communications 18
      public health 18
graphic designs 2
Grasshopper Kangaroo Pack function 72
Grasshopper software 25, 65, 71–3, 75–6
green spaces 1
Guo, Z. 71
Guvenc, Pinar 166–7

handwashing leaflets 89
Hasan, S. S. 65
health and social care 34
health inequalities 12
health objectives 223–4
healthy housing 1
Heathrow Terminal 5 193
HelloMask 23
Helsinki Design Lab 54, 56
Hernandez, Ricardo J. 108
HeyMama 166–7
Hill, D. 252
homes/housing 232
Hong Kong 17
Huang, H. 71
Hunt, J. 52

imperfection in design 35–6
India 17
infectious diseases 1–3; *see also* Covid-19 pandemic
infodemic challenge of Covid-19 79–80
infographics 20
Innovation for Culture programme 200–21
   building common ground 215–20
   building involvement 211–15
   navigation 208–11
   orchestration for 201–5
      as balancing activity 204–5
      origin 202
      processes/disciplines, transcends 202–4
   overview 200
   steering processes 205–8
   steps 205
Innovative Learning Environments 239
international public health communication design 79–95
   Covid-19, infodemic challenge of 79–80
   data analysis 81–6
      for countries 84–5
      framework guidelines employed for 83–4
      language and message framing 82–7
      stages 82
   discussion 92–4
   draft recommendations 92–4
   leaflets on handwashing 89
   limitations 94
   past epidemics/pandemics, lessons from 80–1
   research methodology 81–6
   on social distancing 90
   visual design 86–92
      analysis of 88
      bad practices 89–91
      framework guidelines employed for 83–4
      good practices 86, 89
      mixed practices 92
      ugly practices 91
Introduction to Italian Design (Branzi) 35
IoT sensor 135, 150, 159, 189
Irwin, T. 52–3
IslandWood School, Washington State, United States 240

Jalisco   200
Johal, Sarb   120–1
Junginger, S.   53

Keyholding Company (KHC)   191–2
Krippendorff, K.   55
Kumar, V.   194

Lancashire Resilience Forum   67
Lancaster City Council (LCC)   67–8
Lancaster Design Studios Gather Town space   261–3
laptops   26
large-scale design   2
LCC; see Lancaster City Council (LCC)
LEGO   190
Lego Education   190
Levi Strauss & Co.   192–3
Li, B.   71
Libin, Katya   166–7
Liechtenstein   17
line graphs   19–20
lockdowns   2, 10, 12–13, 18, 24, 37, 57, 65–6, 100–1, 109–11, 114–18, 124, 189–93, 200–1, 223, 267–8
Lowe, Heath   121
Lurås, S.   53

McDonald's   18–19
McDougall, S. J. P.   69
machine learning   192–3
McKinsey & Company   194
Mak, W. M.   69
Manzini, E.   52, 59, 133, 142, 269
Map UI   143, 145
masks   21–3
medical equipment   21–4
MEDIP PRO COVID19(A-7) application   144
Melles, G.   132–3
Merewether, J.   239
Michael Van Valkenburgh Associates (MVVA)   180
Microsoft Teams   258
Mindstorm, LEGO   190
Miro   259
Mixed Reality Game Cards   258
mobile learning   242–3
mobile software   135, 143, 146, 152, 154

Moral-IT cards   258
Mullagh, L.   131
Museum of Disinformation   104
My Vaccine Pass   118, 123

national flooding signage system   69
Natural Connections Demonstration Project   238–9
navigation   208–11
NeighborhoodsNow initiative   165
neighbourhood   232
New York, Covid-19 in (research)   165–84
    cases   166–74
        Family Pockets by Sour project   166–9, 175, 177–83
        South Bronx Community Gardens Activation project   165, 169–75, 177–83
    design of study   166
    findings   174–9
        abstract, tangible   176, 179
        design agency   174–8
        design and power dynamics   179
        designers as catalysts   179
        social innovation lens, design for   174–8
    impact   180–3
        digital as barrier   180–3
        digital as co-design innovation source   183
        research/engagement, community-led modes of   180
    limitations   183–4
    methods   166
    sample/data collection/data analysis approach   166
New Zealand, Covid-19 pandemic in   114–28
    Alert Level System   115–16
        lockdown (alert level 4)   115
        prepare (alert level 1)   116
        reduce (alert level 2)   116
        restrict (alert level 3)   115
        timeline   117
    communication tools   118–21
        health crisis, human response to   119–21
        Unite against COVID-19 campaign   119–22
    contact tracing in   116–17

Covid-19 Protection Framework 117–18
   key components of 118
   stages/characteristics 118
  data visualization 20
  design and development 124–5
  lockdown in 114–15, 117–18, 124
  measures to guide in 115–16
  National Close Contact Service 116
  NZ COVID Tracer app 123–6
   design and development 124–5
   features 123–4
   impact of 125–6
   overview 123–4
  online access to information (website) 126–7
   characteristics 126
   signage, posters and other supporting material 126–7
   visual design 126
  outbreak 114
  state of national emergency declaration 115
  timeline and responses to 114–18
  'Unite against COVID-19' campaign 18–19, 119–22, 126
   human response to a health crisis 119–21
   impact/success of 121
   visual language and details of 122
  vaccinations in 116, 118
  visual system evolution 122–4
New Zealand Public Health System 116–17
Ng, A. W. Y. 69
NHS Covid-19 mobile application 13–14
Nocek, A. 3, 28
NZ COVID Tracer app 118, 123–6
  design and development 124–5
  features 123–4
  impact of 125–6
  overview 123–4

OLE; *see* outdoor learning environments (OLE)
Olson, E. M. 194
Ongkrutraksa, W. 69
online banking 191
online co-design insights 256–7
online tools 38
open-air schools, Germany 240

Open Source Social Distance Signage Pack 70–1, 76
Open Ventilator System Initiative (OVSI) 24
Orbit Privacy App 196–7
orchestration 201–5
  as balancing activity 204–5
  origin 202
  processes/disciplines, transcends 202–4
organizational agility 187–8
organizations, pandemic impacts on 187–9; *see also* business, Covid-19 impact to
Oura's smart rings 17
outdoor learning environments (OLE) 238–47
  for children 238
  Covid-19 pandemic experience 240–2
  and pandemics 240
  in secondary education 238, 242–4, 246–7
   architectural design 247
   educational practice 247
   policy 247
  spaces/uses of 244–6
   agora/forum 245
   colonnaded courtyards 245–6
   palaestra 244–5
   theatre/benches/urban elements 246
  value/advantage of 238–9
OVSI; *see* Open Ventilator System Initiative (OVSI)

palaestra 244–5
pandemics; *see also* Covid-19 pandemic
  designing for and in 13–25
  future, threats of 9
  recovery/resilience, principles for designing 25–7
  stages of 11–12, 132
   adaptation 12, 132
   framework 11–13
   reaction 12, 132
   recovery 12, 132
   resilience 12, 132
Penlon's Prima ES02 24
personal protective equipment (PPE) 21–4, 48
  adaptation stage 23
  China 21

demand for   21
disposable   27
reaction stage   22–3
shortages of   22
sustainable   27
personal ventilator, PersoCO   106–7
Peruccio, P. P.   52
phone alerts   13
PlayingCards.io   258
Poland   17
policy co-design
  building common ground   215–20
  building involvement   211–15
  goals   208
  key performance indicators   208
  navigation   208–11
  orchestration for   201–5
    as balancing activity   204–5
    origin   202
    processes/disciplines,
      transcends   202–4
  physical settings   201
  principles   201
  programme   201
  steering processes   205–8
policy design   53–4, 201–5
Policy Lab   56–8
policy making *versus* policy delivery   53
post-modern design   36
post-pandemic world   187–98
  business resilience   194–7
    design principles to digital
      space   194–6
    fourth order design   196–7
  business transformations   190–4
    digital transformation   190–2
    non-human interactions, increasing
      prevalence of   192–4
    robots/AI, use of   192–4
  Covid-19 impact to traditional business
    structures   187–90
PPE; *see* personal protective equipment
  (PPE)
Prendiville, A.   53
prototyping   176
public/civic sectors, strategic design in   53–4
public health crisis   79, 188, 193
public health messages   18
public spaces/places   232
Pye, David   36

QR codes   118, 124
quarantine   17

Raby, Fiona   36
reaction stage of pandemics   12
  cities and public space   24
  data visualization   19–21
  global branding   18–19
  government communications   18
  graphic design and communication   18
  PPE   22–3
  public health   18
  technology design and use   13–17
  ventilators   23
recovery stage of pandemics   12
RedTab   193
relational design   36
research ecosystems designing   254–7
resilience
  agility and   267–8
  business   194–7
  cities post-Covid-19   223–33
  digital technologies   252–64
  pandemics and   25–7
  principles for   266–71
  South Korea's Covid-19 response   150–5
  stage of pandemics   12
Rhino3D software   65
Rhino software   25, 65
robotics   16–17, 135, 154–5, 159–60,
    192–4, 197
Rush, Auckland-based agency   124

'Safe Korea' bracelet   17
Sangiorgi, S.   53
Scotland
  drone use during pandemic   15–16
  Play Strategy   243
scrubs   22
self-isolation   2
service design   53–4
Shakib, Tony   189
Shenzhen Smart Drone UAV, China   15
signage, social distancing
  automated positioning of   71
  branding   68
  design   69–71
  emergency   68–9
  pack, open source   76
  types   68

Silverstripe   126
Simon, Herbert   110
Singapore
   dog robots in   16
   robots use in pandemic   16
   TraceTogether in   13
Slater, S.   194
smartphones   26
social bubbles   66–7
Social Distance Lab   65, 73–4
   installation   73–4
   results   74–5
   testing   74–5
social distancing designing   12, 25, 65–76
   '1m+'   66–7
   automation using optimization
       software   71–3
   building capacity, limitations on   66–7
   communication material on   90
   full capacity   66–7
   future work   74–6
   human-designed plan *versus* automated
       Grasshopper definition   75
   impact of   67
   measures   25
   overview   65
   plan comparisons   75
   research questions   67–73
   scientific/contextual background   65–6
   signage
      branding   68
      design   69–71
      emergency   68–9
      pack, open source   76
      types   68
   Social Distance Lab   65, 73–4
   in UK   65–6
Social Distancing Lab   68
social gatherings   2
social innovation   131–2
societal unrest   12
Soporte Facial para Pacientes con
      Ventilación Mecanica Invasiva
      (SOFA)   108–9
South America, Covid-19 pandemic
      in   98–111
   care, responses to   107–10
      SOFA, Chile   108–9
      ventilators, Colombia   109–10
   challenges   99–100

   first-line responses design   100–1
   inform, responses to   101–4
      Chilean government website   101–4
      COLEV research project   104–5
   protect, responses to   105–7
      facial shield, Chile   105
      personal ventilator, PersoCO,
         Colombia   106–7
South Bronx Community Gardens Activation
      project   165, 169–75, 177–83
South Korea's Covid-19 response
      (research)   17, 130–61
   background of   130
   case analysis   136–59
      adaptation stage cases, synthetic
         analysis of   144–50, 152
      case selection criteria   136–41
      framework/method   136, 142–3
      reaction stage cases, synthetic
         analysis of   143–6
      recovery/resilience stage cases,
         synthetic analysis of   150–5
      synthesis   153, 156–9
   methodology   131
   purpose of   130
   scope of   131
   social change   131
   social problem-solving design   131–4
      definition/role of   132–4
      promotion of   133
      Seoul Basic Plan for   142
      social innovation   131–2
   suggestions/implications   159–61
   technology trends analysis   134–6
Spaces and Tools for Learning project   241
'Stay alert, protect the NHS, save lives'   18
'Stay home, protect the NHS, save lives'   18
STBY, Design Research agency   200–1
steering processes   205–8
strategic design   50–9
   attributes of   55
   context   50–1
   in Covid-19 pandemic   56–9
      broader adaptations   58–9
      life with disability, experiences
         of   57–8
   definition   54–6
   impacts   56
   potential   52–3
   in public/civic sectors   53–4

super-wicked problems   53
'Suwon City Mask is the Answer
 campaign'   144

Tabletopia   258
Tabletop Simulator   258
Teacher Change project   239
technology design and use, in pandemics
 adaptation   17
 reaction   13–17
  contact tracing mobile
   applications   13–14
  drones   14–16
  robots   16–17
Temple Yoga   190–1
test and trace (T&T)   40
theatre   246
threats of future pandemics   9
'Towards Relational Design' (Blauvelt)   36
traffic signs, UK   69–70
transdisciplinary design   52
transition design   52–3
TSB bank   191
tsunami warning signage   69

UIs; *see* user interfaces (UIs)
UK
 data visualization in pandemics   20
 mask wearing in   22
 strategic design in   56–9
 traffic signs   69–70
 Ventilator Challenge   24
'*Unite against COVID-19*' campaign, New
 Zealand   18–19, 119–22, 126
 human response to a health crisis
  119–21
 impact/success of   121
 visual language and details of   122
United States
 drone use during pandemic   15
 mask wearing in   22
urban density (low/high)   226–7

Urban Design Forum   165
urban form   231–2
urban technology   232–3
user interfaces (UIs)   143

vaccines/vaccinations   11
 development of   2
 efficacy   37
 imperfect and trust, relationship
  between   37
Van Alen Institute   165
ventilators   21–2, 106–7, 109–10
 adaptation stage   23–4
 demand for   21–2
 designs for   26–7
 OVSI   24
 production of   24
 reaction stage   23
Verrall, A.   116
Vikneswaran, M.   69
vinyl floor markings   24
Virtual Tabletop (VTTs)   258
visualizations   19–21, 176
visual language   119–22
Volkswagen   18–19
Voronoi offset   72–3

warning signs   69
Wash Studio, Preston   69
wayfinding graphics   25
well-being   224–5
Whitney, P.   194
WHO; *see* World Health Organisation (WHO)
Wingcopter drone, Scotland   15
World Health Organisation (WHO)   18

zero COVID-19   127
'zero tolerance' policies   12
Zika virus   80
zipline drones   15
Zoom classes/meetings   190–1, 214, 258
Zoom fatigue   252